BLACK '47 AND BEYOND

THE PRINCETON ECONOMIC HISTORY

OF THE WESTERN WORLD

Joel Mokyr, Editor

Growth in a Traditional Society: The French Countryside,
1450–1815, by Phillip T. Hoffman

The Vanishing Irish: Households, Migration, and
the Rural Economy in Ireland, 1850–1914,
by Timothy W. Guinnane

Black '47 and Beyond: The Great Irish Famine in
History, Economy, and Memory, by Cormac Ó Gráda

BLACK '47 AND BEYOND

THE GREAT IRISH FAMINE IN HISTORY, ECONOMY, AND MEMORY

CORMAC Ó GRÁDA

PRINCETON UNIVERSITY PRESS

PRINCETON, NEW JERSEY

Library of Congress Cataloging-in-Publication Data
Ó Gráda, Cormac.
Black '47 and beyond : the great Irish famine in history,
economy, and memory / Cormac Ó Gráda.
p.   cm. — (The Princeton economic history of the Western world)
Includes bibliographical references (p.   ) and index.
ISBN 0-691-01550-3 (cloth : alk. paper)
1. Famines — Ireland — History — 19th century.   2. Ireland — Economic
conditions — 19th century.   3. Ireland — History — 1837–1901.
I. Title.   II. Series.
DA950.7.0366   1998   941.508 — dc21   98-27291

This book has been composed in Sabon

http://pup.princeton.edu

Printed in the United States of America

10   9   8   7   6   5   4   3   2   1

Don lead óg, Ruadhán

CONTENTS

LIST OF FIGURES

ACKNOWLEDGMENTS

Earlier versions of much of the material in chapters 3, 4, and 6 of this book have done the rounds of seminars and conferences in places as far apart as St. Andrew's and Tucson, Osaka and Copenhagen, and Oxford and Boston, and have benefited from the experience. I am grateful to Andrés Eiríksson, to Joel Mokyr, and to Kevin O'Rourke for allowing me to recycle and put my own gloss on findings that originated in joint research with them, and to my collaborators and ex-collaborators on the National Famine Research Project—Catherine Cox, Mary Daly, David Dickson, Andrés Eiríksson, David Fitzpatrick, and Des McCabe—for letting me use a few of our data-bases. Tim Guinnane, Liam Kennedy, Joel Mokyr, Kevin O'Rourke, and David Dickson read most or all of the book in draft form, and offered much sage advice. Heather Griggs, Taylor Anbinder, and Marion Casey generously shared their expertise of nineteenth-century New York history. For help with chapter 6 I owe a big debt to the members of the Department of Irish Folklore, University College Dublin, particularly to Tom Munnelly. For advice, support, and help on specific points I am also indebted to many people, including Gavan Conlan, Margaret Crawford, Kevin Denny, Ronan Fanning, David Fitzpatrick, Roy Foster, Michael Laffan, Liam Mac Con Iomaire, Breandán Mac Suibhne, Ciarán Ó Murchadha, Willie Nolan, Tim O'Neill, Kari Pitkänen, Bob Scally, Peter Solar, Rodney Thom, Bill Vaughan, Brendan Walsh, David Weir, Stephen Wheatcroft, Jeff Williamson, and Kevin Whelan. When this book was nearing completion I spent several weeks as a guest of the Institute of Economics at the University of Copenhagen. Gunnar Persson paved the way for my visit, and for his insights and reactions and hospitality while I was based in Studiestraede, many thanks; thanks also to the Institute's ever-obliging librarian, Vibeke Ring, and to all the Reins, especially Bella-Katrine. Awards from the President's Research Fund and from the Faculty of Arts in University College Dublin provided the funds to employ two research assistants, Mark Duncan and Finian McCaul, for some weeks; to purchase some specialist books; and to check archives. For permission to quote material in their care I thank the Deputy Keeper, An Chartlann Náisiúnta, Dublin, and Séamus Ó Catháin of the Department of Irish Folklore, University College Dublin.

The idea for this kind of book on the Irish famine came from Peter Dougherty of Princeton University Press. I am grateful to him for his judgment and encouragement. Thanks likewise to David Huang and Alice Calaprice at the Press. Finally, Christopher Morash is probably right to warn us (in *Writing the Irish Famine*) that "there can be no innocent narrative of the Famine." We can only keep on trying.

Cluain Sceach, April 1998

BLACK '47 AND BEYOND

INTRODUCTION

> Even the scale of the great famine was not unique when
> seen in the context of contemporary European experience.
> (D. G. Boyce, *Nationalism in Ireland*, 1982)

> [In] no other famine in the world [was] the proportion
> of people killed . . . as large as in the Irish famines
> in the 1840s.
> (Amartya Sen, New York University, 1995)

THE OUTLINE history of the Great Irish Famine is familiar. So are its keywords — Black '47, mass mortality, the potato, emigration, clearances, fever, official neglect. To people not from Ireland it is the defining event in Irish history, while to the nonspecialist in famine history it is probably the best-known historical famine of all. Yet oddly enough, until about a decade ago scholarly accounts of the Irish famine were very few. When Dublin historians Robin Dudley Edwards and Desmond Williams published their classic collaborative volume of essays, *The Great Famine: Studies in Irish History* in early 1957, they had the field to themselves, and for a long time afterwards *The Great Famine* was synonymous with that notable duo and their team. Likewise, Cecil Woodham-Smith's enduring best-seller *The Great Hunger* (1962) risked confusion only with the long poem of the same name by Patrick Kavanagh. In more recent years, though, such has been the outpouring of works on the Irish famine that fresh titles are at a premium. My own earlier choice of *The Great Irish Famine* for a booklet published in 1989 has been recycled at least three times since. Other recent variations include *The Great Famine in Ireland*, *Paddy's Lament*, *The Irish Famine*, *The Famine Decade*, *This Great Calamity*, *This Dreadful Visitation*, *A Nation of Beggars*, *A Death-dealing Famine*, *A People Starved*, and *Fearful Realities*. The imminence of the famine's sesquicentennial — the potato blight which sparked off the crisis reached Ireland in 1845 — was mainly responsible for the heightened interest. By the end of 1995, after a hectic year of famine commemoration involving many publications, conferences, seminars, and radio and television documentaries, a sense that historians had rather neglected the famine in the past had given way to a feeling in some quarters that discussion and research on the subject had reached the stage of rapidly diminishing returns.[1] In reality, this was far from being the case.

Analogies between the Irish famine of the 1840s and modern Third

World famines were an important feature of the sesquicentennial commemorations in Ireland in 1995–97. Links were drawn between the generosity of Irish people toward the victims of disasters such as those in Biafra in the late 1960s, Ethiopia in the 1970s and 1980s, or Somalia in the 1990s, and Ireland's own sad past. Irish president Mary Robinson lent her prestige to this link, reminding the large crowd at the opening of a famine museum in Strokestown in the west of Ireland in May 1995 that "the past gave Ireland a moral viewpoint and an historically informed compassion on some of the events happening now." Elsewhere she wrote that "we can honour the profound dignity of human survival best . . . by taking our folk-memory of this catastrophe into the present world with us, and allowing it to strengthen and deepen our identity with those who are still suffering."[2]

This historical "link" between Irish suffering a century and a half ago and sympathy for the Third World's poor is well meant, but it is largely a modern invention. In the heavily urbanized Ireland of the 1990s, "famine memory' probably owes more to Cecil Woodham-Smith's bestseller, recycled versions of the *saeva indignatio* of journalist John Mitchel, and the discoveries of local historians than to any genuine, unbroken link with the 1840s. A more plausible, though less fashionable influence on Irish benevolence is Ireland's strong tradition of missionary activity. That tradition, now also fading but more than a century old, made missionaries of generations of Irish people, literally or vicariously.[3] The link is direct in the case of the major charity agency, Concern, a reincarnation of Africa Concern, which was established by Irish Holy Ghost Missionaries in the wake of the Biafran famine in the 1970s, while the inspiration for another important charity, Goal, was a television documentary about the efforts of an Irish missionary priest in the slums of Calcutta. A third charity, Trócaire, was created by the Irish Catholic hierarchy. These agencies grew out of an empathy built on personal contacts and associations. The Great Irish Famine had little to do with it.[4]

There are similarities between the Irish famine and modern famines, just as there are similarities between the Irish famine and famines throughout history. All famines produce so many individual tragedies that "in their enormity they wear the air of fable."[5] To the historian and the economist, however, the differences can be as interesting as the similarities. One of the big differences between the Irish famine and most modern famines is that it killed more people. The Irish famine was truly a "great famine." About one million people, or almost one-eighth of the entire population, perished as a result of the potato failures of the 1840s. The cost in deaths of many highly publicized Third World famines in the recent past is modest by comparison. One guess at excess mortality in the famine-affected areas of Ethiopia in 1973 puts it at forty thousand; others put excess deaths in Ethiopia as a whole in 1972–74 at about two hundred thousand. The famine in the Sahel region (Chad, Mali) in 1973–74 killed perhaps one hundred thousand people in an area inhabited by twenty-five million. The toll of the famine in Darfur, western Sudan, in the mid-1980s fell somewhat short of one hundred thousand out of a population of about twenty million. In Malawi (then Nyasaland), official sources put excess deaths in the famine of 1949–50 at a few hundred people at most.[6]

The famines in Biafra in 1968–70 and in Ethiopia in the mid-1980s are exceptional in this respect. One has to reach further back for other disasters on the Irish scale. The Soviet famine of 1918–22, Stalin's Ukraine famine of 1932–33, and the Great Bengali Famine of 1943–44 all killed many more people than the Great Irish Famine, while the Chinese Great Leap Forward famine of 1959–62 is in a macabre league of its own. With the likely exception of 1918–22 in the Soviet Union, though, the proportionate cost in lives of the Irish famine was much greater, distinguishing it from most, though not all, historical and modern famines. In relative terms the Great Finnish Famine of 1866–68 was less than half as murderous: it reduced Finland's pre-famine population of 1.8 million by 5 percent or so.[7] Mortality was greater in Ireland partly because the shock to the food supply was greater and longer-lasting than in most other famine-affected regions. Whereas modern famines typically place only a small minority of the population at risk for a year or two at most, in Ireland the destruction of the potato deprived one-third of the population of virtually their only means of subsistence for several years.

A second difference is that today's famine-stricken areas are located in the most economically backward regions of the world, whereas Ireland in the 1840s was located next to that prosperous region which Prince Albert would soon dub "the workshop of the world." However, economic history suggests the need for perspective here. British workers and their families faced harsh conditions at the time, and mid-Victorian Britain was poor by our own late-twentieth century standards. How poor were Ireland and Britain in the early 1840s compared with, say, Ethiopia or Somalia today? Only the crudest answer is possible. Income per capita in Ireland just before the famine was somewhat less than half that of Great Britain, and incomes in Britain today are perhaps eight to ten times as high now as then. In the late 1980s or early 1990s, moreover, the average purchasing power of incomes in Ethiopia was 2–3 percent of Great Britain's, and in Somalia about 6–7 percent. Taken together, these numbers indicate that Irish living standards before the famine were higher than those of Ethiopia in the recent past, and about on a par with Somalia's. By the same reckoning, living standards in Great Britain in the 1840s were somewhat less than those of Indonesia or Egypt today.[8] This comparison does not mean to absolve contemporary policymakers or public opinion of responsibility, but it is a reminder that the rich world today has a much greater margin to spare than even those who were comfortably off in Britain did in the 1840s.

A third important difference between the Irish famine and modern famines is the philosophical context. In 1847 James Wilson, first editor of *The Economist*, answered Irish pleas for public assistance with the disclaimer that "it is no man's business to provide for another," while the London *Times* proclaimed that "something like harshness [was] the greatest humanity." Wilson held that official intervention would shift resources from the more to the less deserving, since "if left to the natural law of distribution, those who deserved more would obtain it." At the same time, economist Nassau William Senior calmly defended policies that were reducing the Irish to starvation, remarking that they would provide "illustrations valuable to a political economist." Underlying such attitudes was the conviction that overgenerous relief would demoralize the Irish poor and merely postpone the reckoning. For Irish novelist Maria Edgeworth, by then an elderly woman, ideologues like Wilson and Senior, and Charles Trevelyan and Charles Wood at the Treasury in London's Whitehall had "heart[s] of iron—nature[s] from which the natural instinct of sympathy or pity have been destroyed." Close reading of the evidence suggests that the influence of such thinking on public policy during the famine was considerable.[9]

Many people in high places in both London and Dublin in the 1840s believed that the famine was nature's response to Irish demographic irresponsibility, and that too much public kindness would obscure that message. There is some truth, then, in John Mitchel's contemporary claim that "Ireland died of political economy." Later in India similar attitudes would also constrain famine relief. There the machinery necessary to eradicate famine was available long before it was put into use. Why? Because those in power believed that "India would have been pauperised, its work ethic shattered, and an importunate populace of government dependents would have been created." To relieve one famine would only "have postponed a calamitous reckoning when a swollen population multiplied beyond its subsistence." In the Netherlands in the late 1840s, the official stance rivaled Whitehall's for dogma and meanness. But in Russia half a century later, a more benign and relaxed attitude toward relief almost certainly saved hundreds of thousands of lives.[10]

Yet if the Irish poor in the 1840s were at a disadvantage in an ideological sense, in other ways they should have been better placed to resist the threat of famine. Ireland's bureaucratic apparatus, part of the Victorian state, was more sophisticated and far less corrupt than that of, say, Ethiopia or Somalia today. Police monitoring and newspaper accounts of the second harvest failure in the summer of 1846 offered an accurate and timely "early warning system" of looming disaster. Letters were delivered promptly and investigators and inspectors could move about freely and quickly. Moreover, a relatively free press ensured that there was no hiding the Irish famine in the 1840s, as there was in the case of the Ukraine in 1932–33 and China during the Great Leap Forward. A constabulary relatively free from corruption and a hard-working and humane clergy eased the problem of identifying and reaching those most in need. Ireland's communications in the 1840s were more than adequate; its roads were quite good, and many of the worst-affected regions could be — and were — easily reached by sea. Bad weather in the guise of flooding or frost was rarely an excuse for not getting relief supplies to the people. Since the 1840s improvements in transport, particularly the steamship and the railway, have lessened the impact of local harvest failures in many parts of the world, notably in India. Yet even today, poor communications are also seen as exacerbating famine, giving rise to market fragmentation, as, for example, in Bangladesh and in Wollo in the 1970s or Angola and Mozambique in the early 1980s.[11]

Ireland was better equipped to deal with harvest failure than many other famine-affected regions for yet another reason. In the 1840s Ireland was a relatively tranquil place. There was no civil war or invading army. Ireland's reputation for lawlessness and outrage was always exaggerated, but by 1845 crime rates in Ireland were on a par with Britain, and while the famine inevitably brought a rise in attacks against property, never was civil order seriously threatened. This contrasts with the situation in Biafra, Ethiopia, Somalia, or Rwanda in recent decades. "In much of Africa," writes Alex de Waal, "war has become synonymous with famine";[12] "analysis" of famine in Mozambique in the 1980s amounted to "little more than a catalogue of Renamo vandalism." The risk of famine in Angola in the mid-1990s was increased by the land mines (an estimated 10–15 million) left behind by the warring parties. In war-torn parts of the Sudan, land mines were more likely to kill cattle than people, but with potentially grave consequences too for pastoral farmers. Civil conflict also produces its IDPs (internally displaced persons) and refugees; their number worldwide rose from about one million in 1970 to about twenty-five million or so in the mid-1990s.[13] War increases the vulnerability to famine in obvious ways. It destroys crops, deflects economic activity, frustrates relief, and dampens democracy and protest.

In previous centuries the connection between war and famine had been all too familiar to Ireland. The famine that produced "very many deaths, famine and many strange diseases, murders, and intolerable storms as well" in the mid- and late 1310s was exacerbated by the invasion of Scottish warlord Edward Bruce: "For three years and a half, falsehood and famine and homicide filled the country, and undoubtedly men ate each other in Ireland." In 1339 an annalist linked "great war all over Meath between Galls and Gaels" with the destruction of "the corncrops of Ireland" and "famine in the land."[14] In the conquests of Elizabeth in the late sixteenth century and Cromwell in the mid-seventeenth, war and famine were also closely linked. However, Ireland faced no civil war or major unrest in the 1840s. Indeed, some contemporary observers spoke of a delusive calm in Ireland on the eve of the famine. Faction fighting and rural strife, so common in the 1820s and 1830s, had been quelled by an alliance of police and priests, and ordinary crime was also in decline. The inoffensive rising of 1848 lasted only a matter of days and in any case took place when the worst of the famine was over throughout most of the country. Therefore disrupted communications and military distractions were not a factor in Ireland during the famine.

Today serious famines are confined to the world's poorest regions, mainly in sub-Saharan Africa. Excess mortality stems less from the lack of relief than the failure of relief supplies to reach those at risk. As a rule, foreign governments and nongovernmental organizations are on hand to provide the necessary food and medicine, but almost invariably corruption, civil strife, and brigandage stand in the way. Famine-affected regions such as Biafra in the late 1960s, Sudan and Ethiopia in the 1980s, and Rwanda, Somalia, and Angola in the 1990s were no better than war zones, in which international relief sometimes unwittingly fueled and prolonged the conflicts. To oversimplify somewhat: today the famine problem is more one of agency than ideology.[15] In Ireland in the 1840s it was the other way around. Ireland then was not Somalia now.

The recent rush of both general surveys and local studies of the Irish famine rules out the need for another detailed chronological account. This study concentrates instead on fresh perspectives on the famine and on topics hitherto not given their due in the literature. It differs from the earlier literature on the famine in two main respects. First, its approach is interdisciplinary. Its primary inspiration is economic-historical, with the standard sources and methods of the economist and the historian to the fore, but it also applies the tools of the historical demographer and the folklorist to the study of the famine. Its second distinguishing feature is its comparative focus. Most writing on the Irish famine hitherto treats it in isolation; this book takes a different tack, seeking a comparative focus wherever possible, and often matching the Irish experience against what is known about other famines, both historical and modern.

Chapter 1 places the famine in its historical context. It begins with a review of the potato's role in Ireland before 1845. Much about this topic remains hidden, but comparing the potato's progress in Ireland and elsewhere in Europe helps explain why the devastation wrought by *Phytophthora infestans* was so much greater in Ireland than anywhere else. Ireland's climate gave it a comparative advantage in potato cultivation, but weather conditions in 1846 helped propagate the blight. The weather also mattered in another way: it made a nonsense of the choice of public works as the main channel of relief at the height of the crisis in 1846–47. Chapter 1 contains an account of the weather's part in the disaster. It also contains a review of economic conditions in Ireland before 1845 and an analysis of the role of economic factors in explaining differences in the famine's impact across the island. It concludes with a brief chronology of the famine. One of the famine's most important features is its long drawn-out character. Though synonymous with Black '47, it would last for three or four years more.

Chapter 2 focuses on the political economy of relief and public action. Today there is much to be said for economist Amartya Sen's notion that, given good will, preventing famine mortality in the less developed world is "easy" or "elementary." Yet clearly there are limits to what the authorities could have achieved in a backward economy like Ireland in the 1840s or France in the 1690s. Thus historian John D. Post probably exaggerated in claiming that the enormous death toll from an earlier Irish famine, that of 1740–41, was entirely due to a public failure to do anything to safeguard lives. Nonetheless, the historian of the Irish famine cannot ignore Post's broader point, based on painstaking research and extended comparative surveys of the subsistence crises of the early 1740s and 1815–17, that "the success or failure of public welfare and relief measures more than any other variable influenced the relative severity of the national mortality peaks."[16]

Chapter 2 also reexamines the main relief strategies adopted during the Irish famine, paying due attention to the constraints facing officials at the time. Some of these constraints were self-imposed, but others were exogenous. All famines produce problems of agency arising from location and from information gaps. But in Ireland the administrative and ideological constraints of poorly devised and poorly financed relief schemes were much more serious. Funding raises the contentious questions of policy failure and neglect. The belief that the authorities in London did little to prevent the Irish from starving underpins the recurrent claims of genocide from some quarters in Ireland and particularly Irish America. There is a sense in which England "slept." However, two points need emphasizing here. First, any worthwhile definition of genocide includes murderous intent, and it must be said that not even the most bigoted and racist commentators of the day sought the extermination of the Irish. Certainly, stereotypical images of feckless peasants and lazy landlords abounded. They underpinned an interpretation of the famine as a divine solution to an otherwise intractable problem of overpopulation, and justified tough policies. If policy failure resulted in deaths, then (as in the Netherlands in the same years and in India and elsewhere later) they were largely the by-product of a dogmatic version of political economy, not the deliberate outcome of anti-Irish racism. In the late 1840s Whitehall policymakers were no less dogmatic toward Irish famine victims than, for example, Mao Tse-tung would be toward Chinese peasants in the late 1950s. Yet even the toughest of them hoped for better times for Ireland and, however perversely, considered the harshest measures prescribed as a form of communal medicine. A charge of doctrinaire neglect is easier to sustain than one of genocide.[17] Second, modern accusations of genocide underestimate, or overlook altogether, the enormous challenge facing relief agencies, both central and local, public and private, at the time. Nonetheless, there is a case to be answered. The concluding section of chapter 2 assesses the official response against some macroeconomic data, and indeed finds it wanting.

Chapter 3 turns to the analysis of demographic aspects of the famine. In terms of the impact on mortality by age and gender, it turns out that most famines have much in common. In Ireland as elsewhere, the very young and the old were most at risk but, perhaps contrary to expectation, women withstood the disaster marginally better than men. Just as in India in the 1870s, in Russia in the 1920s, and in Bengal in the 1940s, infectious diseases rather than literal starvation were the main causes of death in Ireland in the 1840s. While Karl Marx's remark that the Irish famine "killed poor devils only" is broadly correct, the spread of contagious diseases such as typhoid fever meant that many who were not so poor also died. The crude state of medical science in the 1840s meant that the ultimate Malthusian weapon against overpopulation was a rather blunt one.

The influence of medical knowledge on famine nosologies is an important issue, and one which separates Irish from modern famines. A better understanding of the transmission mechanism of infectious diseases would not have saved the very poor, but it would have prevented many thousands of others from perishing of diseases such as typhoid fever. Another demographic feature of the Irish famine, mass long-distance emigration, also sets it apart from most other major famines. In chapter 3 I argue that the selective character of that migration reduced its effectiveness as a form of disaster relief. Nonetheless, mortality in Ireland and in Britain would almost certainly have been much higher in the absence of the safety valve of long-distance migration. I argue that further assisted migration targeting some of those at greatest immediate risk would have been a sensible policy option.

Chapter 4 examines economic aspects of the crisis hitherto largely ignored in the historiography. These include the role of food markets and of traders, and the impact of the crisis on the landed elite. Merchants, shopkeepers, and moneylenders received bad press at the time. I argue that though they may have behaved ungenerously and even ruthlessly, few of them can have prospered from the famine. The case relies on a combination of price and market data and contemporary business records. On the other hand, Irish landed proprietors are unlikely to have fared as badly as the historiography implies. Most of those who were forced to cede land in the wake of the famine had been in dire financial straits before it. This chapter also offers new perspectives on the distributional consequences of the famine, by analyzing the famine in terms of potential "winners" and "losers."

Chapter 5 shifts the focus to Dublin city. In Dublin, in the mid-1840s a city of over two hundred thousand souls, the famine was mainly an externality brought about by immigration from the countryside. Tens of thousands of refugees from the countryside sought work and relief in the capital, and many thousands more used it as a port of embarkation. A considerable number of immigrants died in the city, but Dubliners themselves were not immune either. The famine's impact is well captured in the records of public institutions such as prisons, hospitals, cemeteries, and workhouses, offering a new perspective on the crisis.

Chapter 6 describes how some key famine issues are represented in folk memory. Ireland's national folklore archive is mainly a product of the 1930s and 1940s. Though the archive is a rich source of evocative cameos and anecdotes about the famine years, the resultant picture is not without its gaps and confusions and evasions. This, and a suspicion of the alleged populist and nationalist bias of folklore, may explain why most Irish historians have given it a wide berth in the past. I argue that such fears of "lies, damn lies, and folklore" are exaggerated and misplaced. An analysis of what folk memory reveals about a series of specific famine-related questions reveals that its focus is for the most part intensely local, and its sympathies are less populist than usually suspected. Moreover, the biases, the myths, and the silences of popular memory are history too, and they offer new insights into Ireland's famine.

Finally, chapter 7 addresses the famine's legacy. This entails considering its long-term impact on survivors, on the economy, and on demography. An important feature of the Irish famine is that its outcome was complicated by its ecological character. *Phytophthora infestans* did not disappear with the famine, and this ruled out a return to an agriculture so heavily dependent on the potato. The outcome was also affected by emigration. If, as seems likely, a poverty trap constrained long-distance movement out of Ireland before the famine, the concentrated outflow of the famine years, by making it easier for others to follow, probably swelled it in later years. The famine was therefore partly responsible for the population decline that persisted for decades after the famine. The main features of Ireland's post-famine demographic regime — high emigration, late marriage, high marital fertility — are as familiar as those of the pre-famine era. However, the famine was not responsible for all of them.

One of the implications of this study is that although the symptoms are similar, no two famines are the same. Reappraising the Irish famine in comparative terms adds useful perspective and some correctives to received wisdoms. An important message of the comparative approach for those Irish historians who have sought to talk down the Irish famine is that, far from cutting the Irish famine down to size, it highlights its significance in the world history of famines.

Note on currencies. In general, the rule followed in this book for the 1840s is £1 = 20 shillings = 240 pence = \$4.80. Or, one pence (d) = 2 cents; one shilling (s) = 25 cents; 4s = one dollar; etc.

Chapter One

CONTEXTS AND CHRONOLOGY

Is iomdha maith fairis san aicme gan chuibheas
Le braon na bó ba leor a milseacht;
Ba rómhaith iad le hiasc is le h-ím glan,
Is níor h-itheadh riamh bia ba shaoire.

[They blended well with the diet of the poor; with the cow's drop their sweetness was enough; they were great with fish and pure butter, and there was never a cheaper food.]
(Lament for the potato, 1740)

THE POTATO

WHOEVER SAYS "Irish famine" says "potato." Without the massive and repeated failures of the potato crop in Ireland from 1845 on, there would have been no great famine. Across Ireland's thirty-two counties mortality was greatest where reliance on the potato as food had been greatest before 1845. The rural poor, who depended on the potato most, suffered most when it failed. Moreover, the impact of *Phytophthora infestans* (the potato blight) on the potato's productivity and reliability ushered in a revolution in Irish agriculture, practically banishing spade (or *loy*) cultivation to marginal upland areas and reducing the appeal of crop rotations linked to the potato. The total area under potatoes dropped from over two million acres (0.8 million hectares) on the eve of the famine to less than half that in its wake. Understanding the "potato famine" means understanding the role of the potato before the famine.

Many fanciful reasons have been given for the slow spread of the potato in Europe — that it was not mentioned in the Bible, that it caused flatulence, that it was poisonous. What is known for certain is that in the eighteenth and nineteenth centuries it played a far greater role in the history of Ireland than in that of any other European country. It prompted or accommodated — interpretations differ — the fastest population growth in the whole of western Europe for several decades between the mid-eighteenth and early nineteenth centuries. Though Irish poets may have occasionally referred to the potato as "*an Spáinneach*" (the Spaniard), to outside observers it came to be known as the "Irish

potato." In nineteenth-century English cartoons the Irish were sometimes depicted as potatoes.

In Ireland today, few remember the potato for what novelist Maria
Edgeworth described as "the thousands of hardy bodies and merry
souls which have blessed the potato."[1] The potato evokes instead one of
the greatest catastrophes of the nineteenth century. But why did the
Irish place more of their trust in the potato than the Scots, the French,
and the Scandinavians? Was it simply because they were poorer? For
how long before the famine had Irish reliance on the root been greater?
Such questions have long perplexed historians, and scholars from Red-
cliffe Salaman in the 1940s, through L. M. Cullen and Austin Bourke in
the 1960s, to Joel Mokyr in the 1980s have shed much light on them.[2]

Recent scholarship shows that Salaman's well-known account of the
potato's diffusion in Ireland exaggerated its precocity and extent. Still,
literary sources leave little doubt that the potato had made important
inroads by the mid-seventeenth century in parts of the south. The anonymous author of the second part of *Pairlimint Chlainne Thomáis*,
which dates from that time, depicts the plain people as threatening to
ruin their exploiters, the millers, by switching from cereals to potatoes.
An extract from a poem written in 1674 to celebrate the wedding of a
young Limerick couple suggests that the culinary status of the potato
was more exalted then than later:[3]

Gurab é an bodach	For he a knave
buanna an bhata	Who wields a stick
bhuaileas dorrann	And strikes with his fist
ar a chaile	His wife
faoi na maluinn;	Under her eyebrow
agus póga	Whereas it was kisses
le pronócum	With formality
nó potáta	Or a potato
mar shalúta	that used to salute her
ria na pósadh	Before their marriage

Another Gaelic poem written in the 1700s drew a topographical distinction between "those who eat porridge" and "the followers of the beloved potato," confining the latter to the mountains and "the farmers of
the grain lands" to the better soils. Perhaps the potato's stronger presence in the southern province of Munster stemmed from its higher population density; other reports suggest a marginal or secondary role for
the potato until the mid- or even late eighteenth century in parts of the
provinces of Leinster in the east and Ulster in the north.[4] By 1740–41

the potato was sufficiently dominant in Munster, at least for poets, to blame it for the disastrous famine of those years. *"Gurb é moladh na marbh mo theastas a photátaí oraibh"* (Let my praise for the dead be my testament to you, ye potatoes) lamented Corkman Séamus Mac Coitir in the wake of that crisis.[5]

These sources suggest that the Irish cultivated the potato as a garden crop from the outset, as a supplementary and seasonal food. In some other parts of Europe the potato seems to have been introduced first mainly as a fodder crop or for distillation, a choice that may have delayed its adoption as human food. Recent research on the spread of the potato in Europe has emphasized its tardy and hesitant adoption, confirming the late Austin Bourke's judgment that "in no country other than Ireland did the potato economy run its full course." Indeed, the Irish helped to popularize the potato in neighboring countries. Thus, according to one account it was introduced into Scotland from Ireland "towards the end of seventeenth century . . . but very sparingly cultivated [there] for more than sixty years"; another dating from 1664 implies that the potato was well known in Ireland before it became popular in England: "These Roots, although they came at first from the *Indies*, yet thrive and prosper very well in *Ireland*, where there is whole Fields of them; from whence they have been brought into *Wales* and into the North Parts of *England*, where they likewise prosper and increase exceedingly. They are in quality temperate, very agreeable and amical to the Nature of Man, and of a good and strong nourishment."[6]

In Year II of the French Revolution, Irish emigré Thomas Keating deemed it his patriotic duty to advise the French on the advantages of the potato and its importance in Ireland:

> To be convinced that potatoes are as nutritious and good as corn bread one needs only to consider the actual state of Ireland. This island contains a little more than three million people, and it is incontestable that two thirds of them eat no more than twelve pounds of bread a year. The Irish live on potatoes, to which they occasionally add a little salt and butter. And yet the whole world knows that the Irish peasants are very strong and very brave. . . .
>
> In order to ensure a supply of this precious vegetable all year long, its culture must be modified to accommodate different varieties. I will distinguish four varieties which are good to eat. First, early white potatoes; second, another white variety which is shaped like a kidney (there are very few of this variety to be found in France at present); third, the big red round potato; fourth and finally, another variety of whites which are big and round. All are very floury and excellent. . . . The third and fourth kinds, that is, the big rounds and the big whites are very rare in most regions of France (I have seen

them only at Avignon). These two varieties should be sown around April 25th.

Until the peace one should rest content with the long red and *noueuses* potatoes, or of some other good variety; but when happy times return, the Republic can import all varieties from Ireland.

There is yet another variety which is very plentiful in France and in England. It is round, white, and very big, of a watery quality and hardly fit to eat, but it is very useful in the farm yard, and particularly for feeding and fattening pigs, very useful beasts throughout the land. And in France where pastures are few, raising this animal can only be very advantageous, because it necessarily reduces the price of meat.[7]

In only one region of France, Alsace in the east, had the potato become a staple before the Revolution. By the 1770s potato output there matched that of grain by weight; in the early nineteenth century, "one could not exaggerate the importance of the potato; not only did it bring security in times of distress, but it was also the key to a real agricultural conquest in the wooded areas of Alsace."[8] Though the potato's lack of storability from year to year was a major drawback, its usefulness in seasons when grain crops failed was an important part of its appeal. Indeed, Bourke reckoned that before 1845 there was a negative correlation between potato and grain yields, meaning that either crop offered insurance in a year in which the other was bad. In Alsace (as in eighteenth-century Ireland) the poor slaughtered their pigs and traded down to potatoes when corn was scarce.[9]

Yet wherever the potato was important, the ravages of *Phytophthora infestans* in the 1840s caused extreme hardship. In Belgium and in Holland they brought considerable excess mortality. In Switzerland, they are described in Jeremias Gotthelf's doleful *Käthi die Grossmutter*, while in those parts of Alsace where the potato bulked largest the blight was greeted like a calamity, though its effects have not been much studied.[10] But nowhere was Ireland's tragedy replicated. The most compelling reason why Scotland did not starve in the 1840s is that the potato's role was not as central there as in Ireland. It was the most important item in the diet of the poor in the west Highlands, but even there it was supplemented by oatmeal and fish. The population at risk in the Highlands area has been reckoned at 150,000, or about 8 percent of Scotland's total of over two million. In Scotland mortality rates rose a little in late 1846 and early 1847, but that increase seems to have owed more to immigration prompted by conditions in Ireland and to outbreaks of fever in urban Scotland than to higher mortality in the Highlands themselves, and in any case the crisis was soon contained.[11]

The potato that reached Europe in the late sixteenth or early seventeenth century was transformed between 1650 and 1800. Particularly significant was the development of varieties lasting into the spring months. Did yields rise in the process? Information on potato yields before the publication of English agronomist Arthur Young's famous *Tour in Ireland* (1780) is very sketchy. In the 1660s, according to one account, the potato could easily yield 160 bushels per acre on good ground, using the lazy-bed method. The standard conversion rates of 4 bushels = 1 barrel = 20 stone (280 lbs) would imply 5 tons per acre, but this must be seen as little more than a guess.[12]

Arthur Young put the average yield in Ireland in the mid-1770s at 52 barrels (of 20 stone), or 6.5 tons per acre. His estimate is based on a tabulation of 47 yields taken on the spot. The numbers do not quite add up; correcting, and adjusting for the inclusion of one observation of 176 barrels in an area where "common crops do not exceed 90 barrels" produces an average of 5.8 tons per statute acre.[13] Over three decades later another English visitor, Edward Wakefield, estimated the mean yield of potatoes at 22,094 lbs per Irish acre. Wakefield's figure is an unweighted mean of yields in seven of his eight "agricultural districts." The yields, a combination of data gathered on the spot and estimates included in some of the earlier county surveys by the Dublin Society, vary significantly both within and across regions. Wakefield produced sixty-nine observations in all, ranging from 10,500 lbs to 35,280 lbs per Irish acre; omitting his lowest ten and highest ten observations, and adjusting his returns for Cork, again produces an overall average of 5.8 tons per statute acre for the 1800s.

On the basis of a thorough canvas of the contemporary literature, Austin Bourke argued for an average yield of around 6 tons per acre on the eve of the famine. This cannot be far from the truth, though some of the evidence reported by Bourke is consistent with a somewhat higher figure. In particular, his summary of the most comprehensive eyewitness evidence on yields in the 1840s implies an average of well over 7 tons per acre.[14] Yet even 6 tons would imply a slight increase in mean yields between Young's time and the early 1840s. Given the huge increase in potato acreage between the 1770s and the early 1840s and the consequent decline in the average quality of land used, this was not a bad achievement. On the other hand, since more productive varieties such as the Cup and the Lumper were adopted in part for their supposedly higher yields, some rise might be expected.[15]

Contrary to common belief, the potato never became virtually the sole means of nourishment of the vast majority of the people of Ireland. Yet before the famine the Irish were Europe's "potato people" *par excellence*. In the early 1840s daily human consumption had reached about 5 lbs (2.3 kilos) per capita, increasing to 10–12 lbs (4.5 to 5.4

kilos) per adult male equivalent for the bottom third or so of the population. In France in 1852 the average daily human intake was only 6 ounces (165 grams); in Norway in the early 1870s, 20 ounces (540 grams); in Holland about 28.5 ounces (800 grams).[16] Among European countries or regions, only Belgian Flanders, Prussia, and Alsace came close. Per capita consumption in Belgian Flanders rose from about 2.2 lbs (one kilo) per head circa 1800 to over double that circa 1845; an estimate of daily consumption in the upland parts of Alsace puts it as high as 6½–8 lbs (3–4 kilos), while one of the potato's share in daily calorific intake in Prussia has it rising from one-tenth (210 kcals) in the 1800s to over one-third (1095 kcals) in the 1840s.[17]

There can be no denying that, given the potato's status as an inferior good, Ireland's enormous consumption stemmed largely from its greater poverty. But price must have mattered too: because they shielded Irish (and British) farmers from low-cost grain producers in eastern and southern Europe, the Corn Laws meant that the potatoes were relatively cheaper in Ireland than on the continent.[18] Habit and taste also probably played some part. Habit led the Irish to master the household technologies involved in sowing and preparing potatoes, and lose the skills and capital required to process grain into bread. Moreover, the Irish liking for potatoes transcended class and religious divides and survived emigration to distant places. Cullen has drawn attention to how Irish expatriates missed their potatoes, citing among others a Kildare-born Quaker in America in 1685 "who dreamed night after night that I left the ship and got home and there I was sacking them in barrell sacks," and a prosperous merchant settled near Cognac in the southwest of France in the 1760s, who asked an Irish ship's-captain to send him "a small quantity between this and Tuesday, as that day we have Messrs Saule and Hennessys families to dine with us." Over a century later, an ambitious analysis of working-class consumption in industrial Massachusetts showed the immigrant Irish consuming more potatoes than either American-born workers or other immigrants earning similar incomes. Potatoes were part of the main daily meal for all groups, but, exceptionally, nearly half of the Irish households surveyed also ate potatoes for breakfast.[19]

An added reason for its greater importance for Ireland is that the island's acidic soil and damp, temperate climate probably gave it a comparative advantage in potato cultivation.[20] It would be tempting to infer Ireland's comparative advantage simply from its relatively high pre-blight potato yields. But the selection bias arising from farmers in different regions devoting only the most suitable land to each crop means that comparing the ratio of potato to grain yields alone is not enough.

Combined with the relative size of Ireland's potato acreage (one-third of all land under the plough or spade), the yield evidence is much more telling.[21] In further support of Ireland's advantage in potatoes, the relative quality of potato ground in Belgium and France was likely to be better. And such comparisons are based on year-to-year averages; an added consideration in the potato's favor in Irish weather conditions must have been greater reliability relative to grain. It must also be remembered that in Ireland the potato played the same role in the crop rotation as the turnip did in the "new husbandry" in England, Holland, and elsewhere: it prepared the crop for grain, and it allowed livestock to grow.

A survey of potato varieties conducted by the French Central Society of Agriculture in 1813 mentioned no less than 115 to 120 varieties. Not to be outdone, an *Agriculturalists' Manual* published by Messrs. Lawson & Co of Edinburgh in 1836 contained a list of 146 potato varieties cultivated at the time. But as a French expert explained in the 1860s:

> The names and varieties, apart from a few exceptions, differ from place to place. The prevalence of synonyms offers a bewildering confusion; varieties and variations come and go, and only five or six of all those varieties in use today will have disappeared in five or six years. Parmentier, who discussed the potato in his *Dictionnaire de Déterville*, informs us that in his time the number of varieties was put at over sixty; but their characteristics seemed to be established so carelessly, that he reduced them to a dozen, and in that dozen, we cannot discover a single variety that we could identify with certainty. In his *Descriptions des plantes potagères*, published in 1856, M. Vilmorin lists over five hundred varieties. With patience and allowing the benefit of the doubt that number might be doubled. . . . But let us set aside such childish games, and let us focus on those varieties that are most highly esteemed at the time of writing.[22]

In general, however, the history of potato varieties has attracted more attention in Ireland than elsewhere. The very detailed French *mercuriales* include potato prices but make no distinction as to variety. There are many names for potatoes in Denmark and in France, but these are generic names like the Irish *fata*, *potáta*, or *práta*.[23]

Cultivating a range of potato varieties reduced year-to-year fluctuations in yield, while it broadened the range of taste and quality. The role of potato varieties in pre-famine Ireland is well captured in William Tighe's magisterial survey of Kilkenny (1802) and more recently in specialist works by Davidson (1935) and Bourke (1993).[24] The following piece of late eighteenth century doggerel gives some impression of varieties popular at that time:

Of potatoes (*apples*) I've enough,
And 'tis well known they're no bad stuff;
Nor do I want a few good beds
Of driest wholesome *English reds*,
With *London Ladies* and *White Eyes*,
And *high-cawls* of a monstrous size;
These I by no means could neglect,
The very name deserves respect;
Had they been wanted half a year,
How aukward *Ladies* would appear
No danger that their price will fall
When maid and mistress have their cawl.
Only for fear to swell my work
I may mention the honest *Turk*;
What tho' not delicate nor sweet
It feeds the pig to serve the fleet
That each marine may fill his maw
And keep the French Regicides in awe.[25]

The Irish poor were well aware of the quality differences between varieties. Poet Brian Merriman included a disparaging mention of the "Buck" in *Cúirt an Mheán-oíche* (The Midnight Court), which was composed about 1780.[26] A fictional chronicle of Wexford life in the late 1810s refers to a spelling contest between two young scholars, after which the loser claimed "that there was no merit at all in the matter, seeing that [his opponent] was luxuriating every day on good *cups*, while himself was merely kept alive on *English reds*." Within a few decades the "Buck" and many other varieties had succumbed to the "Lumper," a watery and tasteless potato introduced from Scotland in the late 1800s. The English writer William Cobbett reported from Waterford in 1834 that "when men or women are employed at 6d a day and their board to dig *minions* or *apple-potatoes*, they are not suffered to taste them but are sent to another field to dig *lumpers* to eat." The Lumper was adopted for its reliability and its flexibility: it could produce high yields on marginal, poorly fertilized ground. But the Lumper, unfortunately, was particularly susceptible when the blight struck in 1845.[27]

On the eve of the famine the potato's yield ratio was low, about seven to one. A low yield ratio, high transport costs, and nonstorability all reduced the potato's reliability as a staple relative to grain. However, massive crop failures were the exception before 1845. William Steuart Trench, before the famine a considerable tillage farmer in the Irish midlands, later held that there is no greater fallacy than to suppose the potato was at that time an uncertain crop. In 1846 Trench had planted over 150 acres of potatoes in the belief that he was staking his capital on "almost a certainty." He was nearly ruined by the famine.[28] The continuous yield data needed to prove Trench's assertion are lacking in Ireland. Peter Solar's analysis of pre-blight French yield data suggest that the failures of 1845 and 1848 were "at the limits of European experience," and that of 1846 was "far out of the range of actual or likely western European experience." The likelihood of such failures occurring back to back was accordingly "very small indeed." Price data offer another approach; since potatoes could not be stored from year to year, their price in any year should reflect the contemporary yield. Figure 1.1a describes the year-to-year movements in Waterford potato prices between 1802 and 1863. Too weak a reed to lean heavily on, perhaps; but the outcome is far from suggesting that year-to-year variability rose in the generation before the famine. Filtering the price series and then calculating and plotting the standard deviation of moving ten-year blocks of the residuals offers a more formal way of addressing the issue. The outcome (fig. 1.1b) corroborates the story.[29] A final, inferential argument against potato yields being subject to subsistence-threatening fluctuations before 1845 is the prevalence throughout most of Ireland of the system of potato conacre. Under conacre, agricultural labor was paid in fertilized potato ground rather than in money wages. Had big fluctuations in potato yields been the rule, the system would surely have given way to a contract more akin to sharecropping, whereby the risk would be more evenly spread between capitalist and laborer.[30]

The earliest estimate of the aggregate acreage under the potato, based on unpublished data collected by the constabulary, dates from 1845. It suggests a total of 2.1 million acres. Two years later, the first official agricultural census returned a total of less than 0.3 million. That huge reduction reflected the ravages of two years of blight. Yields recovered in 1847, however, and prompted hopes that the worst was over. As a result the aggregate acreage recovered to 0.8 million in 1848. Between 1845 and 1848 the reductions in the area under potatoes were smallest in counties that were probably least dependent on the potato before the famine (Carlow, Kildare, Laois, Antrim, Armagh, and Down). The recovery in 1848 was greatest in counties such as Mayo and Clare, reflecting the vain hope that the old system had some life in it yet (see table 1.1). The blight baffled some of the best scientists of the day. They misdiagnosed it in the 1840s, and misunderstood it until the 1860s. Frenchman Alexis Millardet's discovery of a remedy in 1882 was serendipitous; it would take another two decades before fungicidal spraying was universal in Ireland.[31]

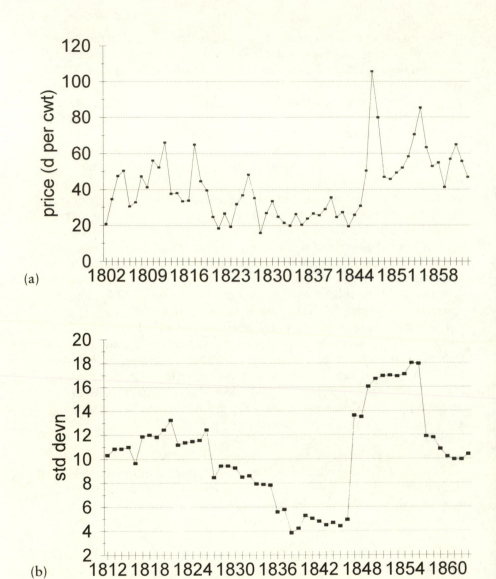

(a)

(b)

Figure 1.1. (a) Waterford potato prices, 1802–63. (b) Waterford potato price variability, 1812–63.

TABLE 1.1
The Acreage under Potatoes in 1845, 1847, and 1848

Counties	Potato Acreage			Decrease (%)	
	1845	1847	1848	1845–47	1845–48
LEINSTER					
Carlow	26,447	6,873	13,668	− 74.0	− 18.3
Dublin	19,064	3,297	[7,778]*	− 82.7	− 59.2
Kildare	27,198	5,570	14,260	− 79.5	− 47.6
Kilkenny	73,715	9,403	27,002	− 87.2	− 63.4
Laois	45,877	8.523	23,416	− 81.4	− 49.0
Longford	27,030	1,414	7,240	− 94.8	− 73.2
Louth	30,129	3,545	11,956	− 88.2	− 60.3
Meath	48,245	4,573	16,705	− 90.5	− 65.4
Offaly	42,055	6,560	20,001	− 84.4	− 52.4
Westmeath	32,168	3,337	13,855	− 89.6	− 56.9
Wexford	74,492	9,860	29,384	− 86.8	− 60.6
Wicklow	27,501	5,204	12,860	− 81.2	− 53.2
Total	473,921	68,159	198,125	− 85.6	− 58.2
MUNSTER					
Clare	89,670	6,129	23,030	− 93.2	− 74.3
Cork	277,070	39,829	103,360	− 85.6	− 62.7
Kerry	78,436	18,319	34,455	− 76.6	− 56.1
Limerick	88,322	12,141	39,019	− 86.3	− 55.8
Waterford	63,212	5,937	[23,934]*	− 90.6	− 62.1
Tipperary	150,956	7,017	[39,303]*	− 95.4	− 74.0
Total	747,666	89,372	263,101	− 88.0	− 64.8
ULSTER					
Antrim	64,304	14.375	37,699	− 77.6	− 41.4
Armagh	47,563	9,652	28,604	− 79.7	− 39.9
Cavan	65,129	5.206	16,236	− 92.0	− 75.1
Derry	65,135	8,991	21,159	− 86.2	− 67.5
Donegal	75,505	10,983	27,884	− 85.5	− 63.1
Down	86,753	13,741	43,506	− 84.2	− 49.9
Fermanagh	39,091	3,681	9,185	− 90.6	− 76.5
Monaghan	45,394	6,436	19,634	− 85.8	− 56.7
Tyrone	67,782	14,101	31,304	− 79.2	− 53.8
Total	556,656	87,186	235,211	− 84.3	− 57.7
Galway	133,272	12,876	39,326	− 90.3	− 70.5
Leitrim	24,971	2,599	8,098	− 89.6	− 67.6
Mayo	147,937	6,674	28,144	− 95.5	− 81.0
Roscommon	52,469	3,916	20,182	− 92.5	− 61.5

TABLE 1.1 (*cont.*)

Counties	Potato Acreage			Decrease (%)	
	1845	*1847*	*1848*	*1845–47*	*1845–48*
Sligo	49,906	3,352	13,262	− 93.3	− 73.4
Total	408,555	29,417	109,012	− 92.8	− 73.3
Ireland total	2,186,798	274,134	805,449	− 87.5	− 63.2

Sources: Mokyr, "Irish history with the potato"; *Agricultural Statistics.*
*Totals for 1849 were substituted for missing 1848 totals.

THE CONDITION OF PRE-FAMINE IRELAND

> In some ways the story of pre-famine times resembles a
> tragedy rising to its devastating climax.
> (T. W. Freeman, *Pre-famine Ireland*, 1957)

Did Irish poverty make a catastrophe like the famine inevitable? For the Irish poor, life on the eve of the famine was at least as grim as for the poor of much of the Third World today. For the bottom one-third or even half of the population, it was harsh and comfortless even by mid-nineteenth century British or west European standards. A stream of official inquiries and numerous travelers' reports highlighted Irish poverty, and the filth, damp and "near-nakedness" associated with it. Already in 1812 Edward Wakefield had found "such various gradations of misery as he could not have supposed possible to exist, even among the most barbarous nations." In 1834 another traveling writer, Henry Inglis, deemed the state of the elderly and infirm poor "shocking for humanity to contemplate, and beyond the efforts of private beneficence to relieve," while most agricultural laborers were underemployed and living "on the very verge of starvation."[32] During the following decade, Frenchman Gustave de Beaumont, German Georg Kohl, budding English novelist William Makepeace Thackeray, American evangelist Asenath Nicholson, and many others followed, with similarly gloomy appraisals. Travelers like these, it is true, tended to visit Ireland in a season when unemployment was high and food supplies low; had they toured in, say, October or November instead of in June or July, their impressions might have been less bleak. Travelers also tended to stick to the main roads where poverty was most in evidence, and where they offered the easiest targets for beggars. Nevertheless, there is no denying the near-unanimity of their impressions. Three public investigations—the ambitious Poor Inquiry of the mid-1830s, the census of 1841, and the Drummond Commission's famous inquiry into landlord-tenant relations, published in the same year as the first attack of potato blight — brought Irish poverty into official focus. The first highlighted the extent of seasonal unemployment and material poverty, the second soberly summarized housing conditions, while the third pointed to the problems of an undercapitalized agriculture. Nor were there any signs of improvement over time, at least insofar as those dependent on labor and the potato were concerned. However, it must not be forgotten that Irish poverty was alleviated by a healthy if monotonous diet and, in most areas, access to cheap fuel in the form of bog peat or turf. Their physical stature and relative longevity suggest that the pre-famine Irish poor were healthier than their lack of material wealth would predict.[33]

The population was overwhelmingly rural and over two-thirds of the labor force relied on farming. Almost two-thirds of the males deriving a livelihood from the land held little or no land themselves. For the remaining 0.6 million males in agriculture, the distribution of land holdings was probably no more unequal than in most European countries, but still the top quarter of farms accounted for 60 percent of the land, and probably an even higher proportion of the best land. Most farms, even excluding mini-holdings of less than an acre, occupied 20 acres (8 hectares) or less.[34] On the eve of the famine, most Irish farmers were tenants operating on short leases and in marginal areas. Many, particularly in the west, held land in common through joint tenancy. The quasi-communal existence that this entailed had its compensations, but the other side of the coin was a lack of privacy and the "perpetual quarrelling and fighting about . . . ducks and pigs, and trespassing on one another's lands."[35]

The Industrial Revolution on the neighboring island had mixed consequences for the Irish economy. The cotton mills of Belfast, Dublin, Cork, and elsewhere weathered the competitive storm reasonably well until the 1810s, and in the northeast a well-established linen industry adapted successfully to the new technology. But the following few decades were tough ones for most textile workers, and indeed for all those relying on their labor alone. Ireland's specialization in foodstuffs meant that it was favored by movements in its terms of trade, an effect reinforced by the Corn Laws. Rents rose in real terms, and most farmers must have benefited too. But this offered little consolation for the landless and the near-landless. There were some signs of economic adjustment before the famine, however. The emigration rate rose, and the rate of annual population growth fell from 1.5 percent or more in the early nineteenth century to about 0.5 percent in the pre-famine decade. In some counties, such as Wicklow and Westmeath, population growth had come to a virtual halt by 1845. Even in county Clare, where numbers were rising fastest, growth halved between the 1820s and 1830s, while in Mayo, if the census is to be believed, it fell by three-quarters. Such numbers indicate that had the potato failure been delayed a few decades the country would probably have been in better demographic shape to cope. The track record of the potato before 1845, the degree of demographic adjustment within Ireland, and the rising demand for labor in regions open to Irish emigration such as Britain and North America mean that a catastrophe on the scale of the famine was neither inevitable nor even increasingly likely. In a might-have-been Ireland without *Phytophthora infestans*, the economy would have progressed slowly and painfully through a period of difficult demographic and economic adjustment. This is not to deny the vulnerability of the economy to a shock such as the potato blight, nor to deny that in the mid-1840s the two or three million people most at risk were in what seemed to many observers like an economic quagmire: badly housed, largely illiterate, underemployed, and for the most part lacking the means to emigrate.

The confiscations of the sixteenth and seventeenth centuries had left most Irish land in the hands of a small elite of English origin. In the mid-nineteenth century that elite still owned the bulk of the country's fixed capital and was still very powerful politically. Three points link it and the famine. First, the live-and-let-live style of management practiced by most landlords before 1845 had failed to control population growth. Proprietors had no more interest than tenants in preventing subdivision, and thus failed in what economist Nassau Senior dubbed "the duty for the performance of which Providence created [them,] the keeping down population."[36] Second, on the eve of the famine a significant proportion of them were in serious financial trouble. Quite how many remains somewhat unclear, but data on rents due on estates managed by the Court of Chancery imply, very roughly, that one owner in twelve was chronically insolvent. Estates in Chancery represented the extremes of indebtedness; the numbers take no account of heavily indebted estates still in proprietorial control before the famine. Moreover, for many tenants an estate being put into the hands of the Court of Chancery was a signal to make things worse by withholding rent. Estates in this category thus stood little chance of proper maintenance and improvement. In 1844–47 the managers of the Court of Chancery spent an annual average of £2,852 (about $13,700), or 0.4 percent of the rent due, on the buildings and land in their care. As a result many properties were in very poor shape by the time they were sold off to new owners. In 1852 the scene at Emo House, the former seat of the Earl of Portarlington, "resemble[d] what might be expected in the neighbourhood of some volcano," and at Sir George Goold's Shanacourt outside Cork City the house was "suffering from want of a moderate coat of paint and white-wash."[37] Naturally the owners of such embarrassed estates were poorly placed to help their tenants when disaster struck in 1846. Relief workers in Westmeath were "dispirited and weighed down by the incubus of the large property of the Earl of Lanesborough, a lunatic, from which they obtain nothing but a host of paupers." In Ballinahinch, the Martins, owners of almost an entire barony, lived on an allowance, epitomizing what a visiting philanthropist dubbed "the disorder and moral disorganization amongst the gentry and landowners." All other landowners in the barony were living on allowances, their estates managed on behalf of their creditors.[38] Third, most Irish landlords were reluctant to live in remote, thinly populated areas. This is understandable, but it meant that the destitute in such areas were even more poorly served and represented when the famine struck. In much of the west a common complaint in the late 1840s was that the lack of a leisured elite meant that farmers and priests were the main spokesmen for those at risk.[39]

During the famine the variation in mortality across the country was significant. Comparing the 1841 and 1851 censuses, which provide data down to townland level, suggests considerable and sometimes anomalous variation at the local level. The range is represented by areas such as south Wexford or north Down, which escaped lightly, and large parts of counties such as Clare, Cork, Leitrim, or Mayo, in which a quarter or more of the people perished. Few areas in Ireland can have escaped the famine as lightly as the baronies of Forth and Bargy in south Wexford in the 1840s. Indeed, a recent account claims that not only did they escape the worst, but that they "actually prospered." These baronies had long been celebrated for their distinctive prosperity; on the eve of the famine, journalist Thomas Campbell Foster noted "an extremely industrious, well-clad, cleanly and thriving people" practicing farming methods far in advance of anything he had seen in the south or west of Ireland. Foster attributed all this to the people of Forth and Bargy being descendants of the soldiers of Strongbow and Cromwell. In 1841 the proportion of Forth and Bargy families living in one-room accommodations (16.9 percent) was less than half the national average, while the percentage of those aged five and above who could neither read nor write was also considerably below the national average (37.5 against 52.7 percent). The population of Bargy rose during the famine decade— from 13,197 to 13,316—while that of Forth fell only marginally, from 24,557 to 24,359. Such near-stasis does not mean that the baronies escaped completely unscathed: it must be compared with the rise of 17.6 percent in their combined populations between 1821 and 1841. The sharp fall in population in the parish of Carne in Forth (914 to

742) was largely due to the bankruptcy of one of its landed proprietors. The Forth and Bargy region was noted for its beans, and was less dependent on the potato than most of the country.[40]

Another area that escaped relatively lightly in the 1840s was the northern half of county Down in the northeast. But even there the crisis had an impact. A reporter for the *Banner of Ulster* was told by "a very respectable authority" in February 1847 that three or four funerals passed his house near the village of Ballygowan daily, and the chairman of Newtownards Board of Guardians resigned in July 1847 in protest against overcrowding in the workhouse and the rigid application of the workhouse test by his fellow board members. And in the electoral divisions of Glaskermore and Loughbrickland in Banbridge union, over one-quarter of the population sought relief through the Soup Kitchens Act of 1847.[41]

The bleak and barren county of Mayo represented the other extreme. Mayo's population dropped by 29 percent between 1841 and 1851, with nearly one hundred thousand of its people dying of famine-related causes. While no part of Mayo can have escaped the famine, the lack of information on migration means that allocating the excess mortality across its parishes and baronies is impossible. Population decline varied widely across the county, but so probably did migration. As explained in chapter 3, the landless and near-landless poor were least likely to emigrate. Perhaps this is partly why the correlation across electoral divisions between measures of poverty such as poor law valuation per capita, numbers on relief during the crisis, or the proportion of small farms, on the one hand, and population loss, on the other, is weak.[42]

Researchers with an eye to local detail have produced evidence of several parishes or regions that seem to have fared "better" or "worse" than might have been expected during the famine. Perusal of the statistical evidence reveals significant variations in population decline across contiguous parishes or electoral divisions, lending plausibility to claims that plentiful fish here, a bad landlord there, or an energetic relief committee or board of guardians somewhere else made a difference. This is the stuff of good local history.[43] However, it must not be forgotten that county- and province-wide patterns override such local variations. There were broad regularities too in the patterns of suffering and mortality, notably a marked east-west gradient in population loss and estimated excess mortality, and these too require explanation. No manageable model of the famine can explain all the variation observed in the record; accounting for the broader patterns and the occasional "anomaly" should be seen as complementary tasks.

Joel Mokyr's classic question about the Irish famine — "Was Malthus right?" — addressed a number of issues best kept distinct. First, was Ireland overpopulated before the famine? Second, were conditions worsening before the famine? Third, was the famine inevitable? Fourth, did the famine work in ways outlined by Malthusian analysis? Answers to some of these questions are complicated by an ambiguity in T. R. Malthus's own teachings and in his writings on Ireland. The accounts of Ireland in the second edition of the *Essay on Population* and in Malthus's parliamentary evidence are bleak and gloomy. However, in 1808 Malthus had sketched the outlines of a more benign prognosis of Irish economic and demographic adjustment. Change would be gradual, he insisted, for "although it is quite certain that the population of Ireland cannot continue permanently to increase at its present rate, yet it is as certain that it will not *suddenly* come to a stop." Moreover, politics mattered: "the causes which independently of soil and climate, have actually determined the chief food of the common people in the different kingdoms of Europe, seem to have been their political state." If only Ireland's Catholic masses were granted their civil rights, "as will make them look forward to other comforts beside the mere support of their families on potatoes," they would forsake their early marriages and higher fertility. Indeed, pre-famine Ireland fits a preventative check or "moral restraint" version of the Malthusian model better than the more famous and harsher "positive check" version. On the eve of the famine, Irishwomen, on average, did not marry until they reached their mid-twenties, and men waited about three years longer than women.[44]

In the generation or so between the battle of Waterloo and the famine, Irish population growth tapered off sharply. By the early 1840s it was down to 0.5–0.6 percent per annum nationally. A big rise in emigration was largely responsible for this, but declines in nuptiality and in the birthrate also helped. The age at marriage and the proportions never marrying rose in these decades, and on the eve of the famine they were about the same as in Britain. These trends would almost certainly have continued and intensified had the potato not failed. Moreover, the evidence is against the gradual intensification of Malthusian positive checks through rises in either noncrisis or crisis mortality. This opens the way for a more benign counterfactual reading of Irish economic and social trends in the nineteenth century. On this reading the famine was not simply bound to happen; had the potato blight somehow missed Ireland, economic adjustment would have come gradually through an increase in the demand for Irish labor abroad and increasing incidence of the preventative check.

But was Ireland nevertheless overpopulated in the mid-1840s in the sense that its high population density had reduced living standards or kept them from rising? An international perspective is suggestive here. On the eve of the famine, Ireland comfortably outpeopled the whole of

Scandinavia, and also contained more people than Benelux. By 1914 both Scandinavia and Benelux would contain more than three times as many people as Ireland. Portugal and Scotland, with far fewer people than Ireland in 1845, would contain more in 1914. The population of England and Wales, less than double that of Ireland in 1845, was eight times as high by 1914. Moreover, land hunger in Ireland was intensified by the greater importance of agriculture as an employer; the proportion of males employed in agriculture there in midcentury (over two-thirds) was significantly higher than in any of the other countries included above except Sweden. Such comparisons have nothing to say about productivity, but the indications are that Irish agriculture before the famine was also relatively undercapitalized. The ratio of horses per agricultural worker is one good indicator of capital intensity. On the eve of the famine that ratio was significantly less in Ireland than in any of the same countries except Belgium, while Irish human capital inputs, as reflected by schooling and literacy rates, were also lower.[45] The implied lack of an investible surplus is consistent with relative Irish overpopulation. So is the rise in average farm income in the wake of the famine. There is some evidence too of a post-famine convergence of Irish incomes on incomes in these other economies. As Ireland lost population between 1845 and 1914, it gained in the standard-of-living stakes not only on Britain, but also on both Scandinavia and Benelux.[46]

In *Why Ireland Starved* Mokyr exploited the regional variation offered by county-level data on a range of pre-famine social and statistical surveys, in seeking to determine whether Malthus was "right." The thirty-two counties provided a convenient cross section for econometric analysis, just large enough for conventional statistical inference. To his surprise Mokyr failed to find any strong connection between land hunger and living standards on the eve of the famine. That result, and the rather weak association between excess mortality during the famine and variables such as the land-labor ratio and potato consumption, suggested, controversially, a rejection of the traditional Malthusian interpretation. However, subsequent research by Patrick McGregor, also relying on county-level data but on a somewhat different set of explanatory variables, seemed to restore the link between population pressure and poverty.[47]

Baronial data offer a finer, previously unexploited, grid. The barony is an obsolete administrative unit introduced in Elizabethan times; at the time of the famine Ireland was divided into 327 of them. The following correlation matrices and regression estimates are based on a subset of 305 baronies. I have excluded the largely urban baronies and a few on which consistent data were unavailable in the sources. The descriptive statistics, grouped below by Ireland's four provinces, show

Leinster to have been the richest in 1841, followed by Ulster, Munster, and Connacht. The human cost of the famine, measured by population loss between 1841 and 1851, was greatest in Connacht and least in Ulster.

The variables which provide the raw material for the descriptive statistics and correlation matrices reported in tables 1.2 and 1.3 as follows:

- Population in 1821, 1841, and 1851 (POP)
- The proportion of families not relying on fourth-class housing (GOODH)
- The proportion of the population that could at least read (LIT)
- Poor law valuation per capita on the eve of the famine (AVPLV)
- The change in the literacy rate between 1841 and 1851 (DLIT)
- The change in the proportion not relying on fourth-class housing (DGOODH)
- Population change 1841–51 (DPOP4151)
- Population change, 1821–41 (DPOP2141)
- A dummy variable set equal to one for coastal baronies (SEA)

Excess mortality is the most obvious measure of the famine's toll. Because migration data are lacking, it cannot be estimated barony by barony. Instead I use population change between 1841 and 1851, a cruder

TABLE 1.2
Descriptive Statistics (Means and Standard Errors) by Province

	Ireland	Leinster	Munster	Ulster	Connacht
DPOP4151	−0.219	−0.199	−0.253	−0.173	−0.285
	(0.115)	(0.118)	(0.107)	(0.102)	(0.89)
DPOP2141	0.202	0.144	0.259	0.183	0.292
	(0.166)	(0.155)	(0.199)	(0.103)	(0.154)
GOODH41	0.642	0.724	0.543	0.697	0.504
	(0.150)	(0.091)	(0.149)	(0.095)	(0.155)
DGOODH	0.206	0.127	0.251	0.230	0.307
	(0.116)	(0.092)	(0.100)	(0.077)	(0.114)
LIT41	0.541	0.585	0.456	0.663	0.376
	(0.139)	(0.074)	(0.088)	(0.142)	(0.082)
DLIT	0.028	0.033	0.024	0.029	0.022
	(0.037)	(0.041)	(0.036)	(0.037)	(0.027)
AVPLV	1.576	2.131	1.288	1.425	0.822
	(0.878)	(0.990)	(0.641)	(0.487)	(0.285)
SEA	0.236	0.127	0.356	0.290	0.244
	(0.425)	(0.335)	(0.482)	(0.457)	(0.435)

Note: See text for explanation.

TABLE 1.3
Simple Correlations between the Variables

A. IRELAND (n = 305)

	DPOP4151	DPOP2141	AVPLV	GOODH	LIT41	DGOODH	DLIT
DPOP4151	1.000						
DPOP2141	0.072	1.000					
AVPLV	0.365	−0.201	1.000				
GOODH41	0.414	−0.281	0.430	1.000			
LIT41	0.405	−0.262	0.429	0.638	1.000		
DGOODH	−0.285	0.242	−0.518	−0.786	−0.391	1.000	
DLIT	−0.240	−0.082	0.077	−0.028	−0.127	−0.036	1.000

B. LEINSTER (n = 118)

	DPOP4151	DPOP2141	AVPLV	GOODH	LIT41	DGOODH	DLIT
DPOP4151	1.000						
DPOP2141	0.223	1.000					
AVPLV	0.317	0.103	1.000				
GOODH41	0.499	0.143	0.155	1.000			
LIT41	0.405	0.136	0.134	0.469	1.000		
DGOODH	−0.253	−0.016	−0.364	−0.559	−0.079	1.000	
DLIT	−0.209	0.231	0.103	−0.266	−0.248	0.044	1.000

C. MUNSTER (n = 73)

	DPOP4151	DPOP2141	AVPLV	GOODH	LIT41	DGOODH	DLIT
DPOP4151	1.000						
DPOP2141	0.236	1.000					
AVPLV	0.355	−0.079	1.000				
GOODH41	0.240	−0.108	0.265	1.000			
LIT41	0.094	−0.089	0.424	0.357	1.000		
DGOODH	−0.240	0.078	−0.252	−0.801	−0.351	1.000	
DLIT	−0.536	−0.368	−0.181	−0.118	−0.102	0.077	1.000

D. ULSTER (n = 69)

	DPOP4151	DPOP2141	AVPLV	GOODH	LIT41	DGOODH	DLIT
DPOP4151	1.000						
DPOP2141	0.199	1.000					
AVPLV	0.349	−0.486	1.000				
GOODH41	0.198	−0.313	0.567	1.000			
LIT41	0.331	−0.278	0.773	0.553	1.000		
DGOODH	−0.215	0.234	−0.380	−0.875	−0.310	1.000	
DLIT	−0.255	−0.166	−0.098	−0.074	−0.392	−0.062	1.000

E. CONNACHT (n= 45)

	DPOP4151	DPOP2141	AVPLV	GOODH	LIT41	DGOODH	DLIT
DPOP4151	1.000						
DPOP2141	0.077	1.000					
AVPLV	0.043	−0.284	1.000				
GOODH41	0.163	−0.304	0.183	1.000			
LIT41	−0.119	−0.271	0.358	0.521	1.000		
DGOODH	−0.234	0.133	−0.103	−0.857	−0.377	1.000	
DLIT	−0.233	−0.100	−0.177	0.050	0.090	0.107	1.000

Note: See text for explanation.

measure but still a fair proxy since its determinants — changes in the death rate, the birthrate, and the emigration rate — were all influenced by the famine. Living standards are captured by indices of housing quality (the proportion of households not living in fourth-class accommodation) and literacy (the proportion of people who could at least read) in the 1841 census, and by poor-law valuation as reported in the 1851 census, divided by the 1841 population. Since land dominated the poor-law valuation, the last of these proxies amounts to a measure of quality-adjusted land per head.

In tables 1.2 and 1.3, the mean values of these variables and the simple correlations between them are reported both for Ireland as a whole and for its four provinces separately.[48] They suggest:

1. A positive association between different measures of material well-being in 1841 and population change in 1841–51. Areas where average living standards were highest before the famine suffered least during the famine.

2. A negative association between improvements in living standards in 1841–51 and population change in the same decade. In other words, crude evidence that the famine targeted the poor and improved the lot of survivors.

3. In the country as a whole, though not in the province of Leinster, a negative association between population growth before the famine (1821–41) and living standards on the eve of the famine.

4. Some sign of "convergence" in the negative correlations between our proxies for living standards in 1841 and changes in living standards during the famine decade. In other words, those areas in which conditions were worst before the famine were those where well-being as defined by housing and literacy made the biggest gains.

Only one of my measures of living standards on the eve of the famine (poor law valuation per capita) comes close to capturing Mokyr's land-based proxies for population pressure. Still, the findings reported below are consistent with a loosely Malthusian perspective on the crisis. They imply that the famine struck hardest in the poorest baronies, and the increase in living standards that followed was greatest where population loss was greatest. Moreover, population growth before the famine was associated with poverty in 1841, if not impoverishment (on which data are lacking at the baronial level). By and large, high population growth before the famine meant high population growth in its wake.

At the provincial level the explanatory variables work best for Leinster and worst for Connacht. The difference is probably connected with the interbaronial variation in mortality (lowest in Connacht, highest in Ulster and Leinster). In general, baronies with a sea boundary fared better, after controlling for poverty on the eve of the famine. This suggests either that access to fish, seashells, and seaweed mattered during the crisis, or that being near the sea meant being nearer relief and employment in port towns. Impact elasticities estimated from regression estimates and reported elsewhere suggest that, across the island as a whole, roughly speaking, a difference of one percent in literacy in a barony in 1841 reduced population loss in the following decade by the same amount, while a 10 percent edge in valuation per head before the famine was associated with a 4 percent rise in population over the same period. Moreover, a one percent fall in population in the 1840s was associated with a 1.86 percent rise in literacy and a 0.3 percent improvement in housing quality as defined.[49]

WEATHER, CLIMATE, AND THE FAMINE

The famine was bound up with Ireland's climate in a number of ways. The Irish climate is moist and temperate. During the winter months, temperature in the west averages 6°–7° C (43°–45° F); in one geographer's evocative account, "in some years December is so mild that almost any garden will have a number of flowers in bloom." Such a climate gave nineteenth-century Irish farmers a comparative advantage in potatoes and in grass. The long growing seasons meant that cattle and sheep could graze virtually all year long. This reduced the attractions of stall feeding and winter dairying. Before the onset of blight the potato was less vulnerable to the rain or lack of sunshine that would seriously reduce grain yields.[50] The demand for agricultural labor depended in large part on the rhythms of the farming season. That demand was lowest in the months between November and February, when there was little productive work to do, with little growth and the ground either too wet and heavy or too hard for digging and ploughing. Joel Mokyr's estimate of 140.5 days as the annual average number worked by male agricultural laborers, based on the Poor Inquiry of 1835–36, reflects these factors.[51]

The evidence in the Poor Inquiry of the mid-1830s is emphatic on the point that there was little work for agricultural laborers between December and March. The reports from county Clare, the focus of much controversy in the early stages of the famine, are unanimous and worth repeating in part. In the parishes of Abbey and Oughtmanagh in the north of the county, "the greater number of labourers [were] altogether out of employment for more than half the year"; in Miltown Malbay in the west "from the month of December until March there [was] nearly a total cessation of agricultural labour"; in Kildysart in the south "from the digging of the potatoes in autumn, and the setting of them in spring, and during the sowing of corn, there [was] little or no employment for the labourer"; in Kilmanaheen north of Miltown "there [was] scarcely any employment for labourers from Christmas-day until St. Patrick's-day, the 17th of March"; and likewise for all other places offering evidence.[52] The constant criticism made against the public works during the early stages of the famine, that they were crowding out private employment on the land, overlooks this key fact.

An added consideration is that though Irish winters were mild by European standards, rain and damp made working outdoors in them for prolonged periods unpleasant and unhealthy. December and January were usually the wettest months, but they often also brought below-zero (0° C) temperatures. That the rural laboring poor were badly clothed and their housing rudimentary is borne out by the famous Poor Inquiry of the mid-1830s. But for many, if not most of them, relatively easy access to fuel in the form of bog peat mitigated the discomforts of secondhand hand-me-downs, and housing consisted of single-room thatched cabins that lacked glass windows, often had mud floors, and "made of sun-dried mud and built with walls the height of a man."[53]

Outside observers and commentators unfamiliar with Irish work routines were liable to misunderstand why "the period [for work] had not yet arrived [though] here we are in the middle of January, the land untilled and choked with weeds and no preparation in the way of seed." A good example is the public works inspector who declared in November 1846 that the thousands he had struck off the welfare lists in Clare "have now gone quietly to till their farms." The combination of poor clothing, cheap fuel, and limited demand for labor explains why the pre-famine poor spent the coldest and wettest part of the winter indoors in semihibernation.[54] Indeed, the combination represented a good example of what development economists call a low-level equilibrium or poverty trap: a labor force too short of capital to be productive at home and too poor to emigrate and be productive elsewhere.

The weather exacerbated the famine in two ways. First, in Ireland the potato had escaped relatively lightly in 1845, but in the following year the weather caused the blight to inflict far more damage there than anywhere else in Europe. In 1846 bad weather had delayed the planting, and drought in the early summer delayed the growth of the tubers; then continuous and heavy rainfall in late July and early August destroyed virtually the entire potato crop, as the wetness caused the spores of the fungi to wash into the soil and attack the bulbs. In France not only did yields fall by less; the aggregate area under potatoes was hardly affected. The average yield in 1845–49 was only one-fifth down on the 1840–44 average, and in 1845–46 only one-third less than in 1843–44. In Belgium the fall in potato yields in 1845 was greater than in Ireland, but the damage thereafter was less, and the reduction in the area under potatoes was also less. In Scotland similar weather patterns meant that yields were affected as in Ireland but, as noted earlier, this mattered less, given the potato's less central place.[55]

Second, the policy of resorting to public works when famine threatened was not new in Ireland. In 1822, 1831, and 1836 public works had been the main channel for relief. On those occasions, however, the threat had been much more limited and had peaked in the "hungry" months of late spring and early summer.[56] Relying on public works in mild weather to stave off a limited crisis was one thing, but relying on them in the depth of winter to relieve a major catastrophe was quite another. Ireland's climate made the choice of public works under the elements during the winter of 1846–47, and to a lesser extent in 1847–48, a tragic mistake. The weather in the late 1840s was not exceptionally cold, as it had been during the last catastrophic famine of 1740–41, when "*a mbeatha go léir gur léirscrios uathu an sioc*" (all their food the frost destroyed). But the winter of 1846–47 was a very cold one, with average temperatures in Dublin between December and February nearly 4° F below the 1830–50 average. As seen in table 1.4, January 1848 was also exceptionally cold.[57]

Bad weather cut the incomes of those relying on piece rates.[58] More generally, being forced to work or even to feign work in the open under "the pelting of the pitiless storm" was much more serious than exceptionally cold or wet weather per se. Some officials admitted as much at the time. Lieutenant Colonel Douglas reported from Nenagh in mid-December 1846 that the snow represented "a frightful aggravation" to the surrounding misery, and pleaded that workers continue to be paid for merely clearing the snow where necessary. A Board of Works inspector attributed deaths in north Mayo at the height of the famine to inadequate food and "exposure to the inclemency of the weather." He ex-

TABLE 1.4
Mean Temperatures (Fahrenheit) in Dublin during the Famine

Month	1845–46	1846–47	1847–48	1830/50
October	49.7	49.6	51.0	49.2
November	44.5	46.8	48.0	45.4
December	41.3	**36.1**	42.8	43.1
January	45.2	41.4	**36.6**	40.9
February	44.0	**37.6**	43.7	43.0
March	42.8	42.6	41.9	45.9
Average	44.6	42.4	44.0	44.6

Note: Coldest temperatures are in bold.

plained that the practice of the Irish peasantry before the potato failure had been "to sit over the fire the entire winter rarely leaving their cabins." A callous Clare landlord would later dismiss complaints about the cold in Kilrush workhouse with the remark that the inmates had been used to sitting "in very large chimneys."[59] Several other accounts referred to the inadequate clothing of those on the public works. According to one from Carrickallen in south Leitrim in February 1847, "the great prevalence of dysentery and fever now existing" could be attributed to "the great want of clothing at present felt among the poor, many of the labourers on the Public Works being almost in a state of nudity." In Kilrush the medical attendant attributed the rise in admissions to the fever hospital in late 1846 to "disease engendered by cold and exposure on the Public Works at this inclement season of the year, the poor being ill clad and not sufficiently clad to sustain them." In Clare a poor man confided that "cold and exposure on the public works, with Indian meal bread and water, was sapping his life up." A medical man in the same county attributed excess mortality to the want of food "together with the exposure to cold and wet to which the peasantry were exposed to an unusual degree," while another report attributed the prevailing sickness to tailors, shoemakers, and other artisans unused to outdoor work "being obliged to go on the roads." A west Wicklow landlord's wife noted of the poor that "their rags [were] hardly coverings for decency." Donegalman Hugh Dorrian's interpretation of official intent, committed to paper a few decades after the event, may have been misguided, but the narrower point about the inadvisability of public works in such conditions holds:

> Here is where the government advisors dealt out the successful blow, and it would appear premeditated, the great blow for slowly taking away human life, getting rid of the population and nothing else, by forcing the hungry and the half clad men to stand out in the cold and in the sleet and rain from morn till night, for the paltry reward of nine pennies per day. Had the poor pitiful creatures got this allowance, small as it was, at their homes it would be relief, it would be charity, it would convey the impression that their benefactors mean to save life, but in the way thus given, on compulsory conditions, [it] meant next to slow murder.[60]

A BRIEF CHRONOLOGY

Unlike most great historical events, the Irish famine had no clear beginning and no clear end. Its long duration marks it off from most other famines and added to the difficulties of coping with it at the time. So

when, approximately, did the famine begin? If famine is defined by excess mortality, the answer must be "not before the autumn of 1846."
This is not to deny the plentiful evidence of privation and fear in the
wake of the first onslaught of *Phytophthora infestans*. As early as November 1845 the London *Times* correspondent in Ireland was outlining
measures needed "to prevent, as much as possible, the horrors, the high
prices, and extortion of a famine"; in January 1846 a well-supported
petition from west Clare pleaded for protection from "the certain and
immediate perils of famine, plague, and pestilence"; and in late May
1846 the poor law guardians of Ballina in north Mayo called for "immediate measures by the introduction of provisions and the carrying on
of public works in this union, to avert the awful calamity which is now
impending." But the evidence for famine-induced deaths before the late
autumn of 1846 is very thin.[61] Some of the credit for this must go to the
relief measures taken by the administration of Sir Robert Peel, including
public works and the creation of public grain depots to meet emergen-
cies. The partial nature of the potato failure was also a factor, however.
The output of potatoes in 1845 had, after all, been only a quarter to a
third below normal, with high yields partly compensating for the damage done by the blight.[62]

News of the much more serious failure of the potato in August 1846
focused the attentions of the Treasury and the officially appointed relief
commissioners under Sir Randolph Routh on the issues of free trade in
grain and facilities for converting the cheapest substitute for potatoes,
maize or Indian corn, into edible meal. But the rapidly worsening situation on the ground, particularly in the west of Ireland, also brought
direct action. It was clear from the outset that the Irish poor-law regime
created in 1838 could not cope. Locally appointed relief committees
and public-works schemes, funded by a combination of local and government contributions, were envisaged as "the principal means of coping with the calamity." As discussed in chapter 2, the policy of reliance
on earnings from "workfare" to induce the inflows of food required to
stave off famine failed on several counts. Moves by some poor law
unions in October and November 1846 at organizing improvised sys-
tems of outdoor relief were not countenanced by the authorities; the
inadequacy of the public works was not admitted until early in 1847.
This delay had disastrous consequences.

The official reaction to early reports of deaths from starvation in the
press was requests for verification. At first such deaths attracted a good
deal of publicity. One of the first was that in late October 1846 of
Dennis McKennedy from Coolasnahee near Skibbereen, an employee on
the public works. A postmortem found no food in McKennedy's stom-
ach nor in his small intestines, but "in the large bowels a portion of

undigested raw cabbage mixed with excrement." Other reports would soon follow, such as that from Lorrha in north Tipperary of the death of a man who had lived for several days "on the refuse of vegetables," or from Dingle in county Kerry of a jury's verdict of death "partly from starvation" on a local man. Early in December, Daniel O'Connell, the "Liberator," was told about the death of "a poor woman, wife of a cottier, on Denis Mahony's property" in Kerry, and Charles Trevelyan, Treasury undersecretary in London, was seeking information from officials on the spot about a woman and three children found drowned in Kilkenny, an event allegedly "brought about by extreme destitution." In west Clare reports of individual deaths from starvation were few before the end of 1846; "it was not contended that death had occurred from starvation." Nationally, such deaths multiplied in early 1847; they then lost their newsworthiness.[63]

The growing crisis is also reflected in the big rise in deaths in workhouses from late 1846 on.[64] Mounting pressure on all of the country's 130 workhouses, each responsible for the poor in a "union" of parishes (hence the administrative term "union"), was reflected in congestion, increasing financial problems, or both. Between early October 1846 and early January 1847, 266 people died in the packed workhouse in Skibbereen, compared to ten in the same period a year earlier, and eleven two years earlier, and by the end of 1846 one inmate in four was suffering from either fever or dysentery. The workhouse was already "full to suffocation" by then. In the South Dublin Union, also full, deaths from dysentery began to mount in late 1846; from December 1846 on the monthly toll was about twenty. In Castlebar, on the other hand, the workhouse remained nearly empty because the guardians had no funds, and local landlords and the authorities haggled about who should relieve the poor.[65]

From late 1846 on, the classic famine symptoms of wandering beggars, roadside deaths, rising crime rates, poorly attended burials, widespread panic about contagion, and mass evictions were commonplace throughout most of the country. Evictions, by forcing more migration, exacerbated the problems. Officials in Dublin were besieged with reports of fever, dysentery, distress, and unrest. While the poor were the main victims, other groups were not immune from the associated infectious diseases. As explained in greater detail in chapter 3, the young and the very old were particularly vulnerable, though it must be noted that mortality in those same age-groups was higher also in normal times. Survival strategies ranged from deception to emigration, from petty thieving to seeking public relief, from rioting to begging. Though larceny and agrarian unrest increased for a time, threats to public order were local and limited.

The course of the famine is well documented. Reduced confidence in the potato and the shortage of seed cut the acreage under potatoes in 1847 to less than 0.3 million (compared to over two million in 1846). The decline was greatest in regions where the potato bulked largest before the famine. Yields were good in 1847 and though output was necessarily low, a plentiful supply of maize convinced many that the worst was over. Hopes that the blight had retreated caused the area under potatoes to recover to 0.8 million acres in 1848. The recovery was greatest in the poorer provinces of Munster and Connacht (for details see table 1.1). The blight returned with full vigour, however, and throughout much of the west conditions in the spring of 1849 matched those of 1847.

Evocative cameos and anecdotes of the famine abound in public and private archives, in literature, in memoirs, and in folklore. An American traveler who had often visited and stayed in the cabins of the poor before the crisis struck now found the gap between herself and them increasingly difficult to bridge. Her comparison has an enduring resonance. The finding that in the Montiaghs on the shores of Lough Neagh a big increase in numbers dying at home preceded the rise in workhouse admissions late in the spring of 1847 suggests how very reluctant the poor of that boggy area were to resort to the workhouse.[66] In west Kerry a new song lamented the young men having lost their spark; there was no talk any more of marriage, but "*tabhair dom an spré*" (give me the dowry) and "*raghad anonn*" (I'm heading off), and good-looking women could now venture out alone at night without fear of harassment. In May 1847 two young country girls went to the shop of a Clonmel hairdresser and sold their hair for 2s 3d (about 55 cents) per head, "an original and extraordinary mode of seeking relief." In Ballykilcline in Roscommon an entire family perished together and remained undiscovered for a week. The men who entered the house "got weak and sick and had to be given whiskey." There were many such accounts of bodies left unburied; others described survivors dragging corpses unaided to cemeteries, and people not yet quite dead being lowered into communal burial pits. The cathartic sociability of the Irish wake gave way to hurried and sometimes furtive burials. In north Cork in April 1849, bodies were carefully concealed for "a space of 13 or 14 days" for the sake of an entitlement to half a stone of Indian meal. Throughout the country there was a sharp increase in petty crimes against property, with jail sentences for offenses such as stealing a basket of turf, stealing a hen, and stealing turnips. A Nenagh magistrate reluctantly sentenced two brothers to three months' hard labor for stealing turnips from a gentleman in Holycross in January 1847, sorry to see such "decent-looking men in the position in which they were." In the same court the theft of two sheep warranted ten years' transportation. To some perpetrators, the risk of jail or prospect of transportation seemed preferable to incarceration in the workhouse. In Limerick in April 1849, it took a court only three days to deal with twelve hundred cases, because nearly all the defendants pleaded guilty in hopes of being held in prison; in this upside-down world two defendants who were set free were recommitted the next day for "an attempt to break into jail." In Cork it was the same story in March 1847; so overcrowded was the courthouse with the diseased and starving that it had to be fumigated twice a day with chloride of lime.[67] Yet amid all the misery, some things went on more or less as before. The first levée of the Earl of Bessborough's viceroyalty in mid-January 1847 attracted the biggest crowd in several years. A few months later, side by side with an account of more vice-regal festivities at Dublin Castle, the *Freeman's Journal* carried reports of inquests into the deaths from starvation of Patrick O'Neill and Bridget Borrane of Bruff and of Michael Kelly of Moate who had died in prison, charged with "breaking a window and stealing bread therefrom."[68]

What of the famine's end? By mid-1851 about one million had died who would not have died otherwise, not counting averted births as deaths. Another million or so had emigrated. As explained more fully in chapter 3, the choice of estimating mortality to 1851 is dictated in part by that being a census year. But few histories of the famine use 1851 as an end date. Canon John O'Rourke ended his pioneering account in 1847; Woodham-Smith ended hers with Queen Victoria's visit in August 1849, while Mary Daly found that "distress remained prevalent in Ireland throughout 1849 and in some cases until 1850." Mokyr and Gray also chose 1850, while the choice of 1852 on the title page of Edwards and Williams was largely dictated by its chapter on emigration.[69] Certainly, in much of Ireland excess mortality remained high in 1849. The average weekly death rate in workhouses rose from 2.5 per thousand in September 1848 to 12.4 per thousand in May 1849; in Ennistymon in Clare in December 1848 it briefly reached 52 per thousand. In the west and the south, according to the poor-law commissioners, the early months of 1849 "were marked by a greater degree of suffering . . . than any period since the fatal season of 1846–47." Evictions were in large part to blame, leaving "many thousands of families shelterless and destitute of fuel as well as food." In unions where the workhouse was full, the homeless were forced to part with some of their food rations for lodging. In the summer of 1849 the workhouses were still full to overflowing, holding 250,000 people. The result was continued recourse to outdoor relief; 784,000 claimants (or one-eighth of the entire population) were so relieved in July 1849.[70]

The end came unevenly. In the province of Ulster conditions had improved considerably by 1849 and by 1850 the death rate had fallen back to near its 1846 level. In west Cork the famine was probably as severe in late 1846 and early 1847 as anywhere else in the island, but by September 1847 "famine mortality had decreased to a minimum."[71] But the bleak picture drawn in other areas by both censal and workhouse data and qualitative evidence cannot be ignored. In January 1849 relieving officers deemed the prospects of Swinford union "gloomy in the extreme," in neighboring Castlebar "as great, if not greater than at the corresponding period last year," in Scariff "confessedly more severe and real than last year," in Ballinrobe "in the ensuing season . . . not less than in the corresponding period of last year."[72] The story of continuing crisis in the west is lent graphic support by the pleas for financial aid in the spring of 1849 from priests in Mayo and Galway to Archbishop Murray of Dublin. Toward the end of 1849 conditions in Mayo had greatly improved; the county surveyor could not see "the least sign of scarcity," and officials and clergymen had told him that the worst was over and that the country was "in process of amendment." Yet Ballina's workhouse experienced another significant peak in mortality in the summer of 1850, as did Killala's workhouse in the early months of 1851.[73]

Other surviving workhouse registers also indicate the protracted nature of the famine. In the first four months of 1849, over twelve hundred people died in the workhouse in Fermoy in east Cork. In Birr (Parsonstown) the weekly death rate of 35.9 per thousand in mid-May 1849 did not match the previous peaks of 67.8 per thousand in April 1847 or 46.8 per thousand in early February 1848, but the number of inmates in early May 1849 (3,007) and the number of deaths (101) in the week ending 19 May 1849 represented all-time highs for the Birr Union. In the unions of Kilrush and Ennistymon the continuing high mortality from infectious diseases, particularly among the elderly and young children, prompted the publication of special parliamentary returns in 1851. In the well-documented case of Ennistymon, over two-thirds of the deaths from dysentery, diarrhea, and typhus in 1850–51 occurred more than a month after admission to the workhouse, compelling evidence that even at that late stage the workhouse was compounding rather than alleviating misery.[74]

Aggregate data reveal that the number of deaths in workhouses was still very high in 1851.[75] However, the total number on relief, indoor or outdoor, fell from just over a million in July 1849 to 0.4 million a year later and under 0.3 million in July 1851. According to the report of the Poor Law Commissioners for 1852–53, the marked shift in the seasonality of admissions into workhouses from 1851 on reflected a return to a new normality: in every year between 1847 and 1850 the number of admissions peaked in late June or early July, but in 1851–52 and 1852–53 the peaks were in mid-February. The commissioners also noted with evident satisfaction that Connacht, the worst-hit province, had recovered sooner from the famine than some pockets elsewhere. The total number of inmates in Connacht's workhouses fell from 42,286 in mid-April 1851 to 26,551 a year later and to 17,389 in mid-April 1853. The fall in numbers was greatest in remote, devastated unions in the west of the province such as Belmullet, Clifden, Newport, and Westport. In Ireland as a whole the number receiving outdoor relief never exceeded four thousand in any week after the summer of 1851; from then on the workhouses were once more deemed to be able to handle pauperism. Inquest judgments of death from destitution fell from 120 in 1851–52 to 35 in 1852–53.[76]

The Irish famine thus raged five years at least. Its long duration made it more like that foretold by the young Joseph in Genesis 41 than most famines on record. In the history of famines in France and England, individual years or pairs of years (1558, 1693–94, 1709–10) stand out. Another example is 1740–41. Most of the mortality caused by the Great Finnish Famine of the 1860s was confined to the spring and early summer of 1868. The latest verdict on the better-known Soviet famine of 1932–33 suggests that it too lasted about a year. Most of India's nineteenth-century famines lasted two years at most, and a recent reassessment of the Great Bengali Famine confines excess mortality to 1943–44. The dates given for the Chinese Great Leap Famine in Western accounts are 1958–61 or 1958–62, but the lion's share of excess deaths seems to have been in 1959.[77]

The long-lasting character of the Irish crisis led to compassion fatigue. An early surge in private charity both at home and abroad reflected an initial eagerness to help, but the efforts of most charities peaked in early 1847 and there was relatively little forthcoming in 1848 and 1849. Members of the Society of Friends worked heroically in 1846 and in Black '47. Then, exasperated at the unfeeling attitude of officialdom, the Society refused to heed government proddings to do more. The British Relief Association, the funds which it amassed mainly during 1847 exhausted, wound down its operations in October 1848. Donor fatigue is also reflected in the records of other smaller local charities such as the Society of Sick and Indigent Roomkeepers, the Mendicity Institution, and the Dublin Parochial Association (see chapter 5).

The flipside of the drop in charitable donations was a less sympathetic public opinion. This was reflected in the very negative picture of Irish irresponsibility and dishonesty painted in the London *Times*, the satirical weekly *Punch*, and elsewhere from early 1847 on. By October

1847, when an order in council requested clergymen of the established church to plead with their congregations for relief for the Irish, the public mood had already shifted. Newspapers contained several letters from protesting rectors and curates arguing that the welfare of their own poor should come first and that the Irish poor did not deserve any more. This "cold and repulsive" response prompted *The Economist* to declare that "charity now seems exhausted."[78] The arrival of thousands of destitute and often sickly Irish in Britain during 1847, with its attendant dangers for public health, did not help.[79] In 1849 all that Westminster would concede was a "rate-in-aid," whereby regions still suffering from famine would be relieved by a transfer of about £0.25 million ($1.2 million) (6d or 30 cents in the pound on a valuation of about £9 million or $44 million) from the better-off parts of Ireland. Irish ratepayers (taxpayers) resisted the measure, claiming that this was a national calamity and that therefore the burden should be shared throughout the United Kingdom. This was surely reasonable, but it must also be said that the taxpayers' resistance reflected a broader reluctance to take responsibility for distress outside their own immediate areas. Though ratepayers in Leinster stood to contribute most, opposition to the rate-in-aid was fiercest in east Ulster, where it had a marked sectarian edge. Meanwhile the *Times* stressed the "moral stimulus" that would result was the "difference between giving alms in the presence of our children and inducing them to contribute out of their own pocket money." The rate-in-aid was forced through Parliament after several months of controversy and agitation. Annoyed by the apparent reluctance of the Irish to help one another, in May 1849 Prime Minister Lord John Russell refused to seek parliamentary sanction for the minimum of £0.1 million (about half a million dollars) deemed necessary "if the house should say that there should be no possible case of starvation in Ireland."[80]

The long-drawn-out character of the famine also entailed years of land clearances and emigration on a massive scale. Comprehensive data on both are lacking. Emigration to North America did not peak until 1851, when it reached almost 250,000, having risen from about 100,000 in 1846 to 200,000 in 1847; it would exceed one percent of the population annually until 1858. Much of this enormous outflow is explained by the famine, but the very size of the outflow in the famine years probably accounts for some of the emigration in following years.[81] The time trend in the number of evictions is less clear, since comprehensive data are available only from 1849 on. One assessment has put the total number of "actual evictions" between 1846 and 1853 at 70,000, with 42,000 of those taking place between 1849 and 1852; another puts the total in the 1846–48 period at 17,000. A recent analysis of data on civil bill ejectments that were entered and decreed revises such findings upward by a considerable margin, and indicates that the number of evictions reached a peak in 1848 in most counties.[82] In north Mayo, as early as mid-January 1847 evictions had taken on the character of clearances; six thousand civil bills had been served at Ballina, and the "persons against whom they were issued abandoned their homes and wandered through the country. No one had any interest in obtaining relief or employment for them, and it was difficult . . . to obtain any information about them."[83] In Kilrush Union in west Clare, notorious for clearances during the famine, at least twelve thousand people were evicted between 1847 and 1850. Hard landlords such as the Marquis of Sligo and Colonel Vandeleur and tough, unsentimental land agents such as Marcus Keane in Clare and John Ross Mahon in the midlands played an important part in the process. Landlord-appointed bailiffs carried out the evictions and the demolition of cabins; the police stood by but rarely intervened.

The mass evictions or clearances continued into the early 1850s. In the early stages evictions were more selective, and some proprietors offered tenants a subsidized passage to America in return for free possession. An absentee Kerry landlord used the crisis as a means of disposing of "some bad tenants" and amalgamating farms. On his 1848 visit, for example, he got rid of "a whole nest of bad & crazy tenants" in the townland of Derivrin, leaving "only four tenants & no partnerships: Moriarty £70, Maurice Connell £90, Horgan, £80; & Connor, £36." Two years later he noted with some satisfaction that "since the potato famine I have emigrated several of the worst tenants & enlarged the farms."[84] But as the crisis deepened, the option of compensation for possession was withdrawn, and in many areas the evictions targeted communities rather than individuals.[85]

Landlords evicted tenants, and tenants got rid of lodgers and laborers. Though the record contains many examples of compassion and of solidarity, there are many, too, of repulsive and inhumane behavior by the not-so-poor against the poor, and by the poor against the poor. In May 1847 the *Cork Examiner* accused some local poor-law guardians of treating workhouse inmates as "some vile, filthy, creeping *vermin*, that it would be well to get rid of, if possible." In Clare a poor relief official, haunted by what he had seen, found that the famine had "hardened the people's hearts against their children and relatives," and concluded that "a reckless, careless and selfish feeling will arise where great want exists."[86] He would not have been surprised at the story, told decades later, of a young lad employed on a public works scheme in Teampall a' Chómaid graveyard in south Kerry. The steward, remembered as Sullivan Dubh, dismissed the boy for continuing to work while his father was being buried nearby. The story was intended to show

how 'the famine and the hardship stifled much of the decency in people's hearts." That the poor were more sinned against than sinning is also the message of a story about Clareman Pat Halpin, who had been charged with manslaughter for "turning out of his house Pat Cahill, who was his lodger, in consequence of which exposure he died" on 11 May 1850. The local police inspector had charged Halpin "not with a view to have him punished, as he was a very distressed man, but with a view to deter others from acting in a like manner." The inspector hoped that the example might deter others from "similar acts of brutality, *as they thought no more of a life of a fellow creature than they would of that of a dog.*"[87] A comparative perspective suggests that big famines everywhere produce their myriad Pat Halpins; kinship and neighborhood ties eventually loosen or dissolve, theft becomes endemic, collective resistance yields to apathy, and group integrity is shattered.[88]

Chapter Two

RELIEF

> [The famine was] primarily a disaster like a flood
> or an earthquake.
> (Rodney Green, in *The Course of Irish History*, 1967)

> Unlike an earthquake, a famine is rarely a sudden
> emergency. It is usually a long-drawn-out calamity.
> (W. R. Aykroyd, *The Conquest of Famine*, 1974)

AGENCY AND VOICE

STRATEGIES FOR preventing future famines and relieving those most at risk in actual famines have been much in the news over the last decade or so. In the recent past, international relief measures have tended to concentrate on food aid, but a strong case has also been made for the alternative of cash aid channeled through public employment schemes. As economists Jean Drèze and Amartya Sen, two of the most influential supporters of the cash-for-work strategy, stress in *Hunger and Public Action* (1989), a major problem with food aid is that much of it never reaches the starving. Several studies of modern famines in sub-Saharan Africa indicate that food aid ends up by benefiting the wealthy and the influential more than the poor, urban dwellers more than country people, and residents more than migrants. Stories abound of injustice and discrimination in the distribution of food during famines past and present. In Finland in 1867–68, those charged with distributing grain were often suspected of keeping some of it for themselves, though such suspicions were hard to prove. In neighboring Sweden in the same years, though in general aid was directed where it was most needed, in some parishes the interests of property-owning taxpayers took preference over those at greatest risk. In tsarist Russia in the 1890s, the substantial farmers (*kulaks*) charged with administering food aid might resell relief supplies or set them aside for their own uses; less sinister but equally problematic was the determination of some village communes to divide aid equally rather than according to need. Sometimes the problem is sheer gangsterism; an abiding image of the Somali famine of the early 1990s is the photographs of the gun-toting "technicals" roaming around in trucks and extracting food and protection money from the relief agencies. When economic backwardness is coupled with civil unrest or warfare, the opportunities for corruption increase. In Biafra in the late 1960s, in Ethiopia in the mid-1980s, and in Sudan in the mid-1990s, relief supplies fueled the soldiers and the military campaigns that were largely responsible for the crises in the first place. Declining real incomes increased the temptation for officials to collude with merchants, providers of transport, and others involved in the market for foodgrains. An extreme example of the leakages entailed in the transfer between donor and victim is offered by the Sudan, where in 1984–86 foreign aid exceeded one billion dollars, or one-seventh of 1985 national income, and yet tens of thousands died of famine.[1] Another problem is that food aid, unless strictly limited to the periods of severe shortfall, risks crowding out food production in the famine-affected regions. This last point has long been urged by critics of the U.S. food aid program PL 480.

In *Hunger and Public Action*, Drèze and Sen argued instead for a system of nonexclusive cash aid in return for work that would enable those at risk to buy food from those who had enough. Such a system requires well-functioning markets in agricultural produce, and they concede that choosing the right people for work "involves a comparatively exacting selection procedure." Drèze and Sen also concede another awkward feature of cash-for-work: it is likely to increase energy requirements at a time when calories are at a premium. In mitigation, they claim that the leakages involved in food aid far exceed the calories sacrificed on this count. They also dismiss the possibility that cash support may divert labor from other activities, particularly crop production, arguing that "vulnerable groups will have very little access to alternative employment, and in fact alternative opportunities may even be *enhanced* by greater security." Properly planned public works programs can enhance social overhead capital and productivity. Nor, they argue, are the logistic difficulties of organizing cash relief more demanding than those of an effective system of food distribution. Cash-for-work is best seen as a strategy for early intervention, being economically less disruptive and quicker to reach those in need. Drèze and Sen offer several examples of successful cash-for-work programs.[2]

In a later study, Sen's support for cash-for-work is more tempered. He concedes that such relief is "arguably more prone to corruption," and that "the visibility of direct food distribution does provide a better check." Moreover, in conditions of severe famine as distinct from endemic malnutrition, food aid may have the advantage of reaching places faster where it is most urgent. This seems to have been the case in Bengal in mid-1943, for example; amid widespread starvation in rural areas, the authorities relied on the Famine Code and its associated pub-

lic works and subsistence wages, but "the only thing to do was to provide food directly at special centres, in the form of cooked meals."[3] Two
aspects of the choice between food aid and public works must be borne
in mind. First, the institutional context in which most famines are likely
to occur means that the problem of agency (i.e., getting the aid to where
it is most needed) is an important one. Second, there is bound to be
some trade-off between the primary goal of saving lives and the secondary goal of keeping the associated problems of crowding-out and moral
hazard under control. In other words, famine relief, like all forms of
welfare, inevitably induces some recipients to take unfair advantage; but
no effective relief effort can completely eliminate such opportunism.

The administrative focus of much writing on the Irish famine means
that public actions aimed at relieving those at risk have been widely
discussed.[4] By and large, historians have been unenthusiastic in their
assessments of the relief effort. Most of their criticisms were anticipated
by people at the time. The main points, now very familiar, focus on
relief being too little, too slow, too conditional, and cut off too soon.
Outgoings on relief, though considerable in terms of mid-nineteenth-
century public spending, seemed small, given the dimensions of the disaster. The authorities underestimated the gravity of the crisis in the
worst-affected areas and overestimated the capacity of such areas to
generate the necessary revenues. A dogmatic obsession with the moral
hazard and "pauperization" arising from gratuitous or overgenerous relief meant that the funds provided were not put to the best use: *The
Economist,* for example, held that government money and private charity had led to an "inattention to cultivation" that aggravated the destruction of the crop in 1846.[5] Nor did ministers see the crisis out; they
declared it over in mid-1847, though, as noted in chapter 1, in places it
would last four or five years more. While conscious of the difficulties of
trying to cope with a disaster on the scale of the Irish famine, most
assessments agree that relief erred on the side of caution and in insisting
too rigidly on the principle of relief being "less eligible" than the lot of
even the most destitute of those seeking to fend for themselves during
the crisis.

From the outset, the authorities in Westminster and Dublin were
faced with the challenge of how best to identify where the poor were
most vulnerable and how to transmit aid from the center to the (sometimes remote) areas most affected. A key part of the strategy adopted
was to create relief committees that would muster help at the local level.
These relief committees were supposed to raise funds locally, submit
proposals for public works, advise on those most deserving of outdoor
relief on the public works, and distribute food gratuitously where necessary. The committees, which were unpaid, were sanctioned by the

queen's lieutenant in each county. Their membership consisted mainly of landed gentry (where present), land agents, traders, clergy, and other ratepayers (local taxpayers) such as the more substantial farmers.[6] The aim was to employ voluntarism and paternalism in economizing on the cost of targeting the needy. That solution certainly capitalized on local knowledge, but the informational asymmetry that gave rise to it placed the onus on local initiative to organize support and seek matching help. This underestimated the burden placed on local representatives. It also created the potential for "agency" problems from adversarial or corrupt relief committees.

Many contemporaries were very critical of the relief committees, and historians have registered and echoed their complaints with varying conviction. Most, implicitly or explicitly, would accept the verdict of John O'Rourke's pioneering *The Great Irish Famine* (1874) that "there did not seem to be much in it." Recently, however, what may be called the "agency hypothesis," which holds that the allocation of relief was characterized by endemic waste and corruption, has been given a new lease on life.[7]

Like modern development experts, policymakers and commentators in Britain and in Ireland in the 1840s debated the most effective means of relief. The main response of Prime Minister Sir Robert Peel's administration to the initial attack of potato blight in 1845 was to target the needy through cash-for-work schemes. It also took the precaution of importing and storing a supply of Indian corn, acting secretly so as not to disrupt private markets. Peel's schemes provided employment for up to 140,000 people at a cost of £0.6 million ($2.9 million). Roughly half this sum was a grant; the remainder was intended as a loan, although it was written off later.

From mid-1847 on, most of the burden of famine relief would fall on the regime established by the Poor Relief (Ireland) Act of 1838, which established parishes called "poor law unions" for the purpose of administering poor relief. People in each union area were entitled to relief in the union workhouse. However, the role of the program in the early stages of the crisis was secondary. The new law, modeled on the English New Poor Law of 1834, had been opposed by many on the grounds that Ireland was too poor for the principle of "less eligibility" to bite; in other words, a relief regime harsher than the least attractive alternative could not be devised. Supporters countered that confining relief entirely to custom-built, prisonlike workhouses would be a sufficient deterrent to would-be welfare cheats. The first workhouses under the new law were opened in 1840; by summer 1845 the system of 130 workhouses was almost fully operational. The workhouse regime included segregation and confinement, physical labor, unpleasant and sometimes inadequate food, and a pauper's uniform. Partly because the poor loathed the new institutions which stripped them of all dignity, partly because some unions sought to keep down rate (i.e., local property-based tax) charges by deterring even very deserving paupers, few workhouses were stretched in their first few years. Thus Carrickmacross Union, with space for five hundred inmates, held only twenty-six on the first day of January 1844; Roscommon Union, with accommodation for nine hundred, held only forty-two. On that same day the workhouses in Dublin, Cork, and Belfast were nearly full. These represented the extremes. In the first quarter of 1844, 50,114 paupers were relieved in workhouses built to accommodate 100,000, and 36,381 remained on the last day of the quarter. Of those relieved, 22,585 were aged under fifteen years; the 15,311 "infirm or diseased" inmates included 1,311 cripples and 1,292 "idiots," and 706 who were blind or nearly so. A striking feature of pre-famine workhouse admissions registers is the under-representation of married couples with young children and of older married people. The registers suggest that marriage in Ireland before the famine, far from causing impoverishment, provided security.[8]

Admissions into the country's workhouses rose after the potato failure of 1845, but by the end of March 1846 they still held fewer than fifty thousand inmates, half their capacity. In some unions, this was because the ratepayers' (i.e., local taxpayers') representatives on the Board of Guardians refused to raise the sums necessary for relief. The authorities disbanded boards in Tuam and Castlerea for this reason, and replaced them by paid officials. The second potato failure in July–August 1846 brought increasing reliance on the poor law. By mid-October, four workhouses were already full, and admissions continued to rise so fast that many of the workhouses in the worst-hit areas were turning away would-be inmates by the year's end. Conditions in the workhouses became critical. On 17 October 1846 Ballina poorhouse already held twelve hundred, "the full number allowed," and the guardians turned away over three hundred more out of consideration for the health of those already in the house. In Castlerea, according to *The Economist*'s reporter on 2 January 1847, "the dormitories resembled pig-styes more than habitations of human beings, and the effluvia from them was overpowering to the highest degree"; "typhus had made its appearance."[9]

The peak in admissions reached at the end of February 1847 thus reflected capacity and public health constraints, not a peak in misery. The mean weekly death rate in the workhouses peaked in early March 1847 at 24 per thousand. In Connacht, the death rate was then 33 per thousand; it would reach 43 per thousand in late April. But as the poor-law commissioners noted in their annual report for 1846–47, statistics gave a very incomplete impression of the "disastrous state of certain individual unions," and mortality in the workhouses as a whole was very much a reflection of a limited number in which pestilence was rife.[10]

The workhouses could have held only a tiny fraction of those needing help from late 1846 on. In such circumstances the power of the "workhouse test" to deter the indolent was beside the point. But making virtual prisoners of hundreds of thousands of people would not have been the best way of dealing with the problem in any case: the mass distribution of food through soup kitchens would have made much more sense. This would have posed its own organizational challenges but, as subsequent experience would show, they would not have been insuperable. Instead, the government resorted to a system of cash-for-work on an unprecedented scale. While numbers in the workhouses rose from forty thousand at the beginning of 1846 to nearly one hundred thousand by its end, numbers on the public works rose from twenty-six thousand at the end of September 1846 to over seven hundred thousand in March 1847. Since most households were allowed only one member on the works at a time, the proceeds reached over three million people. Did they reach the most deserving? The "agency hypothesis" says not, but the balance of claims and counterclaims argues differently. It shows that the problem was less the misappropriation of relief than the reliance on payments for physical labor as the main channel of relief. The public works consumed vital calories, particularly in the adverse weather conditions of late 1846 and early 1847, and they facilitated the spread of disease. The average wage paid on the works, about 13 pence (25 cents) per day, would have been considered good money before 1846. In the circumstances of 1846/47, with potatoes virtually unavailable and substitute foods fetching high prices, it was almost certainly insufficient for household subsistence. Moreover, where wages were paid on a piece rate basis — as stipulated by law — they victimized the weak and the elderly and those who were most in need of help.[11]

Overall responsibility for dealing with the famine rested with government-appointed relief commissioners and their staff.[12] They relied on the locally appointed relief committees, as reorganized during the summer and autumn of 1846, to draw up lists of deserving candidates for work. Committees were instructed not to register landholders unless it was clear that the public works offered them the only prospect of subsistence.[13] The aim was to create the purchasing power that would induce the flow of food to where it was most needed. The relief commissioners believed that the extra cash would induce traders to import food or to retain more of what they might otherwise have exported. It might seem as if the authorities in Ireland in the 1840s had anticipated the policy recommendations of Drèze and Sen. However, there is an important difference. Drèze and Sen's support for the cash-for-work solution presupposes the existence of enough food to feed everybody. Many, if not most, modern famines fulfill that condition, to the extent that they occur in circumstances where an absolute shortage of food is not the fundamental problem. But in Ireland, at least until the arrival of large quantities of maize in the spring and summer of 1847, it was a different story.

In order to monitor problems of corruption and mismanagement and deal with them as they arose, the authorities created a temporary inspectorate involving inspecting officers, works engineers, overseers, and so on.[14] In their reports to Dublin and London, the inspectors, mostly army or ex-army men, often criticized the public works for failing to target the most deserving. They accused landlords of insisting that their tenants get priority, farmers of supporting their sons over more deserving laborers, and priests of impeding their efforts, and they were often especially scathing about the relief committees. Extensive extracts from their complaints were published in the Blue Books and in the press. Thus one inspector deemed relief committees were "a decided curse to the country and the service . . . an area of interested motives and debating societies." Another, in Kilkenny in November 1846, found most of them sending the inspectors "lists of every one that applies," while a third in Waterford got no help from the committees in "finding out men who have been placed on the works, not in need of assistance." In west Clare, Captain Wynne (on whom more later) struck three thousand people off the original lists to make room for the most destitute, but Wynne believed that this still left many landholders who were not "true objects of charity" on the works, bringing farmwork to a standstill. In south Westmeath, an inspector needed the help of the police and some of the local Catholic clergy in checking jobbing and employing the most destitute; in Leitrim, another relied on destitute applicants for work to inform on who should be struck off the lists; a third in east Galway believed one-third of those on the lists were undeserving; in Tinnehinch in Queen's County (Laois), a fourth inspector had been duped into sanctioning work for more than one member of several families. In Roscommon, though huge numbers were employed in every district, "the very poorest [were] in many cases omitted." In Dingle, "farmers have been recommended and the really destitute not attended to." In Glenties in Donegal, a poor-law guardian was employed on the works, and in Dunkinely it was the church clerk. In Galway "one chairman, a man of large fortune," was allegedly forced to resign his seat when it was discovered that he had given priority on the relief lists to those of his own tenants who had paid their rents.[15] Where farmers dominated the relief committees there were frequent accusations, and not just from public works inspectors, of them favoring their own kind at the expense of the truly destitute. In north Donegal, "the applicant for relief presented himself at the committee man's dwelling, got an hour or so at some job, then was supplied with the desired ticket drawn out in favour of some shopkeeper at some distance, and having reached that place, [would] have to await [his] turn." In December 1846 a south Tipperary priest declared himself "completely disgusted at the conduct of some of our comfortable farmers" who, when asked to furnish lists of the poor in their localities, replied with "none but their own friends and dependants, many of whom were admitted to have money funded in the Savings Banks, whilst others were known to possess corn and cattle."[16] But if some committees connived at favoring cronies, others were simply helpless in the face of demands from people seeking to be added to the lists. In west Cork they were accused of placing the elderly and the infirm on the works at the expense of the able-bodied. This may have created the right impression at the outset, but as soon as the old and the sick began to perish on the works, the Board of Works was blamed. Inexperienced and dishonest overseers were also a problem.[17] Folk memory contains references to favoritism and corruption on the public works, though the low wages mentioned in most accounts (typically fourpence per day for men) place the scale of this corruption in perspective.[18]

In February an inspector reported from Ennistymon that "where the family does not exceed three, and one of these only on the work, they are better off than they were before the failure of the crops. There can be no doubt of this where they are earning high wages, as some of them are, for instance, 2s 4d [60 cents] per day." Another reported that three members of the Lisdoonvarna relief committee had obtained jobs as gangers at six shillings a week, and that another member was a check clerk.[19] In Cavan it was alleged that horses and carts belonging to wealthy farmers were being used on the works, while in Wexford a man, his son, and two horses were employed. A relentless critic of the system in Clare found "the determination on the part of committees to take care of their friends" endemic in Mayo too.[20]

Sensationalism and hearsay were grist for the mill. One inspector claimed that the works had produced a big increase in drunkenness from Ennis, and related a story that he had heard from a priest about four brothers spending £1 ($4.80) on drink; "the fact was not then established, but was about to be investigated." Another "discovered a case in Galway where a man upon whom the verdict of death from starvation was pronounced was in possession at his death of 60 sheep and several cows; his name was Mullen, a tenant of Mr. Blake of Castle Grove, from whom I heard the particulars." According to the head of the Board of Works, "a gentleman told [him] he had received a letter from his father, who informed him that there were men employed on the works who were buying sheep!" A complaint from a west Clare land agent that one landlord's tenants were virtually excluded from the works by a coalition of priests and rival landlords could not, on investigation, be sustained.[21] Half-true and tendentious tales of jobbing were repeated in *The Times* and *Punch*, prompting a strong reaction in the letter columns. Such tales prompted one correspondent to declare that sending the Irish more money would be 'about as ineffectual as to throw a sackful of gold into one of their plentiful bogs."[22]

Though favoritism and corruption were an undoubted feature of the public works, quantitative evidence on the extent of jobbing and leakages is lacking. It should be noted, however, that 90 percent or so of the funds channeled through the Board of Works went on wages, not on administration or equipment and animal hire. Moreover, the socioeconomic gap between laborers and farmers, on which much of the criticism rested, must be kept in perspective. On the eve of the famine most Irish farms were small, and the island contained over three hundred thousand "farms" of between two and ten statute acres. But the relief commissioners defined households with even "the grass of a cow" as farmers. It is safe to assume that the bulk of those farmers eager for employment on the works had been hard hit by the crisis. Surely the "penny corruption" of those members (presumably small farmers) of the Lisdoonvarna relief committee willing to labor as gangers for a mere six shillings a week was testimony enough of their predicament. Such a perspective also explains the alarm of Daniel O'Connell, Kerry landlord and nationalist leader, at a proposal in November 1846 that even the humblest stockholders be denied work. As O'Connell complained to his son, "all are nearly equally without provision, and though the cowless creature may be somewhat lower in the scale, yet the wants of the others are equally pressing." To muddy the waters further, the impressionistic evidence of corruption is conflicting, and the loudest complaints from the poor were about delays and bureaucratic obstructiveness.[23] Nor is the picture of the relief committees, even as painted in the almost certainly biased sample in the parliamentary Blue Books, by any means one of universal deception and noncooperation.

Given the problems of bias and exaggeration, a "battle of quotes" supportive and critical of the committees would not produce a conclusive outcome. But some examples of the considerable volume of support for the committees bear noting. A senior official informed Treasury Undersecretary Trevelyan in December 1846 that, as far as he could judge, the Roscrea committee had done a good job of scrutinizing "the state of poverty of the men on the works."[24] A former engineer on the works concluded that "the greater part" of the committees "performed their duty most spiritedly, meeting day after day to help in staving off the impending calamities." The Society of Friends lauded the committee in Castletown, Queen's county, noting that practically everybody "above immediate want" had subscribed something. In February 1847 the Valentia relief committee was "very active." In Dublin "in general" the committees operated "in a regular and orderly manner," while in Roscommon they "generally, under great pressure and difficulties" seemed anxious to follow the rules.[25] Even in Clare, a notorious blackspot, in mid-January 1847 a hostile witness found the committees "in tolerably good order, with the exception of two, which ought not to exist." A few weeks later Major Watson reported from Limerick that the committees under his jurisdiction were discharging their duties "attentively" and "in a satisfactory manner"; in Carlow the committees were "doing their duty very well and firmly"; in Kilkenny "the greatest abuse existed amongst some," while "a few were exerting themselves very much"; in Meath most of the committees were acting "independently and conscientiously"; in Queen's by early January 1847 the committees were "beginning to perform their duties with greater regularity"; in Tyrone a few weeks later they were "active in the discharge of their duties."[26] And there is a good deal more along the same lines.

Moreover, there was a learning process as inspection became more effective and the committees more active. By December 1846, relief committees in Tyrone were giving "every assistance possible"; in Meath most were doing their work with "zeal and integrity"; in Monaghan they were "working better"; in Carlow they were doing their work "generally speaking, well and firmly"; in Waterford they were "improving"; in Cork they had "generally speaking . . . got into a good system," while even in remote Erris the inspector had gotten the committee "to work in a little more regular manner." In east Galway "the committees at length admit the error they committed in not scrutinizing their labour lists; already many improper objects of relief have been removed from the books."[27] It should not be forgotten that the bulk of the sums allocated to the public works was spent between January and March, when the worst of the abuses had been corrected.

During the famine the Catholic clergy played a leading role as conduits of information and social controllers. In the eyes of some inspectors they exaggerated hardship. In east Galway, priests, the "chief actors," represented the people to be literally dying of starvation. In Waterford, where with a few exceptions "the priest is the leading person," they did all they could to crowd the works. In Queen's county a priest urged something "which no judgement could be equal to, viz. pricing the work in accordance with each individual's physical ability to execute it." In Leitrim, an inspector complained of the undue influence of priests and clergymen "as having no stake in country, they are regardless as to the numbers they recommend for employment." In Cork the priests "seem[ed] to make a point of accusing the Board and its officers of supineness." Priests were often berated for "trying to force every person on the lists."[28] However, such criticism did not convince Sir Randolph Routh, chairman of the relief commissioners, who found that the vast majority of priests were behaving "most liberally, and most meritoriously," and working closely with their Protestant peers.[29] Most eyewitnesses concurred. W. H. Smith, a Board of Works engineer, found that the priests' influence over their flocks made their assistance very useful. A team of Quakers investigating conditions in west Clare in February 1847 wrote of the local priest of Kilmacduane near Cooraclare, that "he entered earnestly into the subject of our mission; gave us information on every point we sought; and displayed much good sense, good feeling, and candour in his communications." In the south Tipperary parish of Clonoulty-Rossmore, the parish priest attended presentment sessions, successfully resisted the efforts of local "jobbers," and sought employment for those who needed it most. Local officials relied on the clergy's influence in matters such as convincing people to purchase rye and barley seed and even getting them to pay "this most righteous impost," the poor rate. Lord Monteagle, a Catholic member of the Whig government, wrote that the priests were "labouring like tigers for us, working day and night, and without them we could not move a stroke." Priests from the worst-affected parishes also bombarded the press and officials and bishops with letters and pleas. They replied with alacrity to the questionnaire sent out by the Central Relief Committee in September–October 1847, and to the news that Archbishop Murray of Dublin had funds to distribute in 1849. In August 1847 Bishop George Browne of Elphin issued a questionnaire to priests in his own diocese in anticipation of a meeting between representatives of the hierarchy and the lord lieutenant, in the belief that the replies would highlight the continuing distress. Selections of the returns, many with detailed statistics, were published in *The Freeman's Journal* in late October.

Such reports prompt three concluding remarks about the role of the clergy. First, in a context where some people were bound to see famine relief as a means of patronage, most priests were honest and eager to single out the neediest and to lobby on their behalf. Clerical demands for universal lists might be deemed unreasonable, but they can hardly be called corruption. Second, in an era of evangelical revivalism, some sectarian tension was inevitable, yet there is ample evidence too of clergymen working in harmony or "vying with one another in acts of benevolence." Occasionally, moreover, the unpleasant competition for souls between parish priest and vicar may have benefited the starving materially, if not spiritually. Third, some Catholic bishops left themselves open to criticism for not speaking out more during the famine, and some priests for persisting with grandiose church-building schemes; but on the whole the famine would have been worse but for the clergy's efforts.[30]

The role of another institution, the constabulary, was also important. The crisis would have given a force of ten thousand or so corrupt, heavily armed men ample scope for opportunism. The predations of thuggish policemen such as the *bravi* in Manzoni's *I Promessi Sposi*, which depicts a famine in Lombardy in the 1630s, and Somalia's gun-toting "technicals" in the 1990s immediately spring to mind. However, all the evidence indicates that the great majority of the policemen who served during the Irish famine were honest and well informed; subject to stern discipline themselves, they were in turn feared by the people. The constabulary may not have been directly involved in the administration of relief, except in some of the worst-hit areas, but they were involved in identifying and seeking help for hardship cases and in arranging the burials of the destitute and the abandoned. They assembled information about agricultural yields and acreages. Some of the constabulary's actions, such as overseeing evictions and protecting grain shipments to the ports, probably led to increased mortality, but the point at hand is that they performed these and other duties as ordered. The same holds for tasks such as supporting rate and county cess collectors, protecting cash and property in transit, and keeping order on the public works. The constabulary could not prevent the huge increase in petty crime that peaked in 1847, but they prevented against large-scale rioting and plunder. Mortality and health-related departures from the police force increased markedly in 1847–49. A recent assessment concludes that they "represented great stability in difficult times," that there was "little criticism of their performance," that "as an organization, the Irish Constabulary proved very useful and reliable in some of the hardest years of Ireland's history." It is worth adding that the constabulary, like the Catholic priesthood, was well distributed throughout the country; the poorest province of Connacht contained virtually its population share of both, much better than its allocation of other occupations with a potential agency role in times of crisis, such as schoolteachers and medical practitioners. Mokyr's assessment stands: "By the standards of the time, Ireland enjoyed a fine administration of education, public health, and the police force." From Whitehall mandarin to ordinary policeman, the bureaucracy responsible for the Irish famine was certainly much more honest and probably more sophisticated than its Third World counterparts today.[31]

Captain O'Brien and Captain Wynne

> Even today old-timers here speak of the Year of the Board
> o' Works. That was the year when the government built big
> roads and old roads, drains, ditches, and many other works
> in order to enable poor creatures to earn the pittance that
> would buy them a morsel to put in their mouths. . . . Old
> people used to say that the year after the relief works ceased
> was the worst year of the famine.
> (Folklore from Doolin, county Clare)

I have been arguing that the inadequacy of funds and ideologically constrained policies rather than agency were the real problems facing those
seeking to stave off famine in Ireland. The controversy about agency, as
reflected in jobbing and corruption on the public works, was most intense in Clare. Captain Edward (or Edmond) Wynne, inspecting officer
for west Clare between October 1846 and January 1847, became the
loudest exponent of "agency" rhetoric. Wynne's evidence was reproduced at length in the parliamentary Blue Books. Was Clare, as Chan-
cellor Charles Wood declared, "an exception to what had occurred generally in Ireland"?[32] Or was corruption as pervasive or endemic in Clare
as Wynne claimed? Some insight into this issue may be gained from
comparing Wynne's accounts with those of Captain H.H.D. O'Brien,
his colleague in east Clare.

First, a little background context. Clare was a poor county. A recent
estimate of average annual income in Clare on the eve of the famine
(£6.51, or about $30) places it second only to Leitrim (£5.85) in the
poverty stakes, and at less than two-thirds that of Wexford (£10.23).
Between 1821 and 1841 Clare's population had grown from 208,089 to
286,394, or at twice the national rate, and faster than in any other
county in Ireland. The estimate of the distribution of land and holdings
in the county reproduced in table 2.1 implies that on the eve of the
famine landless or near-landless households accounted for two-thirds of
the population of Clare and that only a small fraction of farms — perhaps a quarter — contained more than fifteen statute acres. There was an
east-west gradient to poverty in the county. Nearly four-fifths of those
living in the barony of Burren in the northwest of the county were completely illiterate, and over two-thirds of households lived in one-room
accommodation. In Tulla Lower, in east Clare, the proportions were
better, but still somewhat over a half and nearly two-fifths, respectively.
The county's supply of medical practitioners in 1841 — forty-seven, or
one per 6,093 population — was lowest in the country. Though poor, the
county was highly politicized; in the late 1820s it had been the cockpit

TABLE 2.1
Land and Wealth Distribution in Pre-Famine Clare

Class (by land value)	Families in Each Class	Persons, (incl. servants)	Irish Acres of Land per Family	Total Acreage per Class
I >100	1,000	12,000	120	120,000
II £20–£100	3,000	21,000	30	90,000
III £10–£20	10,000	50,000	8	80,000
IV Little land	16,000	80,000	4	64,000
V None	16,000	80,000	Waste lands	122,000
Total	46,000	243,000		476,000

Source: "Agricola," *Considerations Addressed to the Landed Proprietors of County Clare* (Limerick, 1832), 44.

of Daniel O'Connell's campaign for Catholic representation in Parliament, and the conversion of tillage land to pasture in the early 1830s had produced agrarian unrest on a mass scale. But the county had been relatively tranquil since then.[33]

The potato's failure was more serious in Clare than in most other counties in 1845, but Peel's measures were enough to prevent any significant excessive mortality. In mid-August 1846 Peel's successor, Lord John Russell, was happy to cite the claim that "the people of Clare were never so well provided for as they have been this season" and that there had been fewer cases of fever than "for many years past."[34] Yet Clare was devastated by the famine. For the county as a whole a recent simulation suggests nearly sixty thousand excess deaths and nearly fifty thousand famine-induced emigrants in a population of about three hundred thousand in 1845.[35] Population change by barony between 1841 and 1851 suggests that the famine's horrors were well spread across the county (table 2.2). In nine of Clare's eleven baronies, the decline in population exceeded one-fifth, the exceptions being Islands in mid-Clare and Moyarta in the south. East Clare lost proportionately far more people than west Clare in the 1840s. This does not mean that mortality was lower in the west, however; population growth there in the 1820s and 1830s had been much faster.[36] Moreover, the relative roles of death and emigration in reducing the populations of the two Clares is unknown.

Accounts by outside commentators describing conditions in Clare during the famine are relatively few. However, a Quaker delegation touring the west of the county in February 1847 found the same story on all lips: with their potato crop ruined and their meager supply of oats used up, the poor were entirely dependent on the public works. Such was the demand for work on the roads that in most cases there

TABLE 2.2
Population Change in Clare Baronies, 1821–51

Barony	Pop. Change, 1821–41 (%)	Pop. 1841	Pop. 1851	Pop. Change, 1841–51 (%)
WEST				
Burren	60.7	12,786	8,744	−31.6
Clonderlaw	48.3	29,413	20,707	−29.6
Corcomroe	54.3	25,979	20,372	−21.6
Ibricken	55.4	25,186	18,674	−25.9
Inchiquin	31.3	21,231	14,467	−31.9
Islands	21.2	29,264	26,498	−9.5
Moyarta	43.9	38,227	33,560	−12.2
Subtotal	42.4	182,086	143,022	−21.5
EAST				
Bunratty L.	34.0	23,535	15,263	−35.1
Bunratty U.	24.6	18,370	11,731	−36.1
Tulla L.	13.7	32,217	19,353	−39.9
Tulla U.	56.3	30,186	23,059	−23.6
Subtotal	30.0	104,308	69,406	−33.5
Total	37.5	286,394	212,428	−25.8

Note: L = Lower; U = Upper.

was a place for only one man per family, though in some a woman, boy, or girl might also be allowed. Men were paid tenpence (20 cents), women eightpence, and children sixpence a day. In pre-famine Clare, a daily wage of tenpence would have been a good wage for a farm laborer, but given the inevitability of days lost through sickness and bad weather, the high cost of basic food, and the large mean family size in the region, it was hardly enough for subsistence. Typically, families earned enough for three or four days' food, but in order to maintain the strength of the breadwinner other members of the household were often forced to reduce their own rations.[37]

Captain Edward Wynne was the most controversial of the scores of military or ex-military men employed by the Board of Works as inspectors and engineers during the famine.[38] Judging from his actions and the comments of others, he was honest and hard-working. He was also arrogant and paranoid, and loathed by nearly all who had dealings with him in the west. Much about him remains hidden or debatable. Though we know that he hailed from a Sligo landowning background, his date of birth and birthplace are unknown, and his career between the sale of his army commission in 1829 and his appointment as temporary inspector for the Board of Works in October 1846 remains a blank. A veiled hint of earlier confrontations in Clare, "none calculated to alarm a man accustomed to a Tipperary or Clare mob," is little help.[39]

Wynne's relations with Clare's relief committees were poor from the start. Where they wanted to interpret regulations liberally, he sought to impose rigid boundaries. Where locals believed that the government would eventually foot the bill for coping with the famine, he saw a conspiracy to defraud the Treasury. Within a few weeks Wynne was complaining of having to deal with "*half gentry, bankrupts in fortune and in character*," upstarts who used the system as a means of doling out patronage, and who had crowded out Protestant clergymen and "gentlemen of character." The result was a classic case of corruption at the local level—favoritism and nepotism on the part of relief committees had "crippled the operation of the Relief Act," leaving thousands of the poorest without work "and dying daily in vast numbers." Wynne complained that his staff could not correct this fatal abuse[40] and supplied officials in Dublin and London with lists full of undeserving names, highlighting apparent inconsistencies and exaggerations.[41]

From the start, Wynne picked fights with priests and threw insults at local politicians. His altercations with west Clare's whiggish parliamentary representatives reached the floor of the House of Commons. Wynne was also an anti-Catholic bigot, yet his superiors in Dublin and London stuck by him, and extracts from his testimony made good copy in the Blue Books.[42]

In early December 1846 an attack on one of his overseers prompted Wynne to suspend the public works in the village of Clare Abbey. His feelings about this standard sanction were ambivalent, vacillating from worry about the consequences for "individuals not concerned in the outrage" to jesting that the sanction might not work, since freedom from the works would give the local people "an excuse to plunder, which indeed they have begun already." Yet the outcome would show how important, if precarious and temporary, a lifeline the works offered the poor. Within a few weeks of the suspension, the sufferings of Clare Abbey's plunderers finally "unmanned" Wynne. Severe hardship in the area was corroborated by another inspector, who found that the poor were "*indeed* suffering most severely, in great measure aggravated by the suspension of the Public Works some time since." On Christmas Eve, landowner Sir Lucius O'Brien complained to Routh that the local relief committee had been stretched to the limit by the suspension; he and others had raised £40 ($190) and asked for a matching contribution. In late December the works resumed and Wynne put on "150 additional men and women."[43]

"Unmanned" was Wynne's own word: indeed, by year's end his earlier bluster had given way to utterances consistent with some kind of mental breakdown. When, some days later, he intimated to the authorities that "the officers of the Board of Works will resign and go away," he may well have had himself in mind.[44] He left Clare under a cloud in late January 1847 after weeks of confrontations and of striking off claimants. A week later he was in north Mayo, berating relief committees there. Wynne's behavior in Clare forced a parliamentary inquiry, and several of the testimonials solicited by him were reprinted in the parliamentary Blue Books. He was warmly supported by his military understudies, but what is significant is that bigger players such as Lucius O'Brien, Colonel Vandeleur, and Captain O'Brien were lukewarm or tempered in their support. Wynne was transferred to Carrick-on-Shannon Union in March 1847, where he presided over the transition from outdoor to indoor relief. There he would achieve further notoriety, though of a different kind.[45]

Captain Henry O'Brien was mainly responsible for the four baronies of east Clare. Like all Board of Works officers, O'Brien had served in the army, having been an officer in the Royal Artillery for twenty-five years. He knew the whole of Clare well, and indeed traveled widely throughout Ireland in the course of his months as inspecting officer. His assessment of the situation both in Clare and in Ireland at large contrasts sharply with Wynne's. While Wynne believed that cheating on the works was endemic and pervasive, O'Brien in effect argued the opposite and was clearly worried about the effect of exaggerated reports of jobbing and laziness on the condition of the poor. In a letter from Limerick on St. Stephen's Day 1846 he summarized his impressions for Trevelyan:

> Much has been written and said against the Relief Committees, and, in several instances, there has been much which is reprehensive; but from what I hear I am inclined to think that the majority have done their duty. The majority, too, of the priests, considering how they are circumstanced, have behaved well; and certainly, the patience and self-denial of the people have been beyond all praise. The labourers work for their wages, but seeing clearly that what they are doing on the public roads is of no clear value, their heart, they say, is not in it. Naturally quick in feeling, and acute in intellect, they have no lively interest in the completion of a task which, though it keeps them from starvation, is manifestly unproductive.[46]

A few days earlier O'Brien had reported that the labor lists in east Clare had been "closely revised," and that he had "reason to believe that very few, if any, persons not really destitute are now employed on the Relief Works." In early March he wrote from Dublin about "the traces of want which are visibly depicted in [the countenances] of the men, women, and children who are congregated on the Public Works in remote districts."[47] Not that O'Brien was blind to fraud; he admitted that the Clare relief committees had made out their lists "without due discrimination," and that "many therefore are now enjoying relief who are not fit objects for it."[48] But the key point was that "the number of destitute is really so great, that the number of those improperly employed bears but a small proportion to the whole." Moreover, O'Brien's observations led him to conclude that as a rule the people were willing to do "more than a fair day's work for a fair day's pay" on the works, and he was quick to dismiss false reports of jobbing and fraud.[49] Nor did he share Wynne's loathing of Catholic priests.[50]

O'Brien's more sympathetic reading of the situation both in Clare and further afield is evident in the excerpts reproduced in the parliamentary chronicles of "measures adopted" to deal with the famine. The emphasis in his account of conditions in an area north of Sligo known as "the Sands" is not on how the poor had been kept from the works, but on how the public works were ill-geared to saving lives. O'Brien drove his point home with several detailed case studies. One described a hut in which he found the mother lying on the ground by the fire, "attenuated and moaning," and two of her teenage sons bedridden with fever. Their illness meant the loss of a shilling a day from the public works. A daughter in her twenties might have been earning about sixpence (12 cents) a day as a substitute, but "as that was nothing among so many," she had stayed at home to care for the others. For O'Brien the conclusion was stark: only immediate relief in the form of food could save such people. Many deserving cases could not make their way to the works, never mind perform work when there.[51] But O'Brien's most striking and telling report, dated 4 January 1847, was not reproduced in the Blue Books:

> I beg to call the attention of the Board to the following facts, from which I apprehend that many persons must soon die of starvation unless some measure for their support in addition to road works is adopted. The present price or meal in the county is 2/6 to 2/8 a stone.
>
> The labourer's weekly wages average 6/-. and the number dependent on each is on average 4½. The quantity of food they contain is therefore less than 1 lb. a day for each member of the family. Now after very careful inquiry I have come to the conclusion that 1½ lbs. per day for each, distributed throughout a family according to age and sex etc. is barely sufficient to keep them in health and the men in working condition.
>
> When five or more in family depend on one man's wages (and there are many such cases) their condition is truly pitiable. The man's strength must gradually fail, and the consequences are but too obvious.

The workhouses are crowded out and yet there are many widows with helpless families left out.

The above cases are far too numerous to admit of being adequately relieved by the efforts of private benevolence. During the last week I saw for the first time symptoms of starvation. This was in the parish of Ogonnelloe, which I had thought well provided for, as the number there employed was comparatively greater than in any other parish in the district.[52]

O'Brien was also concerned to rebut another frequent criticism of the public works in the winter of 1846–47: that they crowded out private employment. In mid-December he found tillage "nearly at a standstill," but for good reason: smaller farmers were being forced on to the works as they exhausted their savings, while the more substantial farmers, who previously paid laborers in potatoes or in conacre, now could not afford the higher money wages needed to support them. Nor was that all. O'Brien had been told by "*really practical* agriculturalists, on whom every reliance must be placed, that hitherto the labourers had but little to do at this period."[53] Early in February he sent Trevelyan his impressions from a tour of the southeast:

Again I find myself differing with many of the inspecting officers as to the extent of land under cultivation. . . . Between Carlow and Tullow, about eight miles, I counted eight ploughs at work. In the next eight miles I saw only four; but the land was not only poor, but in want of general care and proper culture. . . . The small farmers being reduced to destitution . . . falling back, indeed, to their natural position as labourers — flock to the public works, and their land remained untilled. . . . With the cultivation of the potato spade husbandry has disappeared. Beyond fencing, draining, and turf-cutting, I do not see what is to employ manual labour in this country for nine months in the year, and in winter there will be very little, indeed, to give the spade man work.

A few weeks later O'Brien repeated that the high price of manual labor would deter many farmers and "at all events, the tillage which must now be substituted for the culture of potatoes will employ comparatively very few hands."[54]

O'Brien's perspective on county Clare was echoed in the reports of Captain Mann, a member of the local coast guard who was transferred to the Board of Works during the famine. Mann, who "knew everybody personally" and was "much esteemed" in Clare, had no time for the "spouting patriot whose speech is intended to go through the broken pane of glass to the poor creatures outside." Yet his verdict on local efforts in Clare was largely benign. He found the Corofin committee "composed of active and kind resident gentry," and that of Kilfenora "a credit to their country, working and doing good with their subscription,

£160 . . . most benevolent, active, and hard-working."[55] Moreover, he found that reports of hardship from the committees matched the findings of fever hospital officials and the police. When Mann called for more subscriptions in Kilrush in January 1847, he commented on the generosity of the "*generality* of persons about that place." In Quin he found the committee assembled, "distributing Indian-corn meal to the destitute," and the Tulla committee, spurred on by a resident landlord, had set up two soup kitchens. However, in Scariff, "a very distressed district, perhaps the worst in Clare," Mann was met by dissension and apathy, and he was also unimpressed by local efforts in Ennistymon and Miltown-Malbay. On the day of his arrival in Ennistymon, four coffins passed him on the street and the workhouse was full to overflowing. In Miltown, pleas for subscriptions toward a soup kitchen seemed to fall on deaf ears. Yet it is striking that Mann's report did not refer to jobbing in either place.[56]

Reports such as Wynne's doubtless created an impression, convenient to some, that the public works offered a cozy sinecure. However, the balance of the evidence supports Canon John O'Rourke's verdict in 1874 on Wynne's criticism of the relief committees, that "there does not seem to be much in it." Readily conceding that "men of influence" would try to favor their own people, O'Rourke reasoned that "the efforts of such parties would be calculated to neutralize each other."[57] Had the committees succeeded in excluding laborers *en masse*, representatives of the laborers would have spoken up and sought redress, through force if necessary—something for which there had been a strong tradition in Clare. While there were violent incidents on the public works, violence was by no means endemic. Captain O'Brien's calmer assessment of the situation was the more accurate one.

On several occasions before 1845, public works had offered a useful defense against the threat of local famines in parts of the west of Ireland. On such occasions, however, the works had almost invariably been confined to spring and summer, and had operated on a limited scale. Applying the same remedy in the apocalyptic context of autumn and winter of 1846–47 was a grave mistake. Forcing masses of half-starving and poorly clothed people to build roads and break stones in all weathers, often for less than a subsistence wage, was no way to minimize mortality. The system, especially when conducted on a task-rate system, militated particularly against the sick and households containing healthy adult men. As a rule households were allowed one representative on the works; the insouciant claim from Galway in late 1846 that "a young man without incumbrance could maintain himself twelve days on the earnings of a week" ignored the fact that such young men were supposed to support whole families.[58] In Erris and Tyrawley in Mayo, "many of the reported deaths from starvation are among those employed on the public works — feeble and infirm persons making exertions they are unaccustomed to, weakened from previous want of food."[59] Nor did the wages paid always attract the necessary food supplies in the worst-affected areas. In January a Board of Works engineer wrote from Castlebar: "The pressure for employment has now arrived at such a height, that nothing short of universal lists for the entire population will suffice, the blame and odium of refusing to put on more than one-fifth of the destitute being heaped on me . . . the maximum of one to each family is looked upon as useless; and certainly the high price of provisions gives strong grounds for additional demands." A colleague wrote from Ennis that "modes of relief suited to more favoured localities are altogether unsuited to this over-populated district, which now possesses scarcely any provisions; the introduction of large quantities of which by the government, be the consequences what they may, is the only way of mitigating the sufferings of the people."[60] The introduction of task work in parts of Westmeath edged wages below subsistence, leading the local inspector to hope for "greater exertion" the following week. By mid-January "in some districts the men who come to the works are so reduced in their physical powers as to be unable to earn above 4d or 5d per diem. This is evidently too little."[61] The Board of Works in Dublin and the Treasury in London differed on the relative merits of cash-for-work versus food aid. In Dublin, Lieutenant-Colonel Jones realized early on that while the system of task work gave some too much, it deprived those who were too weak of a subsistence wage.[62]

In an account of its activities in December 1846, the Board of Works declared that "no system of Public Works, however zealously or anxiously conducted, no expenditure of money in public employment, however lavish or uncontrolled, can prevent the fatalities that are daily occurring." In other words, the fundamental flaw was not corruption, but relying on the public works as the main means of relief. As early as 2 December 1846 Lieutenant-Colonel Jones of the Board had warned Trevelyan that "in wild remote districts . . . the sides of mountains cannot be cut up with useless roads"; in such districts relief in food or in cash would be necessary. A few weeks later, in the first of a series of panic-laden letters to Trevelyan, he pleaded that "we have arrived at a very important crisis in our operation. . . . The want of food drives everybody to the works; we have neither staff, nor work upon which we can employ them." In its next report the Board looked forward to being "unembarrassed by the necessity of employing the weak and the infirm, and destitute, merely for employment sake," and to being restored to its old responsibilities. In late February, Jones declared that the system of task work "or the one nominally so styled, must soon be exploded," and in their final report the Board again reminded ministers of their expressed conviction of December 1846 that "the question had become one of food, not labour."[63]

The following account captures the impact of public policy in one blackspot in mid-December 1846:

This town (Skibbereen) contains, according to the last census, about 6,000 inhabitants. Of those, more than one-half are totally destitute, having no means to procure food, clothing, or fuel, except their daily hire, which, as I will show, is totally inadequate to supply a sufficient quantity of these to support life. The rate of wages is eight pence per day, and the prices of provisions in this market at present are, for

Indian meal	2s. 5d. per stone of 14 lbs.
Wheaten meal	2s. 6d. " " "
Oaten meal	2s. 9d. " " "
Barley meal	1s. 10d. " " "
Household bread	9d. per 4 lb loaf
Potatoes	None at any price

At these prices you can easily suppose that a working man with a family of six persons (which is about the average number) cannot procure for them even one tolerable meal out of his miserable earnings, supposing him fortunate enough to get employment, and to be able to work every day, which is impossible in this inclement season.

Yesterday morning at daybreak, I saw a gang of about 150, composed principally of old men, *women*, and little boys, going out to work on one of the roads near this town. At that time the ground was covered with snow, and there was also a very severe frost; seeing that they were miserably clad, I remarked to a bystander that it was a miracle that the cold did not kill them, even though they had enough to eat. In less than half an hour after one of them, an old man, named Richard Cotter, was brought on a man's back dying, and I had to give a cart to take him home. In the course of the day, I went out to visit this gang, who were opening a drain inside the fence on the Marsh road, and such a scene I hope I may never again be called upon to witness. The women and children were crying out from the severity of the cold, and were unable to hold the implements with which they were at work, most of them declared they had not tasted food for the day, while others said that but for the soup supplied by the Committee they must starve. The actual value of the labour executed by these could not average two pence each per day, and to talk of task work to such labourers would be too ridiculous.

I could not help thinking how much better it would be to afford them some temporary relief in their own homes during this severe weather, than thus to sacrifice their lives to carry out a miserable project of political economy.[64]

In London, the message took some weeks to sink in. At the sign of early protests from the Board, Trevelyan impressed on them the government's gratitude, arguing that abuse was not so pervasive and that the relief committees should not be dispensed with. In early 1847 Trevelyan was reluctant to reject the principle of cash-for-work. Later he would concede that the works had offered a below-subsistence wage, "melancholy proof of which was afforded by daily instances of starvation."[65] The Temporary Relief Act (10 Vic. Cap. 7) was passed in February.

OTHER OPTIONS

> Pauper, pauper, don't you fret,
> The stirabout you will surely get.
> The meal so thick and milk so sour
> That's what you'll get at the regular hour.
> (Paupers' rhyme in Scariff workhouse)

The Irish poor law was not geared to cope with the crisis that faced it in 1846–47. By mid-October 1846 about one-fifth of union workhouses were full or nearly so, including those in places as different as Dublin and Ballina, Cork and Roscommon, Belfast and Abbeyleix. Ballina's workhouse already contained "the full number allowed," and the guardians were forced to turn away most of the "upwards of 300 more in an abject state of destitution now in the front hall seeking admission." In Clare Ennistymon and Scariff, workhouses were full to overflowing. However, some workhouses in badly affected areas were far from full; Tuam had ninety-nine inmates in a workhouse with accommodation for eight hundred, and the ratios of inmates to places in Westport, Castlerea, and Castlebar were 17, 24, and 26 percent, respectively. Some unions were already in financial trouble before the end of 1846 and refusing admission. The advice from headquarters in Dublin was that they should borrow privately, if necessary, and enforce the rates.[66]

By April 1847 workhouses all over the country, even in less-affected unions such as Newtownards and Ballymena, were full to capacity. Congestion bred contagion, but the record of workhouses on the spread of infectious disease is mixed. In early 1847 the medical officer repeatedly warned the Tralee guardians of the risks in the overcrowded workhouse; by early March the master was in bed with typhus, and "the progressive increase of mortality in the house, as dreaded by the medical officer in his previous reports" was minuted. In Ballina the situation was much worse; in mid-March there were 230 cases of "a malignant kind of fever" in the workhouse, and for several weeks the *weekly* death rate in the house reached between 5 and 10 percent.[67] At Castlerea in April 1847 Count Strzelecki of the British Association found four-fifths of the one thousand workhouse inmates sick; "at the moment of [his] visit, twenty coffins left the house by one door, while by another forty applicants had been refused admittance into it." Nor was high mortality restricted to the west. In February 1847 Lurgan workhouse in county Armagh experienced mortality matching that in Ballina, with dysentery being the major killer; disease and overcrowding forced the temporary closure of the workhouse. More than half the 581 people dying in Lurgan between October 1846 and March 1847 had entered the house in a "healthy" state, a scandalous record that provoked an official inquiry and a verdict of "neglect and discomfort such as I have never seen in any other charitable institution" from its author.[68] On the other hand, the evidence from North Dublin Union at the height of the famine suggests that the great majority of those who died there had been in poor health when admitted. Deaths in the North Dublin Union between February and May 1847 were three times as high as they had been a year earlier, but conditions in the workhouse cannot be blamed for this, since most of those dying were in poor health on entry.[69]

At the height of the crisis, guardians in the worst-hit unions battled against formidable odds. In Tralee the local branch of the Provincial Bank refused further accommodation unless members of the board were prepared to accept personal liability; a group of guardians accepted in early March. A few weeks later the Tralee guardians threatened the only sanction left to them, which was to resign. This forced some help out of headquarters in Dublin. In Ballina the chairman of the board kept the union afloat for several weeks. In Kenmare local traders used the law to threaten the guardians with distraint against their personal property.[70]

From late 1847 on, the poor-law commissioners sought to reduce relief entitlements drastically. The application of the Gregory Clause, a section in the Temporary Relief Act of February 1847 which excluded those holding more than one-quarter of an acre of land from relief, was part of the package. So was the determination to reduce the numbers of "able-bodied" persons given outdoor relief. Others were evicted from the workhouses in late 1847 in order to make way for those among the able-bodied who passed the workhouse test. Thus Margaret Hegarty died on her way home, after she had been forced out of Milford workhouse in late December 1847. Four of Catherine Connolly's children perished on the roadside outside Kenmare after the family had been ejected from the workhouse; she had left them to seek outdoor relief entitlement.[71] Others, perhaps initially better off, risked death rather than surrender their smallholdings and enter the workhouse. The deaths from starvation of several people in the Kilshalvy/Kilturra area of south

Sligo in the spring of 1848 fit this pattern. The Kilkenny family, "by leaving the workhouse [had] brought upon themselves their sufferings." As for May Connelly, "nobody appear[ed] to blame but the poor creature herself for leaving the workhouse." Philip McGowen's wife and child "appear[ed] to have been offered [the workhouse] more than once and refused"; "aversion to enter the workhouse appears to have been fatal" in other cases. The guardians in Boyle argued that most of those who died had refused the workhouse test, adding as a second line of defense that the victims' local representatives rarely attended board meetings. In May 1848 the commissioners issued an order disbanding Boyle's Board of Guardians.[72] In the unions of Kilrush and Ennistymon three years later, continued mortality was also blamed on the reaction of the poor to the workhouse test; such was its deterrent effect that many of them waited outside until it was too late.[73]

In the case of Boyle workhouse, the commissioners intervened against murderously negligent guardians, but their own "less eligibility" welfare stance was also hard and uncompromising. In December 1847, determined to keep numbers on outdoor relief to a minimum at a time when workhouse accommodation could not meet demand, they advised the Ballina guardians to rule out employing paupers on roads left unfinished by the Board of Works or any other roads, "because road making has been proved to be no adequate test of destitution." Instead they recommended stone breaking as "highly effectual," and urged the guardians to seek out "a large supply of hard stone for employing able bodied paupers at task work in breaking stones in return for the rations to be supplied by the union." They specified a workday of eight hours, which made due allowance "for the present season of the year and for the possible circumstance that some of the able bodied paupers may come to the stone breaking from a considerable distance." This did not exclude the guardians from insisting on an even longer workday; eight hours was "in fact merely the minimum." At the same time the commissioners kept urging that indoor-relief for all was the preferred solution.[74]

In some of the worst-hit unions a shortage of funds or of accommodation meant turning away paupers at the height of the crisis. Even before the end of 1846 the commissioners in Dublin were already "earnestly" requesting the Tralee guardians to refuse further applications "however distressful it may be to their feelings." Tralee's medical officer insisted that allowing more in would be disastrous for all. Meanwhile, the rations of those already in the workhouse were cut back to save money. In Tralee in March 1847, treacle, a sugar-based syrup, was substituted for milk in the pauper diet, and the medical officer warned that the overwhelmingly liquid nature of the diet was likely to keep up disease. A month later the bread being given to hospital patients was "*of a very inferior description, very coarse, often half-baked*, and unfit of the use of the sick"; it was likely to induce relapses, and indeed some patients would not touch it. Some months later Ballina's medical officer complained that the recovery of convalescents in the workhouse had been "considerably retarded from want of sufficient nourishment; and in my opinion, the lives of some of them have been lost from the same cause." At the height of the crisis in both Tralee and Ballina guardians were forced to offer personal securities or else dig into their own pockets in order to keep the workhouse open.[75] The medical officer of the Tralee workhouse described the state of its graveyard in April 1847:

> He has visited the grave-yard and made a personal inspection of it, a *duty* he would not willingly undertake again. Tis most revolting to see the body of a child rather grown, dragged quite out of the coffin and lying on the yard totally uncovered, with one leg and one thigh completely taken off and devoured by dogs which nightly prowl about this yard. Many of the coffins are completely exposed to view, and the whole state of the yard is such as to cause much apprehension for the public safety. The effluvia even at present must engender and give disease to those frequenting it on the occasion of the burial of their friends.
>
> The insufficient space appropriated for the interment of the poorer classes in the parishes of Tralee, Rathass, and Cloherbrien is notoriously such as to render it necessary in most cases to disturb the remains of one to make room for another, and many coffins, almost new, containing the remains of only lately interred persons, are to be seen above ground in the burial grounds of these parishes by all passers by.[76]

In different ways, then, the shortage of funds certainly exacerbated the crisis.

With the Poor Law Amendment Act of 1847 the public works were replaced by soup kitchens and the strict enforcement, where feasible, of the workhouse test. The aim of the Temporary Relief Act which underpinned the soup kitchens was "the seeking out of every distressed individual." The commissioners believed that the machinery set in motion to stay the crisis had operated "with more complete effect than was probably ever before affected . . . the administration has been nearly perfect."[77] Many of those employed on the public works resented and resisted the switch in policy. Their resentment — and, it is also worth noting, that of their families — stemmed partly from fear that no alternative relief would be available and partly from a dislike of porridge and the ensuing reduction in status. Such feelings motivated the large band of laborers who marched into Castlecomer on 3 June to protest their dismissal from the public works, and whom weakness from hunger forced "to halt several times on the road." The stigma is reflected in the tone of the folklore narratives recorded in the 1930s and 1940s. Doubtless, some people resisted the regime switch because it reduced their scope for converting relief entitlements from food to semiluxuries such as drink and tobacco and animal feed. But to blame all or the bulk of the protests on such opportunism would be perverse. The overall impression from contemporary press reports is of worry and despair; the nationalist *Tipperary Vindicator* detected "apprehension and terror fill[ing] every mind," while even *The Times* conceded that "the want of more timely notice" had produced "much distress and confusion." Indeed, in many areas there was no proper provision in place for those dismissed from the works.[78]

Though soup was almost nontradable, inevitably there was some cheating; in a few small areas more meals were doled out than there was recorded for population in 1841. Nevertheless, the regional distribution of people dependent on rations was probably a better indicator of privation than that of employment on the public works. As an administrative feat the organization behind the soup kitchens was impressive indeed. In early July 1847 the number of meals provided exceeded three million, representing well over one-third of the population. Relief was highly decentralized, with soup houses in nearly every parish. This was far removed from the huge feeding stations employed in famine relief efforts in Africa in the 1970s and 1980s. The soup kitchens undoubtedly helped to reduce the number of deaths from starvation during the summer of 1847. A drawback was the nutritional content of the stirabout "soup" (known in Irish as *brachán, brot, grutharlach,* or *súp*); the Board of Health linked the rising incidence of "sea scurvy" to the lack of fresh vegetables in the soup. More generally, the complaints of medical officers against undue reliance in some workhouses on a liquid diet probably applied to soup kitchen fare as well.[79]

Falling food prices and the prospect of a good harvest in 1847 prompted the authorities to make relief the sole responsibility of the Irish poor law. The corollary was an end to all outdoor relief, but this did not prove feasible. In November 1847, the lack of space in the Ballina workhouse for "the poor of Erris" prompted the guardians to offer outdoor relief to "destitute poor widows and others described in the 1st section of the amended Poor Law Act." Qualifying adults were granted a pound of maize daily and others half a pound.

For some of the hardest-hit areas a lack of "voice" or representation exacerbated the crisis. Mary Daly has drawn attention to the apparently undue concentration of public works funds in some regions, particularly in counties Clare and Limerick, at the expense of "undoubtedly deprived areas such as Erris, or the Carbery baronies of west Cork." Clare's relief committees certainly had the midas touch when it came to obtaining money under Peel, though the greater damage done by the first attack of potato blight in Clare partly justified its relief entitlements in 1845–46. However, Clare's success was repeated in 1846–47. What was striking about Clare's schemes was less their number than the number involving relatively large sums (notably the £16,658, or $80,000, granted to the barony of Clonderlaw and the £13,620 to Ibrickane for the repair and construction of roads). Table 2.3 below attempts to adjust for "need" by adjusting the sums sanctioned for public works between late September 1846 and late January 1847 for housing quality. Comparing the outcome in the two worst-affected provinces and in Ireland as a whole indeed confirms that Clare, and to a lesser extent Limerick, were "special." Otherwise, however, the allocation of funds across counties seems to have been "fair" enough.[80] Over two-thirds of the total was spent in Connacht and Munster, and by this admittedly crude reckoning even Clare got only twice its entitlement.

TABLE 2.3
Sums Sanctioned by The Board of Works in Certain Counties, 1846–47

COUNTY	Total Agreed (£)	Families (4th Class)	Families (3rd Class)	Families (All)	Total per Family (£)		
					I	II	III
CONNACHT							
Galway	185,911	36,865	30,456	78,368	2.4	5.0	3.2
Leitrim	68,012	11,703	11,844	27,192	2.5	5.8	3.5
Mayo	236,719	41,714	23,859	70,910	3.3	5.7	4.1
Roscommon	130,881	19,766	21,447	46,387	2.8	6.6	3.8
Sligo	81,063	15,010	13,373	32,837	2.5	5.4	3.4
MUNSTER							
Clare	249,758	24,650	16,551	48,981	5.1	10.1	7.0
Cork	328,990	64,080	42,555	149,794	2.2	5.1	3.6
Kerry	144,374	29,730	15,361	51,593	2.8	4.9	3.6
Limerick	187,878	23,961	18,657	56,338	3.3	7.8	5.2
Tipperary	107,077	24,879	30,869	74,570	1.4	4.3	2.4
Waterford	54,649	8,177	13,192	33,878	1.6	6.7	3.2
Munster/Conn.	1,775,312	300,535	238,164	670,848	2.6	5.9	3.9
Ulster/Leinster	776,080	216,396	328,495	801,939	1.0	3.6	1.8
Ireland total	2,551,392	516,931	566,659	1,472,787	1.7	4.9	2.8

Note: "Total Agreed" refers to the amount sanctioned by the Board of Works between 25 September 1846 and 26 January 1847. The next three columns give the number of families (excluding those in incorporated cities and towns) and totals living in 3rd- and 4th-class housing in 1841. Column I gives the amount sanctioned per family, and column II the amount sanctioned per family living in 4th-class housing. Column III assumes that two-thirds of those in 3rd-class housing were very poor. The Board of Works data are reported in IUP6/555–91.

Comparing the numbers employed on the public works in the four provinces in late February also suggests this allocation roughly in proportion to need. Munster accounted for 41 percent, Connacht 28 percent, Leinster 18 percent, and Ulster 12 percent. Two-thirds of Ulster's quota were employed in its poorest counties (Cavan, Donegal, and Monaghan), while Antrim and Down absorbed only 4 percent of its 87,745. Clare again stands out, but not so noticeably: it accounted for one-fifth of Munster's 293,886 and 8 percent of the national total of over seven hundred thousand. The geographical spread of incoming letters to the relief commissioners in Dublin suggests that the poorer counties were well represented, with Munster and Connacht accounting for over 70 percent of all submissions in July–August 1846. However, the remoter regions in those provinces were underrepresented,[81] and remoteness was undoubtedly a problem for some regions as the crisis intensified. The agency problem had a spatial as well as a vertical aspect.

The western end of the Dingle peninsula in Kerry offers a good case in point. The workhouse serving the area at the height of the famine was located in Tralee over 30 miles away. In February 1847 the Tralee guardians advised parish wardens "in and about the electoral division of Dingle" that forwarding claimants for admission "from the distant parts of this union will only be adding to their misery"; in late 1847 the poor of that area were "reduced to such a state of want and weakness as to render them perfectly unable to travel to Tralee." Out west such sentiments got translated into "*Imígh an bóthar agus ná tair arís*" [be off and don't come again] and "*ní linne a luíonn sibh, is ní bheidh sibh ann*" [you are not our business, and you won't stay here]. The chairman of the Tralee guardians explained that before the creation of a separate union for the Dingle peninsula, the poor law was virtually "a dead letter" as far as that area was concerned; geography meant that the workhouse contained hardly any paupers from Dingle, "certainly not a proper proportion."[82] Location was also an added burden for the men, women, and children from the hamlet of Maam Cross in north Connemara seen "wading thro' the snow a distance of 20 miles from their homes to fetch their relief meal" in February 1848. The local poor-law inspector explained that "there was not a single person in that whole district to whom the distribution could be entrusted or who would undertake it," whereupon the official recommended the already hard-pressed constabulary at Maam Cross for the task.[83]

The poor of Erris in north Mayo faced the same problem. They lived at the western extremity of the country's largest poor-law union, and the failure of their guardians to attend union meetings in Ballina was explained by "the long distance from Erris here being upwards of 40 miles [which] renders it impossible to manage properly for that district." In the 1840s it took at least five hours by coach to get from there to Ballina, which may help explain why neither Erris's elected nor ex officio guardians attended meetings on a regular basis.[84] Perhaps it would not have made much difference; if the representative of the British Association is to be credited, most of the Erris guardians could not read or understand official instructions, and could not be trusted. For much of the spring of 1846 they remained both absent and incommunicado, forcing their colleagues in Ballina to repeatedly defer a decision on the need for a fever hospital in Erris. In August the chairman and the local poor-law inspector felt compelled to travel west to see for themselves. They found no evidence of fever or other epidemics, except at the bottom tip of the Mullet peninsula, but they found a potato crop totally destroyed, and were "led to believe that even were the oat and barley crops left entirely for the consumption of the peasantry of Erris, there would not be sufficient to support them for more than three months."

Soon Ballina was regretting its responsibility for Erris. By October 1846 its guardians were complaining of the lack of rates coming in from Erris "while the number of inmates in the house from that district numbers 100." They accordingly refused accommodation in Ballina to 265 applicants who had journeyed all the way from Erris, sending them back home with a week's provisions and insisting that the poor-law commissioners provide them with outdoor relief in their home place. The Ballina guardians thereafter showed little sympathy for the Erris poor, refusing to admit paupers from that part of the union, and passing resolutions "that as we have no funds available for the Electoral Districts of Erris, we suggest that meal be got to support those people from the Commissioners' stores in Erris," and that Erris be separated from the union. Otherwise, they held, "we shall be dragged down by the number of their paupers and by the insufficiency of the rates paid to support them, and we feel that if the rates paid in by other Electoral Divisions be directed to support those hundred of paupers coming from Erris the collection will be paralized throughout the Union." This, however, was unfair; in the first week of November 1847 the electoral divisions of Belmullet and Binghamstown owed only £854 of the £12,303, or about $4,000 of $59,000, of rates remaining uncollected, while Ballina electoral division owed over £3,000 ($14,000). Those in arrears in their payment of the poor rates, the property-based tax that funded relief, included several guardians. The guardians' inability to deal with the western end of the union area was one of the reasons why the elected board "requested to be freed from the very onerous duties which devolved upon it" in late 1847.[85] Only in 1849, much too late, was the original Ballina Union divided into three more manageable unions.

DID ENGLAND SLEEP?

> [T]he mass of the people firmly believe that the money paid
> for the public works will be provided from the general funds
> of the State. They say the loss of the potato is by the hand
> of the Almighty: it is a destruction of property not caused
> by the fault or act of man: a disaster, the sad effects of
> which . . . should be regarded as a great national loss to
> which the whole community must contribute through the
> instrumentality of taxation.
> (Captain O'Brien, Limerick, to Charles Trevelyan,
> 26 December 1846)

> The good faith of the empire should be staked to prevent
> the scenes that have occurred in the west. Surely the
> government of the country will have to answer for the blood
> of the people if the relief provided by the legislature is not
> properly and largely administered.
> (Patrick McManus P. P. Louisburgh, *Freeman's Journal*,
> 8 January 1847)

> At a period when the Parliament could not do half enough
> for Ireland it is not disposed to do half as much as it can.
> (Daniel O'Connell to P. V. Fitzpatrick, 8 February 1847)

> To convert a period of distress, arising from natural causes,
> into one of unusual comfort and ease, by the interference of
> government money, or of private charity, is to paralyze the
> efforts of the people themselves.
> (*The Economist*, 16 January 1847)

Spending from public funds on the Irish famine totaled £9.5 million ($45.5 million). More than half of this sum, including more than £4 million spent on the public works, had been originally earmarked as a loan.[86] Nearly all of it had been spent by the autumn of 1847, and with the winding up of the soup kitchens in October 1847 Westminster left the Irish virtually to their own devices. While the outlay on relief was enormous compared to what had been spent in Europe in the 1310s or even in the 1740s, and probably unprecedented in famine history, contemporary critics of government policy nevertheless expected more. This expectation was widespread at ground level, and is well reflected in the complaints of an engineer on the public works in Clare, that when the numbers on the relief lists reached 35,000 and the daily expenditure £2,000, the cry continued to be for "more, more," and of a fellow worker, depressed at the repeated "cuckoo cry" of "What do the Government intend to do?"[87]

It bears emphasis that criticism of public parsimony was vocal at the time, and the sense that this was "an imperial calamity [to] be borne by imperial resources" widespread. John McHale, Catholic archbishop of Tuam, predicted that "the people's bones, piled in cairns more numerous than the ancient pyramids" would remind later generations of "the ghastly triumphs" of Lord John Russell's "brief but disastrous administration." A few years later another more moderate Catholic voice wondered what the student of history would make of the contrast between "the means at the disposal of the governors, so extended, almost so exhaustible, and then the wretched piteable conditions of the governed." Opposition leader Lord George Bentinck warned ministers that "the time will come when the public and the world will be able to estimate, at its proper value, your management of the affairs of Ireland." Even Trevelyan accepted the need for minimal relief; otherwise "the deaths would shock the world and be an eternal blot on the nation, and the government will be blamed."[88] The accusation of stinginess, well articulated by modern historians like Christine Kinealy and Peter Gray, is therefore not merely retrospective or anachronistic. Nor are remarks such as Joel Mokyr's that half the sum spent on "an utterly futile adventure in the Crimea" a few years later would have saved hundreds of thousands of lives. Many contemporaries made the same point, including McHale and William Smith O'Brien. In O'Brien's version, given in mid-January 1847 in the course of a plea to fellow M.P.s, "if there were a rebellion in Ireland tomorrow, they would cheerfully vote 10 or 20 millions to put it down, but what they would do to destroy life, they would not do to save it."[89]

Nevertheless, there is something to the criticism that the historiography of the Irish famine has paid insufficient attention to economic conditions at the height of the crisis. A key point here is that the early stages of the famine coincided with a poor wheat harvest all over Europe and a monetary crisis in the United Kingdom. The shortage of domestic food supplies in 1846–47 led to significant price increases and trade deficits which in turn brought about an external drain of bullion from the Bank of England. How badly were the public finances affected? What of incomes?

An analysis by Harvard economist Robert Barro[90] of the effects of budget deficits on interest rates in the United Kingdom over two centuries (1701–1918) offers a partial answer to the first question. Barro shows that in years when big rises in government spending were financed by public borrowing, the resulting competition for funds between the public and the private sector may be expected to have increased the cost of borrowing. In Barro's account, such increases, as reflected in the return on consols, were not unusual, but they were nearly always caused by temporary rises in military spending. Only twice in peacetime — in 1836–37 (due to the cost compensating plantation owners in the West Indies for slave emancipation) and in 1909–10 (as a result of legislative deadlock over tax reforms) — did budget deficits due to rises in public spending drive up real interest rates. In Barro's account this particular dog did not bark during the famine. A limitation of Barro's interest rate data is that they are annual. The frequency and timing of changes in bank rate — the interbank rate charged by the Bank of England — in the mid- and late 1840s offer a more sensitive barometer of economic pressure. It is true that the number of changes in bank rate in 1847 (nine) and the peak rate reached in late October 1847 (8 percent) were exceptional. However, they were not the product of relief expenditure, but of the pressure caused by the bust that followed the speculative boom, mainly in railways, in that year. The pressure on the Old Lady of Threadneedle Street was not serious before summer of 1847, and not until early August 1847 — after public spending on relief had come to a virtual halt, and long before the loans in 1846–47 were commuted to outright grants — did the Bank Rate rise above 5 percent.

A classic study of the crisis of 1847 by C. N. Ward-Perkins offers an answer to the second question.[91] Ward-Perkins found that the monetary crisis had little impact on the real economy. He concluded that its impact was exaggerated by special-interest lobbies, inferring from movements in food imports, the tonnage of sea coal entering London, and the home consumption of such semiluxuries as tea, sugar, coffee, and tobacco that "national income cannot have fallen off unduly in 1847–8." Trends in the consumption of some of these items are shown in figure 2.1. Ward-Perkins's case is supported by later estimates of macroeconomic trends. Figure 2.2 plots the movements in GNP, investment, and industrial production between 1830 and 1854. On this reckoning, the crisis of 1847 was minor compared to that of the early 1840s.[92]

Data on public expenditure hardly imply a serious fiscal crisis in 1847 either, and show that expenditure on Irish relief had little impact on the overall budgetary situation (fig. 2.3). The numbers are also a reminder, however, of how small the public sector was in the 1840s. They show that an adequate response to the situation in Ireland would have required a very substantial rise in the portion of spending not accounted for by debt service or defense. Finally, figure 2.4 describes the trend in bank note circulation in the same period.[93] The dramatic fall in note circulation in Ireland between 1846 and 1849 (41 percent) dwarfed that in either England (12 percent) or Scotland (8 percent), and underlines the bigger and more protracted fall in real incomes there.

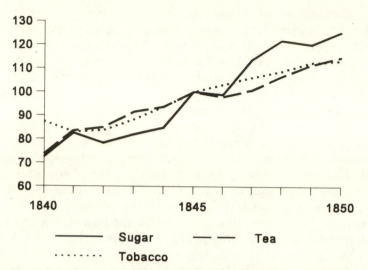

Figure 2.1. Tea, sugar, and tobacco consumption in Britain, 1840–50. (1845 = 100.)

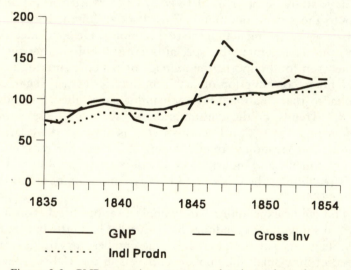

Figure 2.2. GNP, gross investment, and industrial production in Britain, 1835–54. (1845 = 100.)

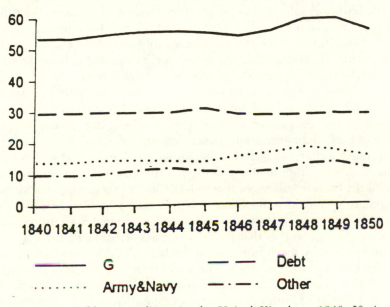

Figure 2.3. Public expenditure in the United Kingdom, 1840–50, in £ million.

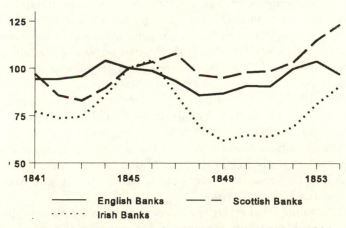

Figure 2.4. Bank note circulation, 1841–54. (1845 = 100.)

In the historiography and popular understanding of famines, the ruling elites of the day often bear a heavy responsibility. Incompetence and a lack of empathy on their part are blamed for most of the mass mortality that occurs. Democracy and the moral force of public opinion are thus weapons against famine, just as economic development is. In his major study of famine in western Europe in the early 1740s, John Post singles out the fate of Ireland and Norway. Mass mortality was present in those countries, not because of their remote locations, but "fundamentally because public administrations either neglected or failed to carry out the elementary welfare service of safeguarding the hunger and starvation." Post is also the author of the definitive study of the famines that followed the harvest failures of the mid-1810s, and there too, "the success or failure of public welfare and relief measures more than any other variable influenced the relative severity of the national mortality peaks." Amartya Sen's assertion that modern famines are in fact extremely easy to prevent is very much in the same spirit. Sen's claim refers to famines in which only a small fraction — no more than 5 to 10 percent — of the population is at risk. The Irish famine of the 1840s was in a different league in terms of both intensity and duration. Given Irish poverty and the lack of effective antidotes to infectious diseases, it was bound to cause significant mortality. Nonetheless, Sen's claim that modern famines reflect a severe indifference on the part of the government in those countries where they occur has a strong resonance for Ireland in the 1840s too. So does economic historian Peter Solar's finding on the basis of a comparative study of distress throughout Europe in the same decade that "relief efforts mattered": the limited resources available were sufficient, if mobilized, "to relieve distress and keep down mortality."[94] In certain respects, moreover, relief, if not prevention, was easier in Ireland in the 1840s than in Ethiopia in the 1980s or in Somalia or Rwanda in the 1990s. Ireland, as part of the United Kingdom in the age of Victoria, was endowed with a relatively sophisticated and efficient bureaucratic structure. Good road and postal communications and an extensive and relatively free press ensured that trouble spots were identified quickly. The absence of civil strife meant that it was easier to identify and reach those at risk.

The Irish famine relief effort was constrained less by poverty than by ideology and public opinion. Too much was expected of the Irish themselves, including Irish landlords. Too much was blamed on their dishonesty and laziness. Too much time was lost on the public works as the main vehicle of relief. By the time food was reaching the starving through the soup kitchens, they were already vulnerable to infectious disease, against which the medical science of the day was virtually helpless.[95] Too much was made of the antisocial behavior inevitable in such crisis conditions. Too many people in high places believed that this was a time when, as *The Times* put it, "something like harshness is the greatest humanity." These included the people who declared the crisis officially over three or even four years before it was really over. From spring 1847 on, most of the English print media conveyed an impression of the Irish poor as devious, violent, and ungrateful and of famine relief as a bottomless black hole. Irish landowners were hardly blameless in their responses to the crisis, but the sense that, particularly in the worst-hit areas, as a group they were shirking their responsibilities only made matters worse for those needing help most. In effect, the poor were being made to pay for the perceived sins of the rich.[96] By 1849 the government was unwilling to concede even the £100,000 ($480,000) deemed necessary to prevent further "possible case[s] of starvation in Ireland."

Most important, public spending on relief went nowhere near the cost of plugging the gap left by the failure of the potato. Given the potato's lowly status before the famine, even relative to maize, putting a value on the missing potatoes offers a lower-bound measure of that gap. Comparing the average pre-famine harvest of about thirteen million tons with the outcome between 1845 and 1850 suggests a cumulative shortfall of over fifty million tons of potatoes over the period. Discounting by one-half in order to allow for some fat in the economy and the reallocation of labor to other crops after 1846, and calculating at a deliberately low price of 3d per stone, still implies a shortfall worth about £50 million ($240 million) in money. Given the higher cost of substitute foods and the inevitable costs and leakages in distributing them, it is doubtful whether expenditure of even that order would have staved off all excess deaths. Probably not even a Joseph Stalin could have extracted the necessary sum from Ireland's middle classes and landlords in the 1840s. Nor should the burden of such a transfer, an annual 2 percent or so of British national income or of about 20 percent of public expenditure over the six-year period, be underestimated. No quasi-independent Irish administration led by some Daniel O'Connell or some latter-day Henry Grattan could have generated it. But in the circumstances, the political arithmetic never even came close to adding up: exchequer spending on famine relief between 1846 and 1852 totaled less than £10 million ($48 million). Bearing in mind the relative wealth of the United Kingdom in the 1840s and Russia in the 1890s, that sum compares poorly with the 150 million rubles (about one percent of GDP) spent by the tsarist authorities during the much less threatening Russian famine of 1891–92.[97]

Chapter Three

THE DEMOGRAPHY OF THE IRISH FAMINE

> The movements of a population in times of calamity are
> governed by a natural law: if plague exists in the towns, the
> inhabitants, to escape its ravages, fly to the country; if
> famine visits the country, to supply their wants the rural
> population flock to the towns; . . . and if both famine and
> pestilence come upon the land, then emigration is the only
> way of escape which presents itself.
> (1851 Census of Ireland, *General Report*)

> A man found dead in the fields would probably be
> mentioned in the police returns as having died of starvation.
> (Lord John Russell, in the House of Commons,
> 9 March 1847)

THE TOLL IN LIVES

IN ENGLAND reputable estimates of the aggregate number of
births, deaths, and marriages are available for each year from the
mid-sixteenth century on. In France similar series reach back to the
seventeenth century. These make it possible to generate plausible estimates of the demographic impact of the last major famines to strike
those countries. Good estimates may also be produced for the major
famines in Iceland in the 1780s and in Finland in the 1860s.[1] However,
most historical famines defy such demographic precision. William
Chester Jordan, historian of the great European famine of the 1310s,
found that "rural society came through the crisis with a far less inten-
sive demographic shock than urban areas," but then all he could say
about the towns was that there was enough evidence "to suggest an
urban collapse of 5–10 percent in 1316, the worst year of the famine in
terms of harvest shortfalls." Hard demographic data on "the black
years of King William" in Scotland in the 1690s are not quite so scarce,
but on the fundamental question of what proportion of Scottish people
succumbed the latest research is necessarily inconclusive. Similarly, surviving records allow only a crude guess — between 250,000 and 400,000 —
at the toll of an earlier great Irish famine, that of 1740–41. In that case
the paucity of direct sources has prompted inferences from chimney-tax

data. Turning to the present century, estimates of excess mortality during the Ukrainian famine of 1932–33 range from three to ten million, while estimates for the Chinese Great Leap Forward famine of 1958–62 (fifteen to thirty million) reveal inconsistencies in the underlying data and puzzles in the resulting outcome. Estimates of mortality from recent African famines are also subject to a wide margin of error.[2]

As we have already seen, many aspects of the Irish famine are extremely well documented. This does not hold for its demographic toll. The lack of hard, reliable data induced historian Kevin Nowlan to declare in his ghost-written introduction to one of the classics of Irish famine historiography that "all that matters is that many, many died."[3] Yet Nowlan's counsel that precision was not to be aimed at did not prevent his fellow-contributors from suggesting several estimates, ranging from one-half million to one million. Some revisionist accounts later proposed half a million, while Woodham-Smith suggested 1.5 million. Nowadays, however, most accounts accept a figure of one million, or slightly above it. This number excludes some tens of thousands of emigrants who died from famine-related causes either in transit or soon after reaching their destinations, and those who died of famine-related causes after mid-1851. On the other hand, it includes about fifty thousand victims of cholera in 1849, some of whom would have died in any case, famine or no famine. Since the 1950s careful and cautious estimates of aggregate excess mortality have been supplemented by analyses of spatial and temporal patterns of mortality and migration. The age and gender composition of mortality have also attracted some attention. But research has been constrained by demographic data that are flawed and partial.[4]

Before and during the famine, Ireland lacked a system of civil registration of deaths and births. The parish registers of the Catholic church rarely include the necessary burial data, and their completeness in other respects is questionable and their survival patchy in the worst-hit areas. Yet the record is not completely silent. Three data-rich Catholic parish registers from county Offaly indicate that the average annual number of deaths in 1847–49 was 75 percent higher than in 1841–46. Data on a larger sample of parishes in the same county indicate a drop of one-third in births and one-half in marriages over the same period. In general, the lack of burial data does not mean that Catholic records are worthless, since the timing and the depth of the crisis are also reflected in their marriage and baptism records. For example, an analysis of some north Armagh Catholic registers indicates a drop of nearly half in the number of marriages in 1847–48, and a drop of nearly two-fifths in the number of births.[5]

TABLE 3.1
Burials in Ballymodan and Kilbrogan by Age and Gender, 1843–51 (percentages in parentheses)

Age (Years)	Males			Females		
	1843–45	1846–48	1849–51	1843–45	1846–48	1849–51
0–9	34 (36)	51 (30)	24 (25)	27 (28)	40 (29)	21 (23)
10–19	18 (19)	29 (17)	19 (20)	13 (13)	21 (15)	15 (16)
30–49	8 (9)	19 (11)	11 (11)	17 (17)	13 (10)	12 (13)
50–69	13 (14)	29 (17)	24 (25)	20 (20)	27 (20)	19 (21)
70+	12 (13)	43 (25)	18 (19)	21 (21)	35 (26)	25 (27)
Total	94	171	96	99	141	92

The established Protestant (Anglican) church recorded the burials of its members, and its registers survive in considerable numbers. Records such as those found in the registers of two neighboring parishes of Ballymodan and Kilbrogan in county Cork are very revealing in this respect. These were then largely urban parishes, with almost two-thirds of their people living in the economically depressed town of Bandon. About one in four of the population of the two parishes in the 1840s was Protestant. The registers confirm that Bandon and the surrounding countryside were very badly hit by the famine.[6] Among Bandon's Protestants the death rate was almost three-fifths above its immediate pre-famine level during 1846–48. As seen from table 3.1, the crisis increased male mortality more than female, but there were no striking changes in the incidence by age. Parish registers also imply excess mortality in Dublin's Protestant community, though on a much smaller scale (see chapter 5).

Contemporary local tabulations of deaths are few. An unusually detailed return of mortality in six west Cork parishes prepared by J. J. Marshall, a public works inspector, returned a toll of 7,332 in a population of about 45,000 between September 1846 and September 1847. Adjusting for noncrisis mortality suggests that the famine killed over one-tenth of the population in the six parishes in that twelve-month period. Marshall's return also contains data on emigration, and its parish-by-parish breakdowns throw some important new light on the workings of the famine at the local level.[7] Another useful return is that compiled by Thomas Synnott, driving force behind the Catholic-run Central Relief Committee, from replies to a questionnaire circulated to Catholic priests in late 1847. This partial return produced a total of 35,166 deaths from starvation to 25 September 1847 and another 94,007 from famine-related diseases.[8]

However, such data are too scarce for inferences about excess mortality for the island as a whole. Estimates of aggregate mortality rely instead on the 1841 and 1851 census reports, assumptions about population growth to 1846 and net emigration thereafter; they estimate mortality as a residual. The two most widely cited estimates of excess mortality, independently derived but similar in methodology, argue for about one million. Neither made allowances for famine-related mortality occurring after April 1851, for averted births nor, as noted above, for mortality on emigrant ships or in destination ports. Nor did either rely on the mortality data compiled by William Wilde, noted Dublin surgeon and medical census commissioner in 1851.[9]

Wilde's tables are unparalleled in detail for their day. They provide mortality-by-cause cross-tabulations county by county, year by year, and disease by disease. They are broken down by gender, by age, and by season, and there are separate entries for rural and civic areas and for workhouses and hospitals. Modeled on the nosology devised by Wilde for the 1841 census, the data represent the best that nineteenth-century medical science had to offer. Yet Wilde's tables also suffer from well-known problems, set out in some detail in a paper by Sir William MacArthur forty years ago. They contain several puzzles and surprises. Some, such as the 17 women aged 55 years and above (plus another 114 aged 50–54 years) reported to have died in childbed between 1841 and 1851, or the 1,376 people who allegedly succumbed to cholera in 1841–47 (plus a further 2,502 in 1848), though that particular outbreak of cholera did not reach Ireland until December 1848, or the two youngsters of 5–9 years (plus another fourteen aged 10–14 years) who fell victims to "intemperance," are unimportant in themselves, but hint at bigger, though perhaps less obvious errors. Yet the tables' most serious failing is that because much of the data was collected retrospectively from survivors still living in Ireland in 1851 they grossly underestimate true mortality. In Wilde's own words "no pen has ever recorded the numbers of the forlorn and starving who perished by the wayside or in the ditches, . . . whole families lay down and died".[10] For this reason alone, the reported death toll from literal starvation—just over twenty thousand—is certainly far too low. In his classic account MacArthur warned "against accepting the figures of mortality at their face value, and against basing any theory on the relative proportions of the several groups, because the possible error in each of the totals is so large that any deductions drawn from the differences between them would not only be valueless but actually misleading."[11] The warning is well taken, but the temptation to experiment with these figures persists. Mokyr[12] has also dwelled on their shortcomings but has shown that, handled with due care, the tables have their uses. He subjected an amended version of Wilde's data to regression analysis in order, for example, to distinguish between the impact of particular diseases on excess mortality across counties. Broad consistencies between findings based on some of Wilde's numbers and features of famine mortality elsewhere will continue to tempt historians into trusting Wilde sometimes in cases where such comparisons are impossible.

Famine deaths are attributable to two broad classes of causes. The first closely depends on nutrition and includes deaths from literal starvation and hunger edema, and from infectious diseases such as dysentery. The second is indirect: death is due to the disruption of the normal operation of society, and the failure of associated support networks. Overcrowding and migration allow diseases which are not very hunger-sensitive, such as typhoid fever and cholera, to take their toll. Wilde's tables refer to all these diseases. In the following discussion, I argue that while the tables are quite misleading as a guide to the famine's aggregate toll, they contain some useful messages about the characteristics of famine mortality. Table 3.2 reproduces the numbers of reported deaths of five mainly famine-related causes in Ireland's four provinces between 1846 and 1851. These are what are described in the report as dysentery, diarrhea, dropsy, starvation, and fever. "Fever" presumably includes deaths from both typhus and relapsing fever, as well as from typhoid fever.[13] The sum of reported deaths under these headings — slightly over four hundred thousand — is a serious underestimate, but the implication that the famine was roughly twice as likely to kill people in the provinces of Munster and Connacht as in Ulster and Leinster is perhaps not too far off the mark. Two other plausible nosological points emerge from these raw, uncorrected data. First, the graver the crisis, the more likely was starvation to have been the proximate cause of death. The percentage of deaths included in table 3.2 due to starvation was four times as high in Munster as in Leinster and seven times as high in Connacht as in Ulster. County data reinforce that pattern. Starvation accounted for 0.6 percent of reported deaths from these five causes in Antrim (excluding Belfast and Carrickfergus) and 1.2 percent in Wexford, two of the counties least affected by the famine, but 11 percent in Cork (West Riding) and nearly 15 percent in Mayo. Second, the more serious the crisis, the lower the proportion of famine-related deaths due to fever: across provinces it ranged from 47 percent in Connacht to 61 percent in Leinster. The range is even better reflected in, for example, only 39 percent of deaths in Kerry (in the province of Munster) from these five causes being attributed to fever as against 59 percent in Dublin (in Leinster) and 65 percent in Belfast (in Ulster).[14]

Table 3.3, also derived from Wilde, shows the increase in reported deaths by age between 1841–45 and 1846–51 in two of the worst-

TABLE 3.2
Reported Deaths from Some Famine-Related Causes (by province,
1846–51)

	Males	Females	% Female
LEINSTER			
Dysentery	6,612	4,664	41.3
Diarrhea	4,798	3,395	41.4
Dropsy	3,885	3,507	47.4
Fever	24,739	22,666	47.8
Starvation	620	420	39.6
Total	40,654	34,652	46.0
MUNSTER			
Dysentery	25,038	18,982	43.0
Diarrhea	9,359	7,045	42.9
Dropsy	5,011	3,536	41.5
Fever	46,667	41,074	46.8
Starvation	5,451	3,895	41.7
Total	91,526	74,532	44.9
ULSTER			
Dysentery	6,823	5,561	44.9
Diarrhea	5,326	3,991	42.9
Dropsy	4,373	3,730	46.0
Fever	21,543	20,275	48.5
Starvation	754	411	35.3
Total	38,819	33,968	46.7
CONNACHT			
Dysentery	14,753	10,859	42.4
Diarrhea	4,310	3,095	41.8
Dropsy	2,780	1,840	39.8
Fever	24,603	20,462	45.4
Starvation	5,937	4,295	42.0
Total	52,383	40,551	43.6
Ireland total	223,382	183,703	45.1

affected counties, Mayo and Clare. As far as the overall ratios are concerned, again MacArthur's warning is apposite, but it is the shifts across
age that are of interest here. The relatively light impact of the crisis on
infants may be explained by the likelihood that fewer of them were
born. This could have stemmed from declines in both the desire and the

TABLE 3.3
Reported Deaths by Age in Mayo and Clare, 1846–51, as a Ratio of 1841–45

Age (Years)	Mayo		Clare	
	Males	Females	Males	Females
<1	2.11	3.29	2.18	2.65
1–4	3.36	3.85	3.48	3.92
5–9	5.93	5.46	6.80	6.87
10–19	7.56	7.21	7.55	7.17
20–29	4.66	4.68	4.49	4.79
30–39	5.15	3.97	5.20	4.11
40–49	5.12	4.43	5.65	4.66
50–59	4.95	4.85	5.36	4.52
60–69	4.28	5.07	5.24	4.35
70–79	3.60	4.29	3.51	3.63
80+	3.43	3.70	2.98	3.01
Total	4.12	4.48	4.46	4.50

Source: 1851 Census, Tables of Death.

capacity to bear children. The latter is often associated in the literature with famine amenorrhea, or a malnutrition-induced loss of fertility in women. The implication that those most affected by the catastrophe were young children and adolescents (i.e., those aged 5–19 years) is interesting—though from a comparative perspective, again not so surprising. The numbers also imply that men in their thirties and forties were most at risk compared to women in the same age brackets.

Figure 3.1 compares the age distributions of reported deaths from the same five causes between 1841 and 1851. The implication that diarrhea victims were much more likely to have been children than those dying of dropsy or fever is perhaps less surprising than the implied high share of infants and children among the starvation deaths. The age distributions of reported deaths from diarrhea and dysentery are quite similar. A further interesting implication of Wilde's tables is that men and women in the prime of life (aged 15–54 years) accounted for 53 percent of reported fever victims, but only 35 percent of reported dysentery victims and 28 percent of reported starvation victims.

Most of the victims of famines in the past have been either young or elderly. Whether the very young and the very elderly were *relatively* more vulnerable during famines than in normal times remains rather a moot point. Wilde's flawed data suggest not (see table 3.3). This too is the tentative message of some Protestant parish registers in Dublin city (discussed in chapter 5), but the records of the city's biggest cemetery at

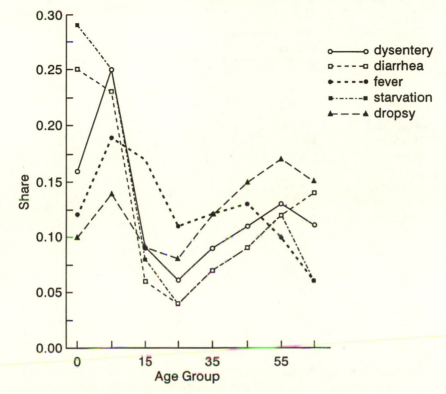

Figure 3.1. Death from famine-related causes by age.

Glasnevin show a big proportionate decline in the proportion of infant burials and a rise in the shares of all other age groups, with the biggest proportionate rise in the 5–14 year age group. The Bandon parish registers also indicate that the elderly were the worst sufferers, though not by a big margin (see table 3.1). How do these Irish patterns compare with those found elsewhere? In south Asia in the nineteenth and early twentieth centuries, perhaps contrary to expectation, the biggest proportionate increases in mortality also occurred in age groups where normal mortality was light, that is, among older children and adults. Again, in Japan in the famine year of 1837, people aged under five years and over seventy-five were relatively less affected, and in both Finland in the late seventeenth century and in Darfur in western Sudan in the mid-1980s child deaths rose more than infant or adult deaths.[15]

Table 3.4 is also derived from Wilde's tabulations. It compares the female shares of reported deaths from smallpox and consumption with

TABLE 3.4
Female Percentage of Deaths in Connacht and Munster, 1841–51,
Tabulated by Cause of Death

	All	Workhouses & Hospitals	Non-Institutional
CONNACHT			
Fever	45.4	47.9	44.6
Dysentery	42.4	45.3	37.3
Diarrhea	41.8	45.3	37.4
Starvation	42.0	38.1*	42.0
Smallpox	49.8	45.7	49.9
Consumption	50.7	48.3	50.8
MUNSTER			
Fever	46.8	48.9	45.1
Dysentery	43.0	46.3	39.4
Diarrhea	42.9	46.9	37.8
Starvation	41.7	37.8	41.8
Smallpox	48.8	49.2	48.8
Consumption	49.7	48.2	49.9

*Very few observations.

the female shares of deaths from fever, dysentery, and starvation. Small-pox and consumption are included as crude controls, since deaths from them are less likely to have been famine related. Note that the female shares in these cases are close to half. The implied female shares of deaths from starvation, dysentery, diarrhea, and even fever were significantly less, supporting the hypothesis, discussed at greater length below, that in Ireland in the 1840s men were relatively more likely to succumb to famine-related diseases than women.

Wilde's Tables of Deaths can be adjusted for underreporting, though at the cost of debatable assumptions about the variation in underreporting and emigration across counties. Table 3.5 summarizes the range of results produced by one such exercise. The weighting schemes reflect the distribution of reported deaths by cause in counties with the highest death rate (Mayo) and the highest migration rate (Tipperary/Clare); deaths which would have occurred in the absence of famine are excluded. The adjustments increase the proportion of famine-specific diseases such as starvation and dysentery and reduce the shares of more traditional causes of death such as consumption and infirmity. They suggest that every disease listed by Wilde contributed something to excess mortality during the famine. Thus the famine's physiological impact on the population at large went far beyond the direct and immedi-

TABLE 3.5
The Main Causes of Famine Mortality (in percentages)

	Mayo Weights	Tipperary/Clare Weights
Hunger Sensitive	40.8	29.0
Dys/Diarrhea	28.2	21.1
Starvation	9.1	3.6
Dropsy	2.0	1.4
Marasmus	1.6	2.7
Partially Sensitive	29.5	36.1
Consumption	4.6	6.9
Other	24.8	29.2
Not very Sensitive	29.7	35.0
Fever	27.5	29.7
Cholera	5.7	7.0
Infirmity, old age	−3.5	−1.7
Total	*100.0*	*100.0*

Source: Mokyr and Ó Gráda, "Famine mortality and famine diseases."

ate effects of famine diseases. Table 3.5 also indicates that, roughly speaking, two-thirds of famine mortality was due to diseases that were the result of poor nutrition, and one-third from those resulting from the indirect effects of the crisis on personal behavior and social structure. In particular, fever and cholera had little direct nutrition sensitivity.[16]

Other data corroborate another important message of Wilde's tables: no county in Ireland was immune from the crisis. Though for a largely urban county such as Dublin the famine invites analysis as an externality brought on by immigration from rural areas (see chapter 5), poor law and prison records suggest that mortality in Dublin was not confined to immigrants. The admission books of the North Dublin Union distinguish between inmates born in Dublin and others. The number of Dublin-born inmates dying in the workhouse rose from 186 in 1845 to 322 in 1846 and 632 in 1847, before falling back to 312 in 1848.[17] As noted above, Dublin parish registers also indicate increases in mortality in several Protestant parishes in the late 1840s. A third source of data on Dublin deaths during the famine is the burial records of the city's biggest Catholic cemetery in Glasnevin. The records distinguish between burial plots that were paid for and pauper plots. Both categories showed a big rise in the spring of 1847, though the number of pauper burials continued higher than before, while — the cholera-induced spike in 1849 apart — burials in paid plots quickly returned to their pre-crisis norm (see the appendix to chapter 5). The surge in the pauper burials preceded the rise in other burials.[18] As in Dublin, the authorities in Cork and Belfast sought to limit and control the immigration of famine victims from the countryside by imprisoning beggars and vagrants.

A Belgian chronicler wrote of the Great European Famine of the mid-1310s that "men and women from among the powerful, the middling, and the lowly, old and young, rich and poor, perished daily in such great numbers that the air was fetid with stench."[19] Almost certainly the chronicler allowed his class bias to exaggerate the vulnerability of the "powerful" and the "middling" relative to the "lowly." In the case of Ireland, Karl Marx's claim that the Irish famine killed "poor devils only" is much closer to the truth, in the sense that the poor and the marginalized were the first and always the most likely to die. A report that three people had been buried without priest or ceremony in Skibbereen in west Cork in December 1846 was accompanied by the observation that "this mortality is confined to a certain class of persons, who are always to be found in and about towns in Ireland, such as the laboring people and beggars." At this stage "the country people" — code for landholders — had simply fallen back on the grain in their barns and held on to the rent.[20]

Still, the better-off were not immune. The poor were the main targets of disease such as mild typhoid fever in normal times, but during the famine "when fever attacked the higher classes it was universally of a much more fatal character than amongst the poor."[21] At greatest risk were those who came into contact with the diseased in the course of their work. In Waterford in May 1847, "fever and pestilence have been doing the worst here among the upper classes, while famine and destitution are quickly thinning the numbers of the poor." In Mayo in February 1848, "all who mingled with [the poor] might be said to carry their lives in their hands." Landlords, priests, and doctors died in numbers. Casualties among the gentry during the spring of 1847 included Thomas Martin, proprietor of the huge Ballinahinch estate in Connemara, Mr. Gregory of Coole Park (father of the sponsor of the notorious Gregory Clause), Lord Lurgan, and Stepney St. George of Headford Castle.[22] Many clergymen of all denominations died. In Cloyne and Ross, perhaps the worst-affected diocese, seventeen Catholic priests had died by late November 1847 "by reason of their attendance on the suffering poor." Cork and Ardfert accounted for eight more and Limerick for another five.[23] Workhouse officials suffered too; 164 of them died of fever between 1847 and 1849. In that way, half the paid staff of the North Dublin Union contracted fever at the height of the famine, and nearly half of those died of it. Valentine Flood, an eminent anatomist who had been working for the Board of Health in Tipperary, was only one "among the many voluntary victims offered by [the medical] profession to the Moloch of typhus contagion." Long gaps in the records of the Dublin Sick Poor Institution in 1848 were blamed on the "almost contemporaneous" deaths of two doctors there. In Ireland as a whole, nearly two hundred doctors and medical students died in 1847, three times the pre-famine average. Physicians could not even immunize or cure themselves, and indeed mortality in the medical profession was higher than in the population as a whole. The high mortality explains why "the horror of contagion (among the Irish poor) in general amounts to a perfect monomania."[24] In its inability to distinguish fully between rich and poor, the ultimate weapon against overpopulation in the Malthusian armory was a blunt one.

THE ROLE OF MEDICINE

During the Irish famine, professional medicine and medical men served little purpose. A scientific understanding of how contagious diseases were transmitted was still some decades away in the 1840s, and the relevant curative measures almost a century away.[25] The treatments and cures recommended by doctors were of little benefit, if not positively harmful. The following account of the treatment of famine-related diseases in Dublin is instructive:

> Plenty of nourishment and the free use of stimulants were found to be absolutely necessary. Wine was freely given, and with the best effects. General experience was decidedly opposed to the use of bleeding in any form. In some cases of local congestion the application of a few leeches, or the abstraction of a small quantity of blood by cupping-glasses, was found beneficial. Mercury was only given as a mild aperient or alternative, and sometimes, combined with Dover's powder, in dysentric cases it acted beneficially. Opium does not appear to have been very generally employed; "it was only useful for allaying the vomiting of the secondary fever." "A combination of morphia and tartar emetic was found so valuable in cases of excitement and delirium, that it was styled a specific in the North Union sheds."[26]

Another Dublin practitioner met cases of "tenderness of the epigastrium by small blisters and sinapisms," an unlikely remedy which often resulted in "haemorrhagic eruptions on the parts they were placed upon, perfect patches of extravasation marking for days after the size and place of the sinapisms, and looking as if the patient had been painted with blood." This same doctor described bleeding a man who fainted after the removal of six ounces of blood. In late 1848 the Board of Health recommended a variety of powders for cholera victims: they included a compound of chalk and opium — "one powder every half hour until the looseness ceases" — and pills of mercury and opium. Against dysentery and diarrhea, the eminent physician William Stokes recommended doses of a concoction of whiskey and laudanum diluted in two gallons of water, to which two pounds of logwood in chip had been added before boiling and cooling down.[27] His clinical experience led a fellow-practitioner to surmise whether "the epidemic, like the ague, owes its origin to terresterial miasms?" The link between malnutrition and fever was controversial. Against surgeon Dominic Corrigan's mantra of "no famine, no fever," the editor of the *Dublin Medical Press* declared that "it could easily be shown that famine and destitution are more frequently the effect than the cause of fever."[28]

The majority of those contracting fever recovered from it, but it is important to remember that when the disease struck there was little that medical knowledge *per se* could contribute. Isolation in fever hospitals was the main institutional remedy for fever. Modern medical wisdom would not rate the diagnostics or treatments of mid-nineteenth-century Irish practitioners highly; indeed, some of them (such as cupping) were likely to weaken already weak patients, and some (such as mercury) were positively harmful. Though they were slow to say so, doctors simply did not know how to prevent or cure infectious diseases. Accounts of the activities of medical personnel stress their commitment and heroism,[29] but results are quite another matter. Medical treatment is unlikely to have saved many lives during the famine.

How much difference would better medical knowledge have made to those at risk? Would the famished simply not have died of something else? These are difficult questions, awaiting considered answers.[30] Since the 1840s medical technology has made massive strides both in diagnosis and treatment. First came the medical breakthroughs associated with Louis Pasteur (1822–95) and Robert Koch (1843–1910), and their demonstrations that the transmission mechanism for diseases such as typhus and dysentery was through microorganisms, not through noxious odors or "bad air." Curative measures for infectious diseases came much later: effective antibiotics and antibacterials against typhus, typhoid fever, dysentery, and malaria have been available only since the 1940s. The same holds, broadly speaking, for the disinfectants and insecticides that control or eradicate the flies, fleas, lice, and ticks that cause these diseases. Even more recent are mass vaccination campaigns against measles and meningitis, diseases more likely to be lethal in famine conditions. Finally, the technology for supplying clean water and rehydrating dysentery victims has also advanced in recent decades. Yet it is important to note that better medical knowledge is not only a matter of effective cures but also of understanding the transmission of the infections that were killing people. Long before the cures just listed, preventive measures such as using boiled water, washing clothes, and taking care with personal hygiene were available as corollaries of the medical breakthroughs of Pasteur and Koch.

Reliable famine nosologies to compare with those reported in table 3.5 are scarce. However, the registration data available for India from the 1870s on, though less detailed, are almost certainly more accurate than Wilde's data and provide cause-of-death information on several famines. Cause-of-death records from the Russian famine of 1918–22 also survive, though they are more problematic. Table 3.6 suggests that in both India and Russia infectious diseases continued to dominate during famines, decades after the implications of the germ transmission theory had been absorbed by medical experts and public health officials. In India, by and large, typhus, typhoid fever, and malaria were more important, and dysentery less important, than in Ireland; the outcome in Saratov *gubernaia*, source of the best Russian data, closely mirrors Ireland. The 1918–22 outbreak of typhus in Russia was the greatest in the history of that disease.[31]

Information on the causes of death in Warsaw's Jewish ghetto before its destruction by the Nazis in July 1942 affords further insight into the role of medical science in preventing deaths from infectious disease. As the death rate there quintupled between 1940 and 1941–42, the proportion attributed to starvation rose from one percent to 25 percent. The share of typhus remained small, however. The data bequeathed by two other twentieth-century European famines—those in occupied northeastern Italy in 1918 and in the western Netherlands during the starvation winter of 1944–45—tell similar stories. In both cases mortality rose significantly, with starvation accounting for a big share of the rise and infectious diseases counting for relatively little. Finally, in Greece in 1941–42 another famine produced by wartime conditions resulted in no murderous epidemical outbreaks either.[32]

Why the differences and what are the implications for a counterfactual Ireland in which the authorities understood the germ transmission theory? Part of the answer is that before the war both the Dutch and the Jews of Warsaw had enjoyed universal literacy, clean running water for drinking and washing, sufficient changes of clothing and bedding to ward off lice, housing that was easier to keep clean, soap and disinfectants, good cooking facilities for what little food there was, and good medical advice.[33] The preventative measures implied by the new medicine had become part of their daily routine, and must have continued to be so when famine struck. But neither Russia in 1918–22 nor Bengal in the 1940s acted out the lessons of Koch and Pasteur. Such comparisons would seem to indicate that the new medicine would not have been enough to affect the Irish "Tables of Death" much. Unlike the Dutch

TABLE 3.6
Causes of Excess Deaths in Ireland, Russia, and India

A. IRELAND AND RUSSIA

Cause of Death (%)	Ireland		Saratov 1918–22		Petrograd 1918–22		Moscow 1918–22[a]		Moscow 1918–22[b]	
	(a)	(b)	(i)	(ii)	(i)	(ii)	(i)	(ii)	(i)	(ii)
D/D/G	28.2	21.6	20.1	19.7	12.0	10.4	18.0	16.0	−1.8	−1.3
Cholera	5.7	7.9	6.5	5.1	2.1	2.0	0.9	0.7	2.9	1.4
Fever	27.5	30.8	21.9	24.1	23.0	19.3	22.4	24.6	37.2	37.8
Respiratory	4.6	5.0	10.8	9.8	18.4	19.3	19.8	20.2	4.0	12.6
Starvation/scurvy	12.6	7.4	21.5	5.5	36.7	12.8	–	–	–	–
Other/unknown	21.4	27.3	19.2	35.8	7.8	36.2	38.9	38.5	57.7	49.5
Total	100.0	100.0	100.0	100.0	100.0	100.0	100.0	100.0	100.0	100.0

TABLE 3.6 (cont.)

B. INDIA

Cause of Death (%)	Bombay 1877	Berar 1897	Berar 1900	Punjab 1900	UP 1908
D/D/G	9.7	30.4	37.0	3.0	−1.2
Cholera	16.5	12.1	9.6	7.6	4.6
Fever	45.9	29.0	23.9	72.2	90.9
Respiratory	–	–	–	–	–
Starvation/scurvy	–	–	–	–	–
Other	27.9	28.5	29.5	17.2	5.7
Total	100.0	100.0	100.0	100.0	100.0

SOURCES AND NOTES: D/D/G = Dysentery/Diarrhea/Gastroenteritis; (–) = not known, not given. *Ireland*: Mokyr and Ó Gráda, "Famine mortality and famine diseases," with (*a*) Mayo and (*b*) Tipperary weights. "Starvation" includes dropsy and marasmus. "Respiratory" includes only consumption. *Saratov, Moscow, and Petrograd*: Derived from Stephen G. Wheatcroft "Famine and epidemic crises in Russia," 340; id., "Famine and factors affecting mortality in the USSR: The demographic crises of 1914–1922 and 1930–33," CREES Discussion Paper No. 21, University of Birmingham, 1982, appendixes, pp. 17–18. I am grateful to Stephen Wheatcroft (pers. comm., April 1998) for the estimates for Moscow and Petrograd. (*i*) 1918–22 averages calculated directly from 1918–22 values without weighting for separate years. (*ii*) 1918–22 averages calculated for the entire five year period.

D/D/G figures include deaths from typhoid and other water and food borne diseases. *Fever* includes typhus and para-typhus, the common diseases of infancy, smallpox, pyaemia, and erysipelas. *Respiratory* includes normal tuberculosis and other respiratory diseases but excludes non-respiratory tuberculosis. *Other* includes nonrespiratory tuberculosis, syphilis, anthrax, rabies, and unspecified micro-organisms, as well as specified non-micro-organism apart from starvation/scurvy, and all unknown. *India*: Maharatna, *Demography*, table 2.6, pp. 46–47. I subtracted cause-specific death rates in baseline years from rates during famine years to get excess mortality by cause. I then calculated the percentages of the totals explained by the different causes. Maharatna's D/D/G totals are for diarrhea and dysentery.

[a]Excess deaths in comparison with 1923 levels.
[b]Excess deaths in comparison with 1914 levels.

and the Jews of Warsaw, the pre-famine Irish poor knew or cared little about hygiene. For people who went barefoot much of the time, who relied on old or secondhand clothes, and who often shared their accommodation with pigs and poultry, it was a luxury few of them could afford. Their thatched cabins and clustered settlements made the spread of disease more likely. The contrast between Ireland and Warsaw or the Netherlands was probably intensified by the onset of famine. In the latter cases, hunger may have made people cold and less likely to shed or change their clothes, but there still was clean water and adequate medical care, and cleanliness and hygiene were easier to maintain. The lack of mobility enforced by the Nazis may, perversely, have reduced the spread of disease in Warsaw and in Holland. The Irish poor, inured to poor hygiene in normal times, would have found it even more difficult to stay clean during the famine. In principle, as the North Dublin Union's Catholic chaplain explained, there was "a *famine disease* that may be *prevented* but not *cured*." The trouble was that the damage had already been done before "the warm clean clothing, the abundant and wholesome food, and the medical skill and attention of [the] workhouse" could have much effect. Aykroyd's account of Bengal a century later probably holds for Ireland in the 1840s too: "Patients did not care how dirty or naked they were. Those with famine diarrhoea would repeatedly soil their beds and pay no attention to the protests of attendants . . . a pathological condition induced by starvation."[34] In such circumstances better medical knowledge alone would not have been enough to eliminate mass mortality. Indeed, though Irish public health officials and others in the 1840s had no inkling of the transmission mechanism discovered by Pasteur and Koch, they had an intuitive sense of the importance of cleanliness in the homes and yards of the poor, as well as of the link between contaminated water and diarrhea. A good example is the Dublin doctor who had warned the wealthier classes in 1843 that "foul air, want of cleanliness, [and] bad or insufficient food, so derange the natural processes of nutrition and secretion that new concentrations are formed from the blood, the results of which are dangerous and destructive of human life." But given Irish poverty and the social disruption caused by the famine, such intuitions served little purpose.[35]

The comparisons suggest that in Ireland in the 1840s poverty would have constrained the impact of better medical knowledge. This is in line with a broader point about the historical role of breakthroughs in medical science. It is well known that in the developed world of the nineteenth century mortality from several infectious diseases began to decline before the discovery of effective science-based medical treatment. Improved nutrition and better hygiene were at least partly responsible for this. In today's less developed world, however, it is the other way around; the decline in mortality from specific causes such as gastroenteritis, malaria, and tuberculosis has tended to lag behind medical technology. Even in the 1990s dysentery and typhoid fever remain serious threats. Thus economic and political progress are a precondition for modern health technologies playing their part in improving the health of the masses.[36]

These comparisons do not rule out a role for the new medicine in Ireland in the 1840s. Though the insights of Koch and Pasteur could have done little for the poor, they could have prevented many comfortably off, well-nourished people from succumbing to contagion. This implies another important difference between the Irish famine and today's famines: in today's famine-threatened regions elites are largely protected against the big killer diseases such as typhus, malaria, and dysentery. Medicine has thus probably made famine mortality far more class-specific than it was in the nineteenth century. Comparing the fate of clergy and medical personnel during the famine with that of modern Irish volunteer aid workers makes the point; since the 1960s several Irish aid workers have been attacked by famine fevers, but happily none has died of famine-related illnesses. Marx's quip about the Irish famine killing "poor devils only" holds truer still for modern famines.[37]

FAMINE AND GENDER

In the wake of a tour of the west of Ireland in 1849 a sympathetic and humane English observer noted: "No one has yet I believe been able to explain, why it is, that men and boys, sink sooner under famine, than the other sex; still, so it is; go where you will, every officer will tell you, it is so. In the same workhouse, in which you will find the girls and women, looking well, you will find the men and boys, in a state of the lowest physical depression; equal care in every way being bestowed on both sexes."[38]

If estimating excess mortality during the Irish famine is a very tricky business, estimating the relative impact of the crisis on men and women and on different age groups is more difficult still. Any such exercise for the country as a whole hinges on necessarily debatable assumptions about normal mortality rates, deficiencies in the 1841 census, and emigration before and during the famine period. The quantitative evidence is somewhat limited, but most of what is available supports the claim that men were worse hit than women, though by a narrow margin. An indirect estimate for the country as a whole also found that men were a little — but only a little — more likely to succumb than women. The eve-

TABLE 3.7
Gender Ratio of Reported Deaths in 1851 Census

Year	Rural Areas Male/Female	Civic Areas Male/Female	Public Institutions Male/Female
1845	1.13	1.10	1.05
1846	1.17	1.07	1.09
1847	1.25	1.13	1.11
1848	1.20	1.11	1.14
1849	1.22	1.07	1.09

Source: 1851 Census, vol. 5(2), 674–76.

ning out in the gender ratio between older men and women in the 1840s is consistent with women's stronger survival capacity. The gender ratios implied in Wilde's Tables of Death (table 3.7) is also consistent with a slight male edge in mortality during the famine years. So are the Bandon burial data described above, and the data in some Protestant parish registers in the south side of Dublin. Marshall's return of mortality in six west Cork parishes between September 1846 and September 1847, discussed above, also implies that male deaths exceeded female; it listed totals of 3,136 children, 2,396 men, and 1,800 women. Workhouse records tell the same story. In Wicklow, for example, 1,916 males and 1,733 females succumbed to infectious diseases between 6 June 1841 and 30 March 1851. In Manorhamilton workhouse on 1 April 1847 the guardians resolved that "as the boys appear in a very delicate and sickly state, their rations be increased."[39] The relative advantage of women during the famine years must be seen against their relative deprivation, marked in nineteenth-century Ireland in normal times.

What of other historical and modern Third World famines? The big drop in the sex ratio in Iceland in the wake of the catastrophic famine of 1783–84—843 in 1769, 784 in 1785, 839 in 1801—suggests that males suffered more than females. An analysis of the Japanese famine of 1837 based on Buddhist temple registers returns the same verdict. In Finland in the 1867–68, though in general excess mortality was nearly proportional to "normal" mortality across ages and for both males and females, adolescent and young adult men were more likely to succumb, as they were in Holland in the "hunger winter" of 1944–45. The study of Indian famines returns a mixed verdict; in most of the subcontinent males were at a relative disadvantage, but in the Punjab in the 1890s and in 1900 female mortality exceeded male.[40]

A recent study by U.S. anthropologist Donald K. Grayson finds that women are more likely than men to survive when conditions are at their

worst. Grayson's claim is based on his analysis of the 87-member Don-
ner party who were caught in a blizzard in the mountain passes of the
Sierra Nevada as they attempted to travel from Illinois to California
during the winter of 1846–47. Nearly half (40) of the group never
made it; over four-fifths of those aged over fifty years and nearly two-
thirds of children under five died. But nearly twice as many males (30 of
53) died as females (10 of 34). Grayson also studied the fate of 429
Mormon immigrants from Europe who left Iowa City for Utah with
handcarts in 1856. Sixty-eight died en route, the death rate among the
men being three times that of the women, and mortality was highest
among older people.[41]

Was this female resilience the product of physiological or cultural
factors? First, in support of a physiological interpretation, Grayson
stressed female advantages in conserving body heat and energy, while
allowing that male work patterns exposed them to greater dangers
and energy use. Second, the demographic literature notes that the
greater amount of body fat stored by healthy females allows them to
withstand deprivation longer. A recent U.S. textbook reports that
body fat accounts for 27 percent of the body weight of the average
20–24 year old female compared to only 15 percent of that of
the average male of the same age. Muscle, an encumbrance in famine conditions, accounts for 36 and 44.8 percent of female and male
body weights, respectively.[42] Third, famines universally reduce the
birthrate. The associated fall in maternal mortality is not enough to
account for the gender mortality gap, but freedom from the discomforts of pregnancy and the reduced need to care for and feed very
young children surely also count. In support, comparing reported
deaths by age in 1846–51 and 1841–45 implies that women's relative advantage during the famine was greatest in the 30–49 years
age bracket (table 3.3). Fourth, further insight into the issue of
gender and famine is offered by research into the animal world. It
turns out that the verdict of zoological research, both in laboratories
and in the wild, is virtually unanimous: the gender gap reported in
several studies of famine also applies to dimorphic mammal species
(i.e., species in which males are bigger than females). Among
Siberian deer, for example, the harsh winter of 1976–77 "produced
a particularly high mortality differential between stags and hinds."
In U.S. experiments with rats subjected to complete starvation for
six days, males used up more body protein and less fat than females. Studies of a wide range of species including voles, lions, rein-
deer and caribou, elk, musk oxen, wildebeest, and kangaroos corroborate these findings. Why? Because when food is short the larger
body size of one gender (in most cases males) — dimorphism — makes

them more likely to starve.[43] Surely there is thus a physiological presumption in favor of relative female advantage in *Homo sapiens* too?

An alternative, cultural interpretation of relative female advantage proposed by David Fitzpatrick points to the likely improvement of women's entitlements relative to men's during famines. The point is that during famines traditional female skills or attributes such as cooking, affection, and consolation are at a premium. The result is a relative increase in women's entitlements as reflected in food consumption. So far, hard evidence for this interesting hypothesis is lacking. Workhouse guidelines were far from uniform; most unions seem to have stipulated less food for women than men, but some did not. Yet, as noted above, women withstood the workhouse regime better. Moreover, the cultural hypothesis is also consistent with scenarios where women are more likely to die; different assumptions about living standards and mortality could produce both a greater reduction in women's entitlements and a better survival rate. It all depends on three factors: how close each gender was to the subsistence threshold before the famine; how sensitive population is to declines in consumption; and how far the entitlements of each gender fell. None of this rules out a role for culture too. So far, though, the zoological and biological evidence described above make the physiological explanation more convincing.[44]

THE FAMINE AND EMIGRATION

> *An chuid aca imigh ó Éirinn*
> *Is iad is fearr saol mar a mheasaimse*
> *Tá 'rán acu is im is tae*
> *Is níl leite bhuí 'n aonchor dá theannadh leo.*

> [Those of them who left Ireland had the best of it in my
> opinion; they have bread and butter and tea, and nobody is
> forcing yellow meal on them.]
> (From a Cork famine song, late 1840s)

"To go a thousand *li* in search of something to eat; to go off in all directions in order to find nourishment": so went one description of the movements of population induced by a massive famine in eighteenth-century northern China. Most famines induce people to move temporarily in search of food and work and in order to escape disease. Much of the movement is from rural areas into the towns, and when the worst is over most of the surviving migrants return home.[45] Some of the migration during the Irish famine followed this pattern, as the cities and bigger towns were swollen by the arrival of largely unwelcome migrants seeking charity and work. The result was an increase in the populations of many towns. In April 1847 a local newspaper contained the following description of the inflow into Cork city: "The incursion of rustic paupers into the City continues unabated . . . they wait on the outskirts of the town till dark, when they may be seen coming in droves, the bedclothes strapped to the shoulders of the father, while the children carry pots, pans, jugs, old sacks and other articles. On an average about 300 of these miserable creatures come into the City daily, who are walking masses of filth, vermin and sickness."[46] However, a distinction must be made between such local, largely temporary, movements and permanent long-distance migration. In Scottish history the "ill years" of the 1690s rank among the most disastrous on record. A succession of poor harvests accompanied by high prices cut the population by 5–15 percent. The fall was not all attributable to deaths and averted births: there was significant emigration to Ireland. The size of the migration will never be known exactly, but even a conservative guess of fifty thousand would mean about 5 percent of the Scottish population at the time. Again, the so-called Great Highland Famine of the 1840s killed very few people but produced a huge increase in emigration, mainly to North America. But permanent migration on such a scale in the wake of famines is unusual.[47]

A key feature of the Irish famine was that well over a million people left Ireland for good between the mid-1840s and the early 1850s. Some of these would have left in any case; after all, migration had been substantial in the early 1840s. But most of the mass emigration of the late 1840s was part of the famine tragedy. It was push migration with a vengeance, and its tragic character has been rightly at the center of historical writing about it. Yet two points often missed in the historiography need emphasis here.

First, fewer perished in transit than might have been expected in the circumstances, or implied by many popular accounts. The famine migration occurred just before steamships won out over sail on the north Atlantic route. Much has been written about the terrible conditions and high mortality endured by Ireland's "economic refugees" on the long crossing. Robert Scally offers an eloquent summary:

The miserable epic of the Atlantic crossing in these years has been told so often and well that it hardly seems necessary to recount its dreadful details. Flanked by Skibbereen and Grosse Isle at either end of the voyage, the "coffin ship" stands as the central panel of the famine triptych, depicting bondage and fever in the steerage, wailing children and mothers' pleas from the darkness below decks, heartless captains and brutal crews, shipwreck, pestilence, and burial at sea. In its own smaller scale, the memory of the emigrant steerage has long been held, like the slaves' "middle passage" and the trains of the Holocaust, as an icon in Ireland's oppression.[48]

This account is an apt reminder of the harsh conditions faced by many passengers in the later 1840s, and of the exploitation endured by some at the hands of unscrupulous shipowners and agents en route and at either end of the voyage. Indeed, an Irish landlord, surveying the scene on the quay in Limerick in August 1850 remarked in his diary, "They may talk of the horrors of the middle passage, but I cannot think there is much difference between the accommodation for the whites & the blacks." Yet analogies with slaves and Holocaust victims ring false, and not only because most Irish emigrants made it safely to the other side.[49] It remains true that the mortality on the Canadian route—about 20 percent—in 1847 was very high. That route, serviced mainly by old timber hulks, produced rates rivaling those on slaving ships plying the Atlantic route then and earlier.[50] The less regulated Canadian route, favored by both poorer emigrants relying on their own resources and by landlords with an eye to a bargain, accounted for a significant proportion of the outflow in Black '47. Indeed, about half of those participating in one landlord-funded emigration scheme from Strokestown in Roscommon died in transit to the New World.[51] But the notion that such mortality was the norm—as implied, for example, in the claim in the *Irish Press* in December 1994 that "at least [one million] fled the country on the aptly named coffin ships"—is a myth. Those Strokestown emigrants were far from being typical. The great majority of those forced out in the late 1840s made it safely to the other side. Migrant mortality on the passage between Europe and New York between 1836 and 1853 may be inferred from contemporary passenger lists. Table 3.8 compares the mortality rate of a sample of Irish emigrants bound for New York with that of samples of French, German, and English emigrants. What is most remarkable about the numbers is that neither the Irish as a group nor the famine years stand out; the record of German ships in 1847 and 1848 was much worse, and curiously 1849, not 1847, produced the highest mortality overall. While the death rate out of Liverpool, the departure point for most of the New York-bound Irish, was higher in 1847–48 than in 1845–46, the average mortality rate was still less than 2 percent. Admittedly, the New York passenger lists cannot tell the full story, but after 1847 it was the American ports that dominated and, given the tragic and chaotic contexts of the journeys, it is the low overall mortality which is significant.[52]

Second, in the absence of long-distance emigration as an outlet, many more would have perished, either in Ireland or in Great Britain. There is

TABLE 3.8
Mortality on New York-Bound Ships

Year	Irish Ports		Liverpool		France		Germany		London	
	MR	Obs.	MR	Obs.	MR	Obs.	MR	Obs.	MR	Obs.
1845	—	—	0.76	13	0.61	8	0.96	5	3.57	1
1846	—	—	0.91	18	1.18	11	1.07	13	1.28	5
1847	1.33	5	1.64	22	0.83	6	3.77	5	1.09	3
1848	2.74	5	1.54	39	1.35	11	3.36	2	1.04	2
1849	3.36	14	3.34	61	1.74	7	1.51	8	0.56	1
1850	1.16	7	1.49	57	0.55	3	4.41	3	1.89	2
1851	0.67	16	1.18	94	0.79	12	1.05	8	0.52	8
1852	3.59	2	0.88	67	0.74	16	0.55	3	0.96	12
1853	0.62	5	1.73	54	1.30	18	1.01	27	1.23	10

Source: Derived from data kindly supplied by Raymond Cohn.
Key: MR = mortality rate; Obs. = number of ships.

thus a sense in which mass migration may be regarded as a form of disaster relief. Still, it was not the very poorest who left. In March 1847, in a frequently cited passage, the *Cork Examiner* noted that "the emigrants of this year are not like those of former ones; they are now actually *running away* from fever and disease and hunger, with money scarcely sufficient to pay passage for and find food for the voyage." Nonetheless, though hard data distinguishing between the socioeconomic backgrounds of those who died and those who emigrated are lacking, it seems fair to assume that the latter were mostly people of some modest means. Many contemporary accounts refer to small farmers "with interests in their farms" and "small sums of money at their disposal" leaving or planning their departure. In west Kerry, for example, farmers swapped their holdings with their more prosperous neighbors for the passage money to America. In the words of the inimitable storyteller Peig Sayers, "Isn't that how the people got the big farms around here, since all those who had any standing left would find neighbours willing to trade their land in return for a passage to America" (my translation). Around Skibbereen a good many were giving up their land and preparing for departure; these were the "substantial farmers, who still have a little means left." In early April 1847 in a village not far from Galway city, sixteen young women, most of whom could command a dowry of £20 (almost $100) each, were about to leave for America.[53] For most of the landless poor, with no savings or liquid assets to fall back on, the cost of a passage across the Atlantic remained too high. The emigrants were therefore more likely to be from artisanal or small-farm than from purely proletarian backgrounds.

An account in the *Freeman's Journal* of a "wretched looking" Roscommon woman who had sought refuge for herself and six children in a night asylum in Dublin is illuminating in this respect. She had been put into custody by the keeper for failing to account for a large sum of money in her possession. The magistrate evinced surprise at the family's condition, "while she had so much money about her." The following is the woman's account: "She lived in the county Roscommon, and her husband held about ten acres of land, but he died last Shrovetide; she had no means of sowing a crop, and she gave up the place to a collector of poor rate, who gave her £15 for it; she got £5 for a mare, and £4 for a cow, 10s. for a cart and harrow, and more money for other things, and this made up all she had; she was about going to America, but she would not be taken with her children for less than £27." When this woman's eldest boy, a thirteen-year-old, corroborated her story, the magistrate deemed it "evidently true," and discharged her.[54]

The passenger lists mentioned earlier offer some insight into the quality of the New York-bound component of the famine migration. First, they suggest a fall in the share of unaccompanied individuals during the famine; 50.8 percent of those reaching New York in 1846 traveled with at least one other individual with the same surname, compared to 57.9 percent in 1847–51. This, and the accompanying shift in the age composition of the migration, reflects the more family-oriented character of the famine outflow. The share of females was largely unaffected by the famine, however. Those describing themselves as laborers and servants dominated both before and during the famine, but there was a significant rise in the percentage of self-declared farmers, from 6.1 percent in 1846 to 11.2 percent in 1847–51. The passenger lists offer little direct information on the county origins of emigrants, but the shifting regional distribution of the outflow from Irish ports is consistent with rises in the shares of the worst-hit provinces of Munster and Connacht.[55]

While life in America in the 1850s almost certainly marked an improvement on conditions in Ireland even before the famine, Irish immigrants fared poorly in terms of occupational mobility or wealth accumulation. Joseph Ferrie's recent analysis of the immigrant experience in the U.S. in the 1840s and 1850s is relevant here. Ferrie, who matched hundreds of individual records in trans-Atlantic passenger lists with U.S. manuscript census data in order to construct a profile of immigrant occupational and geographical mobility, interprets his overall results as evidence of the flexibility and adaptability of both the immigrants and the antebellum U.S. economy. The Irish fit the claim to the extent that though they remained German and British immigrants in 1860, as they had been in 1850, they had converged on the British and the Germans in a relative sense (table 3.9). Nevertheless, the absolute gap in terms of

TABLE 3.9
Mean Wealth by Ethnicity, 1850–1860 (in U.S. dollars)

	British	Irish	German	All
Mean real estate wealth, 1850	388.5	109.6	289.4	270.1
Mean real estate wealth, 1860	1,398.8	461.4	1,149.1	1,048.4
Mean personal wealth, 1860	507.3	229.5	595.3	441.8

Source: Ferrie, "Wealth accumulation," 6.

real estate wealth between them and German and British emigrants widened during the decade, and the gap between the Irish and British in both years was wider than the gap between British and Irish income per capita. The Irish were also slowest to make the occupational transition between laborer and nonlaborer. Precisely why they were slower to "better themselves" remains unclear. One reason, as Ferrie notes, was probably their lack of means on arrival.[56]

Lack of means and poverty are relative. During the winter of 1846–47 the chief of the Board of Works in Dublin referred to the "great delusion" about emigration. It was not the poorest who were about to leave, he complained, but "all the small farmers [who were] hoarding all the money they can procure in order to make a stock for the spring, when they intend to bolt, leaving the landlords in the lurch." Some smallholders, barred from the public works, deemed emigration a better bargain than running down their assets in seeking to make ends meet at home. In the Skibbereen area in February 1847 the larger farmers were saving up the proceeds of selling corn and planning "on the first opportunity [to] escape from the famine-stricken island to the unblighted harvests of America." From Sligo too in March 1847 there was "much emigration going on and in contemplation." The paupers were heading for England and Scotland, those with money for the States, "many carrying away large sums, and taking French leave of their landlords, with several years' rent unpaid, and some clandestinely transferring the possession of their holdings to others whom it is not easy to evict." Even in the neighboring Ballina Union, the board of guardians fretted about the implications for rate collection of "persons who have left their holdings for America and other places."[57] An engineer on the public works claimed that as a consequence of not getting work on the public works, those with some stock or savings emigrated. In the words of Lamie Murray, general manager of the Provincial Bank of Ireland, "the best go, the worst remain."[58]

Which regions supplied the most emigrants? Answers to this question come at a cost. One approach is to rely on county estimates of excess

TABLE 3.10
An Estimate of Excess Mortality (DR) and Emigration (EM) by Province,
1841–51 (in thousands)

Province	Population	Emigration	Deaths	EM (%)	DR (%)
Ulster	2,386	291	184	12.2	7.7
Munster	2,396	333	383	13.9	16.0
Leinster	1,974	171	193	8.7	9.8
Connacht	1,419	246	240	17.3	16.9
Ireland total	8,175	1,041	1,000	12.7	12.2

Source: Ó Gráda and O'Rourke, "Mass migration."

mortality by historical geographer S. H. Cousens, grossed up to produce
an aggregate of one million, and to combine those data with a counterfactual no-famine estimate of the population in 1851. Assuming an annual no-famine population growth rate of 0.5 percent for the country as
a whole during the 1840s, and allocating county shares in proportion to
county growth rates between 1831 and 1841, produces counterfactual
estimates of county populations yielding an aggregate no-famine population of just under 8.6 million. Then subtracting the adjusted excess
mortality figures yielded one estimate of excess emigration by county
during the decade. The implied provincial emigration and death rates
are given in table 3.10. The numbers rely on the dubious assumption of
underenumeration across counties, but they are consistent with qualitative accounts: Connacht was most severely affected by the potato blight,
followed closely by Munster, with Leinster and Ulster being the least
affected. The data suggest that the death rate in Leinster exceeded Ulster's, but that Ulster's emigration rate was higher than Leinster's. Otherwise, the ranking of provinces by death rates is the same as that by
emigration rates.[59]

However, the correlation between emigration and death rates is not
strong across counties. Consequently, counties such as Clare and Galway, with high death rates, also tended to have a low ratio of emigration to deaths. Counties with low wages and high potato consumption,
and counties registering large declines in the acreage under potatoes in
1845–47, had higher death and emigration rates. However, the ratio of
emigration to deaths was higher in richer than in poorer counties, again
supporting the intuition that the poorest died rather than emigrated.
Finally, county migration rates (as reflected in age-cohort depletion
rates) were much more sensitive to the cross-county variation in wage
levels after the famine than before it. One plausible interpretation of
this pattern is that the famine removed a poverty trap that had prevented some of the poorest from emigrating before 1845.[60] At the local

level, the returns from west Cork cited earlier also record an inverse relation between mortality and migration in 1846–47; in Goleen (where the poor-law valuation per head was £0.59, or about $3.00) the mortality rate was 18.8 percent while the emigration rate was 0.9 percent, but in Kilcoe (valuation per head £1.03 or $5.00) the numbers were 9.8 and 4.1 percent.[61]

Because emigration did not target those who were at the greatest risk of dying, it was an inefficient form of disaster relief. Nonetheless, without the emigration option, famine mortality would surely have been higher. It is unlikely, though not inconceivable, that the absence of distant outlets for emigration would have increased mortality by more than the number of frustrated would-be emigrants. A more plausible outcome would be the death of a fraction of those forced to remain. In addition, some migration would have been diverted to the already crowded cities of Ireland and Great Britain. As things stood, famine immigration placed considerable strains on the cities of Dublin and Liverpool, for example, and much of the excess mortality in Dublin was due to it. Famine-induced immigration from Ireland had imposed demographic strains on England in the eighteenth century, and the rise in mortality there in the 1840s probably stemmed in part from Irish immigration. Most of the huge increase between 1841 and 1851 in the number of Irish-born living in Britain—from 417,000 to 727,000—happened in the wake of the potato failure. The concentration of much of that increase in the run-down sections of a small number of big towns aggravated its impact; in 1851 four cities (Liverpool, Manchester/Salford, Glasgow, and London) contained over three hundred thousand Irish-born, or well over two-fifths of Britain's total Irish. Many Irish fleeing from famine died in Britain in 1847, prompting middle-class sympathy at first and, soon, widespread fear and resentment.

English vital statistics are consistent with a famine effect in the late 1840s. Its precise size cannot be gauged, but fitting polynomial trends to the annual series of births and deaths[62] and adding dummy terms for 1846–50 produced the results summarized in table 3.11. The sum of the coefficients on the dummy terms for 1846–48 in the first regression—just over 110,000—provides a rough estimate of excess mortality in England and Wales in those years. The estimated sixty thousand excess deaths in 1849 are better explained by the cholera outbreak that struck eastern Scotland first in October 1848 and then spread south and west. The shortfall in registered births in 1847–48, calculated in the same way, was about fifty-five thousand. These are substantial numbers, representing over one-quarter of the annual death rate in the mid-1840s, and one-twentieth or so of the birthrate over the years in question.

TABLE 3.11
Estimating Excess Deaths and Births in England in the
Late 1840s

Regressor	Deaths	Births
CONST	306,854.6*	495,241.5*
T	−11,328.4*	−9,659.1*
TSQ	1,859.7*	1,264.9*
TCUB	−89.4*	−41.1
TQUAD	1.448*	0.476
DUM46	27,596.9*	—
DUM47	54,961.4*	−34,820.9*
DUM48	28,100.6*	−20,233.8*
DUM49	61,315.8*	−13,136.1
DUM50	—	−5,902.6
R^2	.964	.977
D-W	2.09	2.43

Note: Asterisked coefficients carried t-ratios of over two.

The greater impact of the crisis of the 1840s on deaths than on births is probably a signal that most of the excess deaths were among the Irish immigrants. Frank Neal's recent assessment of the evidence in both England and Wales leaves absolutely no doubt that the great majority of those dying from typhus and dysentery were Irish. In Liverpool alone, pauper burials, mainly of Catholics, rose by nearly five thousand in 1847. Horace Mann's statistical analysis of mortality in the London slum of Church Lane in the 1840s reports an increase in the numbers dying there from eight in 1845 and thirteen in 1846 to fifty-two in 1847, "when the Irish migration may be taken to have set in." Cities like Manchester and Leeds also had their Church Lanes. Given the state of medical knowledge, it is hard to see how the English themselves could have remained entirely immune from the diseases introduced by the Irish. However, the implied averted births are more likely to have been in the native English population, reflecting what Wrigley and Schofield have dubbed England's "low pressure" demographic regime.[63]

In Scotland the late 1840s have been described as years "of quite exceptionally lethal character more redolent of the seventeenth century than of the nineteenth." The rise in mortality was considerable; the Highlands escaped largely unscathed, but in Glasgow burials doubled in 1847, and across the country as a whole mortality in 1846–48 was 50 percent higher than normal. South and east of the Highlands at least, the rise could not be blamed directly on the potato failure. Typhus was the main killer, and urban areas suffered more than rural. Bad sanitation in the cities would have been enough to trigger off disease, but immigration, temporary or permanent, is the more likely culprit. Immigration from Ireland into lowland Scotland—about 110,000 in the 1840s—far exceeded immigration from the Highlands, and mortality was particularly high in regions such as the west lowlands and the western borders where the Irish presence was strongest. But the data base is too slender to say more than that.[64] For Great Britain as a whole, it seems safe to conclude that some tens of thousands of famine refugees perished in the late 1840s.

As noted earlier, before the famine wealthier counties in the north and east of Ireland supplied most of the trans-Atlantic emigration from Ireland. Emigration may thus have increased the inequalities between Irish regions in the manner posited by Cousens over three decades ago.[65] The famine is likely to have produced a radical shift in the regional origin of Irish emigrants, but hard data on this are scarce. Official emigration statistics begin only in 1849, and in any case they are an unreliable guide on origin for some decades after that, while passenger lists provide only very partial data on regional origin. The issue is an important one, however, because the variation in the roles of excess mortality and emigration across counties and provinces has a big bearing on our understanding of the famine; hence the importance of other sources that shed some light on regional origins. One such source is the records of the Emigrant Industrial Savings Bank, established by a small group of philanthropic Irishmen in New York City in 1850.[66] The data refer to accounts opened during the bank's first few years, which provide the name and date of arrival of thousands of Irish-born account holders (as well as much other detail). Table 3.12, which is derived from this

TABLE 3.12
Emigrants and Population by Region

| Province | Percentage of Emigrants | | Percentage of Population, 1841 |
	Pre-1846	1846–52	
Leinster	30	29	24
Munster	20	37	29
Ulster	35	20	29
Connacht	15	14	17
Mayo-Galway-Clare-Kerry	7	15	15

Source: New York Public Library, Emigrant Savings Bank Archive, II.1. Based on all those emigrating before the end of 1852 who had opened an account by the end of June 1854.

source, highlights the difference in the regional origins of those arriving and staying in New York before the famine and those arriving from 1846 on. Before the famine, Ulster and Leinster were overrepresented, and Munster and Connacht (particularly Galway, Roscommon, and Mayo) underrepresented. The numbers imply that before the famine, the New York Irish were disproportionately from the east and north of Ireland, though Sligo and Leitrim had also provided a higher than expected share. If Sligo is excluded from the reckoning, the number of account holders from the rest of Connacht more than tripled, though admittedly from a very small base. The weak representation before 1846 of counties like Clare, Kerry, and Mayo, which were devastated by the famine, is also noteworthy.

Finally, some features of the shifting distribution are worth noting. Munster, which, though relatively poorer, had been greatly underrepresented relative to its population before the famine, was overrepresented during the famine. The same could not be said for Connacht, but the greatly increased representation of four west-coast counties — Mayo, Galway, Clare, Kerry — is also important. For emigration to have been a truly effective remedy during the famine, however, the outmigration from the poorer counties would have to have been higher still.

How representative was the small minority of Irish immigrants who took out accounts in the Emigrant Savings Bank in the early 1850s? A preliminary canvass suggests that people with proletarian, blue-collar occupations were very much to the fore among both male and female account holders. The sums deposited by those opening accounts suggests people of modest means.

New York's Famine Irish

> New York City you will find a busy place. . . . The sooner
> you get out of it the better.
> (Advice to intending Irish immigrants, 1851)

New York was the main port of entry into North America for Irish famine emigrants both during and after the famine. Modern cliometric research confirms the accuracy of contemporary advice to would-be immigrants not to stay long in New York and, indeed, most of the new arrivals seem to have followed this counsel.[67] Nonetheless, New York's population grew rapidly during the 1850s and with it its number of Irish-born. By the mid-1850s greater New York contained almost as many Irish-born people as Dublin. The recent arrivals, like other immigrants since, did most of the city's "rude and heavy work." A guide for prospective immigrants described their occupations thus:

> [T]hey are generally employed in buildings, either as masons, bricklayers, plasterers, carpenters, or as helpers and hodmen; they are found portering on the quays, repairing, cleaning, and watching the city; sawing wood, carrying packages; serving as waiters, hostlers, barkeepers in the hotels and boarding-houses, eating-houses, and provision shops; owning or driving carts, cabs, hackney coaches or omnibuses; working as hostlers, trafficking in the vegetable and fruit markets; carrying newspapers, dealing in paper, owning small fishing or ferry boats; at work in the tailoring "sweating shops," in the printing offices, founderies; digging foundations or blasting rocks up town, mending the streets, digging sewers, and laying water or gas pipes for the corporation or other companies; plying on the river as firemen or boatmen, in the thousand canal and steam boats that flit to and fro on the Hudson and "East River"; attending the merchants' auctions in Pearl Street, and buying an odd damaged bargain in a small way, which is peddled at good retail profit in the suburban districts of the city; having a fruit and temperance stand in the summer season in a recess of the street, &c. &c.[68]

Little wonder, perhaps, that most of the Irish did not tarry in New York. It is worth reemphasizing that those who made the voyage there were typically people of *some* modest means, who presumably could afford to escape further inland. Emigrants whose passages were paid by landlords or by the state, and who arrived virtually penniless, could not. Only a small share of all passages overseas were so financed, certainly no more than 4 or 5 percent.[69] But they raise an interesting question: Suppose more of the really destitute had been helped in the same way? How different would the character of the famine outflow have been?

Here we offer a partial answer by taking a closer look at the Irish community of New York's Sixth Ward in the 1850s. The Sixth Ward was located in lower Manhattan, east of Broadway and north of City Hall, and encompassed today's court district and much of Chinatown. In 1855 the area contained about twenty-five thousand people. Many of the Irish living in the "Bloody Ould Sixth" in these years had formerly been smallholders or laborers on landed estates in south Kerry and in Sligo. Their landlords had paid their passages. As a result most of the Kerrymen and Kerrywomen who settled in the Sixth Ward had been born in a small, impoverished Irish-speaking area in south Kerry (encompassing the parishes of Kenmare, Tuosist, and Bunnawn), while the majority of the Sligo immigrants had lived on or near that county's northwest coast, with particularly heavy representations from the rural parishes of Drumcliff, Ballysodare, and Ahamlish. The architect of the Kerry assisted emigration scheme, William Steuart Trench, reported:

"We have not lost one single man I should wish to keep. . . . We lose none but abject Paupers — other estates, where no assistance is given, *retain their paupers* whilst *all the respectable Tenants are moving off.* . . . Scarcely any *Tenants* yet have gone, and no Tenants of substance. Those who are running for their lives are the cottiers and paupers."[70] That the Kerry emigrants arrived in a destitute state is borne out by several contemporary press accounts. One described tenants and their families "without a penny of money . . . mak[ing] their way on foot from Kenmare to Cork . . . from whence their passages were paid to Liverpool, and thence to New York," another "groups of these hapless beings . . . penniless and without physical energy to earn a day's living . . . congregated about the Park and in Broadway, looking the very picture of despair, misery, disease, and want." According to yet another, the U.S. Commissioners of Immigration forced the carrier of one shipload of Kenmare emigrants to pay twenty-five dollars per head for their maintenance out of public funds.[71] Presumably arriving in New York together made it more likely that former neighbors would stick together initially in the United States. Perhaps it also reduced their mobility later. Counties Sligo and Kerry were heavily overrepresented relative to their populations in the Sixth Ward in the 1850s, and Ireland's poorest counties were better represented there than in overseas migration as a whole.

It does not seem too fanciful to argue that the poverty trap which prevented more of their compatriots from leaving Ireland during the famine prevented some of these inhabitants of the Sixth Ward from moving beyond it. The same holds true for many more of New York's huge Irish population in the 1850s. Yet in economic historian Joseph Ferrie's sample of antebellum immigrants, which links passenger lists and manuscript census data, less than one-fifth of the Irish who arrived in the port of New York between 1840 and 1850 remained there on census day in 1850.[72]

The Sixth Ward, a largely working-class area of tenement buildings, included the Five Points (to the north of today's Foley Square), a neighborhood with a very seedy reputation. Charles Dickens's *American Notes for General Circulation* (1842), local journalist George Foster's *New York by Gas Light* (1850), and other reports in a similar vein conjured up an image of a violent and depraved population living in a virtual no-go slum area. To the evangelical missionaries who sought to reform its inhabitants, the Five Points was "a synonym for ignorance the most entire, for misery the most abject, for crime of the darkest dye, for degradation so deep that human nature cannot sink below it."[73]

The new social history of the 1970s generated a revisionist literature on the heavily Irish Sixth Ward. Carol Groneman Pernicone's unpublished dissertation contrasted the gap between the negative contemporary assessments by Dickens and others and the picture gained from an investigation of contemporary census data. Her main source, the original manuscript sheets of the New York City census of 1855, implied the presence of strong family ties among the Irish immigrants, as reflected in the high percentage of co-resident teenage children. About two-thirds of Irish teenagers lived at home, compared to about one-third of German and native-born teenagers. The census also indicated the dominance of nuclear family households, augmented, perhaps, by a boarder or two. It also confirmed the unskilled character of the Irish labor force. Pre-famine immigrants were more skilled than recent arrivals, but there was a negative assocation between skills and age. This curious outcome is presumably a reflection of selection bias — a tendency for the better qualified and the more talented to leave — in migration out of the Sixth Ward.[74]

The 1855 census revealed Irishwomen as specializing in the sewing and dressmaking trades (25.7 percent of the total), in domestic service (36.3 percent), and in taking boarders (31.9 percent). Groneman Pernicone's research offered a useful corrective to those earlier accounts which tarred the entire population of the area with the same brush, but is probably marred somewhat by undue reliance on the 1855 census, an imperfect enumeration which was most likely to miss the more marginalized and unattached sections of the population.[75] An even more revisionist gloss on the Sixth Ward Irish is offered by a recent archaeological survey of one of its most impoverished corners near the Five Points. In this federally funded exercise in "the archaeology of domestic trash," the Irish struggle for stability and even a modicum of respectability is revealed in the "pretty things" they left behind. Objects such as transfer-printed tableware, olive oil and gin bottles, plain flowerpots, even a little bowl depicting temperance crusader Father Mathew, it must be said, cannot have cost much. This interesting study goes farther than Groneman Pernicone in its critique of the earlier sensationalist literature, and even exaggeratingly refers to the Five Points as a "mythic slum."[76]

The marriage registers of the Church of the Transfiguration of Our Lord, located on the corner of Mott and Cross Streets, a few blocks from the Five Points, offer one useful source of information on the local Irish community, which was overwhelmingly Catholic. Church records for the 1853–60 period report the ages and addresses of most couples, as well as their places of birth.[77] Connacht and Munster, the two poorest provinces, supplied the bulk of the migrants, and three counties — Sligo in Connacht, and Kerry and Cork in Munster — supplied nearly half of the brides and grooms in these years (table 3.13). The records

TABLE 3.13
The Regional Origins of Parishioners

Province	Male	(%)	Female	(%)	Total	(%)	Ratio to Population
Leinster	116	16.3	119	16.0	235	16.1	119
Munster	299	41.9	307	41.2	606	41.6	253
Ulster	69	9.7	80	10.8	149	10.2	64
Connacht	229	32.1	238	32.0	467	32.1	329
Ireland total	713	100.0	744	100.0	1,457	100.0	178

Note: The ratio is per million population.

reflect not only a tendency for Irishmen to marry Irishwomen, but the remarkable strength of regional and local networks within the Irish community. Most marriages involved couples from the same or from neighboring counties in Ireland. This was particularly so for well-represented counties such as Sligo and Kerry. More than two-thirds of men reported as born in those counties married women from the same county, and most marriages involved couples from the same corner of the same county. Ten of the fifteen grooms born in Tuosist married women from the same parish, and three more married women from the neighboring parishes of Bunnawn and Kenmare. Eleven of the twenty-nine grooms born in Ahamlish married women from the same parish, and another four married women from Drumcliff. Men and women who married in their mid- and late twenties were slightly less likely to "marry out" than others. Table 3.14 summarizes the geographical pattern for the group as a whole.

TABLE 3.14
Marrying "In" and Marrying "Out" in the 1850s

Age Group	Own County	Neighboring County	Other
Men			
<25	141 (48.6)	59 (20.3)	90 (31.0)
25–29	118 (63.8)	24 (13.0)	43 (23.2)
30 +	145 (50.6)	69 (24.0)	73 (25.4)
All	404 (53.0)	152 (19.9)	206 (27.0)
Women			
<25	213 (52.2)	87 (21.6)	108 (26.5)
25–29	96 (59.3)	19 (8.3)	47 (29.0)
30 +	44 (47.3)	20 (21.5)	29 (31.2)
All	353 (54.1)	116 (17.8)	184 (28.2)

Source: Transfiguration Church parish registers.

TABLE 3.15
Remarriage Patterns

Age	Men		Women	
Group	Remarried	Married a Widow	Remarried	Married a Widower
<30	30	3	28	9
30–39	60	15	42	18
40+	50	28	21	15

Remarkably, in about one marriage in every four, grooms and brides-to-be gave the same address to the church clerk. This is hardly evidence of cohabitation; cohabitation, if practiced, would certainly have been concealed from the local priest or parish clerk. A more plausible explanation is that it reflects the tendency of immigrants from the same region in Ireland to live in neighboring apartments in tenement housing. Certain addresses turn up repeatedly in the records. For instance, thirteen men, mostly with different surnames and mostly from county Cork, married out of 5 Mulberry Street in the 1850s. The twelve men who married out of 22 Mulberry Street had come from a range of Irish counties, but those living in 20 Mulberry Street were mainly Sligo people, while between 1853 and 1856 three men, all from Rahamlish in county Sligo, married out of 10 Franklin Street. Eight grooms were supplied by 31 Baxter Street, all from Kerry or west Cork, and five of them married women giving the same address.

The registers also give the ages at marriage in most cases, and show that the immigrants married young. According to the Transfiguration Church registers, the age at first marriage for women was about 23 years; for men 25.2 years.[78] Nearly one-third of first-time brides were under twenty-one and over two-fifths of first-time grooms were under twenty-four. The remarriage prospects of men and women cannot be judged directly from the data, but many of those marrying in the Transfiguration Church had been previously married. Widows who remarried were also younger than widowers (33 years versus 36.5 years). Note too the high mortality rate hinted at—though not proven—by these numbers: one in six of the men and one in nine of the women had been married before (see table 3.15).

Finally, the total number of paupers "shoveled out" by Lansdowne, Palmerston, and Gore-Boothe cannot be known with precision, but it certainly did not exceed more than a few thousand. The significant numbers of men and women from Kerry and Sligo marrying in the Sixth Ward suggests that a significant proportion of the paupers remained in New York's slums instead of heading farther west. Nor does the 1855 census leave little room for success stories among them in terms of skills acquisition. Taken together these bits of information suggest that an increase in the share of assisted emigrants would have further impaired the geographical and occupational mobility of the Irish as a group. As matters stood, the Irish fared poorly relative to British and German immigrants in the 1840s and 1850s. Further assisted emigration would have made their record seem even worse, and would have intensified poverty and overcrowding in places such as the Sixth Ward. On the other hand, it would have made emigration a more effective form of disaster relief.

Though the Sixth Ward was undoubtedly an overcrowded, mainly working-class slum, hundreds of its Irish-born inhabitants opened accounts in the Emigrant Savings Banks in the 1850s. The regional origins of these account holders matches those of brides and grooms in the church records quite well. Moreover, the occupational profile of account holders reflected the social mix of the population rather well. Comparing the occupational profile of Sixth Ward Irish male account holders with the results of Groneman Pernicone's analysis of the Sixth Ward Irish as a whole implies some bias in the former toward a residual "other" category containing sales and clerical workers, petty entrepreneurs, storekeepers, and white-collar workers. This is to be expected. Still, the savers were mainly unskilled workers and petty traders. They included 89 laborers, 36 domestic servants, 24 washerwomen, 19 porters, 13 fruit dealers, 12 seamstresses, 12 peddlers, 18 tailors, 9 junk dealers, and one teacher. Martin Hogan from Limerick described himself as a "fireman in Sweeny's saloon," while John O'Donoghue from Longford was a "barkeeper at John Dempsey's." John Shea of Tuosist distributed handbills, Jeremiah Daly of the same place sold matches, and Bridget Gilmartin from Ahamlish "picked hair."

A comprehensive history of assisted emigration during the famine remains to be written. Some projects, such as Major Denis Mahon's in Strokestown, ended in disaster and earned lasting notoriety. Others were efficiently managed; the crown-financed emigration from Ballykilcline, next to Strokestown, seems to have been a model of its kind. The assisted emigration of over three thousand people from the Lansdowne estate in 1850–51 or so was the most ambitious project of all. By scrimping on maintenance and concentrating the emigration on the low season, the organizer of the Lansdowne project kept its cost down to a modest £10,000 or so. He and his employer were criticized at the time, not unfairly, for their stinginess.

Yet surely the broader implication of these efforts is that further projects, properly timed and more humanely managed, would have been a viable form of famine relief. The possibilities must be kept in proportion. First, assisting people to emigrate in 1847–48 would not have eliminated the need for other kinds of public relief during the winter and spring of 1846 and 1847. Nor, second, could the very young and the very old have traveled; neither could heavily pregnant women or the mothers of very young children. Third, the absorptive capacity of the New World and particularly its cities was limited. In the late 1840s the total population of North America was not much more than twenty million, and only 10 percent of the total lived in towns and cities. Fourth, in the early months of 1847 the capacity of the passenger trade, and of shipping in general, was already sorely stretched and probably subject to rising costs at the margin.[79] Moreover, a significant increase in immigration from Ireland would undoubtedly have prompted increases in mortality in U.S. cities like they did in Liverpool and Glasgow. Further immigration would have intensified anti-Irish feeling, already at an all-time high; in the New York mayoral election of 1854, the anti-immigrant Know Nothing candidate, James Barker, obtained about 31 percent of the popular vote and came in second in a four-way race. In the same year Know Nothing candidates won the mayoralties of Boston, Philadelphia, Chicago, and San Francisco. No modern anti-immigrant movement in the developed world matches the Know Nothings at their peak in electoral support. Such considerations mean that mass migration was no panacea. Nevertheless, the assisted migration of even one hundred thousand destitute famine victims in 1847–48 would almost certainly have saved thousands of lives in Ireland itself. An outlay of public money of, say, £1 million ($4.8 million, or about 0.2 percent of U.K. national income or 2 percent of public spending) would have easily covered the cost of such a plan.

Chapter Four

WINNERS AND LOSERS

> The state of changes necessarily acts upon all classes, and
> the entire earnings of the poor being insufficient to procure
> food, the country tradesmen, such as tailors, shoemakers,
> etc. are nearly entirely without employment, and of course
> destitute, while the shopkeepers are daily going to ruin, as
> no one of any class thinks of purchasing an article beyond
> indispensable necessaries.
> (A report from west Cork, February 1847)

> When the country tailors and shoemakers are obliged to go
> to road-work, or find it more profitable than their trades,
> there must be great local distress.
> (Sir Randolph Routh on conditions in Clare, February 1847)

ENTITLEMENTS

IN A SERIES of influential and important publications, economist
Amartya Sen has argued that modern famines are not so much
crises in the total availability of food as in its distribution. Sen instances the Great Bengali Famine of the early 1940s as a "boom" famine, brought on by wartime inflation and the precautionary and speculative hoarding of foodstuffs. In Ethiopia in 1973, he argues, "famine
took place with no abnormal reduction in food output, and consumption of food per head at the height of the famine was fairly normal for
Ethiopia as a whole."[1] Such claims have not gone uncontested,[2] but they
have some resonance for Ireland in the 1840s also. One of the most
evocative images of the Irish famine is of a people being left to starve
while their corn was being shipped off under police and military protection to pay rents. Indeed, Drèze and Sen write of "English consumers
attract[ing] food away, through the market mechanism, from famine-
stricken Ireland to rich England, with ship after ship sailing down the
river Shannon with various types of food." Not all the food left: even in
Skibbereen in December 1846, despite all the horrors described in the
media of the day, "there was the 'extraordinary contradiction' of a market plentifully supplied with meat, bread, fish, in short everything," and
it was alleged that dragoons guarded three hundred tons of Indian meal

as the poor sank "from famine to fever and from fever to the grave."[3] Policymakers opposed interference in the grain trade on the grounds that free trade would help stabilize consumption. Critics claim that in Ireland, as in India later, allowing grain to flow freely out of the country was often one of the main causes of suffering during famines. Ravallion's study of the grain trade in India in 1892–1914 finds that foreign trade was a slow and far from perfect consumption stabilizer: in the short run only about 7.5 percent and in the long run only 30 percent of an output reduction would have been passed on in reduced exports.[4]

In Ireland during the famine years, food imports dwarfed food exports, but in the months between the second potato failure of the summer of 1846 and the arrival in quantity of a cheap substitute, maize, in the spring of 1847, the story of "perverse" food flows has some appeal. Annual data suggest that the failure had an immediate negative impact on grain exports (see table 4.1), but quarterly data show that exports of oats in the second half of 1846 were still significant (table 4.2). On the import side, arrivals of U.S. maize in Cork, the main port of entry, totaled 567,253.5 bushels in 1847, but less than 3 percent of this (16,576 bushels) arrived in January and February. Another 89,480 bushels arrived in March, but the bulk of the inflow (394,138 bushels) came during the following three months. Moreover, several ships laden with maize, including the *Sun* from New York with 116,034 bushels on board, made stops in Cork in February and March without landing any of their cargoes. A temporary embargo on grain exports coupled with restrictions or prohibitions on brewing and distilling[5] — a time-honored

TABLE 4.1
The Irish Grain Trade, 1843–48 (in 1,000 quarters)

Year	Exports	Imports	Surplus	Maize Imports
1842	2,538	280	+2,258	20
1843	3,206	74	+3,132	3
1844	2,801	150	+2,651	5
1845	3,252	147	+3,105	34
1846	1,826	987	+839	614
1847	970	4,519	−3,549	3,287
1848	1,953	2,186	−233	1,546
1849	1,437	2,908	−1,471	1,897
1850	1,329	2,357	−1,028	1,159
1851	1,325	3,158	−1,833	1,745

Source: BPP 1852 (LI); see also Bourke, *Visitation of God*, 168.
Note: 1 quarter = 2 barrels. The barrel, a weight measure, varied by type of grain. Thus a barrel of wheat weighed 20 stone (1 stone = 14 lbs), of barley 16 stone, and of oats 14 stone. For details see Wakefield, *Ireland, Statistical and Political,* vol. 2, 197.

TABLE 4.2
Grain Exports from Ireland to Britain, 1846–47 (in quarters)

Period	Wheat	Barley	Oats	Wheat Flour	Oatmeal
1846:1	82,368	33,069	283,524	299,854	278,139
1846:2	48,574	16,338	216,016	260,340	114,879
1846:3	33,871	15,264	223,299	82,924	86,818
1846:4	21,917	28,183	236,012	110,462	73,311
1847:1	6,825	2,226	87,622	45,869	20,848
1847:2	39,852	7,377	55,792	98,538	26,943
July–Dec. 1845	223,116	66,863	703,314	605,917	452,144
July–Dec. 1846	55,788	43,447	459,311	193,386	160,129

Note: See note in table 4.1

stratagem — or else a more vigorous public commitment to buying up and redistributing Irish and foreign grain in late 1846 or early 1847 might have alleviated starvation in these crucial months. Once maize became available in quantity, importing it duty-free while exporting high quality grain was a sensible alternative.[6]

The entitlements approach is a useful reminder that the Irish famine was in part the product of maldistribution and greed. Yet it offers at best a partial understanding of the crisis, for at least three reasons. First of all, it relies too much on an oversimplified but enduring, populist image of the famine as starvation in the midst of plenty. And dwelling on the exported grain masks the reality that, taking the period of the Irish famine as a whole, the issue of grain exports is of more symbolic than real importance. This may be seen by assuming that the transfer of all the exported grain from farmers to the starving masses had been costless both in terms of resources spent on collection and future output foregone. Alas, the ensuing increased supply of food would have made only a small dent in the gap left by *Phytophthora infestans*. On the eve of the famine the potato harvest yielded about twelve to fifteen million tons annually, half of which went to human consumption.[7] Thus the 430,000 tons of grain exported in 1846 and 1847 must be set against a shortfall of about twenty million tons of potatoes in those same years. Allowing the exported grain four times the calorific value of potatoes, the exported grain would still have filled only about one-seventh of the gap left by the potatoes in Ireland in these two crucial years. Thus, though official neglect and endemic injustice played their part in Ireland in 1846 and 1847, there is no denying that the Irish famine was, at least in those years, also a classic case of food shortage. Only by adopting an all-U.K. perspective to the problem in those years might an interpretation stressing entitlements instead of food availability at the height of the famine be defended.

A second difficulty for the entitlements approach is its somewhat ahistorical character. It ignores the inequalities at the roots of Irish society in normal times: before the famine, few of those at risk in Skibbereen in late 1846 would have been able to afford the meat, bread, and fish referred to above.[8] The exported corn belonged not to the landless or near-landless masses, but Ireland's half a million farmers, who would certainly have resisted the lower prices that an export embargo would have brought in its train. Third, the long drawn-out character of the Irish famine also mattered. The transfer implicit in the entitlements model instead of being once-off would have become a kind of repeated struggle after each harvest, with unpredictable consequences for the farmers' output reaction.[9] Nevertheless, the persistence of destitution and famine throughout much of the west of Ireland during 1849 and 1850, despite plentiful supplies of food, would seem to fit the entitlements approach well enough.

The context of the entitlements model, in its starkest and simplest form, is of a shift in distribution or in the terms of trade between food consumers and food producers. It is consistent with no output change, and in this sense may be interpreted as a *zero-sum* game. This prompts the question: Who were the winners and losers in the Irish famine? The rest of this chapter may be interpreted as offering an answer to this question.

Perhaps the least affected group were export-oriented manufacturers in the cities. Their workers relied less on the potato than the rural masses, and their markets were largely unaffected. At the other extreme, the landless poor and cottier smallholders who perished were the most obvious losers. Next in line were the several hundred thousand people who were forced to emigrate, already described in chapter 3. What of farmers and landlords, and of traders, shopkeepers, and moneylenders? In Bengal in the 1940s, according to an official source, "larger landholders benefitted from the situation, since they could sell most of their rice at an enormous profit. . . . The famine thus principally affected one section of the community—the poor classes in rural areas."[10] For Irish farmers, however, the outcome was not so straightforward. There were gains to farmers in terms of lower rent, but losses in terms of a lower-yielding potato crop and a higher efficiency wage for farm workers. Holders of large, pasture-oriented farms suffered least, as the data on livestock and butter exports indicates (table 4.3). For cattle exports, the late 1840s were relatively good years. Nor was the decline in sheep exports in 1848 due to the failure of the potato: sheep murrain was responsible. Given that potatoes were the main input into pig fattening, it is hardly surprising that pig exports plummeted. The importance of the potato and of tillage generally for most Irish landholders probably means that farmers as a group did not benefit during the famine. The

TABLE 4.3
Agricultural Exports, 1840–50

Year	Live Sheep (I)	Pigmeat (II)	Live Cattle (III)	Butter (IV)	Grain (V)	Pasture (VI)
1840	132.7	76.2	114.3	88.1	76.4	100.9
1841	101.6	77.6	120.2	80.8	93.6	95.3
1842	90.6	77.7	109.1	92.7	83.3	99.8
1843	84.8	89.6	104.1	99.1	113.1	102.4
1844	87.0	82.3	95.2	96.9	131.3	103.0
1845	100.0	100.0	100.0	100.0	72.0	122.5
1846	134.7	95.7	159.7	101.4	36.4	117.3
1847	168.4	28.8	163.6	88.8	75.2	123.7
1848	132.8	23.4	266.8	100.3	52.4	117.8
1849	125.2	22.2	174.9	89.5	45.6	113.7
1850	91.9	33.4	154.2	94.9	72.3	120.0

Source: Derived from Solar, "Growth and distribution," 114, 159, 160, 189, 253.
Notes: Columns I–IV have been reset at 1845 = 100, while V and VI are set at 1840–45 = 100.

eagerness of so many of them to flee is also significant. The fate of farmers in the longer run is discussed in chapter 7.

LANDLORDS

> At this period of such misery and famine, I should not like to put such a number of starving creatures loose on the world, without any means whatever of feeding them.
> (A Roscommon landlord, March 1847)

> We feel that *the people must die off* . . . and it is not the first landlord I have heard say as much. This is a blessed famine, God be praised!
> (William Carleton, *The Squanders of Castle Squander*, 1852)

How badly did the famine affect Ireland's ten thousand or so landlords? Curiously enough, the specialist literature on Irish tenurial relations and landed estates offers little guidance. Well-known studies of the management of the London Companies and Downshire estates concentrate mainly on the pre-famine period, while Vaughan's masterly account of the Irish land tenure system begins in the 1850s; and neither McCarthy's monograph on the Trinity College estates nor Proudfoot's analysis of the Duke of Devonshire's Waterford estates, both of which straddle the whole nineteenth century, contains more than a few pages on the famine.[11]

Impressionistic accounts of landlord hardship are plentiful, however. One described the Blake family of Renvyle in north Connemara as "looking forward to starvation" in May 1847, another noted the relief of Hyacinth D'Arcy, former owner of a neighboring estate and founder of Clifden, at being offered a position as a school inspector at a salary of £100 a year. Folklore recalls the owner of a small estate in east Galway being "worse than any one else in the place because he had nothing. He used to go from house to house begging and he would stay for a time in each house. The locals respected him because he was not too bad to them when he had the chance." These are atypical, but there are many reports too of debts or encumbrances, and of falling revenues and increasing outlays;[12] and the significant declines in landlords' net income in the late 1840s and in the value of their most important asset, land, tell their own stories. One way of interpreting the resort to eviction on a mass scale from 1847 on is as another signal of the pressure that the famine placed on landlords.

Several landlords succumbed to famine fever, as already noted in chapter 3. How many lost their properties as a result of the crisis? Why did they do so? Some accounts dwell on the generosity and sense of responsibility of individual proprietors. It was claimed that one of the Martins of Ballinahinch "contracted a debt for food to support her famishing tenantry in the years of famine; a prompt payment was demanded, but, with the characteristic humanity of her family, she would not press her dependents in distress, and a sheriff's execution swept the mansion and demesne of Ballinahinch. This was the flash that disclosed the coming ruin."[13] The impact of the Great Famine on landlordism is difficult to separate from the creation and early history of the Incumbered Estates Court, established in 1849. One of the few concrete policy recommendations of the Devon Commission, appointed by Parliament to survey and recommend improvements to the Irish land system in the early 1840s, had been that "every facility consistent with safety should be given for bringing [encumbered] estates to an early sale, rather than allowing them to remain for years the subject of expensive litigation."[14] Both Whig and Tory ministries were committed to the creation of a special institution for the sale of heavily mortgaged land with the minimum of red tape. The measure introduced by Sir Robert Peel in 1846 lapsed with the collapse of his Tory administration in July, but the Whig ministry that followed was formulating its own version from late 1846 on. Their first measure, introduced in March 1847, produced fears of an ensuing glut in the land market and was withdrawn in July. A second bill, passed in 1848, proved a dead letter, but under the Incumbered

Estates Act of 1849 a creditor could petition for a sale when encumbrances exceeded half the estate's net rent, or the annual rent less
taxes and fixed charges.[15]

The decision to establish the Incumbered Estates Court was undoubtedly linked to the problems posed by the famine, and in the early years
some of its business was undoubtedly a by-product of the famine. How
much is a moot point, but I argue here that the bulk of the encumbrances on affected sales could not have been caused by the famine
alone.

Landlord bankruptcies in the wake of the famine are frequently highlighted in the literature. Some accounts stress the precarious status of
many affected estates before 1845, but others imply that it was the
impact of the famine itself on landlord incomes that did the damage.
Thus R.D.C. Black has claimed that "the rise in poor-rates and the decline in rent receipts served to send many proprietors into the Incumbered Estates Court once its operations began in 1849," while Donal
McCartney also makes the link between the ruin of some landlords and
"about a quarter of the land of Ireland chang[ing] hands as a result of
the working of the Encumbered Estates Act" in the following decades.
Again, F.S.L. Lyons links the demise of "many of the old landlords" to
"the crushing burden of paying vast sums in poor relief at a time when
rents drastically diminished." The Incumbered Estates Act of 1849, he
suggests, "enabled numbers of them to dispose of their estates to a new
type of owner who knew the value of money." The same link between
the famine and landlord bankruptcy has been highlighted by several
other historians.[16]

The overall impression given by such accounts is that much — if not
most — of the Court's early business was famine-inspired. Indeed, Lindsay Proudfoot infers from K. T. Hoppen's summary that "up to one-
quarter of all land changed hands as a result of Famine-induced bankruptcy among landowners."[17] A corollary is the claim, implicit in the
extract from Lyons above, that the landlord class was too prostrated
and poor to buy land on offer at bargain prices, and that their place
was taken by grasping businessmen and lawyers.[18] It is not hard to
imagine how the presence of the Court might have forced an already
heavily indebted estate over the top, or tempted nervous creditors to
seek their money back. But that is not the same thing as saying that the
famine was responsible for what happened. The Court would have had
plenty to do in any case. The circumstances have produced a *post-
famem ergo propter famem* interpretation of events.

Quite how many estate owners were in serious financial trouble before 1845 remains somewhat unclear. Data on rents due on estates managed by the Court of Chancery imply, very roughly, that one owner in

twelve and one acre in twenty had become chronically insolvent before 1845.[19] The embarrassed estates were well spread throughout the island and not confined to the poorer counties. The provinces of Leinster and Munster accounted for over twice as much of the rent due as the more marginal province of Connacht in 1844, roughly the same as their proportions of the Poor Law Valuation and estimated rent due.[20] Estates in Chancery represented the extremes of indebtedness; the numbers take no account of the large number of heavily indebted estates still in proprietorial control on the eve of the famine.

An estate being put into the hands of the Court of Chancery was a signal for many tenants to stop paying rent. While the D'Arcy estate, sold in August 1850 to the Eyre family, was in the Court's hands, arrears worth eight years' rent accumulated; in the case of the Percival estate the arrears due in 1849 were 7.5 times the annual rent of £800.[21] Moreover, the numbers suggest that estates in Chancery stood little chance of proper maintenance and improvement. In 1844–47 the managers of the Court of Chancery spent an annual average of £2,852, or 0.4 percent of the rent due, on buildings and the land in their care — "a state of things which," according to *Thom's Directory*, "would necessarily require a heavy outlay by the incoming purchasers."[22] As a result, many properties were in poor shape by the time they reached the Incumbered Estates Court. In 1852 the scene at Emo House, the former seat of the Earl of Portarlington, "resemble[d] what might be expected in the neighborhood of some volcano," and at Sir George Goold's Shanacourt outside Cork City the house was "suffering from want of a moderate coat of paint and whitewash."[23] Naturally, the owners of such embarrassed estates were poorly placed to help their tenants when disaster struck in 1846.

There is no definitive answer to the question why so many estates were in trouble before the famine struck. On the basis of an analysis of a relatively small number of Irish estates, historian David Large blamed the expense of family settlements, but there are striking examples of reckless spending on estate houses too, and there can be little doubt but that "the cumulative cost of an aristocratic life-style drove many owners of estates to the moneylender."[24] Landlord indebtedness was by no means a uniquely Irish feature, however. In England around this time it was commonly held that land was mortgaged to about one-half its value, or that servicing debt absorbed about half the gross rental income. Nor did debt necessarily entail mismanagement and insolvency. After all, most growing businesses rely on high debt-to-equity ratios as they wait for their ventures to succeed. Imagine a dynamic computer company with a debt-to-equity ratio of 50 percent which fails as a result of an utterly unanticipated worldwide crash in the hardware market. In such circumstances it would be unfair to berate the management for its rashness. Similarly it would be wrong to blame the failure of an Irish landed estate on a high debt-to-equity ratio alone: it depends on whether the debt had been contracted for productive purposes. Given the circumstances of most estates presented to the Estates Court, though, they hardly deserve the benefit of the doubt in this respect. In the 1840s Irish estates were worse positioned than their English counterparts in that a higher proportion of English rental income was spent on maintaining and improving estates, in that the prospects of English agriculture were arguably better, and in that selling English estates was easier.

Though the issue deserves more detailed analysis, the verdict of the specialist literature is that conspicuous consumption and poor estate management rather than bad luck or investment plans thwarted by the famine were responsible for the lion's share of estate indebtedness.[25] When the famine was over, the pro-landlord *Mayo Constitution* conceded that the demise of ancient landed families was due to debts of many past generations. The record is full of examples of landlord extravagance in quest of a quality of life set by their peers across the Irish Sea. The behavior of Cork landlords prompted the historian who knows them best to surmise that "although the fateful events of 1845–49 pushed the encumbered landowners of Cork over the brink of disaster, it was as clear as their best-polished silver by the early 1840s that the long-awaited day of reckoning with their creditors was close at hand." In other words, the famine only forced changes that were inevitable in any case: "the incubus of a largely bankrupt or debt-ridden landlord class was cast off by the operation of the encumbered estates court in the 1850s."[26]

Before the famine the only way of recovering money lent on landed security was by a bill in Chancery or Exchequer. But this was a tedious and ruinously expensive route. The vast quantity of legal documents accumulating in the Court's record office within a few years of its opening for business prompted the London *Times* to comment: "What an antiquity of troubles, what a prescription of impossibility do those figures denote — 100,000 documents and muniments of title! Surely when the work is done, this mountain of spent and refuse legality will be committed to the flames like the books of the sorcerers. Let them no longer burden the earth, and crush the energies and intellect of man."[27] Complex and defective legislation allowed huge debts on landed property to accumulate and delayed the sale of such property. As Donnelly explains, "there was no single, simple, and complete register of settlements, mortgages, and judgements. Instead, there were separate registers in different courts and in the registry office of deeds."[28] And yet landlords found ways of borrowing; the ability of so many to accumulate such debts offers a paradoxical reminder that Ireland before the famine was not short of idle capital.

The Incumbered Estates Court opened for business in late 1849. It did its work smoothly, selling off land in lots of several hundred acres rather than in whole estates in order to maximize sales revenue. The following analysis is based on a record of its sales between 1849 and the end of 1855, by which date the bulk of sales forced by the famine should have been conducted. Certainly the character of the Court's business had evolved by the mid-1850s. An official inquiry suggested that by then its transactions were no longer mainly or even largely due to landowners being driven to the Court by pressure from their creditors, and that petitioners tended to be owners seeking the benefit of the parliamentary title obtainable through the Court.[29] Including sales up to 1855 is thus likely to provide an upper-bound measure of total sales forced by creditors in the wake of the famine.

The results offer their own perspective on the regional incidence of the famine. Traces of the east-west gradient evident in maps in the 1841 census and in the distribution of relief rations at the height of the crisis are also evident here.[30] Sales were disproportionately concentrated in the provinces of Munster and Connacht, west of an imaginery line from Waterford to Ballyshannon. The pattern is not clear-cut, however. An interesting implication is how little of county Donegal was processed in the Court, and how landed proprietors in Kerry, Leitrim, and Clare, three counties devastated by the famine, also escaped relatively lightly. On the other hand, there are anomalous baronies with particularly high sales in other counties. One estate accounted for nearly all of the land sold in the Tipperary barony of Iffa and Offa West. It belonged to the Earl of Glengall, while nearly all the land sold in the northern baronies of Antrim Lower and Toome Lower belonged to the Earl of Mountcashel.

The results suggest that landlords were not as badly hit by the famine as sometimes thought. The O'Brien rentals imply that only about one Irish townland in eight contained land auctioned in the Incumbered Estates Court between 1849 and 1855. Almost certainly, a higher proportion of Irish land was seriously encumbered before the famine.[31]

Moreover, the indebtedness that forced proprietors to the Court dwarfed any outlays attributable to the famine alone. In mid-November 1849, the petitioners against the Earl of Portarlington—whose estate was one of the first to be presented to the Court—claimed debts of £700,000 ($3.6 million) against lands started to yield only an annual £33,000 ($158,000) in rent. Lord Oranmore and Browne (Dominick Browne) had accumulated debts of over £200,000 ($960,000) on an estate with a pre-famine rental of less than £5,000 ($24,000), and in the case of the Earl of Aldborough debts of £151,478 were supported by a rental of £2,629.[32] True, these are rather spectacular examples. Yet a more systematic analysis of the return of over sixteen hundred cases pending before the commissioners shows that debts many times the declared rental were typical (see below). Those cases represent more than half the total presented to the Court in that period. Does their residual quality mean that they were more encumbered than the average? Clearly, the delay attaching to cases presented in the first few years and still outstanding in 1854 *could* reflect the greater encumbrances on them. However, a year-by-year analysis of the ratio of debt to rent due rules this out as a serious bias. Between 1850 and 1853 three-quarters of the estates presented had debts exceeding ten times the declared rent due on them, and the median ratio of debt to rent was 14–15 years. The declared rents typically referred to pre-famine conditions; whether such rents could have been recovered in the conditions of 1850 at least is open to question. This lends a conservative bias to the ratios reported. The share of estates with debts of ten years' rent or more was down in 1854, supporting the claim that more landlords were by then using the Court to gain parliamentary title. Yet the proportion of estates owing twenty-five times or more the rent due hardly fell over the period (see table 4.4). Such estates can be deemed bankrupt de facto, since few

TABLE 4.4
Ratio of Debt to Rent Due on Encumbered Estates by Year of Presentation

Ratio	1849–50	1851	1852	1853	1854
0–4	3.4	4.9	6.6	6.0	11.8
5–9	20.8	20.8	20.7	19.8	29.5
10–	21.6	27.8	20.7	23.2	16.1
15–	16.8	13.7	13.8	18.8	11.8
20–	11.3	10.2	9.0	9.1	6.3
25–	7.6	7.4	4.8	4.7	2.8
30–	6.8	5.6	6.2	7.7	6.7
40–	2.9	1.8	4.5	3.4	3.1
50–	2.6	2.5	4.1	1.0	1.6
60+	6.1	5.3	9.7	6.4	10.2
10+	75.8	74.3	72.7	74.2	58.7
25+	26.0	22.6	29.3	20.2	24.4
Median ratio	15	14	15	15	12
Total	380	284	290	298	254

Source: Computed from BPP 1854–55, *Report of H.M. Commissioners Appointed to Inquire into the Incumbered Estates Court . . . with an Appendix Containing Evidence and Returns* (1938), vol. 19 [.527], table 2.

estates sold through the Court fetched more than twenty-five years' purchase.[33]

The important point about these ratio distributions is that, even bearing the possibility of some bias in mind, they are much too large to have been caused by the famine. Even a landlord who had received only half the rents due to him during the worst famine years (say 1846–48), and who had been responsible for a significant share of the rates burden in his area, would not have accumulated debts anything on that scale.[34] Even in the worst-affected poor-law unions the rates rarely exceeded four or five shillings in the pound (or, since the valuation approximated the gross rental, about one quarter of the normal gross rent) at the height of the famine. So even if a landlord was responsible for rates on half of his land, rates would have absorbed at most about one-eighth his normal receipts. The famine, then, might have cost some landlords in the worst-affected areas as much as two or three years' rent, a small fraction of the median above.

British public opinion was extremely critical of the performance of Irish landlords during the famine.[35] The landlords' defenders pictured them as squeezed by the pincer movement of lower rents and higher outlays both on relief and taxation. The impact of the crisis on aggregate rents received can only be guessed at, but the records of individual estates suggest that landlords may have been less affected than sometimes claimed. On eight Cork estates described by Donnelly, the average gap between rents due and received between 1845 and 1853 was only 16 percent. The record on another four estates described by Vaughan is even better: receipts as a percentage of rents due hardly fell. On the Devonshire estate, rent receipts fell back by 30 percent between 1845 and 1849, but surpassed their previous peak again in 1854.[36] Such data suffer from a likely selection bias: the rentals of estates whose receipts fell more drastically are less likely to have survived. Moreover, outlays on poor rates (local taxes) and, in many cases, on relief mounted during the famine. However, neither increased outlays nor reduced incomes can account for the staggering debts of most estates processed. Even in the worst-affected regions, poor rate outlays accounted for only a fraction of rents due.

The new historiography of Irish land tenure demolished the populist perception that evictions were common between the mid-1850s and the outbreak of the Irish Land War in 1879.[37] The myth that the famine was mainly responsible for the ruin of many Irish landlords, equally pervasive, has proved more enduring. However, the massive indebtedness of those landlords who succumbed in its wake suggests that the famine's true role was that of a catalyst: getting rid of landlords who were doomed in any case. This prompts two concluding speculations. First, it is doubtful whether any landlord who was free of debt and owed no rent in 1845 succumbed during the famine. Second, there was bound to have been a negative association between financial embarrassment and outlays on relief in the late 1840s. Debts accumulated in the years before the famine must have prevented many landlords from playing a more active part in limiting mass mortality during the famine.

TRADERS AND MARKETS

> The depopulation of some parts of the country is so
> complete, between the workhouse on the one hand and
> wholesale emigration on the other, that trade may be
> said to be almost extinct.
> (*Freeman's Journal*, 23 April 1849)

In a passage in Alessandro Manzoni's *I Promessi Sposi* (1840) describing a famine in Lombardy in the 1630s, a character in the street in Milan complained, "There's no famine at all really. . . . It's profiteers, cornering the market." "And bakers," added his companion, "hiding their stocks of grain. Hanging is the only thing for them." Manzoni, a product of the liberal enlightenment, did not believe such stories, but they are the stuff of fiction and oral history about famines everywhere. Ireland is no exception: the sense that traders profited from the miseries of famine is a driving theme in fictional works such as William Carleton's novel *The Black Prophet* (1847) and Liam O'Flaherty's *The House of Gold* (1929). Famines elsewhere yield similar stories. Many accounts of the greed of Malawi's maize traders in 1949 survive, and in India, where scarcities were so beneficial to usurers that they allegedly used sorcery to induce droughts, many accounts condemn the activities of traders during famines. In 1985 millionaire grain barons were accused of hoarding grain in the Sudan.[38] History also records many examples of real or alleged exploitation by traders and merchants. In eighteenth-century China the government was faced with the speculative activities and cynical manipulation of prices perpetrated by firms like the great rice-brokerage houses (*mi hang*) of Hankou or Suzhou. The *mi hang* liked to drive up prices by spreading false information about weather conditions. A royal declaration issued in Paris during the famine of 1693–94 attacked grain merchants for hoarding grain, "sure of the shortfall in consumption caused at the frontiers by the soldiers of our armies," while in mid-January 1694 a factory inspector denounced several citizens of Rheims for "holding large quantities of grain in their barns which they refused to expose to sale." A historian of the Iranian famine of 1870–72 finds that "the responsibility . . . can be squarely laid at the door of senior bureaucrats, landlords, grain dealers and high-ranking religious officials who engaged in hoarding and market manip-ulation." When Richard Cobb claimed that deaths from famine in years 3 and 4 of the French Revolution "serve as a condemnation of the sub-sistence policies of the Thermidoreans, who represented a sudden return to a free economy and to the lifting of restrictions from the primary producers," he was echoing a common theme in the historiography.[39] Another historian, Stephen Kaplan, eloquently describes the situation in mid-eighteenth century France:

> In most of the cases the rioters, men and women, blamed their distress first of all on the merchant: anyone engaged, professionally or opportunistically, in the traffic of grain. The fact that the harvest might be patently bad or the supply notoriously short in a given area no more justified the maneuvers of the traders than it made the concomitant rises palatable. . . . Even in the midst of obvious scarcity, the consumers of each village, bourg, and town believed that if the grain "of the place" were properly used and honestly apportioned, there would be enough, albeit barely, for everyone at prices which would be onerous but accessible.[40]

Similar accounts survive from Ireland in the 1840s. For example, the *Waterford Freeman* (3 October 1846) claimed that "merchants [were] closing their stores, already counting their gains, and gloating over the misery by which they hope to enrich themselves." Some months earlier around Loughrea it was "well known that speculators have made large purchase of oats, and are overholding oat-meal in store at Galway to raise the price of that article, and realize exorbitant profits." In West-meath "1s 6d a stone [was being] demanded by a man of the name of Swayne," while "in the large village of Portroe the provision dealers [were] charging £1-4-0 for a cwt. of oatmeal with two securities- and 20 percent for every day the notes remain unpaid after being due." In Carlow in January 1847 it was alleged that "the millers and dealers united to spread alarm among the farmers to induce them to bring their grain to market, which they were always holding back in hopes of higher prices." Indeed historian Mary Daly surmises that "there are so many references to farmers holding grain off the market in the autumn of 1846, in the hope that prices would rise even further, that they can-not be discounted."[41] The huge rise in grain prices in Cork in late 1846 prompted one of Treasury Under-Secretary Charles Trevelyan's infor-mants to tell him in late December 1846 that "£40,000 to £80,000 were spoken of as being made by merchants" there, and to hope that ministers would intervene to check "the extortionate prices." Bess-borough, the Lord Lieutenant, informed Prime Minister Russell a few weeks later that "there is no great doubt that the merchants in the great towns have taken advantage . . . , and in some places are keeping up the prices by the most unfair means."[42]

As Jean Drèze and Amartya Sen point out, the workings of traders and markets during famines remains a topic "that is not always approached dispassionately." Economists and historians remain divided on the issue. The founder of classical economics, Adam Smith, was unequivocal about the cause of famines, at least in Europe since the sixteenth century:

> Whoever examines, with attention, the history of the dearths and famines which have afflicted any part of Europe during either the course of the present of that or the preceding two centuries . . . will find, I believe, that a dearth never has arisen from any combination among the inland dealers in corn, nor from any other cause but a real scarcity, occasioned sometimes, perhaps, and in some particular cases, by the waste of war, but in by far the greater number of cases, by the fault of the seasons; and that a famine has never arisen from any other cause but the violence of government attempting, by improper means, to remedy the inconvenience of a dearth.[43]

For Smith, political meddling had long been the cause of famines, not markets or traders. Thomas Malthus, whose second publication was inspired by a near-famine in England in 1799–1800, agreed. On the other hand Amartya Sen blames much of Bengal's tragedy in 1943–44 on vigorous speculation and hoarding on the part of producers. Farmers, he claims, exacerbated the crisis by holding back the rice crops they had grown in 1942–43: "The normal release following the harvest did not take place. A moderate shortfall in *production* had by then been translated into an exceptional shortfall in *market release*."[44] Something similar was often alleged during earlier Indian famines. A contemporary observer compared the speculation during the famine of 1860 to "the excitement due to South Sea Schemes of railway manias." In western India, "dearth was of such obvious advantage to the usurers that it was commonly believed that they used sorcery to prevent rain from falling." Martin Ravallion's pioneering econometric analysis of markets during the famine of Bangladesh in 1974 might be interpreted as lending support to those who blamed "hoarders, profiteers, and black marketeers [for] creating the crisis conditions."[45] He found that "stockholders had over-optimistic price expectations during the famine" and that "price series for all districts exhibit quite strong localized effects of the 1974 famine," so that "excess mortality in Bangladesh during 1974 was, in no small measure, the effect of a speculative crisis."[46]

In the discussion of markets and famines, two issues sometimes get confused. The first is whether markets worked efficiently, that is, responded in the standard, predictable manner to relative price signals. The second is whether markets, even though functioning in textbook fashion, exacerbated the crisis. I am mainly concerned with the first issue here. There are several ways to interpret the claim that markets worked poorly during the Irish famine. The failure could have been temporary (e.g., early on, as in late 1846, when the trade in Indian meal was new); it could have been partial (e.g., restricted to remote areas); or it could have been intertemporal (e.g., agents hoarded, or held on to their stocks for too long).

Though the famine was over before the completion of the Irish railway network's main trunk routes, communications within the country were not bad by the standards of the time, and much of the population lived within easy reach of seaports.[47] In theory, competition between ports and between grain merchants might therefore have been expected to keep down monopoly power. Here I offer some tentative clues to the question, Were markets derailed as such accounts imply? Before doing so, three simple points based on elementary price theory are worth bearing in mind. First, supply shocks might well have caused monopoly suppliers of food to increase their prices *less* than firms in a competitive industry. Second, higher prices induced by supply shocks would have *reduced* the profits of monopolists. Third, the drastic fall in the purchasing power of their customers should have induced meal merchants — other things remaining the same — to reduce, not increase, their prices (assuming that grain, unlike potatoes, was not an inferior good). These theoretical points suggest that some contemporary observers may have mistaken adverse supply shocks for monopoly power. On the other hand, some of the criticism may have referred to trades (such as that in Indian corn) that were unfamiliar, and therefore more amenable to exploitation.

Few of the business accounts of famine traders that might shed light on these possibilities have survived. Before turning to the records of two such traders, let us take a look at food price data from the period. Such data are plentiful, but must be handled cautiously. There are well-known pitfalls involved in comparing pairwise movements in prices or the variation in prices across markets or regions: high correlations do not prove market integration.[48] However, *changes* in correlations during crises probably arise from those crises. In a well-integrated market with a modicum of interregional trade, persistent price differences between regions stem largely from transport costs. Therefore, if markets continue to function well during a harvest failure, the price variation (as measured by the standard deviation) across regions such as counties or provinces should remain the same. However, if markets become more segmented, a rise in the standard deviation might be expected.

TABLE 4.5
Markets and Famines: A Simple Model

	A	B	C	D	Mean	σ
P_N	2.0	3.0	4.0	4.5	3.38	0.96
T	2.5	1.5	0.5	0.0		
$P_{F(1)}'$	3.0	3.5	4.0	4.5	3.75	0.56
$P_{F(2)'}$	8.0	7.0	4.0	4.5		
$P_{F(2)}$	7.5	6.5	5.5	5.0	6.13	0.96
$P_{F(3)}'$	2.0	3.0	5.0	6.0		
$P_{F(3)}$	2.5	3.5	4.5	5.0	3.88	0.96

Note: See text for explanation.

This may be stated somewhat more formally in terms of the Law of One Price, which argues that in a well-integrated market, persistent price differences between regions stem largely from transport costs. Let T be a vector of the (constant) costs of shipping grain from a region to the most expensive region, and P_N and P_F be vectors of normal and famine grain prices, respectively. Then the Law of One Price implies that the standard deviation of prices across regions, σ, will reflect T. Normally—and this certainly holds true for the Irish famine—P_F will exceed P_N. However, unless T changes, with well-functioning markets arbitrage will produce $\sigma(P_F) \leq \sigma(P_N)$.

A simple example illustrates. Let $P\,N$ be a vector of prices in four regions A to D in normal times (see table 4.5). Assume that transport and distribution costs, T, do not change: this is a reasonable assumption where the railway is the dominant mode of interregional communication. Given T, these prices reflect the Law of One Price. Next, let $P_{F(1)}'$ and $P_{F(2)}'$ describe what prices would be in the absence of trade in two situations of harvest failure, $F(1)$ and $F(2)$. In $F(1)$ the failure is most serious in food-exporting areas. Unless T is affected, the higher prices obtaining in regions A and B will cause food to remain in them, and prices will remain at $P_{F(1)}'$. In $F(2)$, the failure in the supplying areas is such that reverse flows of food from normally deficit regions are necessary to reflect the Law of One Price. Such flows would establish an equilibrium vector such as $P_{F(2)}$. In $F(3)$ the failure is most serious in the consuming areas. In the absence of trade prices would be at $P_{F(3)}'$, but trade flows lead to the equilibrium vector of $P_{F(3)}$. Note that σ, the standard deviation of prices across regions, is the same in $F(2)$ and $F(3)$ as in N, and less in $F(1)$ than in N. By the same token the Law of One Price implies a fall in the coefficient of variation of prices across different regions. A rise in σ would be consistent with the failure of the Law of One Price to operate, through markets becoming more segmented. We shall now apply this simple, partial test of how markets behave during crises to Irish markets for potatoes in the 1840s.

As already noted in chapter 1, most potatoes grown in Ireland before the famine were for domestic or local consumption. One of the potato's disadvantages is that it was relatively costly to transport; Hoffman and Mokyr reckon that before the famine, 2.5 percent of the potato's value evaporated with every mile it traveled. Nevertheless, there was an active local trade in potatoes in Ireland before the famine, and most towns had their potato markets. Internal trade was probably mainly local and by horse and cart, though the coastal trade in potatoes covered significant distances (e.g., from Iveragh in Kerry to Cork city), and canals and navigations were also used to carry potatoes. A good deal of evidence on potato prices survives in both the general and specialist press and in the Blue Books. Did the same hold during the famine?[49]

Table 4.6 reports evidence from three examples of regional price data. Section A summarizes data contained in a parliamentary report on potato prices in almost four hundred Irish towns between 1840 and 1846. The numbers are not ideal for our purpose; they extend only as far as the harvest of 1845, the first to be affected by blight. A further problem is that they refer to the highest prices paid, and therefore may well reflect a range of qualities and varieties across the country. In partial mitigation, because they refer to the prices paid in a single week in January, they have the advantage of controlling for seasonal variation. In general, the observed interregional price gaps are smaller than what transport costs would indicate. This suggests that trade in substitutes for the potato such as grain helped to arbitrage away disequilibrium differences. In all four provinces, prices were higher in 1846 than in any other year, as expected. In three of the four provinces, however, the standard deviation was also highest in that year.[50]

Section B of table 4.6 is derived from a "return of the price of potatoes agreed for the last contract entered into by each Board of Guardians in Ireland previously to the 1st of May in the years 1844, 1845, 1846," also printed in the Blue Books. The Guardians' preoccupation with economy means that these data should refer to inferior if not identical potato varieties.[51] Unlike the data in section A, however, the prices do not refer to a uniform date. The results reported below refer only to unions where prices refer to the first four months of 1845 and 1846 or later, which restricts the number of usable observations to thirty-six, since the standard deviation in 1846 is not much bigger than that for 1845. Finally, the data in section C refer to potato prices in over thirty Irish towns in 1848–51. In this case the standard deviation was lowest when the average price was highest.

TABLE 4.6
The Regional Variation of Potato Prices in the 1840s

A. *Market town data, 1840–46*

Province	Obs.	1840	1841	1842	1843	1844	1845	1846
(i) Mean price per stone (pence)								
Leinster	126	3.09	3.02	3.02	2.66	2.92	2.98	4.68
Munster	76	3.09	2.87	2.95	2.73	2.70	2.82	3.76
Ulster	87	2.70	2.59	2.66	2.21	2.32	2.56	4.12
Connacht	98	2.74	2.62	2.78	2.19	2.26	2.48	3.37
Ireland	387	2.83	2.70	2.78	2.38	2.49	2.65	3.94
(ii) Standard deviation								
Leinster		.874	.763	.843	.702	.704	.629	.973
Munster		1.162	.872	.850	.786	.734	.792	.842
Ulster		.653	.570	.665	.736	.596	.492	.882
Connacht		.737	.689	.778	.618	.563	.551	.843
Ireland		.974	.824	.892	.835	.794	.755	1.158

Source: Derived from data in BPP 1846a.

B. *Poor law union contract data, 1845–46*

	1845	1846
Price per stone (pence)	3.12	5.22
Standard deviation	.615	.778

Source: Derived from data in BPP 1846b.

C. *Town price data, 1848–51*

	1848	1849	1850	1851
Price per cwt. (pence)	58.06	49.55	42.37	43.38
Standard deviation	7.04	9.12	8.40	7.09

Source: Thom's Commercial Directory, 1852, p. 242, and 1853, p. 298.
Notes: The 1848–50 data refer to thirty-two towns; those for 1851 for the same towns minus Mohill and Wicklow. One stone = 14 lbs.

If there is a message in these results for how the market (or markets) for potatoes worked in Ireland before and during the famine, surely it is one more consistent with orderly than segmented markets in the wake of the blight. Though the standard deviations in sections A and B are higher in 1846 than earlier, the rises are small.[52] Section C includes 1848, when the ravages of blight were particularly severe, and the outcome is consistent with normally functioning markets in that year.

Data on grain prices also survive, and are probably of higher quality in that a grain crop such as wheat or oats was more homogeneous than the potatoes underlying the information above. Let us use grain prices first to take a closer look at the situation in those crucial weeks in late

1846 and early 1847. We compare oatmeal prices in a few towns for which more or less continuous weekly market data are provided in the *Farmers' Gazette*. Prices are usually reported as a range, and the series used here represent the midpoint in the range reported (except in the case of wheat in Dublin, where I use the market average given). We first compare trends in the price of oatmeal (pence per cwt.) in Cork, Dublin, and Galway between mid-1846 and the end of 1847 (fig. 4.1). The comparison suggests that while there were occasional local blips, short-term fluctuations were very similar. If anything, Cork prices tended to be lower than those in either Dublin or Galway. A more direct look at those Cork traders is provided by comparing the prices paid for Indian meal on the Cork and Liverpool corn markets[53] between July 1846 and June 1847, as reported weekly in the *Mark Lane Express*. The outcome in this instance (described in fig. 4.2) does not so readily absolve Cork traders. It suggests a significant wedge (10–15 percent) between prices in the two ports until mid-December 1846, and a whittling away of that gap to a few percentage points thereafter. The earlier wedge could have been the product of collusion between grain merchants, as alleged, but it could also have reflected the initial inability or reluctance of most traders to engage in what would have been an unfamiliar commodity.

More formal econometric analysis confirms the impression left by figure 4.1. I estimate the following error-correction model for Cork-Dublin and Galway-Dublin:

$$dP_{it} = a.P_{i,t-1} + b.P_{DUB,t-1} + c.dP_{DUB,t} + g.dP_{DUB,t-1} + e_{it} \tag{1}$$

or

$$dP_{it} = a[P_{i,t-1} + b/a.P_{DUB,t-1}] + c.dP_{DUB,t} + g.dP_{DUB,t-1} + e_{it} \tag{2}$$

where P is price, DUB is Dublin, and i is Cork or Galway. The RHS terms may be broken into two components; the first, $[P_{i,t-1} + b/a.P_{DUB,t-1}]$, is the error-correction element, which measures adjustment to an existing disequilibrium, while the second, containing the dP_{DUB} terms, measures the response to current changes in P_{DUB}. $a < 1$ implies that the adjustment to disequilibrium is working in the correct direction. Estimating this error correction model (ECM) for the eighty-two weeks between early June 1846 to the end of 1847 called for linear interpolation for a small number of observations missing in the *Farmers' Gazette*. The results, using log values of prices, are shown in table 4.7A. In both cases the almost identical values of the coefficients on P_i and P_{DUB} imply full adjustment in the long run. The result for Cork, for example, suggests that a quarter of the adjustment to disequilibrium occurred within one period (i.e., a week), while over half the

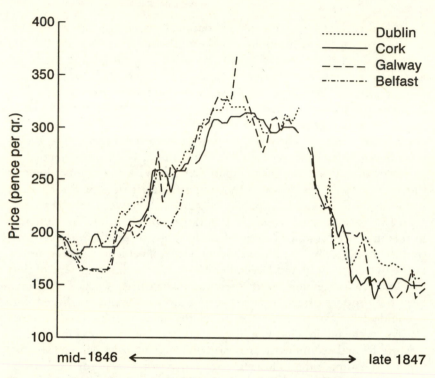

Figure 4.1. Oatmeal prices in Dublin, Cork, and Galway, 1846–47.

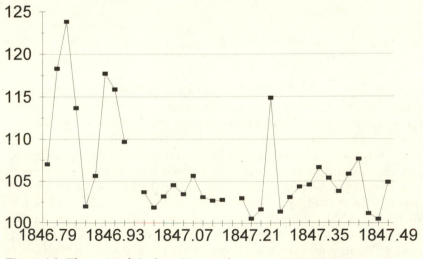

Figure 4.2. The ratio of Cork to Liverpool maize prices, 1846–47.

TABLE 4.7
Estimating the Error-Correction Model

A. OATMEAL

	CORK	GALWAY
$P_{i,t-1}$	$-0.24687\ (-3.26)$	$-0.24281\ (-3.12)$
$P_{DUB,t-1}$	$0.24473\quad(3.25)$	$0.24079\quad(3.12)$
$dP_{DUB,t}$	$0.31505\quad(3.27)$	$0.61662\quad(4.97)$
$dP_{DUB,t-1}$	$0.28263\quad(2.71)$	
$F(3, 75)$	11.85	14.63
DW	2.07	1.98

B. OATS

	DUBLIN	CORK
$P_{i,t-1}$	$-0.13401\ (-2.45)$	$-0.25140\ (-3.61)$
$P_{L,t-1}$	$0.13603\quad(2.45)$	$0.24726\quad(3.59)$
$DP_{L,t}$	$0.11425\quad(0.80)$	$0.38487\quad(1.59)$
$DP_{L,t-1}$	—	$0.34761\quad(1.47)$
$F(2, 100)$	$3.03\ [.053]$	$F\ (3, 98)\ 5.00\ [.003]$
DW	2.23	1.98

Notes: t – statistics in parentheses. P_i is the lowest price quoted in Dublin and Cork, as reported in the *Farmers' Gazette*. P_L is the London price given in the *Mark Lane Express*.

response to a change in P_{DUB} occurred within two weeks. The results for Galway are similar. Comparing movements in the price of oats in Dublin and Cork with those in London over a longer period (all of 1846 and 1847) produces the results in table 4.7B, which once more suggest rapid erosion of disequilibrium gaps.

A direct look at the situation in Cork is provided by the surviving letters of two leading Cork merchant firms, R & H Hall and J. N. Murphy. The letters of Robert Hall[54] capture the trends in the city's grain market at the height of the crisis very well. R & H Hall were commission agents: their speculation in the grain trade went no further than discounting traders' bills. As early as 21 August 1846 Robert Hall was telling his London correspondent, James Prevost, that "if any of our friends should float a cargo of Galatz, which seems to be liked here just as well as Tuscan, I shall be happy to take charge of it, and have little doubt of being able to obtain a good price." This offer was not taken up, and the initiative was left to Cork merchants. Though the price of maize had already reached £15–£17 ($72–$82) per ton by late October, it is worth noting that Hall could not get a buyer at first for a London factor offering a "small cargo of Tuscan" loading in Leghorn:

"what two months may produce none can tell." A day or two later Hall was offering 45s ($10.90) per quarter for 480 lbs (or £10 10s, or $50, per ton), cost, insurance, and freight for the shipment, and in mid-November suggesting to Calcutta correspondent that he "safely send 100 tons" at £10 ($48) per ton, adding that he had sold about 200 tons at £11 per ton of Tuscan Indian Corn for a Leghorn client and that "for the next ten months all sorts of grain cheap must be imported here." In the following weeks more Irish buyers were tempted to make offers, but most were too timid to be executed. Given that the market price of maize in Pisa, not far from Leghorn, rose from 9.67 Tuscan lire per sacco (or $30 per ton) in early October to 11.33 lire ($36 per ton) a month later, and 15 lire ($47 per ton) by year's end, Irish bids were not allowing a sufficient margin for freight and insurance.

Still, a frustrated Robert Hall complained to his Leghorn correspondent that "if your Black Sea merchants continue refusing the high prices now going out for wheat, they may next year find themselves in the position they were in last year, for undoubtedly the quantity to come forward from America will be enormous, not half the wheat taken out of bond in August has yet gone into consumption, and you know well what a change any little panic would create, so that though a large import of foreign wheat must be required for this country, yet I do not think it safe to speculate on too high prices." Most of Hall's orders remained unexecuted, and little maize arrived in Cork.[55] Only traders such as Daniel Lane and Samuel Allen, who set what turned out to be realistic limits or allowed factors at the point of sale full discretion, found satisfaction. Hall vainly sought to entice foreigners to take the risks by shipping the grain over for sale on the spot. Big money was made on forward contracts in the following weeks, and though prices had given way a little by February 1847, Hall was still seeking offers of forward contracts then. On 27 February 1847 he wrote to his contact in Leghorn telling him that he had got "as high as 72s ($17) per quarter cost, freight, and insurance" for two cargoes of Indian corn from Bayonne within the previous ten days. Such a price should have seemed more attractive to Italian sellers; in Pisa on 3 March maize fetched 19.5 lire per sacco (about 55s or $13 per quarter).

A week later, maize had become "dull" in Cork, in consequence of "arrivals rather exceeding the demand." On 15 March 1847 a London factory was informed that there was "no buyer here for your Salonica Indian corn at near your limits, over forty vessels with maize have arrived within the last three days."[56] A severe winter had delayed American exports by a few weeks, but by March maize was crossing the Atlantic in quantity. On 26 March 1847 the *Freeman's Journal* reported that about 160 ships had arrived in Cove within the previous fortnight, with "beneficial" results. Panic had seized the market, and by 27 March maize had fallen from 72s per quarter to 50s per quarter. Hall told his Leghorn friend, Lloyd, that "if this should continue, we shall have many failures amongst second class houses, which I hope won't involve any of our friends." It was "almost impossible to get an offer for a floating cargo at present . . . so many parties have been caught at high rates." Banks were "very tight on the corn men which will not tend to advance prices"; "some parties . . . must sell."

On 11 May, Hall confided to Prevost in London that "banks here are as tight as ever and it should be indeed a first rate house that I would put myself in the position of sending out an order for," but a few days later continental demand brought a temporary reprieve, and Hall sold a cargo of maize from Trieste at 66s ($16) per quarter. "We can assure you the utmost was obtained for this cargo. . . . The sample was placed in the hands of Mr. O'Hea and every broker here by David Hall, who evinced the greatest interest to get you the highest rate, it was only when all failed that we, by agreeing to take half payment in bills, succeeded in making the sale." By month's end the trade was very "dull" again, and the arrival of four American vessels laden with about 1,200 tons maize did not help. On 4 June 1847 Hall hoped a Bristol correspondent had "not suffered much from the failures which I hear have taken place in Dublin," and explained that "there will I fear be more failures throughout Ireland this year than have taken place for many years, the Banks give no accommodation." The overall impression gained from the Hall letters is of a trade in which the bolder speculators who bought forward in October and November made huge speculative profits, while some of those who tried their luck later had their fingers burned. Moreover, the profits of the early birds prompted the surge in imports from early 1847 on. But the impression gained is not of a closed, cartelized market. The impact of trends on the London grain market is also evident from these letters. Cork merchants read the *Mark Lane Gazette*, and "excited accounts" from London led Cork traders to revise their bids for fear of nonexecution.

Throughout late 1846 and early 1847, the Cork merchants and distillers, J. N. Murphy & Co.,[57] toyed almost continually with the idea of entering the trade in maize, without ever quite managing it. At first they sought to use spare capacity in their distillery at Midleton to grind maize, but some or all their insurance companies proved unaccommodating. Then they contemplated a purely trading role, contacting London correspondents for occasional information and quotations of grain and maize prices. As prices mounted, the lure of the business increased, and on 4 December 1846 Murphy sent off two inquiries about shipments from southeastern Europe. On New Year's Day 1847 they informed their New Orleans correspondent that importers of maize had been making vast sums of money, and regretted not handling an October order. Still, they expected "a serious decline in prices in May as the quantity to about and previous to that period will be large." Two weeks later Murphy was seeking information on Galatz Indian corn for spring delivery and what would be the probable rate of freight. Next day they informed an Antwerp correspondent that "things are very feverish with us, bread stuffs are becoming higher every day," adding that "in fact our prices are regulated by the London market." On 28 January 1847 Murphy offered the Antwerp correspondent to do "the best we can to dispose favourably of any cargoes you may consign to us. In this case we would suggest your fixing the lowest price you would take, and at the same time instructing us where to send the vessel on, if we could not realise it." And on 1 February 1847 they sought pro forma terms for maize from New York and New Orleans dealers, adding that "our ideas, we must confess, are rather low compared with present very high prices at this side of the Atlantic." However, by 19 February 1847 Murphy was informing Fraser in Antwerp that they had decided not to take up the corn business, recommending Messrs Burke instead.[58] In late April they informed their New York correspondents that "we have not yet been tempted to operate in Indian corn. Although the fall on this side has been considerable we expect it will be still lower. Therefore we prefer looking on for the present." By June 1846 they were looking forward to the next season, inquiring of Messrs H & J Johnston & Co. of London "what [was] doing in Indian corn for forward delivery—or Archangel oats?" and in July they handed a New York firm a big order for "Indian corn of the growth of 1846 to be shipped on vessels of form 200 to 350 tons each for Cork and to stand free on board including freight to Cork but not insurance £6. 10. 0 per ton." However, Murphy's low limits and special conditions meant that none of their orders was executed in the 1846–47 season either. It was not until 1847–48 that they got involved in a substantial way in the trade in Indian corn.

The letters of both R & H Hall and Murphy & Co. reveal a cautious approach to profit-making in the southern capital. The brave few who took the risks made a lot of money. If Murphy & Co. and, by extension, other Cork grain and flour merchants are to be criticized, it must be for being overly cautious in an admittedly risky business.[59] But this raises the question: Why not blame the seasoned traders in maize in the Mediterranean and in the New World for not taking their chances?

Finally, what of speculative hoarding? Modern evidence suggests that hoarding can exacerbate famine situations. Sen blames the situation in Bengal in 1943 largely on "speculative withdrawal and panic purchase of rice stocks . . . encouraged by administrative chaos," while speculative withdrawals of foodgrains were also important in Bangladesh in 1974. In the case of Bangladesh the signals on the rice market gave the impression that rice was much scarcer than it really was, with the result that the increase in the price of rice was much greater than it should have been.[60] In an earlier test of hoarding in potato markets, prompted by McCloskey and Nash's analysis of late medieval corn prices, I compared the seasonal rises in prices from autumn trough to summer peak before and during the famine. Unlike grain, potatoes could not be stored from one year to the next; potatoes "hoarded" at the beginning of the season must be disposed of before its end. If we assume consumption smoothing through a roughly constant demand from month to month while the supply lasted (i.e., until, say, the end of May or June), then the seasonal prices must reflect the disposal of the stock over the harvest year. I simply assumed that if prices rose less from trough to peak during the famine than before, then traders were hoarding. The outcome of this admittedly limited test did not support the hypothesis that speculation made a bad situation worse, since, if anything, seasonal price rises were greater during the famine than before.[61]

The raw material for a more direct test may be found in the pages of Cork city newspapers, where returns made to the mayor of the quantities supplied and price obtaining on each market day were reported. Such data were first collected in October 1840 in response to repeated complaints against forestalling.[62] The markets of Cork, then Ireland's second city, obtained their potatoes both coastwise and from the interior; according to *The Economist* (20 June 1846), the city was "the chief market for potatoes in Ireland." Nevertheless, the market absorbed only a small fraction of production in its wider hinterland. The combined annual sales on the city's six markets—about 40,000 loads (one load = 9 cwt)—would have been enough to provide every man, woman, and child in the city 1.5 lbs of potatoes daily for most of the year. The supply may be gauged against the estimated 277,078 acres under potatoes in county Cork on the eve of the famine.[63] Assuming a yield of six tons an acre implies that Cork's potato markets would have absorbed only 2 percent or so of the county's production. Nor was the city's supply of potatoes limited to the county; the coastwise trade in potatoes extended from Iveragh in Kerry to Waterford. Such arithmetic exaggerates the subsistence character of the potato, however, since Cork's producers also supplied numerous towns and villages in the county.

The reports refer to six city markets. Five of them—Harpur's Lane, Barrack Street, Capwell and Evergreen, North, Blackpool—operated daily from Monday to Saturday, while the smallest at Leitrim and John Street operated only on Saturdays. Saturday was the busiest day by far,

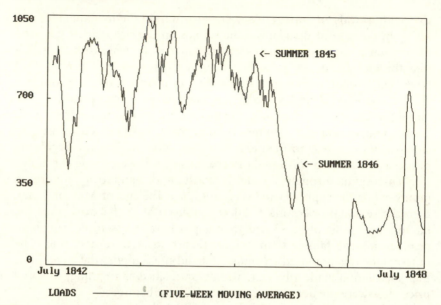

Figure 4.3. Potatoes supplied to Cork's markets, 1842–47. The numbers to the left are loads (one load = 9 cwt).

usually accounting for nearly half the week's sales, followed by Wednesday and Thursday. The data used here were taken from the *Cork Constitution*, a Tory newspaper published three times a week. The data refer to 1842–48. The *Constitution*'s coverage was by no means complete, but enough information is provided to infer something about the size of the market and its evolution during the famine period. I plugged short gaps in the data by applying the pattern of sales in complete weeks,[64] and resorted to simple interpolation in the case of some weeks when data were not reported (fig. 4.3). Only in two extended periods — for six weeks in November–December 1842 and January–July 1847 — did the *Constitution* fail to report from the potato markets. I filled the first gap by assuming a weekly delivery of nine hundred loads; the second is a direct reflection of the famine and followed a ten-week period when weekly supplies averaged only about thirteen tons. This resulting series allows us to compare the disposal of the crop in good and bad years.

For the years immediately before the famine, the outcome shows a market which spread sales well over a harvest season beginning in early autumn. The slight tendency for supplies to fall over the season is as might be expected, as is the lull in business around Christmastime. What of the famine period? Figure 4.6 shows a similar pattern in the harvest years of 1842–43, 1843–44, and 1844–45. The pattern in 1845–46 reflects the blight, but indicates that the proportion of sales early in the season was higher than before. In 1846–47 sales between July and December were far less than normal, and market reports for the first of 1847 are lacking, presumably because the volumes involved were very small. But again sales were proportionately higher early in the season. Only in 1847–48 is there any hint at all of potatoes being held back till late in the season, but it is only a slight hint, and the amounts involved were only a fraction of the pre-blight norm. These data cannot tell us what was going on in the minds of potato sellers. We cannot rule out the possibility that some of them would have loved to speculate but sold quickly for fear that their supplies would not keep. In these data, actions speak louder than intentions, and if the evidence does not conclusively rule out speculation or hoarding on the part of potato suppliers, it certainly argues in that direction.

The perspectives on markets and traders in the 1840s offered by the analysis of the data discussed above—potato and grain prices, merchants' letters, potato sales data from Cork—provide no definitive, dogmatic answers. They do not rule out individual instances of profiteering. Particularly in those extensive regions where traders were few and their customers often ignorant and desperate, only a Dr. Pangloss would deny the likelihood of exploitation. Nor do they prove that food always moved speedily where market signals beckoned. Still, the balance of our evidence is in that direction. During the Irish famine at least, markets worked more smoothly than might have been expected on the basis of a reading of qualitative and fictional accounts of markets and famines.

MONEYLENDERS

> The Pawn offices are so stocked with Goods that
> 10 shillings could scarcely be raised on the
> value of five Pounds.
> (Letter from Milltown, county Kerry, 20 November 1846)

Trends in both note circulation and the value of bank stock imply that the famine years were difficult ones for Ireland's joint-stock banks. However, the joint-stock banks had few direct dealings with the masses most at risk. What of those individuals and institutions who provided credit to the poor? In the following pages I discuss three institutions who specialized in trading with the poor, pawnbroking, loan fund banking, and savings banks. In Ireland, pawnbrokers operated under relatively liberal laws enacted by the pre-1801 College Green parliament,

TABLE 4.8
Pawnbroking During the Famine

Year	Tickets Issued	Sums Lent (nearest £)	Average (pence)
1843	10,517,022	1,458,839	33.3
1844	11,501,108	1,603,789	34.2
1845	13,039,882	1,849,758	34.0
1846	14,161,152	1,922,343	32.6
1847	11,081,865	1,293,332	28.0

Source: IUP, Famine volumes, IV, 406–7.

which allowed them to charge higher effective rates than their British counterparts. Perhaps the size of Ireland's legal pawnbroking sector — nearly five hundred establishments on the eve of the famine — owed something to these laws. Yet there was also a widespread feeling that those laws did not adequately protect the "needy and ignorant" who resorted to the pawnshop, and pawnbrokers were widely reviled. A parliamentary inquiry in 1837 noted "odium and discredit attached to the trade at present" and "the disreputable character of many persons engaged in the trade." Some sense of the extent of the business before and during the famine may be obtained from table 4.8.[65]

The regional spread of pawnbroking was very uneven. Just before the famine, Dublin city alone accounted for nearly one-third of pledges made, and the province of Connacht less than 3 percent. Though pawnbrokers might be found throughout most of the island, they had not yet made their way into some of the most backward areas in the early 1840s. Several poor-law unions could not claim a single legal pawnbroker; the two in Boyle and Carrick-on-Shannon unions were established only in 1848, and they declined "the filthy and valueless rags presented for their acceptance by the poorer classes." In Mayo, pawnbroking was a recent introduction, and "not always within reach of the poor"; in the barony of Erris "there never was one. The trade is unknown." Nonetheless, pawnbrokers' humble clients everywhere were from the strata most likely to be hurt by the famine. The typical pledge was in clothing and for the equivalent of a few days' wages. Many pawnshops combined lending money with a trade in secondhand clothes.

How did pawnbrokers fare during the famine? The account of "Distress indicated in the clothing of the peasantry, and pawnbrokers' returns" in the parliamentary Blue Books contains many reports from pawnbrokers in late 1848 and early 1849. These reports usefully capture both the patterns of the business in normal times — its seasonal rhythms, the type of good pledged — and the variation in the regional incidence of the famine. A pawnbroker in Gort in county Galway, for example, feared that many of his clients would fail to release their pledges and complained about the poor quality of the articles offered. A Roscommon pawnbroker believed that "pawnbroking must become extinct for want of purchasers of the forfeited goods"; before the famine, about 2 percent of goods were forfeited, but in late 1848 forfeitures were about 30 percent. In late 1848 pawnbrokers' premises in Tralee were "filled with wearing apparel of every description, homemade clothing materials, feather-beds, bedding, and tradesmen's tools of every kind." A "most respectable" pawnbroker in Fermoy (in Cork) related the increase in pledges in 1846 to "the destitution which commenced in that year," and the subsequent fall-off in business to the lack of suitable articles to pledge. A pawnbroker in Tipperary town reported a decline of more than half in the profits of his own concerns, while those in Roscrea (in north Tipperary) claimed that their stocks of unclaimed pledges were more than twice what they ever had been before. The sole registered pawnbroker in the Castlerea union area produced monthly returns and gave the following summary account of business:

> In 1844, might lend nearly the entire value, and goods would be nearly all released. In 1845, any thing that remained unredeemed, would bring more than its value, the attendance was so large at pawn-office auctions.
>
> In 1846, a large stock remained unredeemed, and could not make sale of it, in consequence of the want of means among the class of persons who usually bought those goods.
>
> In 1847, stopped receiving most kind of goods or clothing, sickness being so prevalent among the class of persons that were compelled to apply.
>
> 1848, has taken less this year, and still a large stock remains unredeemed — what were pledged during the above years.[66]

Several pawnbrokers also supplied monthly returns of pledges received and returned between 1843 and 1848. Some of these are described in figure 4.4. This shows that pledges usually mounted in the lean summer months, and redemptions tended to exceed pledges in the autumn. Only in one case (Gort) did the number of pledges exceed returns throughout, though in others (e.g., Tralee) they did so in most months. In such instances, pawnbrokers were presumably content to combine moneylending with merchandising secondhand goods. For Loughrea's sole pawnbroker, whose pledges were usually redeemed within the year before the famine, the crisis brought a huge cumulative excess of pledges over redemptions, which he sought to reduce during 1848. In Tralee, on the other hand, an annual build-up in pledges over returns (about five thousand in 1844–46) was normal, but the reduced demand for secondhand goods brought this to a halt in 1847 and 1848. In general, the onset of

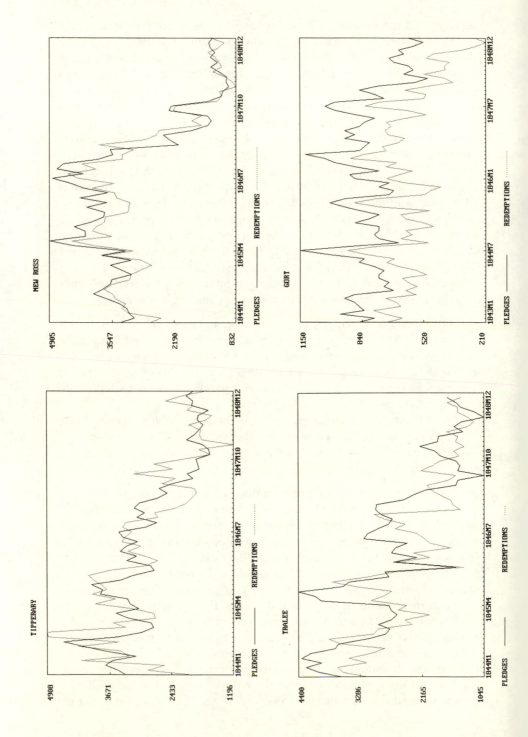

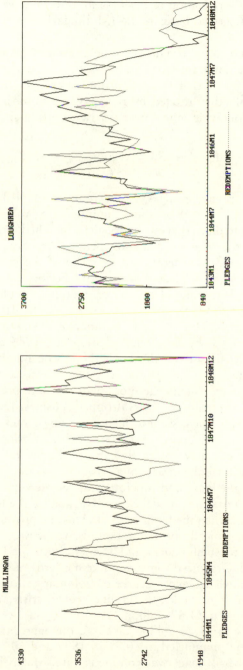

Figure 4.4. Sample of monthly pawnbrokers' pledges and redemptions.

the famine provoked a jump in pledges in late 1846 and early 1847, followed by a reduction in business in 1847 and 1848. In only one of the towns described in figure 4.4 (Mullingar) is there no obvious "famine effect."

The pawnbrokers' responses to the crisis may be modeled in a simple error correction framework (table 4.9). The underlying logic is that when they found that the proportion of pledges being redeemed had begun to fall, they reacted by reducing the number of pledges. I estimated the following model for the pawnshops in six different locations in Ireland:

$$dP = a + bP_{t-1} + cR_{t-1} + d.dR_{t-1} + e.dR_{t-2} + .. + g.JAN + .. + h.NOV + u,$$

where P represents pledges, R the number of pledges redeemed, and $JAN, FEB, \ldots, NOV$ seasonal dummies. Log values of P and R were used. The outcomes suggest that pledges matched returns in the most of the towns, the obvious exception being Gort. Seasonal patterns were broadly similar. In general, half or more of the shifts in returns were matched by shifts in pledges in the same period.

While the increasing likelihood of default prompted pawnbrokers to lend less, the erosion of the stock of pawnable assets reduced the demand for loans. The aggregate number of tickets issued by legal Irish pawnbrokers fell by over one-fifth between 1846 and 1847, and the total lent by almost one-third. Neither those numbers nor individual accounts support the claim that the famine was a golden opportunity for pawnbrokers. Surely the most plausible interpretation of the numbers is that as creditworthiness dropped, business fell back in tandem.

Pawnbrokers, then, seem to have been one group of traders who did not fit the model implied by writers such as Carleton and O'Flaherty. Their depictions may accurately capture the mentality of these traders, but they misjudge the impact of a crisis such as the famine on them. The evidence of the loan funds operating under the aegis of the Loan Funds Board does not fit the model either. The goal of the loan funds, a recent phenomenon when the famine struck, was the provision of small investment loans, typically of a few pounds, to artisans and traders in the towns and to smallholders and farmers with modest holdings in the countryside. Organized somewhat like modern credit unions, they relied on local knowledge and a degree of voluntary effort for their success.[67] For the loan fund banks, the famine spelled crisis and sometimes ruin. After peaking at £1.87 million ($9 million) in 1845 and falling back only slightly to £1.78 million in 1846, the aggregate value of loans issued by them plummeted to £0.86 in 1847 and £0.72 in 1848. The fall in the number of loans was commensurate. Meanwhile, the number of

TABLE 4.9
Modeling Pawnshops' Response to the Famine

Variable	Tralee	Loughrea	Gort
a	0.192 (0.37)	−0.092 (−0.17)	2.304 (4.72)
P_{t-}	−0.357 (−3.56)	−0.148 (−1.60)	−0.655 (−5.51)
R_{t-1}	0.392 (3.09)	0.159 (1.16)	0.322 (4.41)
dR_t	0.522 (4.62)	0.496 (4.84)	0.295 (4.27)
JAN	—	—	—
FEB	—	—	—
MAR	—	—	—
APR	—	—	—
MAY	—	0.084 (1.47)	0.074 (1.91)
JUN	—	0.664 (1.18)	0.098 (2.46)
JUL	−0.135 (−1.84)	0.107 (1.88)	0.095 (2.33)
AUG	−0.107 (−1.37)	−0.080 (−1.35)	−0.029 (−0.69)
SEP	−0.131 (−1.69)	−0.084 (−1.49)	−0.098 (−2.35)
OCT	−0.145 (−1.88)	−0.114 (−1.94)	—
NOV	—	—	—
n	59	71	71
Period	1844:1– 1848:11	1843:2– 1848:12	1843:2– 1848:12
F	4.62 [0.000]	5.00 [0.000]	4.72 [0.000]

Variable	New Ross	Mullingar	Rathkeale
a	−0.081 (−0.28)	0.243 (0.28)	0.587 (0.36)
P_{t-1}	−0.500 (−3.89)	−0.528 (−4.53)	−0.543 (−4.29)
R_{t-1}	0.512 (3.74)	0.505 (4.16)	0.471 (1.79)
dR_t	0.581 (5.07)	0.652 (6.74)	0.569 (2.11)
JAN	—	0.130 (2.67)	—
FEB	—	—	—
MAR	—	—	—
APR	—	—	—
MAY	—	—	—
JUN	—	—	—
JUL	—	—	—
AUG	—	−0.099 (−2.20)	−0.315 (−3.21)
SEP	—	−0.160 (−3.52)	−0.291 (−2.77)
OCT	—	−0.070 (−1.42)	−0.290 (−0.26)
NOV	—	−0.120 (−2.52)	−0.216 (−2.12)
n	59	59	59
Period	1844:2– 1848:12	1844:2– 1848:12	1844:2– 1848:12
F	9.68 [0.000]	11.92 [0.000]	7.43 [0.000]

Note: See text for explanation.

societies transmitting accounts fell from 260 in 1845 to 232 in 1847 and 178 in 1848.[68]

The famine also dealt a severe blow to Ireland's fledgling savings banks, which as in Britain, targeted the small saver. The records of a few survive. Sums deposited in the Thurles Savings Bank fell from £10,108 ($48,500) in 1845 to £2,823 in 1849, while the number of depositors fell from 868 to 337, the huge gap between withdrawals and deposits causing reserves to fall by two-thirds. The records of the smaller Carrickmacross savings bank, linked to the Shirley estate, also survive. In 1845 it had 179 depositors. Sixty-two of them held less balances of than £20 ($96), and a further eighty-three between £20 and £50. Until late 1845, when deposits totaled nearly £6,000, deposits usually had exceeded withdrawals. Thereafter withdrawals exceeded deposits in each quarter, with net withdrawals in 1846–48 totaling over £4,000. The famine put an end to the bank, which accepted no further deposits in 1849 and 1850. Aggregate data tell broadly the same story: total balances in Ireland's savings banks fell from £2.92 million in 1845 and £2.86 million in 1846 to £2.41 million in 1847 and £1.33 million in 1848.[69] Overall our findings are not robust enough to reject outright the hypothesis that the greed of millers, meal merchants, moneylenders, and the like exacerbated the famine, but they hardly support that hypothesis.

In the end it is difficult to pinpoint any major group of economic agents who benefited from the Irish famine while it lasted. Laborers, emigrants, landlords, farmers, traders, moneylenders: individuals in each category no doubt found ways of taking advantage of the crisis, but none of those categories, taken as a whole, escaped unscathed. On the other hand, most of those who survived the famine ended up being materially better off than they would have been had Ireland been spared *Phythophtera infestans*. Laborers operated in a tighter labor market, and the rise in the land-labor ratio benefited farmers. Most of those who emigrated during the famine or immediately in its wake earned more than they would have in an imaginary blight-free Ireland in the 1850s. Traders benefited from rising demand. Even landlords, buoyed by the rising demand for meat and dairy products and brutally freed of thousands of nonviable tenants, soon saw their rents recover and their tax bills decline. But that is really another story.

Chapter Five

FAMINE IN DUBLIN CITY

> The City of Dublin is in a position peculiar to itself, as
> compared with other towns of the empire. It is a metropolis
> for the poor, not for the rich.
> (Report on Dublin hospitals, 1854)

DUBLIN: THE FACE BEHIND THE GORGEOUS MASK

THE GREAT FAMINE'S demographic and economic impact differed significantly across Ireland's counties and provinces. As explained in chapter 1, variables such as measures of average income and of reliance on the potato, of the labor-land ratio, and of urbanization help explain a good deal of the intercounty variation in excess deaths.[1] The greatest horrors were reserved for rural areas in the west and south, and the familiar horrific depictions of roadside deaths and hinged coffins mostly refer to them. One does not so readily associate *that* Great Famine with Ireland's cities. Indeed it is sometimes argued or implied that the largest of them, Dublin, was largely immune from the disaster. For example, in *Why Ireland Starved* Joel Mokyr concluded that Dublin may have been the only county of the thirty-two to have been spared excess mortality. In their history of Arthur Guinness's brewery, Patrick Lynch and John Vaizey wrote:

> The areas unaffected directly by the Famine were the maritime economy centred on Dublin, Cork, and Belfast. . . . Initially, in 1848, the worst famine year, trade improved temporarily in the maritime economy because of the profits earned from the importation of corn. . . . Dublin soon recovered from the depression; by late 1848 the boom had resumed. The "scarcity of provisions" which ended in the autumn of 1847 was not sufficiently long in duration to reduce the sale of porter, and it may be doubted whether the distress among the working class was prolonged or widespread. The Great Famine had taken place as though it were a war in a neighbouring country, while Dublin was a brightly lit, comparatively well fed, slightly anxious neutral country.[2]

Lynch and Vaizey here acknowledge that rising food prices caused some hardship in what they dub "the maritime zone" in 1847, but their main emphasis is on how that zone (Dublin included) escaped the worst of both the famine and the trade cycle downswing which caused greater problems in England in 1847–48. For Lynch and Vaizey, Dublin was spared the famine because it was part of a commercial economy; its links with Liverpool and London meant much more to it than its links with Galway or Cork.

A little historical context is necessary. In the mid-eighteenth century, Dublin city contained about 130,000 people, making it a major city by European standards[3] and bigger than any city in Britain except London. Dublin's population had more than doubled since 1700, but most people continued to live in the overcrowded, disease-ridden old city.[4] Both the pace of population growth and congestion seem to have declined somewhat in the second half of the eighteenth century. The Reverend James Whitelaw, who surveyed Dublin meticulously in 1798 and counted 180,000 inhabitants (excluding military personnel), claimed that "a great number of houses, that once teemed with population, are no longer to be found." Armed with the four-sheet map of Dublin produced by London cartographer John Rocque in 1756, Whitelaw had sought out certain courts and backyard dwellings, but found them mostly in decay or converted into warehouses. Whitelaw's account of conditions in the Dublin slums in the 1800s nevertheless conveys the impression of acute overcrowding:

> In the ancient parts of this city, the streets are, with a few exceptions, generally narrow, the houses crowded together, and the reres, or back-yards, of very small extent. Of these streets, a few are the residence of the upper class of shop-keepers, and other engaged in trade; but a far greater proportion of them, with their numerous lanes and alleys, are occupied by working manufacturers, by petty shop-keepers, the labouring poor, and beggars, crowded together, to a degree distressing to humanity. A single apartment, in one of these truly wretched habitations, rates from one to two shillings per week; and, to lighten this rent, two, three, and even four families, become joint tenants. As I was usually out at very early hours on the survey, I have frequently surprized from ten to sixteen persons, of all ages and sexes, in a room, not fifteen feet square, stretched on a wad of filthy straw, swarming with vermin, and without any covering, save the wretched rags that constituted their wearing apparel. . . . The crowded population, wherever it obtains, is almost universally accompanied by a very serious evil; a degree of filth and stench inconceivable, except by those who have visited those scenes of wretchedness.[5]

The Act of Union of 1800 is frequently held to have hurt Dublin by depriving it of the business and prestige associated with the College Green parliament. The trend in population growth does not bear this out: Dublin grew faster in the two decades after 1800 than in the two decades before it. The rate of growth then declined from 0.9 percent in 1798–1821 to 0.6 percent in 1821–35, and the population of Dublin

TABLE 5.1
The Population of Dublin in 1841 and 1851

Ward	Area (acres)	Valuation (£)	Pop. 1841	Pop. 1851	Pop. Change (%)
NORTH					
Arran Quay	540	29,041	25,610	30,148	17.7
Inns Quay	218	34,592	18,331	21,533	17.5
Mountjoy	217	34,296	13,502	14,305	5.9
North City	77	38,155	16,410	15,307	−6.7
North Dock	509	40,564	12,574	17,211	36.9
Rotundo	136	39,707	10,638	11,019	3.6
Total	1,697	216,355	97,065	109,523	12.8
SOUTH					
Fitzwilliam	203	38,770	6,918	8,825	27.6
Mansion House	115	35,199	11,507	12,475	8.4
Merchants Quay	313	23,672	23,616	24,907	5.5
Royal Exchange	71	40,547	14,557	14,137	−2.9
South City	51	44,547	10,705	10,101	−5.6
South Dock	263	38,212	9,574	14,156	47.9
Trinity	152	40,306	14,034	15,955	13.7
Ushers Quay	571	30,841	22,264	24,931	12.0
Wood Quay	157	23,112	22,486	23,351	3.8
Total	1,896	315,206	135,661	148,838	9.7
Total Dublin	3,593	531,726	232,726	258,361	11.0

Source: Derived from the 1851 Census.

city and county combined declined between 1831 and 1841. When the famine struck Dublin, its inner suburbs had a population of about 240,000 souls, or about 3 percent of the island's total.[6] It still remained the island's major port. The relative importance of migration, births, and deaths in determining Dublin's pre-famine demography remains to be discovered, but information on the ages of first-time mothers in the Rotunda lying-in hospital suggests that an increase in the mean age at first marriage was partly responsible for the shift. Dublin's occupational profile on the eve of the famine reflected the city's commercial and metropolitan role. Though it could boast several considerable manufacturing concerns in the 1840s, traditional occupations dominated and the Industrial Revolution had failed to make a lasting impact there.

Dublin's poor continued to be concentrated in the dilapidated and congested old city. Congestion was greatest in the inner city wards of North City and South City, where density exceeded two hundred people per acre (see table 5.1), rivaling the levels achieved in London's slums.

In the Liberties to the south and west of the city's core, the workhouses and attics of former artisans were converted into rack-rented housing accommodation. Elsewhere houses on formerly fashionable streets were converted into tenements. On the eve of the famine, one observer, with some honest exaggeration, might still describe Dublin as "notoriously the worst sewered, lighted, cleaned, and watered city in the empire."[7] Some of that squalor would persist after the famine. In the early 1860s a City Hall official spoke of the housing of Dublin's poor in terms reminiscent of Whitelaw's depiction of the Liberties six decades earlier or Thomas Willis's account of his own northside parish of St. Michan's in the 1840s:

> We may safely venture upon the average of eight persons to each house, which gives us 64,000 people out of a population of 249,733, 50,000 at least of whom reside in a fetid and poisonous atmosphere. The dwellings of the poor are chiefly confined to about 450 lanes, courts, and alleys, and about sixty streets. The worst districts are the Liberties on the south, and the parish of St. Michan on the north side of the city. . . . The entrance to the courts is very narrow—a sort of great stench valve, or over-ground sewer. As a general rule, there is a green slimy steam oozing from a surcharged and choked-up cess-pool, through which the visitor is compelled to wade.[8]

Still, comparing data on inhabited houses and population parish by parish in the 1821 and 1841 censuses suggests that overcrowding was, if anything, slightly less by the latter date.

In pre-famine Ireland it was the poverty of western counties like Mayo and Clare, not Dublin, that struck foreign observers most. Yet if Dublin poverty had more in common with that of, say, the East End of London than the west of Ireland, the advantage over their rural compatriots did not rest unambiguously with the poor of Dublin. The Dublin poor were probably less well fed and less healthy than country people, and in the eighteenth and nineteenth centuries they lived short and harsh lives.[9]

In early modern Europe, subsistence crises tended to kill more people in the cities than in the countryside.[10] In eighteenth- and early nineteenth-century Ireland, remote rural areas were most likely to be affected. However, outbreaks of famine fever were nothing new or unusual in Dublin. In 1801 "the sufferings of the poor. . . and the dangers to which the higher or wealthier classes of society were consequently exposed" prompted a number of "reflecting philanthropists" to take action. The philanthropists, who included banker John David La Touche, Arthur Guinness Senior, and Quaker merchant Samuel Bewley, formed a committee that would purchase a site ("the orchard of the widow Donnelly") for a new fever hospital on the southwestern outskirts of the city. The site was on Cork Street, across the road from the Society of Friends burial ground. The hospital, two separate but linked plain three-story buildings with 120 beds, opened its doors to patients in May 1804. Its capacity would increase to 220 beds a decade later, and additional temporary accommodation was improvised more than once in times of crisis.

The Cork Street Fever Hospital's annual reports convey the impression of recurring crises in the city. In 1810 a formidable and extensive fever created considerable panic, and in 1814 excess mortality was such that eighty funerals took place on a single Sunday. Data on the numbers admitted to, and dying in, the fever hospital in 1817–19, in 1822, and in 1826 (in particular) suggest that those too were crisis years in Dublin. In the early 1840s annual admissions averaged about twenty-five hundred and deaths about two hundred.[11] Given such a track record it is inconceivable that Dublin should have been untouched by the famine.

In effect, the famine could have affected ordinary people in a city like Dublin in two distinct ways. First, it could have done so by reducing the purchasing power or entitlements of Dubliners to the food produced outside the city. The potato failure certainly had an impact on the terms of trade facing urban dwellers. Yet though Dublin, like all Irish towns, had its potato markets and its market gardens, the failure was clearly less of a problem for Dubliners than for those living in more potato-dependent rural areas. Dubliners did not starve like Mayomen or Cork-women. Nonetheless, because of Dublin's role as a service and distribution center, the reduced purchasing power of people living outside Dublin must have had an impact on business in the city. Migration offered a second transmission mechanism; the famine could have affected Dublin as an externality, that is, as an event occurring outside the city but making its impact through migration into Dublin and the consequent the spread of infectious diseases such as typhoid fever. This mechanism was a classic one in the history of famines; throughout Europe in 1740–41, for instance, epidemics were "inescapably tied to the wave of itinerant vagrants and beggars who crowded into the towns."[12]

Let us take first the immunity of the so-called maritime economy. Direct evidence on short-term fluctuations in economic activity in that economy in the 1840s is not so plentiful. However, almost by definition, a good guide would be the trend in bank-note circulation and bank profits. These hardly support the claim that the maritime zone escaped lightly in the late 1840s. As noted in chapter 4, Irish bank-note circulation plummeted during the famine. Figure 5.1 traces the value of the stock of the Hibernian Bank and the Royal Bank of Ireland—two banks catering to an almost exclusively Dublin clientele in these years—and the Bank of Ireland, Ireland's quasi-central bank, in the 1840s. All three

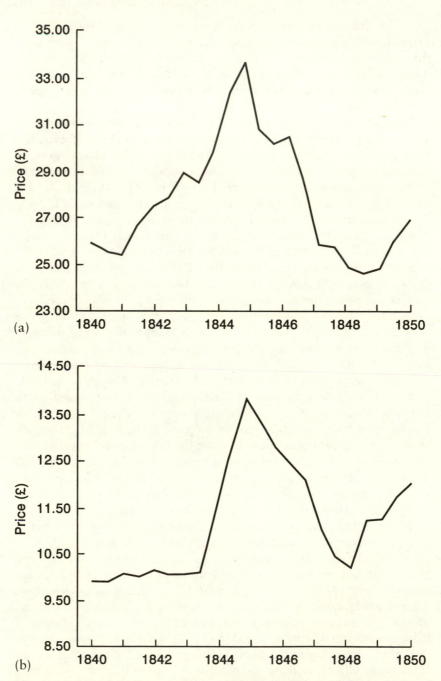

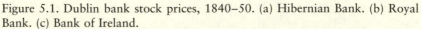

Figure 5.1. Dublin bank stock prices, 1840–50. (a) Hibernian Bank. (b) Royal Bank. (c) Bank of Ireland.

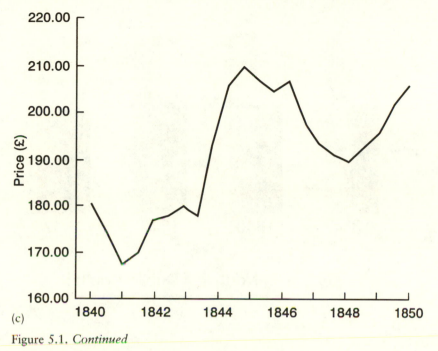

(c)

Figure 5.1. *Continued*

show the effects of the famine. The records of a humbler lending institution already encountered in chapter 4—the pawnshop—are also telling. That the rise in pledges was faster outside Dublin in 1844–46 is partly a reflection of the more complete diffusion of the pawnshop in the metropolis before the famine. But the numbers reveal a drop both in the total number of pledges accepted in Dublin and in the average size of a pledge in 1847 (fig. 5.2). The drop in pledging in Dublin in 1847 (19.7 percent) was far less than for Ireland as a whole (32.7 percent), but it was still significant, reflecting reductions in the supply of both loans and pledgeable goods. Taken together, the banking and pawnbroking numbers show that the Irish subsistence and maritime economies—if that distinction is insisted on—were much more interdependent that Lynch and Vaizey admit.

The trend in the price of bread in Dublin in the mid- and late 1840s provides some indication of the trend in entitlements. Dublin was a bread-eating as much as a potato-eating city: in 1841 the city had ten flour merchants and over a thousand bakers and confectioners. Since money wages are unlikely to have risen, the hefty rise in the price of a 4-pound loaf—from 7d (14 cents) in 1844–45 to 7.5d in 1846 and 9.5d in 1847—must have hurt the entitlements of the Dublin poor. However,

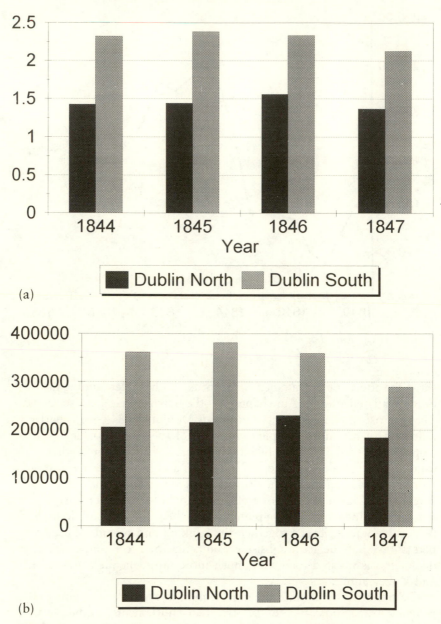

Figure 5.2. Pawnbroking and the famine in Dublin, 1844–47. (a) Articles pawned, in millions. (b) Sums lent, in pounds. (c) Average sum lent, in pence.

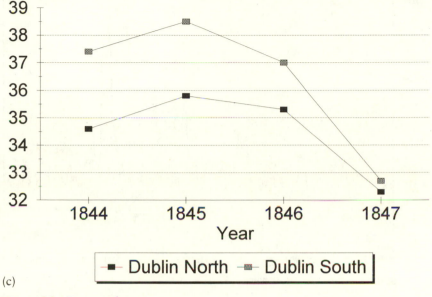

(c)

Figure 5.2. *Continued*

the price fell back to 8d in 1848 and 5d (inferior quality) to 6.5d (best quality) in 1849. Moreover, the *proportionate* rise in the price of bread between 1844–45 and 1847 was dwarfed by the rises occurring in 1799–1800 and 1815–17, and the 1845–47 rise in London was greater than that in Dublin. Finally, the rise in the price of bread was also small compared to the rise in potato prices.[13] In sum, in Dublin the shock to the entitlements of the poor was much less in the countryside.

FAMINE MORTALITY IN DUBLIN

The famine did not last as long in Dublin as in rural Ireland, but it was quite intense for some months. According to a Dublin physician, the very lowest estimate of the number contracting fever in Dublin was forty thousand. The pressure peaked in June 1847, and then declined gradually; by February 1848, the epidemic may be said to have ceased.[14] Several sources — burial records, censal evidence, religious records, poor-law registers — imply excess mortality in Dublin during the famine. On 13 February 1847 the *Dublin Evening Post* reported that burials in two of the city's cemeteries (Glasnevin and Golden Bridge) had risen by one-third between January 1846 and January 1847, while burials in pauper plots had almost doubled. Detailed information on burials in

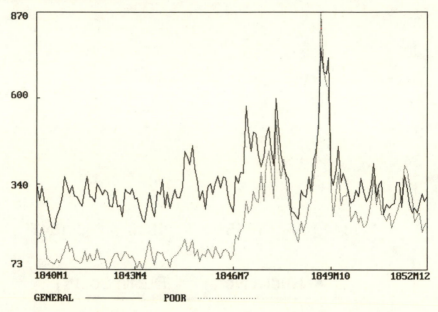

Figure 5.3. Numbers of monthly Glasnevin burials, 1840–52.

Glasnevin's Prospect Cemetery survive. Its registers distinguish between burials in paid plots and pauper burials for those who lacked the funds for a plot. Figure 5.3 presents a summary statement of the trend in both categories. The implied differential impact of the famine is striking, but clearly both groups experienced excess mortality in 1847. Also noteworthy is the huge increase in deaths during the short-lived cholera epidemic of 1849. Censal returns show that in the city as a whole, burials rose from an annual average of 6,758 in 1839–41 to 9,150 in 1841–51. If half the excess was attributable to the famine, then this would mean about 20,000 out of, say, 300,000 — a small fraction of aggregate mortality, and small relative to other places, but hardly negligible, either.

William Wilde's Tables of Death also indicate excess mortality in Dublin. These tables suffer from well-known weaknesses of misreporting and underrecording (see chapter 3), but they are reliable enough to carry the points being made here. Figure 5.4 describes reported deaths from starvation, fever, and dysentery per ten thousand population in four counties: Tyrone, Cavan, Mayo, and Dublin during the 1840s. While they indicate that few died of starvation in Dublin during the famine, they also show that the incidence of fever and dysentery, higher in Dublin than in the countryside in normal times, rose dramatically there in 1846 and 1847. By 1848 — almost as bad a year for excess mortality as 1847 in badly hit counties such as Mayo and Cavan—the worst seemed to be over in Dublin. However, a serious cholera epidemic brought further panic and crisis to the city for a few months in late 1848 and early 1849. Wilde also provides data on deaths in work-houses and fever hospitals from famine-related diseases. These recorded over four thousand people dying of fever in the city's fever hospitals, jails, and charitable institutions, and another two thousand succumbing to dysentery or diarrhea in the city workhouses.[15]

The Tables of Death also include an abstract of all deaths occurring during the previous decade, on which inquests were held.[16] Most deaths by starvation or by exposure and cold were famine-linked, since they occurred in 1846 and subsequently. Thirty-nine of the all-Ireland total of 2,148 deaths deemed to have been from starvation took place in Dublin city and county, and twelve of the total of 805 deaths were from exposure. Had deaths been distributed proportionate to population throughout the island, Dublin's shares would have been about three times the actual level—another indication that while Dublin escaped lightly, it did not escape scot-free.

Other evidence also suggests that Dublin suffered in this period. For poor-relief purposes the city was divided in two by the Liffey.[17] By the end of 1846 nearly half of the two thousand inmates in the South Dub-lin Union were ill, mostly from dysentery and fever of a very fatal form. That did not prevent the guardians of the North Dublin Union from accusing their southside colleagues of turning people away and turning others out prematurely, and in late 1846 and early 1847 several city parishes formed committees to set up soup kitchens. In the urban part of the South Dublin Union the rate per pound struck on 17 June 1847 was three times that struck in early 1846; north of the Liffey the rise over roughly the same period was even steeper, from 6d (12 cents) to 20d.[18] An editorial in *The Freeman's Journal* (4 January 1847) noted:

> To the poor and unfriended the crowded city is as a desolate wilderness. They are surrounded, it is true, by human beings enjoying, perhaps, wealth and comfort, and luxury, but they might as well be surrounded by so many corpses. . . . We find that the citizens of Dublin have a more intimate knowl-edge of the want, and misery, and suffering of the cottier population of Skib-bereen, of Mayo, and of Clare, than they have of the more appalling destitu-tion of the hundreds of human beings who are huddled together in the lodging houses of Dublin. Be it our task to inform them of the misery that surrounds their happy and luxurious homes. We have assumed a holy work.

In early January 1847 a police report describes several attacks on bakers' shops and bread carts, some successful: "men from the country" seem to have been responsible.[19] Around the same time, a parish relief

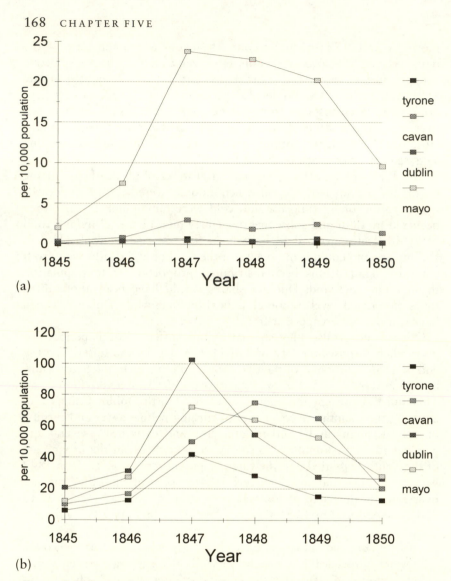

(a)

(b)

Figure 5.4. Comparing reported deaths from (a) starvation, (b) fever, and (c) dysentery in Tyrone, Cavan, Mayo, and Dublin counties, 1845–50 (per ten thousand population).

officer, overwhelmed, according to the *Freeman's Journal*, by the misery he witnessed, was driven to suicide. A month later, the deaths in quick succession of John and Ellen Mulherin, a married couple living in squalid conditions in a yard of a house at 6 Hendrick Street (in the northwest of the city, between Blackhall Place and Smithfield), caused a stir in the neighborhood. The Mulherins' case is interesting, since

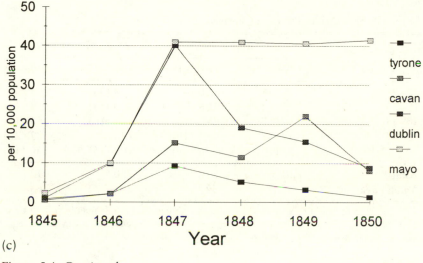

(c)

Figure 5.4. *Continued*

according to the police it was the first case of that kind in Dublin. A coroner's jury returned a verdict of deaths by destitution on the couple, who had fled from immediate death by famine in Leitrim some months previously, bringing their four children with them. Bad weather had prevented John Mulherin from taking up a job in Cabra; he had been fasting several days when he died, and those responsible for relief in the local parish (St. Paul's) were evidently distressed and embarrassed by the deaths.[20] The jury exonerated St. Paul's, but took the opportunity to plead for an improvement in the nutritional content of soup kitchen fare generally.[21] Conditions worsened in the city in early 1847.[22]

Morbidity and mortality in Dublin rose during the famine. But perhaps those who died were, like the Mulherins, famished famine immigrants?[23] Were Dubliners largely immune, as Lynch and Vaizey claimed? Burial data are silent on this aspect, but another demographic source, parish register data, indicates that the crisis was not confined to immigrants. Canon law obliged Catholic parishes to record marriages and baptisms, but not burials. However, the registers of the established Protestant church contain some useful data. Just before the famine, about one-fifth of Dublin's inhabitants were Protestants. Protestants dominated its professional and business community, but the city also contained many thousands of working-class Protestants. Anglican parish registers, many of which survive, allow extra insight into how Dubliners fared during the famine.[24] The registers of the established church tend to be better kept and more detailed than Catholic registers. Because they

TABLE 5.2
Burials in Five Dublin Protestant Parishes in the 1840s

Age Group	Males		Females	
	1844–45	*1846–48*	*1844–45*	*1846–48*
0–9	276 (45)	330 (40)	258 (35)	293 (32)
10–29	82 (13)	116 (14)	100 (14)	132 (14)
30–49	106 (17)	142 (17)	120 (16)	155 (17)
50–69	95 (15)	154 (19)	143 (20)	182 (20)
70+	61 (10)	76 (9)	109 (15)	150 (16)
Total	620	818	730	912
Annual average	197	329	234	365

Notes: Percentages in parentheses. These cross-tabulations exclude mainly stillborn and deserted infants and a few unidentified strangers whose ages were not given in the registers. St. Peter's data refer to 1844–45 and 1846–47 only.

include burials, and usually note the ages of the deceased, a sense of the pattern of mortality by age and gender may be inferred from them. Some of the records in the registers of five Dublin parishes—St. Peter's, St. Catherine's, St. Luke's, St. Mark's, and St. Mary's—are summarized in table 5.2. St. Catherine's and St. Luke's were southside parishes with substantial working-class Protestant populations; the socioeconomic composition of St. Peter's, a huge parish, was more mixed, but its registers show similar patterns to St. Catherine's and St. Luke's. Before the famine, female burials outnumbered male in all three, a reflection of the female preponderance in these parishes' populations (58 percent in St. Peter's, 53 percent in St. Catherine's, 57 percent in St. Luke's). A few more common features emerge during the famine period. First, mortality rose in all three parishes at the height of the crisis, with St. Catherine's being least affected. In St. Peter's and St. Luke's, mortality almost doubled between 1844–45 and 1846–47. Second, as already noted in chapter 3, males seem to have been worse hit than females—a common demographic feature of subsistence crises in history. Proportionately, the very young seem not to have been so badly hit. A decline in the number of births might partly account for this, though at least in the case of the St. Luke's registers there is a strong suspicion of a significant proportion of infant deaths going unrecorded. The mortality data in St. Luke's during the famine years also include many inmates of Cork Street Fever Hospital; whether many or most of those unfortunates had lived in the parish beforehand is unclear. Otherwise, across these three parishes the incidence by age differed. In the largely working-class parish of St. Mark's (which incorporated the south docks area) and the more affluent St. Mary's, the effects of the crisis are less evident. In St. Mary's the parish vestry meeting of 6 April 1847 voted for the appointment of "a fit and proper person to inspect the poor deceased in this parish so as they may be provided with coffins and interment also to inspect all nuisances and report the same to the officer of health who shall define his duties." The famine also increased mortality in the Religious Society of Friends. The number of burials in the Society's Cork Street Cemetery averaged thirteen or fourteen in 1841–46 and 1851–55, but twenty-five in 1847–51.[25]

While Catholic registers are unhelpful on the issue of mortality, they reflect the famine in other ways. The quality of Dublin registers, where baptisms reflect births with a lag of a few days, is generally good. Figure 5.5 describes trends in the large Catholic parish of St. Andrew's, Westland Row, whose registers seem to have been well kept in this period. St. Andrew's was located on the less impoverished southeast side of the city. Its registers show that both marriages and baptisms were subject to strong seasonal patterns; marriages were few in March (Lent) and December (Advent), and baptisms peaked in the spring. Month-to-month movements were somewhat erratic, but showing the data in six-monthly blocks reveals that typically baptisms were more frequent in the first half of the year than the second; for the years indicated here, only in 1848 was that not so in Westland Row. Also important are the sharp declines in the first half and, especially, in the second half of 1847. What caused the falling off in births? Experience elsewhere suggests that a reduction in fertility induced by hunger is the most plausible explanation. The data thus imply that in Westland Row privation must have set in about mid-1846, with recovery by mid-1847. The number of marriages in Westland Row also dropped significantly (from an average of 352 in 1843–46 to 294 in 1847).

Other registers tell slightly different stories. In St. Michan's on the north side, the second half of 1847 and the first half of 1848 saw a drop of about one-quarter in the number of baptisms. In the rural parish of Rathfarnam, the drop over the same twelve-month period was even greater—about one-third. In St. Audeon's parish (about one-tenth the size of Westland Row), the number of baptisms fell heavily in 1848 and had not recovered by 1850. In St. Michael and John's, the registers suggest a slight dip in 1847, but they are in very poor condition and any count must be approximate. Overall, the parish registers imply that the number of baptisms was affected most in late 1847 and early 1848. This suggests that privation was greatest in early and mid-1847 in Dublin. Comparison with other parish register data provides a reminder that Dublin escaped lightly compared to other parts of the country. Registers showing declines of 30–50 percent in births in 1847 and 1848 are not unusual.[26]

Few people literally starved in Dublin in the 1840s. But as noted

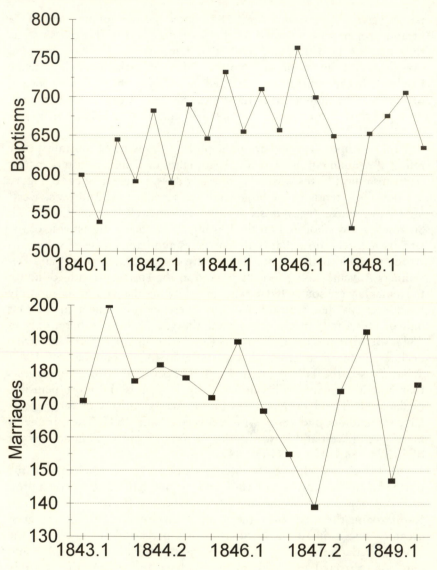

Figure 5.5. Baptisms (a) and marriages (b) in St. Andrew's, Westland Row, 1840–49.

earlier, in the past rural subsistence crises had often affected the metropolis indirectly, through contagious fevers arising from immigration. That had happened in the early 1800s and again in 1817–19, when "the fever entered the city by the great avenues leading from the north and south, particularly the former . . . propagated by 5000 beggars, who first conveyed the contagion from street to street."[27] Dublin, resembling a gigantic refugee camp during the famine years,[28] could hardly have escaped a similar fate then. As late as the spring of 1850 the Liberties were crowded with fever-stricken "*strangers* from different parts of the country, especially Mayo, Galway, and other western counties . . . all presented the same listless, stupid, care-worn aspect, and the same miserable squalid appearance." One-third of the patients in the Cork Street Fever Hospital in early March 1850 "consisted of persons none of whom had been more than four or five months resident in Dublin."[29]

The famine reduced the populations of most smaller Irish towns, the main exceptions being those containing workhouses. Bigger towns and cities tended to attract country people seeking relief, however, and the populations of several (e.g., Galway, Cork, Limerick) rose between 1841 and 1851. Dublin's population grew more than most, from 232,726 to 258,361, or by 11 percent, between 1841 and 1851. The increase was marginally greater north of the Liffey than on the south side and, on the surface at least, was accompanied by an increase in congestion in the poorer areas: the correlation between proportionate population growth and 1841 population density across the city's fifteen electoral wards was +0.846. Yet the increases were greatest in North Dock, South Dock, and in Fitzwilliam, three of the more prosperous wards in terms of valuation per capita. The 1851 total includes 11,250 inmates of public institutions such as workhouses and prisons. If they are left out of the reckoning, the old congested inner city probably gained very little population in the famine decade. The occupational profile of the city was also affected by the famine. However, some of the shift in women's work had less to do with the famine than with the decline of textile spinning.

As figure 5.6, based on information about the birthplaces of the capital's population in 1841, 1851, and 1861 (in percentages), implies, the huge rise in 1851 in the proportion of Dublin residents born elsewhere in Ireland was largely the product of famine immigration. The immigration stretched the facilities offered by the city's relief institutions to the limit. The low starvation rate explains why starving country people headed for the city, but the steep rise in reported dysentery and fever deaths in Dublin in 1847 followed in their wake. Immigration was probably largely responsible for the rise in deaths from typhoid fever.

The rest of this chapter relies for the most part on the records of some well-known and not so well-known Dublin public institutions for further insight into the workings of the famine in the city. But before turning to them, let us briefly consider another source of impressions of Dublin during the famine years. Several foreign travelers have left eye-

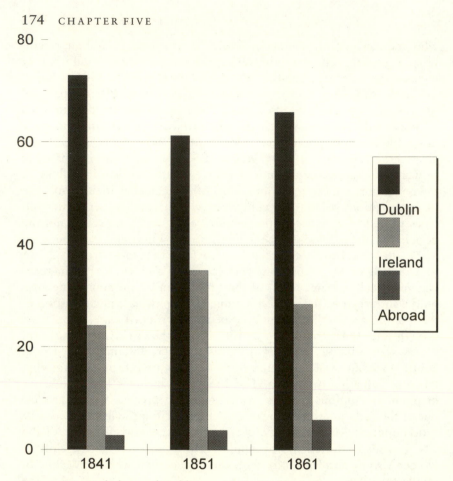

Figure 5.6. Birthplaces of Dubliners, 1841–61. Vertical numbers indicate percent of total.

witness accounts of Ireland during the famine, and most of them passed through Dublin. A rich source, surely, on the famine in the metropolis? Yes and no. One drawback is that though most accounts contain descriptions of misery, dirt, and begging, such descriptions were also the stock in trade of pre-famine travelers. As Alexander Somerville noted, the hordes of beggars he saw in Dublin's streets in January 1847 have always abounded in Ireland. Only when an extra layer of observation is added, such as that provided by eccentric American evangelist Asenath Nicholson, are they revealing. Any travel writer visiting Ireland before the famine might have described "the dreadful importuning, falling upon their knees," but the "lasping their *emaciated* hands," and the "*glaring* eyes fixed upon me, [which] were quite too much" bespeak famine, and are pure Nicholson. Again Lord John Manner's description of unwashed barefooted children puddling about in the black slime in the shadow of Christ Church in August 1846 might have been taken out of Whitelaw or Willis, but the added information that "their potatoes, most of them bad, were selling for a shilling a stone" reflects famine conditions.[30]

A second problem is that though most travelers began their tours in Dublin, they did not stay there long; and those who lingered lacked comparative perspective. Nevertheless, John East, traveling from Kingstown to Dublin and from there on to Drogheda in April 1847, usefully admitted noting so many symptoms of national wealth and prosperity as to make him suspicious of previous reports from Ireland. And Nicholson remarked that cases of death were not so common in Dublin as in many cities. Yet the first sign of starvation she saw was in Kingstown, a man "emaciated to the last degree; he was tall, his eyes prominent, his skin shrivelled, his manner cringing and childlike; and the impression then and there made never has nor ever can be effaced." Asenath Nicholson, an astute observer, had the common touch and sympathized with the poor; and she found that during the famine the "comfortable classes" of Dublin, "whatever hospitality they might manifest towards guests and visitors, had never troubled themselves by looking into the real home wants of the suffering poor."[31]

AN INSTITUTIONAL PERSPECTIVE

The Rotunda

The first of the institutions with some famine records is the Dublin Hospital for Poor Lying-In Women, or the Rotunda, for a century previously a haven for Dublin working-class mothers-to-be. Like most of Dublin's charity hospitals, the Lying-in Hospital had originally been located in the city's south side, on what would later become South George's Street; it had moved across the Liffey to its present location on Parnell Square in 1758. Mothers typically spent about a week in the hospital after giving birth (compared to a day or two in the United States and two or three days in the United Kingdom today). The proportion of Rotunda infants dying in that week after birth had been very high indeed at first—one in five in the 1760s—so high that the early history of the hospital could hardly be deemed a success. According to one expert, for some decades "the hospital instead of answering the original intention of its benevolent founder viz. the saving human lives, had quite a contrary effect."[32] By the 1790s, however, the mortality rate was down to 35.6 per thousand and to 8.8 per thousand by 1830–37.

TABLE 5.3
Inferring Child Mortality, c. 1820–50

Number Alive	1824	1845–47	1847–49
Second-time mothers			
0	20 (3.9)	38 (3.7)	26 (3.7)
1	222 (43.3)	426 (41.2)	314 (45.1)
2	271 (52.8)	571 (55.2)	356 (51.1)
Third-time mothers			
0	10 (3.0)	25 (3.7)	20 (4.1)
1	84 (25.4)	119 (18.4)	106 (21.5)
2	138 (41.7)	270 (41.8)	356 (41.1)
3	99 (29.9)	232 (35.9)	165 (33.4)

Note: Percentages in parentheses.

Mothers died in numbers too, particularly when puerperal fever struck. The data have been periodically tabulated by the Rotunda's historians.[33]

For a relatively short period in its history—a period that straddles the famine—the records also permit us to infer something about deaths outside the hospital.[34] Between the 1820s and the 1840s, the ward-books contain details for each mother of previous births and the proportion surviving. These data give some impression of child mortality during a difficult period for Dublin's poor. The mortality rate is not observed directly. It can only be inferred, on certain simplifying assumptions, but it turns out to have been very high indeed.[35] Table 5.3 reports the results of an analysis of information given in the ward books about mothers giving birth for the second and third time. This suggests some improvement in conditions between 1824 and 1845–47, but carrying the comparison through the famine years suggests a deterioration between 1845–47 and 1847–49. Note in particular the drop in the proportion of mothers with all children surviving between 1845–47 and 1847–49. Mothers suffered too, particularly in 1847. Most maternal deaths were diagnosed to puerperal peritonitis. If peritonitis was indeed the cause, then, strictly speaking, they need not have been linked to the famine. Puerperal peritonitis, which would continue to prove quite a scourge in the Rotunda in the 1850s and 1860s, was due to lax hygiene on the part of medical personnel. However, the authorities may well have mistaken famine fever for peritonitis since, as the Master noted in the ward-book at the end of 1847, "the disease was not confined to the Hospital as some of the women attended at their own homes were attacked and rapidly sunk with all the symptoms of fever upon them."[36]

The hospital registers also show the effect of the famine, though not markedly. Thus of almost forty-four hundred women giving birth in

1843–44, thirty-six died. Of about four thousand giving birth in 1847–48, seventy-eight died. Forty-two children died in the hospital in 1843–44, forty-seven in 1847–48. The incidence of stillbirths was, if anything, lower during 1847 and 1848. (Using 1845 for comparison purposes would be misleading since there was a serious outbreak of puerperal fever in March 1845, killing nine women and forcing the hospital to shut its doors for two weeks.)

Interestingly enough, however, the Rotunda was unaffected in another sense: it remained overwhelmingly a haven for Dublin mothers during the famine. The records bear no trace of a rise in the share of mothers from the country (always a tiny fraction). Perhaps this was because pregnant women were less likely to travel, but perhaps also it was immigrant mothers were consigned to the workhouse.

What of the total number of births? A reduction in the number of births invariably follows famines, since severe hunger reduces both the capacity and willingness to reproduce. What happened in Dublin during the famine? The records of the Rotunda are a tempting guide, given their wide coverage and focus on those most at risk. They are also a treacherous source, given that the hospital always operated close to capacity in normal times.

History tells us that subsistence crises tended to reduce the marriage rate. Parish register data imply that the famine also did so in Ireland. Now, if those most likely to postpone marriage were the young, a rise in the mean age at marriage would have resulted. From the Rotunda ward-books we can calculate the mean age of first-time mothers from the early 1810s on. The estimates are crude averages: I have not attempted to sort out married and single mothers. However, it is fair to assume that the age at marriage would have been about a year less than the age at first birth. Early marriage is indicated, but with signs too of a significant rise between the 1810s and the mid-1840s. However, the average was unaffected by the famine, remaining at just over twenty-four years between 1845 and 1848.

In sum, while the rise in Rotunda perinatal, maternal, and child mortality rates, and the reduction in the number of admissions, might be put down to the famine, the Lying-In Hospital nevertheless seems to have been insulated somehow from the worst of the famine.[37] Not so the next two institutions.

Cork Street Fever Hospital

When famine fever struck in early 1847, the pressure put on the city's accommodations for fever patients was enormous for a time. Relatives of those stricken by fever would go from hospital to hospital seeking a place for them, sometimes in vain. Many of those taken in were released too soon, "shadows in human form, in a state of the greatest debility," and relapsing fever was common.[38]

Institutions such as the Cork Street Fever Hospital bore the brunt of the pressure. As noted earlier, this hospital was founded in 1804 on an open three-acre site at the south end of Cork Street.[39] Interestingly enough, there was nothing remarkable about either admissions or deaths at the Fever Hospital during 1845 or for most of 1846. The fever of 1846 was "on the whole low, often typhoid; consequently it did bear depletion." However, as the number of cases began to mount in late 1846, the Hospital Board sought advice from its physicians as to whether the fever in Dublin was contagious or merely arising from dysentery. In January 1847 tents were erected for an extra two hundred patients, and fever patients were placed in them on the grounds that they were less affected by the elements than those suffering from dysentery. The pressure for space continued to mount, and "crowds of applicants constantly beset the gates." Four long wooden felt-roofed sheds, 140 feet long by 20 feet wide and 7.5 feet high, were erected on the grounds in May at a cost of £1,060. These contained 280 beds; the mortality rate in the sheds would prove higher than in the hospital itself. Meanwhile, temporary accommodations were also erected by the two city poor-law unions and others (including a massive temporary hospital in Kilmainham that could hold 990 people at a time). The city's sheds and hospitals admitted 14,766 patients in all during the peak month of March 1847.

Cork Street Fever Hospital took in 4,874 fever cases in 1847, compared to 4,555 in 1846 and 2,954 between 1 April 1845 and 31 March 1846; between 1847 and 1850 admissions totaled 14,722. An unknown proportion were relapses. The crisis in Dublin was exacerbated by arrivals from the countryside, who "overcrowded the lower class of lodging house in the city, and thus spreading contagion."[40]

The Westmoreland Lock Hospital

The beginnings of the Westmoreland Lock Hospital may be traced back to the 1750s. Originally located south of the city in Donnybrook, "the Lock" switched sites with the Hospital for Incurables on Townsend Street in 1792. This "monument of moral degradation" continued to operate into the 1950s under the name of the Hospital of St. Margaret of Cortona. The building was demolished in 1955. Though the Lock originally housed both male and female victims of venereal diseases, from about 1820 on it catered exclusively to females.[41] It was state supported from the outset, receiving a grant of £2,500 a year in the 1840s. In the nineteenth century nearly all of the Lock's inmates were prostitutes. In their brief but useful account of the Lock in the 1800s, historians Warburton, Whitelaw, and Walsh put the "more extensive propagation of the venereal disease" and the "increased profligacy of manners amongst the lower order of females" down to the large military presence in the capital. Nearly half a century later, Under-Secretary Thomas Larcom linked a demand for continued public support for the Lock Hospital to Dublin's having "the largest garrison of the British army at home or in the colonies." Another sixty years later the Lock's physician could infer the floating population of prostitutes in Dublin — about one thousand — from the Lock's intake.[42]

The Lock Hospital was a rough place, reluctantly entered. Typically, inmates submitted to treatment (usually mercury treatment) and recuperation for 2–3 months, though some absconded prematurely and others were sent out for bad conduct (fighting, swearing, starting fires, breaking windows, and so on) or for refusing to undergo medical treatment. Dosages of mercury provided respite, but of course were very damaging to health in the long run. After the cure, places were found for some of the patients in one or the other of the many "magdalene" asylums in the city. A few proceeded to the Lying-In Hospital, to the poor house, to Cork Street Fever Hospital, or back to the care of relatives. The destination of the great majority is unknown, though the high incidence of repeat cases implies that it was back on the streets. The Lock's visitors' book suggests that the hospital was clean and tidy. The visitors normally dropped in several times a year. On 1 August 1843 visitor Ninian Crawford found "the patients out of bed were at work, and in most of the wards one reading the Bible for the others." On 6 March 1847 more of the patients were in bed than usual.

The Lock's inmates were typically young and single. Women who became prostitutes "ceased being virtuous" at an early age, and the work span of the average prostitute was short, 8–10 years. In 1842–45, for example, three-quarters of the Lock's inmates were aged between seventeen and twenty-five years. Most of them had been born in Dublin or bordering counties or had been living there. Tables 5.4 and 5.5 set out the details from the Lock's registry of patients admitted before, during, and after the famine. Before the famine the Lock Hospital catered overwhelmingly to women from Dublin and its immediate hinterland. The famine changed this radically. Despite capacity problems — it could accommodate slightly over a hundred inmates at any time — the Lock's annual intake rose from an average of 744 in 1842–47 to a thousand in 1848–52. The average then fell off to 488 in 1853–56.

Perhaps it is not too farfetched to see the effect of the famine also in the age composition of the inmates. There was a reduction in the average age and a rise in the proportions of very young women. The in-

TABLE 5.4
Where the Lock Women Had Come From, 1842–69 (in percentages)

Region	1842–43	1844–45	1846	1847–48	1849–50	1853	1855–56	1860–69
Dublin	77.4	83.0	55.4	47.0	39.8	30.6	43.4	50.2
Hinterland*	10.1	7.3	16.0	18.0	18.7	19.7	17.7	15.5
Other Leinster	6.3	4.9	12.0	16.0	20.4	23.8	17.5	12.9
Munster	1.4	1.0	3.1	6.2	5.5	7.8	6.4	6.1
Connacht	0.4	0.3	3.7	4.0	5.5	5.8	5.2	2.5
Ulster	2.7	1.7	3.0	5.7	6.7	5.6	5.0	5.4
Elsewhere	1.8	2.1	6.7	3.2	3.5	6.7	4.7	6.8

Notes: = Kildare, Meath, Wicklow. The 1860–69 data refer to first admissions only, the rest to all admissions.

TABLE 5.5
Women's Ages at the Lock Hospital

Age Group	1842–43	1844–45	1846	1847–48	1849	1850	1853	1854	1855–56
>17	2.6	3.5	4.3	6.7	5.3	5.4	6.0	4.9	5.2
17–19	25.0	24.6	25.6	26.0	27.8	28.7	32.8	30.9	30.9
20–24	49.6	47.6	47.5	46.9	47.6	48.8	47.5	48.1	46.2
25–29	14.4	14.4	13.4	13.8	12.3	12.6	10.0	13.2	11.9
30+	8.4	9.9	9.2	6.5	7.0	4.4	3.8	2.9	5.7
Mean (yrs.)	22.2	22.5	22.0	21.6	21.6	21.3	20.8	20.9	21.3

mates in 1847–48 included an 11-year-old, three 13-year-olds, five 14-year-olds, fourteen 15-year-olds, and seventy-six 16-year-olds. The drop in the mean age after 1845 is clear, but it persisted after the famine was over. Why? It was due mainly to the big drop in the number of women aged thirty years or more. The years 1847–48 saw a peak in the proportion aged sixteen years or less. Is this because some younger women were driven on to the streets by hunger? Or is it because some of the older and weaker women succumbed to the famine, or ended up in the workhouse instead?

Tables 5.3 and 5.4 also show that neither the age composition nor the regional pattern returned to a status quo ante. The famine may thus have been seen as having had a ratchet effect on Dublin's market in prostitution — as it did on other features of Irish life.

The North Dublin Union

The North Dublin Union workhouse, one of "a group of huge, gloomy edifices" located on the northwestern outskirts of the city, had been the city's House of Industry until 1838. Both travel writer J. G. Kohl and budding novelist William Thackeray visited it on the eve of the famine. Thackeray was shown old men in considerable numbers and at least four hundred old ladies sitting demurely on benches (some of whom stood up when the visiting party entered, to Thackeray's embarrassment). He also noticed lots of young, healthy females with sly "Hogarthian faces," as well as eighty babies in the nursery attended by their mothers.[43] The subject of an official investigation in the early 1840s for its allegedly high child mortality rates, this enormous institution could hold two thousand inmates. The open door policy that allowed in Thackeray and Kohl may have been part of a public relations exercise.[44]

The North Dublin Union began to fill up in late 1846, and soon the guardians were forced to convert the dining hall into a dormitory. In late 1847 it expanded its capacity from two thousand to four thousand places. Its admissions registers, which survive, show that old people were overrepresented among the inmates, that older inmates were more likely to be men, and that younger adults more likely to be women. The preponderance of females among those aged ten years or older was partly a reflection of the city's demographic structure: in 1841, 56 percent of Dubliners aged ten or more were female. Deserted wives and young widows were common. The small proportion of women declaring a living spouse — only 37 percent of those in their thirties, 25 percent of those in their forties — is striking.

The famine affected the age and gender composition of admissions in the North Dublin Union less than in workhouses served by a largely

TABLE 5.6
Age Distribution of Admissions to the North Dublin Union, Novembet 28, 1844, to Feb. 10, 1845, and Dec. 28, 1846, to Feb. 13, 1847 (percentages)

| | 1844–45 | | | | 1846–47 | | | |
| | Dublin-born | | Non-Dublin | | Dublin-born | | Non-Dublin | |
Age Group	M	F	M	F	M	F	M	F
0–9	29.2	20.8	6.2	7.0	30.3	23.6	7.0	5.6
10–19	12.1	10.9	9.2	4.2	21.0	20.1	14.1	12.1
20–39	29.3	41.7	27.7	43.7	26.2	36.9	25.1	48.5
40–59	18.5	13.0	26.2	18.3	14.2	13.0	32.7	22.9
60+	10.8	13.5	30.8	26.8	8.2	6.5	21.1	10.8

rural hinterland. Neither the proportion of women nor the age composition of the inmates in the union changed much between 1845–46 and 1846–47 (see tables 5.6 and 5.7). Yet the intake of the union, located in an area on the city's outskirts long heavily settled by people moving into the city, was certainly swollen by famine immigration. Some guardians complained about the increased burden; they were supported by the *Freeman's Journal*, which noted how taxes bore down on the city's citizens as "the Famine precipitates the country on the city."[45] It was claimed that of those inmates admitted in the first quarter of 1847, fewer than two in every five had been born in the union. But how much of this was famine induced was a controversial matter. The union's admission records fail to provide a direct, conclusive answer since they do not distinguish between recent arrivals and longtime immigrant resi-

TABLE 5.7
Deaths of Inmates Admitted to the N.D.U. in January–April 1847

| | Immigrants | | Dubliners | |
Age-Group	Males	Females	Males	Females
0–5	19 (22)	18 (19)	60 (52)	65 (50)
6–19	9 (10)	13 (14)	9 (8)	15 (12)
20–29	2 (2)	3 (3)	2 (2)	7 (5)
30–39	3 (3)	7 (8)	11 (10)	5 (4)
40–59	21 (24)	21 (23)	17 (15)	18 (14)
60+	33 (38)	31 (33)	16 (14)	19 (15)
Total	87	93	115	129

Note: Percentages in parentheses.

dents during the famine period. However, for some time after the union's clerk first began to take down the birthplaces of new inmates in November 1844, he also noted how long those born elsewhere had been resident in Dublin. A comparison suggests that (a) the proportion of Dublin-born inmates was much higher before the famine (about two-thirds), and (b) the proportion of elderly men and women among the immigrants was lower and that of teenage immigrants was higher during the famine than earlier. Thus the union's records offer strong hints of the impact of immigration on the city.

Finally, table 5.6 provides a breakdown by age, gender, and birthplace of about four hundred deaths occurring in the North Dublin Union at the height of the famine. The numbers refer to deaths among those admitted during the first four months of 1847. The high percentages of infants and young children among the Dublin-born and of older people among the immigrants are the most notable features. Most of those who died in the North Dublin Union at the height of the famine were already in bad health on entry there; so if the union did not cure them, at least it was not responsible for killing them, either. Nor did a preliminary investigation of deaths suggest that inmates died sooner after admission as the crisis worsened. Of those admitted in January 1847 who would never leave the workhouse again, over one-third would die within a month, a proportion replicated among the entrants of April 1847. Some of the sick passed on their ailments to the union's personnel, however; "within a year one-half the entire paid staff contracted fever, and of these more than half died." Ignorance about how infections spread, as noted in chapter 3, prevented these people from protecting themselves.[46]

The Sick and Indigent Roomkeepers and Other Charities

The charity known as the Charitable Society for the Relief of Sick and Indigent Roomkeepers (of All Religious Persuasions) was founded in Dublin in 1790. Before the famine in a typical year it raised and spent £2,000 ($9,600) in helping the Dublin poor. In an era renowned for sectarian tension, the society united Catholics and Protestants in day-to-day management, charity giving, and endowments; for several years the famous Carmelite friar Father John Spratt shared the work of joint-secretary with a succession of Protestant clergymen.[47] A well-connected charity, the Sick and Indigent relied on subscriptions, donations, bequests, charitable sermons, and an annual grand ball for its funds (the Dublin balladeer Zozimus contributed ten shillings—a substantial sum at the time—at the ball of 1841); its activities and allocations were constrained by its monthly receipts. In the late 1830s its income seems to have been affected by the introduction of the Poor Law. In September 1841, for example, it was reduced to an outlay of less than £17 ($82) on sixty-three families (about one-tenth of the average monthly outlay) due to exhausted funds.

Curiously, though the Sick and Indigent stepped up its activities during the famine, the change was hardly dramatic. The annual general meeting held on 19 January 1848 resolved that "owing to the great destitution and misery now prevailing to so alarming an extent in this city, the Trustees, notwithstanding the liberality of the friends and subscribers of the Society, have to deplore the inadequacy of the funds placed at their disposal, to alleviate the distress of *all* the deserving objects of relief." In its report for 1847 the society also voiced its frustration at the lack of funds. The month-by-month records of income suggest a burst of enthusiasm followed by donor fatigue. The annual total given in donations rose from £210 (about a thousand dollars) in 1844 and £235 in 1845 to £357 in 1846 and £307 in 1847, but fell back to £181 in 1848 and £225 in 1849. Moreover, £278 of the £674 collected in donations in 1846–47 was raised in December 1846 and January 1847; donations were reduced to a trickle during the rest of 1847. Taken alone, the numbers do not reflect so well on the generosity of better-off Dubliners: but perhaps they were dispensing their charity elsewhere.[48]

The professed aim of the Dublin Parochial Association, formed at a meeting of clergymen of the Established Church on 27 March 1847, was to relieve Dublin's poor through the medium of Protestant parish clergy without religious distinction, in the process "equalising the distribution of charity through the City."[49] Its founders claimed that parish clergy were best qualified to identify and assist cases of hardship not dealt with by public agencies. At the outset its most active members, joint secretaries the Reverends Edward S. Abbot, William Maturin, and Charles Stuart Stanford, were among the city's most active Protestant clergymen.[50] The plan was that each of the twenty-one metropolitan parishes subscribe £1 ($4.80) annually to the Association; clergymen belonging to member parishes would then present lists of individuals relieved to a monthly meeting held in Christ Church, and be reimbursed. How far the Parochial Association succeeded in its aims may be judged from the data discussed below. The Association (which survived until recently) relied on subscriptions from parishes and individuals, and from the proceeds of charity sermons. However, soon after its foundation it obtained £100 from the National Club in London, and in November 1847 it informed the Club that it had spent £126 8s 6d on 2,253 individuals of whom only 511 were "Romanists." In a city where nearly four-fifths of the population was Catholic, and where the poor

TABLE 5.8
The Dublin Parochial Association: Donations by Parish

Parish	Allocation (£)	Population (1841)	Catholic (%)	Illiterate (%)
Included				
Grangegorman	27.9	5,643	74.8	26.6
St. Andrew's	23.9	7,634	64.1	16.8
St. Ann's	30.2	8,808	55.1	17.5
St. Audoen's	11.6	3,966	79.4	26.5
St. George's	37.1	20,749	57.4	17.3
St. John's	31.3	3,931	79.1	24.4
St. Mark's	3.1	15,234	77.2	27.9
St. Mary's	44.0	23,904	72.8	17.2
St. Michael's	12.1	1,271	87.5	31.3
St. Michan's	55.0	22,793	87.1	33.0
St. Nicholas Within	26.8	1,694	73.6	25.4
St. Patrick's	30.8	2,044	72.7	27.7
St. Paul's	27.0	8,422	76.9	27.4
St. Peter's	64.0	41,650	63.4	19.5
St. Thomas's	32.1	22,008	66.6	22.6
St. Werburgh's	29.4	2,969	64.8	17.8
Not included				
St. Bride's	0	10,629	68.8	24.9
St. Catherine's	0	20,749	74.9	34.3
St. Luke's	0	4,802	85.5	39.6
St. James	0	14,226	77.8	35.3
St. Nicholas Without	0	11,967	87.5	33.5

Note: The allocations refer to totals from the beginning to the end of 1848. That for St. Peter's includes the 31.5 allocated to St. Stephen's (the "pepper-cannister" church).

were even more likely to be Catholic, such a bias is hardly reassuring. In practice the Dublin Parochial Association seems to have been a Protestant charity run mainly for Protestants. By the end of February 1849 it had spent £561 6s 9d aiding 3,931 families consisting of 19,655 individuals. An analysis of its spending (table 5.8) suggests that the bias in allocation toward poorer parishes was modest, and some of Dublin's poorest parishes never joined the association.

The Dublin Sanitary Association was active in the city during the later stages of the famine. A product of the enlightened middle-class self-interest mentioned earlier, it was created by a number of gentlemen in July 1848, its professed aim being "controlling the rise in mortality in Dublin, by adopting measures to protect the most miserable."[51] As a defense against the threat posed by the onset of cholera, it advocated the creation of special hospitals for victims. It urged an inspection system that would seek out those suspected of having the disease—a plan taken up by the South Dublin Union from July 1849. To the poor it counseled hygiene and sobriety. It campaigned for the cleaning up of the Liffey, "the monster nuisance of Dublin."[52]

Prisons

"No task," declared the inspectors-general of Irish prisons in their twenty-sixth report, "can well be more discouraging and, indeed, melancholy than that of attempting to detail the history of Irish prisons for the year 1847." In the following year the number of criminal cases dealt with passed one hundred thousand. The "calamitous visitation" of the previous few years, not "a general demoralization" of the people, was mainly to blame for the rise, but a temporary halt to the transportation of convicts and the passing of the Vagrant Act (on which more below) made matters worse. The biggest increases were in crimes such as larceny, indebtedness, and, especially, vagrancy. The famine prompted not only more crime and more convictions throughout Ireland, but a big increase also in deaths in prisons and in prison hospitals (deaths rose from 43 in 1845 and 103 in 1846, to 1,140 in 1847, 1,051 in 1848, 1,293 in 1849, falling off to 597 in 1850). Most of these deaths occurred outside Dublin, but the increase in crime swelled Dublin's prison population too, and during the 1840s 106 inmates died of fever, dysentery, or diarrhea in the convict depots in Smithfield and the Richmond, twenty-eight in the Kilmainham county jail, and another seventeen in Grangegorman.[53]

Not all the increased intake was due to conventional crime; thousands of beggars were committed to the prisons of Dublin under the Vagrant Act, but without an apparent diminution in their number in the streets. Most such beggars had come from the country, of course: according to the Mendicity Association, over 6,000 of the 7,698 committed in 1849 were strangers without any legitimate claim on the city of Dublin.[54] Why strict application of the Vagrant Act failed to deter begging, the executive of the Mendicity Association did not feel themselves competent to decide. As noted in chapter 1, the famine had also allegedly prompted many young workhouse inmates to commit petty offenses in the hope of being transferred to a jail, in the belief that prisoners were better treated than workhouse inmates. An account of the dietary regime in prisons and workhouses throughout Ireland in March 1848 suggests very similar dietary regimes in Dublin, with bread, milk, and stirabouts (porridges) of Indian and oatmeal dominating in both, but with the prisons having a slight edge. In their report for 1847 the inspectors of prisons recommended a reduced diet for juvenile offenders as a remedy for this abuse.[55]

TABLE 5.9
The Regional Background of Grangegorman Inmates

	1844–45		1847–48	
Place	Total	(%)	Total	(%)
Dublin	49	16.4	76	8.8
RofL*	77	25.7	199	23.1
Munster	66	22.1	302	35.0
Ulster	91	30.4	176	20.4
Connacht	16	5.4	110	12.7
Total	299	100.0	863	100.0

*RofL = Rest of Leinster.

The intake of convicts in Grangegorman, a holding prison on the city's north side for women mostly bound for transportation to Australia, almost tripled between 1844–45 and 1847–48. The regional distribution of the intake changed, with remarkable rises in the shares of Connacht and Munster, and a fall in those of Dublin and Ulster (table 5.9). The proportion of first-time convicts also rose considerably, from 26 to 42 percent (table 5.10). Both point to the economic character of crime in the late 1840s.[56]

TABLE 5.10
Number of Previous Convictions, Grangegorman, 1844–45 and 1847–48

	1844–45		1847–48	
Number	N	(%)	N	(%)
0	78	25.7	360	41.6
1	104	34.3	243	28.2
2	58	19.2	143	16.5
3	26	8.6	61	7.2
4	20	6.6	16	1.8
5	5	1.7	8	0.9
6	1	0.3	3	0.3
7	2	0.7	1	0.1
8	2	0.7	1	0.1
9	1	0.3	0	0.0
"Often"	6	2.0	28	3.2
?	0	0.9	1	0.1
Total	303	100.0	865	100.0

The registers of Newgate, an old, dilapidated, and deformed jail in the northwest of the city, inhabited in the 1840s mainly by men, women, and children charged with less serious crimes, also survive.[57] A comparison between Newgate's intake on the eve of the famine (March–July 1845) and at the height of the crisis (March–July 1847) also reflects the impact of the famine. Data on the gender, age, height, literacy levels, and recidivism of those committed are available (table 5.11). These show a rise in the share of non-Dubliners and a striking increase in the proportion of teenage males and of females in their early twenties between 1845 and 1847.

The average adult height of a population is a good indicator of its health and net nutritional status during childhood and adolescence. Research on the height of the pre-famine Irish reflects rather well on their relative nutritional status. The Newgate prisoners were no exceptions in this respect.[58] The numbers in table 5.11, section C, refer to the estimated heights of nonliterate Dubliners and echo the standard findings that country people were taller than townspeople, and those with some schooling were taller than those without any. In regressions of height on age and proxy variables for literacy and place of birth (not reported here), the ability to read and write added another 0.6 inch to male heights, though little to female, while birth outside Dublin was worth a further 0.6–0.8 inch. Comparing estimates of the height-by-age of the Newgate inmates in 1845 and 1847 indicates an increase of 0.3–0.4 inch in the mean adult height of both male and female inmates. The implication that the famine prisoners hailed from a healthier background than the typical pre-famine Newgate inmate is both plausible and significant.

Comparing the intake at the Richmond convict depot in March–April 1846 and March–April 1847 (table 5.12) again confirms that the rise in crime in Dublin during the famine was largely the product of immigration from the country. It also indicates that both before and during the famine, Dublin-born criminals were younger than those from outside the city. Some of those convicted were very young indeed; they included an eight-year-old boy sentenced for "skating." The numbers also indicate an increase in teenage crime during the famine.[59]

In mid-December 1846, when it seemed as if farmers throughout much of rural Ireland were making little preparation for the following season's grain and potato crops, two prominent Dublin businessmen, Jonathan Pim and Francis Codd, wanted the implications of this inactivity discussed at a meeting of the city's Chamber of Commerce. They were given short shrift; the matter "appeared to the meeting to be more of agricultural than mercantile interest and was accordingly dropped."[60]

Table 5.11
Newgate Prisoners, 1845 and 1847

A. Characteristics

	1845		1847	
	Male	Female	Male	Female
Number	417	279	742	397
Leinster	85	84	179	104
Munster	21	15	44	27
Ulster	12	10	42	17
Connacht	10	14	26	9
Recidivists (%)	23	34	28	29
Litscore	1.22	0.84	1.15	0.92
Dubliners (%)	65.2	54.3	57.9	58.4

B. Age distributions (%)

	Males		Females	
Age Group	1845	1847	1845	1847
<15	12.2	11.7	1.1	3.5
15–19	25.4	33.5	10.8	12.3
20–24	23.2	20.3	25.8	32.5
25–29	14.4	13.3	24.4	17.9
30–34	7.4	7.8	15.8	19.9
35–39	3.8	3.8	6.5	3.5
40–44	5.5	4.0	6.5	3.0
45–49	4.1	2.3	2.2	1.8
50–54	1.9	2.2	5.0	2.8
55–59	1.4	0.8	0.4	0.3
60+	0.7	0.3	1.8	2.5

C. Estimated Heights (in inches)

	Males		Females	
Age Group	1845	1847	1845	1847
16	59.99	60.35	58.36	57.98
18	62.58	62.99	59.29	59.18
20	64.31	64.64	59.94	60.06
21	64.89	65.36	60.17	60.39
22	65.34	65.85	60.34	60.65
23	65.65	66.08	60.49	60.88
No.	417	743	279	397

Notes: Litscore is the sum of 2s (Read and Write), 1s (Read Only), and 0s (Neither) divided by the number of inmates. The data refer to March–July in both years.

TABLE 5.12
Origins of Richmond Inmates, March–April 1846
and 1847

Region	1846	1847
Dublin	205 (69)	174 (56)
Rest of Leinster	51 (17)	94 (30)
Munster	12 (4)	9 (3)
Ulster	6 (2)	11 (3)
Connacht	3 (1)	11 (3)
Other	18 (6)	12 (4)
Total	295	311

Events would prove that Messrs. Codd and Pim had every right to worry, since the famine proved a more serious affair for business in Dublin than the Chamber or the government imagined. This was not the "brightly lit, comparatively well fed, slightly anxious neutral country" imagined by Lynch and Vaizey. Nevertheless, the institutional sources described above suggest that migration was a more important mechanism than reduced demand in spreading the famine to the city. In the end, Dublin may have escaped rather lightly, but clearly it was not immune, and if Dublin was not immune, few places in Ireland were.

APPENDIX: A NOTE ON THE GLASNEVIN BURIALS

The Catholic cemetery in Glasnevin, the biggest on the city's north side, had been opened in 1832. The cemetery contained a section for the burials of the poor, where plots could be purchased for 1s 6d per head. Table 5A.1 compares the age and gender distribution of burials there in 1843–44 and in 1847.

TABLE 5A.1
Causality Test Results, Glasnevin

Test Statistics	General on Poor	Poor on General
Serial Correlation (F version)	1.65 [0.086]	1.86 [0.047]
F-statistic of zero restrictions on the coefficient of deleted variables: (4, 132)	6.12 [0.000]	1.37 [0.247]

Figure 5.3 on p. 166 indicates a big rise in both poor and general burials in the summer of 1847. It is not clear from the graph whether the rise in "poor" deaths preceded that of "general." An econometric technique called "vector autoregression" provides an answer to whether poor deaths caused general deaths in this sense. The exercise involves regressing the monthly total of general deaths on lagged values of both general and poor deaths, and then testing for whether exclusion of the lagged poor deaths makes a difference in the statistical sense. If deletion of the "poor" burial term makes a statistically significant difference, then we can say that poor burials caused general burials in this special sense. Such causation is often called "Granger-causation," after econometrician Clive Granger.

I regressed monthly burials against lagged values of itself and poor burials, adjusting for different month lengths and adding monthly dummies. Three lags got rid of first- and second-order serial correlation. The results suggest causation in the sense of Granger. On the other hand, reversing the procedure does not support the hypothesis that general burials Granger-caused the poor burials.

Table 5A.2 reports the age and gender distribution of burials both before and at the height of the famine. The increase in the share of poor burials is to be expected, but the most noteworthy feature is the drop in the share of infant burials in both categories. This is most plausibly explained by the amenorrhea effect mentioned earlier. Note, too, the doubling of the shares of 5–14-year-old children in the poor plots.

TABLE 5A.2
The Age and Gender Distribution of Burials in Glasnevin, 1843–44 and
1847 (in percentages)

	Males		Females	
Age	1843–44	1847	1843–44	1847
(a) General				
<1	20.9	14.4	16.9	11.9
1–4	28.3	20.2	20.6	20.1
5–9	4.4	6.1	4.9	5.9
10–	4.0	4.4	4.4	5.7
20–	6.6	6.3	8.1	6.7
30–	8.2	8.7	9.5	8.2
40–	8.0	8.5	7.7	8.6
50–	6.5	10.9	9.0	9.8
60–	6.3	10.4	9.0	11.5
70–	4.2	6.6	5.9	7.4
80+	2.6	3.4	4.0	4.1
Number	3746	2778	3446	2747
(b) Poor				
<1	32.4	16.3	25.8	12.0
1–4	22.0	22.3	22.5	18.2
5–9	3.0	7.2	2.3	7.1
10–	3.1	5.3	2.9	5.9
20–	5.3	7.0	6.7	8.0
30–	7.2	7.4	7.1	8.1
40–	6.4	9.1	5.5	8.2
50–	6.8	8.8	8.9	9.8
60–	7.6	8.9	9.0	11.2
70–	3.9	5.9	4.6	6.8
80+	2.3	1.9	4.5	4.5
Number	1242	1823	1412	2088

Chapter Six

FAMINE MEMORY

> If we fail to teach history, the vacuum will be filled
> with racialist folklore.
> (Irish journalist Eoghan Harris, 1996)

> As in the triumph of Christianity, the old religion lingered
> latest in the country, and died out at last as but paganism —
> the religion of the villagers, before the advances of the
> Christian Church; so, in an earlier century, it was places
> remote from town-life that the older and purer forms of
> paganism itself had survived the longest.
> (Walter Pater, *Marius the Epicurean*)

HISTORY AND MEMORY

THE CASE for folk memory or oral tradition as a window on the past is a double one. First, in poor and largely illiterate societies oral documentation may substitute for the lack of written evidence. Africanist Jan Vansina, one of the best-known supporters of the oral record as a resource for historians, insists that it is not necessarily untrustworthy as a historical source, even if "what one does reconstruct from oral sources may well be of a lower order of reliability."[1] Because famines usually occur in contexts where written documentation is scarce, several famine specialists have invoked oral tradition as a second-best strategy. Recent studies of famines or near-famines in Malawi and in Alaska offer good examples.[2] In Malawi, Megan Vaughan found that "people calculate their ages by reference to [the famine of 1949], and women consciously keep the communal memory of the event alive when they sing the pounding songs they composed then."[3] However, oral sources are arguably more than mere substitutes for the written word. Oral traditions, Vansina claims, have their own value as correctives on other perspectives, providing a more intimate insider view of events and attitudes, and giving a voice to people ignored in the written record. Another supporter, Gwyn Prins, praises oral history for "its detail, its humanity, frequently its emotion and always its scepticism about the entire historiographic undertaking."[4]

As evident from earlier chapters, the Irish famine is one of the better-documented famines in history. This is explained by its timing (very late by west European standards) and its geographical setting (in a region of the United Kingdom, then the "workshop of the world"). Official sources, business and institutional records, correspondence and other private papers, and newspaper reports abound, offering ample raw material for both analytical and narrative accounts. Thus the case for folk memory is less pressing on the first count. However, folklore may still have a part to play on the second. Though memories recounted much later may fail to reveal the true feelings of those at risk, they may capture them better than the standard documentary sources. Moreover, folklore is also about normative beliefs and semipublic attitudes, as exchanged between people — an important topic for famine historiography. Thanks largely to the Irish Folklore Commission, Ireland's holdings of such material are relatively rich. The Commission was founded in 1935, and its collections, mostly dating from the 1930s, 1940s, and 1950s, include local recollections of traditional customs and beliefs, of folktales, and of historical events such as the Great Famine. At its best, the record is vivid, eloquent, and compelling.

Yet, ironically, Irish historians remain unconvinced of the value of this source. The gap between the *pietas* of the Irish folklorist toward the oral record and the skepticism of the historian is very wide indeed. There have been exceptions,[5] but in Ireland most historians would probably sympathize more with antiquarian John O'Donovan's claim in 1835 that oral tradition "is a blundering Booby who has a cloudy memory and muddy brains," or with eminent folklorist Richard Dorson's surmise that "to the layman, and to the academic man too, folklore suggests fallacy, wrongness, fantasy, and distortion."[6] There are, admittedly, some good reasons for this.

First of all, the evidence of much folk memory is flawed and confused. It is also often — consciously or subconsciously — selective, evasive, and apologetic. It is short on analysis and context, and usually innumerate (or anumerate). A good case in point is the issue of wage levels on the public works during the famine. In the folklore archives by far the most commonly quoted wage was fourpence (8 cents), far below the average on the works at their peak in late 1846 and early 1847 (see appendix at end of chapter). One account from Ballyferriter in west Kerry doubled the confusion by implying that this was a generous payment: "fourpence a day was what they got and they earned a fair penny. Some of them earned enough to bring them to America."[7]

Amusing examples exist of narrators hoodwinking folklore collectors.[8] Collectors, on the other hand, may have avoided important but potentially embarrassing questions. The narrators' social background may also have given rise to unsuspected biases. For instance, none of the many accounts of the poor law and the workhouse reproduced in two recent compendia of Irish Folklore Commission material refers to workhouse inmates as family members or even relations, and only once is there mention of a family member relying on a soup kitchen. This silence could mean that the descendants of inmates were not represented among the narrators, or it may simply echo the shame of people forced to rely on workhouse relief or the soup line. There are occasional mentions of family members who had been employed on the public works but, significantly, they refer mostly to people who served as foremen or clerks.[9] We return to this issue of bias later.

Second, chronological confusion can be a problem too, and the longer the interval between the event and the memory, the more likely the distortion of impressions and attitudes. O'Donovan, frustrated in his quest for the origins of place names in Donegal, concluded that "the natives [r]elate many wild stories about the O'Donnells, but so confuse periods and persons, that it is not worth while to take down any of them for any purpose than to shew what an unsafe historian oral tradition is."[10] The Irish famine offers a possible case in point, since most of the Folklore Commission material about it was collected in the 1930s and 1940s, almost a century after the event. The gap was too much for one Westmeath informant who, confusing 1845 and 1879, claimed that "the 'Scotsdown' was the name of the potato that failed — that was the potato in general use at that time. The ordinary people had no early potatoes. The potato that was sent in relief was mostly the 'Champion.'"[11] The comment that "at that time a person would pay a shilling to the Land League and would get a Land League card in return" refers to the 1880s. Again, the claim from the Béara peninsula in west Cork that those who stole during the famine were known as Whiteboys seems dubious.[12] But it turns out that this is not a fatal shortcoming.

A more serious question is whether the evidence of "the ballad singer and the unknown maker of folk-tales"[13] is to be trusted when it comes to analyzing popular feelings about an emotive topic such as the Great Famine. In defense of folk tradition, it must be said that it tends to do a good job of preserving the memory of particular events and tragedies, at least for a few generations. Moreover, some of its silences are eloquent. The record is rich in its condemnations of local landlords, merchants, and officials. Landlords such as Lord Lansdowne of south Kerry, Wyndham Goold of Limerick, Sir Richard O'Donnell of Newport (Mayo), Lord George Quin of east Clare, and Lord Ventry and Betsy Barry in west Kerry are singled out for their cruelties. In Greencastle, county Tyrone, a group of local traders came to be known as the three extortioners, while in Ballymoe in east Galway, Seán Rua Flynn was remembered for being charged with distributing meal but feeding some of it to his cattle instead and letting more rot in his stores. Yet the record is by no means uniformly negative: folk memory is kind to many landlords, such as Cronin Coltsman of Knocknagree in northwest Cork, the Bournes of Rossport in northwest Mayo, the Fitzwilliams in south Wicklow, Baroness de Clifford of Tuam, Charles Tottenham of Kiltyclogher, county Leitrim, and Freeman Dave of Kanturk in north Cork.[14] More strikingly, resentment against high-ranking politicians in Dublin and Westminster is rather muted. Political leaders and administrators such as Peel, Russell, and Clarendon, or even the notorious Sir Charles Trevelyan, almost never feature. Is this because they had been forgotten by the 1930s or the 1940s, or is it because they had not featured during the crisis? A plausible interpretation of the silence about key figures in both contemporary political controversy and in the historiography of the period is that they were remote and unfamiliar to the underclasses most at risk. Again, several graphic contemporary depictions of the starving and dying in the 1840s have survived in print. However, some clichéd references aside, they are surprisingly few in folk memory; twentieth-century images of bloated bellies or skeletal emaciation find virtually no echoes in the folklore material collected in Ireland.[15] Is this because folk memory is squeamish? Or is it because people succumbed to typhus and dysentery sooner in Ireland in the 1840s than in Ethiopia in the 1980s or Somalia in the 1990s?

The reliability of oral tradition hinges ultimately on the reliability of people's memories of things they witnessed and heard. Autobiographical memory has been the subject of a substantial body of psychological research in recent decades. The research stresses the reconstructed character of such memory: it is adapted to the current needs of both the subject and his audience. Autobiographical memory can thus never be entirely truthful or objective. In the words of a leading expert, it will tend to reflect the beliefs and understanding of the rememberer and preserve only some of the main details of experienced events." Nevertheless, anecdotal memories tend to be accurate, and "do not violate the meaning of the recalled episode; in fact, if anything they seem to emphasize the meaning." Modern research thus urges critical distance, but is broadly supportive of richness of memory as a source.[16]

In defense of famine folklore, it must also be said that it is remarkably free, or almost free, of populist myths such as that of Queen Victoria's miserly donation to famine relief. In one of the two references to Victoria's meanness that I have found in the archives, her alleged donation of £50 ($240) to Ireland was compared to the £5,000 she contributed toward the construction of the Grand National Race Course near Liverpool. In the other reference, "what relief she allowed would come to about a quarter of what was needed by the starving people."[17] For the most part, folklore's focus and concerns — and the targets of its anger — are purely local. One interesting exception from Carna in south Conamara is worth giving:

> *Ins an drochshaol chua scéala go bunáite ríochta na hEoróipe.* . . . During the bad times the news went out to most of the kingdoms of Europe that Ireland was in a bad way, and that people there were starving for the want of food. The Turk heard the story and it caused him great anguish to hear that some of them were dying of starvation. And he sent yellow meal to Ireland to help out, and the saying 'that it would move the Turk' [*go scrútad (scrúdfadh) sé an Turcach*] dates from that time. The Turk was so moved when he heard about Ireland that he sent food there.

> The provisions arrived in Ireland, but the people who appointed themselves administrators of it — meal and clothes — kept most of it for themselves and let many of the poor who needed it most die of starvation, and indeed it turned bad in the end.

The Sultan did send help,[19] but the saying almost certainly predates the help by several centuries.

The objective of this chapter is twofold. First, it seeks to show some advantages and drawbacks of folklore as a source for famine history. It does so by focusing on a set of issues that bear largely on attitudes and feelings about the tragedy. Second, it sets out what has survived of the famine in contemporary song and verse in the Irish language. We will see that a good deal of useful material has survived unnoticed — a reminder that perhaps another reason why historians give Ireland's folklore record a wide berth is that the best of it is in Irish.

THE FAMINE IN FOLK MEMORY

In the past few years, several studies have followed the lead taken in Roger McHugh's contribution to Edwards and Williams's *The Great Famine.*[20] McHugh's research was based entirely on replies to a specially constructed Folklore Commission questionnaire and a series of special reports from the Commission's own fieldworkers in 1945–46. His study relied exclusively on this material; unfortunately, he could not consult the other scattered but voluminous evidence on the famine in the Commission's archive, mostly collected in the 1930s. This is not a criticism of McHugh, since the material was not indexed until much later, and the Commission lacked the resources to appoint a librarian until after McHugh had written his chapter. Still, the result was that McHugh thereby left out of account much of the richest material. Nor could he include material from *Bailiúchán na Scol* (the Schools' Collection), the mass of material collected in Ireland's national schools in 1937–38.[21] McHugh also faced a further constraint: the Folklore Commission questionnaire was rather narrowly conceived,[22] and many of those respondents who clung strictly to its brief found little to report. The best replies interpreted the questionnaire as an open invitation to describe any surviving famine folklore deemed worth reporting. Naturally, the responses to the questionnaire varied greatly in quality. The weakest of them are banal and vague, and several respondents could provide little or no information.[23] At its best, however, the material is very rich, and the sheer bulk of the Folklore Commission's contribution is remarkable. Its 1945 questionnaire alone yielded over thirty-five hundred pages of material, mostly handwritten, from over five hundred informants. The average age of the informants was 73–74 years. Only one or two were old enough to remember the famine, but most had known close relatives or neighbors who had lived through it. The regional spread of the information was as follows: one informant in four lived in Connacht, nearly two in five in Munster, and one in five each in Leinster and in Ulster (a majority of them in Donegal). About one respondent in four used Irish, but these were more voluble than the rest, since they accounted for over two-fifths of the information. The proportion of all famine material in Irish would be higher still. The average quality of the Irish-language material is undoubtedly richer than that of the English. Whether this was because the most skilled and experienced collectors concentrated their efforts on Irish speakers, or because folk memory about the famine and about the past generally was more likely to survive in Irish-speaking areas, is a moot point.[24]

Roger McHugh was more concerned with folk tradition as a source of evidence about what happened in the 1840s than as a clue to popular attitudes, then and later. His chapter therefore included sections on the blight, on famine food, on relief and public works, on disease, on death and burial, and changes in the countryside after the famine. Some of these topics were not explicitly addressed in the questionnaire, which McHugh had no part in constructing. McHugh's contribution is by far the most evocative in Edwards and Williams's self-consciously dry collection of essays. It still deserves careful reading. What follows complements McHugh, since it focuses largely on aspects not treated by him, and relies in part on material not used by him. A comprehensive analysis of all the folklore material is overdue, but that is not attempted here. Instead, I dwell on five issues that bear on private or semipublic reactions to the famine.

Oral memory on the famine is at its best when dealing with details and anecdotes rather than generalizations like those just quoted. Asides

such as "*Dá neosfainnse dhuitse cá bhfuil uaghanna daoine atá curtha
. . . ní raghfá thar doras amach istoíche* (if I told you where people were
buried, you would not venture out at night)" from an eighty-five-year-
old west Cork farmer to a visiting collector capture the horror of the
famine as vividly as James Mahony's famous woodcuts in *The Illustrated London News*.[25] The same old man noted that so poor were people in that area before the famine that old women would put shells on
hens' feet to prevent them from scratching the soil. The claim from Cill
na Martra near Macroom that, when the potato failed, poor women
sought permission from farmers to pick charlock (wild mustard) in their
fields before the cabbage matured could hardly have been made up later.
Similarly, an account from Waterford related how a farmer allowed the
poor of one townland to help themselves to charlock one Sunday morning as long as they did not touch the oat stalks. Another brief cameo
describes how a west Cork priest helped an orphaned child to carry his
mother to the local graveyard. No sooner had the priest allayed the
youngster's fear that they would be alone at the funeral than a troop of
sheep in a field nearby began to follow them.

The fear of contracting fever might mean that there was little communication between neighbors. According to an account from Dromore
West in Sligo, "if somebody died in a house, the corpse was left unburied unless there was somebody in the house able to carry in one way
or another the corpse to the graveyard and do the burial."[26] Or take the
following short depiction from Menlough (Mionloch) near Galway City
of the blight: "*A 'chéad bhliain gon ghorta lobh na fataí ins na poill
. . . .* In the first year of the famine the potatoes rotted in the pits. It was
Thomas Ward from Mionlach who first found out. He went out to the
garden for potatoes for a meal. He stuck his spade in the pit, and the
spade was swallowed. The potatoes turned to mud inside. He shrieked
and shrieked. The whole town came out. All the potatoes were in the
same way."[27] The great Kerry storyteller Peig Sayers (1873–1958) gave
the following Synge-like account nearly fifty years ago:

> *Do ghoill an droch-shaol ana-mhór ar Chillmhicadomhnaigh . . . .* The bad
> times hit Cill Mhic a' Domhnaigh very hard. Three houses were knocked
> down on people who had died of the fever. There was an uncle of himself
> there and the house was knocked down on him and his family.
>
> The Cam got its share of hardship too. Bríde Sheáin, I don't know what
> they called her husband. They were eking out a living as best they could on
> limpets and periwinkles from the strand and other gleanings, but in the end
> the troubles got to them. The husband and the children died. The eldest
> daughter — she was sixteen — held out longest, and her mother was doing her
> best for her. But one day when she came to the house with some supplies for

her she was dead. The mother set aside whatever things she had, got some water and washed her, and dressed her up. She then went out to the garden where there was a little haycock, and gathered enough hay to twist a rope. She put her dead daughter on her back, holding her up with the rope.

Nora Landers, down here in Baile an Ghleanna, saw her passing east with her load. . . . Nora turned round and took seven potatoes from a little mound set aside for seed, and didn't bother with a skillet or an oven, but stuck them under the cinders. She then kept a lookout so that she could intercept Bríde on her return journey.

Bríde was carrying her load until she reached the chapel, but having reached it the poor woman couldn't make a hole. Éamon [Sheehy] saw her and came to her.

"It's a terrible story, Bríde," he said.

"Christ's story was worse," she replied.

Gregory Ashe saw her too and he came over and together they buried her daughter. I don't know whether the others had coffins, perhaps the father had one. When they had put the last sod on her, Bríde said:

"God bless you now, and all of you. Nobody else will join you now. There is only me left and there will be nobody to look after me to bury me here or somewhere else." She used the ditch for support on her way out, and made her way back very slowly. Nora was before her.

"My God," said Nora, "you have had a terrible time, and life is harsh and dark, but come in awhile, and if you'd like to stay the night in the corner you are more than welcome."

The poor women entered, and sat up by the fire. Nora offered her the potatoes and a little mug of milk, which she took.

"Poor Bríde," she said, "you have had a lot to endure, but you must resign yourself, for we will all get our crosses to bear."

Bríde held up the potato and looked at it. "Well, thank God that it wasn't you I buried today," she exclaimed.

Nora never forgot that remark until her dying day. Bríde lived on into old age, making her living from spinning and winding.

Don't they say that no matter where in Ventry churchyard, big though it is, you might dig a hole, you would find bones, because they were buried there without coffins or sheets?[28]

Several accounts of lone survivors carrying corpses on their backs for burial survive.[29] But the image of Bríde Sheáin having to carry the corpse unaided is a powerful one, and the effect is strengthened by Peig's repeated references to people and places recognized by both the narrator and collector. This feature — obviously a rhetorical device — prevades the folklore. The following account, taken from Stiofán Ó hEalaoire of Doolin in west Clare in the 1930s, is another good example. Ó hEalaoire (1858–1944) spent most of his life in his native townland. A poor man, he lived alone in a cottage with a leaking roof, and owned "a cow, a half-tame white cat, and five or six hens." This is his account of the famine:

> *Do bhí sé thíos insa Mhuí Mhuair an t-am a raibh* . . . . Down by Muí Mór when the big house was a poor house, there was a man hired there to carry the people who died to the graveyard. He had made a trench in the graveyard, and he never closed it, nor did he put the dead in there more than once a week, since they used to die of hunger lying on the roadside by the gate in the hopes of getting something to eat. People who were not dead at all but close to it, he would put them in his wheelbarrow and carry them to the trench. He would let them down among the corpses and allow them to die there. That is how it was without a word of a lie!
>
> There was a man in this place in those same Bad Times, and he went stealing turnips for his supper. It is said that the man who owned the garden caught him in the act, and he mustn't have given him the turnip, because he was found dead the following morning in a neighbour's cabin. And he was the fine man! I didn't know him myself, but I often heard my mother talking about him.

Ó hEalaoire may have added a few embellishments but the drift of his account of the famine is plausible. Claims that people were taken away for burial or even dumped in graves while still not quite dead are plentiful.[30]

Another example comes from Colm Ó Caoidheáin of the townland of Glinsce in the parish of Carna, south Conamara. Ó Caoidheáin, an able storyteller, was about fifty years old when quizzed about the Famine by collector Séamus Ennis in 1945. Before the cataclysm, he claimed, Carna was full of people: "They lived so close to one another that men would chat from house to house without ever coming to the door (*bhíodar ann chomh gar dhá chéile go mbíodh fir ag comhrá ó theach go teach ann gan thíocht go doras féin*)." But they were reasonably well provided for; Glinsce, where Ó Caoidheáin lived, was known as Baile na mBrochán (Stirabout Town), because, "they always had an ample supply of stirabout there and rye porridge and every kind of complicated food (*mar bhíodh brochán á ól ann agus prásc seagail agus chuile short beatha ba choimpléacsaí ná chéile ar bord i gcónaí*)." Still, the potato must have bulked large too, because the area suffered badly during the famine. This is how Ó Caoidheáin describes how his grandmother lent a helping hand to neighbors:

> *Bhí líon tíghe anseo thiar ar a' Muing i mBaile Leitreach Árd* . . . . There was a household west here in Muing in the townland of Leitreach Ard—

Tomás Sheáin Uí Chaoidheáin's family — and they were hit by the bad illness because of hunger, the cholera,[31] God help us. But Griallais's daughter (she was my mother's mother) heard that there was nobody looking after them, so she went to them, and what she saw when she entered the house was them all bundled up together under their bedding on the verge of death. The old man was the liveliest of them, but even he was barely able to talk to her. Well, she had brought a few gurnet with her and she boiled them, and she mixed some of the yellow meal that she had also brought through the juice of the gurnet, and gave it to them to drink. She saved them all from death, attending to them regularly until they were strong enough to look after themselves. And they always acknowledged afterwards that she had saved their lives.[32]

Oral tradition, as is shown below, certainly will not tell all. Yet cameos such as those just given surely *do* reveal an important part of what it was like to have been there. Certain topics and motifs also crop up repeatedly in the folklore accounts. Rather than attempt to offer a compendium or undigested sample of all the material collected, the rest of this chapter looks at a few interesting and recurrent themes that bear, directly or indirectly, on people's feelings about the famine.

FAMINE MORTALITY

As explained in chapter 3, estimating the mortality caused by famine is often a tricky and contentious business. The Irish famine's cost in deaths cannot be estimated with precision. This is mainly because deaths were not registered and emigrants were only imperfectly counted at the time; small, inevitable inaccuracies in the 1841 and 1851 census totals compound the problem. Nevertheless, demographic historians estimate that the famine killed about one million people. This makes no allowances for averted births, or for excess mortality after 1851 — an aspect emphasized in some recent accounts.[33] While few places can have escaped scot-free, even within those provinces there was considerable local variation.

The mass mortality of the famine years left its mark on folklore. According to an account from Dingle, up to two hundred people from the area died on the roadside. Another from Croom in county Limerick describes "emaciated corpses, partly green from eating docks, and partly blue from the cholera and dysentery."[34] But what is more striking is how frequently the belief recurs in folklore that some particular area escaped lightly or suffered less during the Great Famine than surrounding parishes and other regions. Thus we hear that the famine "to all appearances" did not affect Cloyne in the Cork barony of Imokilly, "to any great extent"; in the Rosses in Donegal, although "probably one of the most barren districts in Ireland there [were] very few stories of any deaths from famine," while Grange near Clonmel escaped more lightly than "*furmhór na tíre*" (most of the country), and an informant from Seskin near Carrick-on-Suir claimed that there were no deaths in that townland. In Ballymoe in Galway there was a saying still current among the older generation in the 1940s, "that God spare Ballymoe parish from any threatened calamity as he did at the time of the Famine." A Cork informant had "always heard that the people . . . were very lucky in the famine period . . . and though in dire want and low rate of living that at least no one really died of hunger as so many did in several parts or all over the whole of Ireland." He noted that "two people, men, died in Knocknagree but they were not of Knocknagree."[35] There is a strong local tradition on the Aran Islands that its people were spared the worst of the famine, partly because the potato blight was less severe there.[36] "Nobody died here, because the turnips came, I heard," claimed an old Ballyferriter man in 1945.[37] In 1938 a schoolchild was told by a relation in nearby Cill Maol Céadair that "*ní raibh an gorta chomh holc ins an áit seo agus do bhí sé in áiteanna eile*" (the famine was not as bad here as in other places), a message echoed by a girl from Liscarney farther east. In 1950 an informant from Greencastle in Tyrone confided that she had "never heard her people or her grandmother say that any people died of hunger in the parish. But she said she heard that some children died." Around Muigh Ros in south Conamara "*in aimsir a' droch-shaoil ní ru go leor daoine a' fáil bháis leis an ocras sa gceanntar seo. . . . Mhaireadar go mór níos fearr in aice na faraige ná mar bhíodar in áiteachaí eile ar fud na tíre*" (during the famine, there weren't lots of people dying of hunger. They survived much better near the sea than in other places). The following is an account from An Fhaill Mhór in south Kerry:

> *Bhíodh brioscaí 'á thúirt amach siar anuas as na Cumaraibh . . . .* Biscuits were being given out down from the Cumaraibh, and they fought bitterly over them as they were doling them out, and they used to get a small can of soup once a week with the biscuits. But things were not so bad in the valleys here, because they had the goats' milk.
>
> The three townlands which best withstood the Famine — An Ráth, Míll a' Ghoilín, and Buail' Uí Chaoil — were those in which the potato did not fail; they were the townlands that kept the place going. People from Beara, I would imagine, came in this direction looking for potatoes; but when things got bad the locals could not give them any, because they hadn't them for themselves.[38]

In part, such examples are genuine reflections of the regional dimension to excess mortality noted above. Thus the reference to the Rosses is supported by censal data: the population of the parishes of Templecrone and Tulloghobegley, which encompass a considerable portion of the district, fell only very slightly between 1841 and 1851, from 18,891 to 18,574.[39] Again, the population of the Aran Islands fell by only 9.5 percent between 1841 and 1851, less than that of any other Galway barony. Mortality in the townland of Tullagher, county Leitrim, was indeed low, as claimed.[40]

But perhaps the belief that one's own area was spared the worst recurs too frequently to be plausible. The folkloristic impressions are often not supported by contemporary censal data. Thus, for example, those who perished in Fintown in central Donegal were supposedly mostly "*bacaigh is lucht siúil*" (beggars and travelers), yet the population of Fintown fell from 180 in 1841 to 93 in 1851. In Inishowen in Donegal it was claimed that deaths from starvation were much fewer "than elsewhere particularly inland because people could live on shore food," but the baronies of Inishowen East and West lost 13 percent of their combined population between 1841 and 1851, only slightly less than the rate experienced by the rest of county Donegal. "It is said that nobody died of starvation on the Great Blasket," yet the island's population fell from 153 to 97, and the number of inhabited houses from 28 to 17. An informant from nearby Cill Maol Céadair had not heard of anybody dying of starvation there during the famine, "but some of them converted. They took the gruel." However, numbers in the parish fell from 2,333 to 1,534. In Dubh Thuama in northwest Mayo, "the Famine did not affect people as much as it did elsewhere. Fish was plentiful"; yet according to the census of 1851 the population of the townland of Doohooma had fallen by more than half (from 455 to 218) since 1841.[41] The population of the parish of Cloyne, mentioned above, fell from 6,726 in 1841 to 5,148 in 1851, that of the barony of Ballymoe in Galway from 28,666 to 21,388. That of the huge parish of Muigh Ros fell from 11,969 in 1841 to 8,558, and that of the townland of Seskin (in the parish of Kilsheelan) fell from 377 to 289. Again, popular memory suggests that Newcastle West in Limerick escaped lightly during the famine. Yet while it is true that the town's population rose from 2,917 in 1841 to 5,248 in 1851, the 2,846 inmates in the town's workhouse more than account for the increase, because the workhouse had barely opened when the 1841 census took place. In the rural part of the parish, population fell from 1,925 to 1,104. Emigration and averted births in the 1840s are unlikely to account for such shortfalls.

Another possibility is that folk memory erred in equating famine deaths with starvation. There is a local tradition that there were no deaths from starvation during the Great Famine in Killaloe, county Clare. The claim, repeated in Roy Foster's mold-breaking *Modern Ireland*, creates the impression that Killaloe escaped lightly, an impression strengthened by Foster's reminder that "some local landlords behaved well." Perhaps they did, but the claim that Killaloe escaped lightly ignores the 113 deaths recorded in Killaloe's temporary fever hospital, which did not open until November 1847, about a year after deaths from fever and dysentery began to mount in badly affected counties such as Clare. It also ignores the hefty drop in the town's population from 2,783 in 1841 to 2,218 in 1851, and in the rural part of Killaloe parish from 2,948 to 1,666. Killaloe's defective baptismal records also bear the scars of the famine, and the harrowing account left by the local curate of his daily routine offers ample corroboration.[42]

Given the probably huge variations in emigration from parish to parish, population loss is an admittedly poor index of local variations in excess mortality. We have been measuring one crude yardstick against another. Yet the comparisons, taken together, suggest that folk memory is of dubious value as evidence of the regional incidence of famine mortality. The problem is that "lacking corroborative historical evidence, we cannot judge whether the folk memory is telling the truth or or not."[43] Unexpectedly, perhaps, folk memory often errs on the low side. Yet the very unreliability leaves food for thought. Is it an echo of a half-forgotten, subconscious communal scruple about famine deaths? Or is it that people thought that support networks remained more resilient in one's own area than in others?

HUNGER AND THEFT

> Although it was not uncommon to hear of sheep, cows, and even horses being stolen, killed, and eaten by the famishing people, I heard of no instance of highway robbery or personal violence.
> (A Dublin Quaker in Erris, May 1847)

Famine folklore is replete with references to thieving by the hungry and to the preventive measures taken by farmers and others.[44] The references are all, or nearly all, to the theft of food (usually potatoes, turnips, cabbage, or butter) or livestock. Colm Ó Caoidheáin from Carna explained how the hungry poor did their thieving at night, muffling their spades with cloth as they dug. In Dún Chaoin in west Kerry, thieving was also a nocturnal activity. Local men headed for the mountain to steal sheep, and farmers in the habit of leaving firkins of butter in bog holes overnight (in order to increase their weight) now had to guard them. In neighboring Ballyferriter people stole turnips, even though they cost only 1.5d a stone (3 cents for 14 lbs). The man guarding them at night used a buffalo horn (*adharc bó fiain*) to frighten off intruders. In nearby Feothanach a girl was made to stay home from mass on Sunday to mind the turnips. Lord Dunsandle employed an armed guard to protect his turnips. In Ballymara in Galway, people who owned sheep also had to remain up during the night to watch them.[45] In Laois hungry children stole turnips from the fields on their way to school. In southwest Kerry farmers sought to prevent the poor from lifting leaves from their cabbages. In Grange near Clonmel farmers erected huts to prevent people from stealing their turnips. In Mayo they erected man traps in potato fields — "a hole about eight feet deep and two feet wide was dug filled with water and concealed with brambles and grass etc." Monaghan had its man traps too.[46] In Cill Ghallagáin (Mayo) a man who caught two boys stealing his seed potatoes took them back to his house and tied them up like cattle. In Westmeath, "there was a desperate pack of fellows around Horseleap. They used to steal sheep and skin them in the graveyard on the big flat tombstones." An informant from the Béara peninsula told of how his mother, when a young girl, had spent many nights guarding the potato garden. An elderly grandfather in Baile'n Sceilg in southwest Kerry had a gun with him at night when protecting his cattle, and he was not alone in this. In Creeslough in Donegal the landlord employed a man with a gun to prevent the poor from gathering shellfish.[47] Béal Átha an Ghaorthaidh in west Cork produced an amusing, though probably apocryphal, tale about how three brothers outwitted the wife of a Bandon innkeeper "in the bad times" and ended up not paying for the lavish meal they had just consumed.[48]

In Galway city a woman stole some of the newly purchased meal that Colm Ó Caoidheáin's grandfather was carrying on his back; she had cut a hole in the sack and used her apron to collect the escaping meal. A Ballyferriter man who was transported as a convict to Australia for stealing and killing a bullock became rich there, "and he had a pair of horses for transport." Another man named Houlihan from the same parish decided to leave Kerry voluntarily after ten of his seventy sheep were stolen in one night — he returned many years later. There is much more in this vein.[49] A few Uíbh Ráthach men who had brought some potatoes to Cork coastwise were confronted by people who were "grabbing them from the boat and stealing them from others who had just bought them." To make matters worse, the Kerrymen returned home to find that their own potato gardens had been plundered by their neighbors.[50]

In this case the folklore captures events of the kind that left their mark on the crime statistics of the day. The accounts are vivid, if somewhat bloodless and sanitized. Rarely are either victims or aggressors named. And though the community at large may have been more indulgent of such thieving during the famine than of crime in ordinary times, occasional clashes and feuds between neighbors and their descendants are bound to have ensued—and to have lasted. The record is also silent on these. Perhaps a steadier focus on such issues on the part of the collectors would have extracted more information about them.[51]

A related aspect of this evidence, which deserves further analysis, is the narrator's perspective. The eighty-six-year-old woman from Ballykilcline (Roscommon), who in 1957 remembered her father boasting that he kept his family alive by thieving food during the famine, reflected the perspective of those most at risk. According to her, "his mother made a big pocket for him inside his coat and he used to steal oatenmeal and put it in this big pocket and bring it home and that's how he kept his family from starving and he was only a very young lad at the time." In a similar vein is the report of a sixty-five-year-old Wicklow woman that her grandfather stole a leg of mutton from a well-to-do farmer during the famine because his family was hungry.[52] Such revelations about ancestors stealing are very rare. In a majority of cases, such as those from Meelick in Clare that "people had to take in turnips, otherwise all would be stolen," Tuamgraney in the same county that "the people remained up all night in turn minding their turnip crop," or around Westport where people made sure that they traveled in daylight and "in considerable strength" when returning home laden with flour, the perspective would seem to be that of the haves rather than the have nots.[53] Here is another instance where the perspective of folk memory confounds expectations of a relentlessly populist bias.

THE POTATO BEFORE THE BLIGHT

Several accounts recall the bountiful potato crop of the last pre-famine year, and some explain the potato blight as a visitation on people who squandered the crop when it was plentiful. In Ballymoe in County Galway, for example, the yield was so great that men made little of their bounty; in Sligo they piled potatoes along the ditches; in Leitrim "the crop was so plentiful . . . that people could not get sale for them, and it was said that they slept on the bags at Mohill market." Near Mullingar, there was "such a plentiful crop of potatoes that when they had them dug they didn't know what to do with the ones they didn't want, and they filled gaps with them, and they put more of them in heaps in the fields and set fire to them and burned them." In Carrigeen in north Wexford "people thought the blight was a visitation from God because of the careless way they treated the potatoes." In west Kerry "the year before the Famine was a great year for potatoes, and Eamon used to say that the people were over-confident." In Cratloe in east Clare "the year previous to the first famine year was a great one for the potato crop. So plentiful were they that the potatoes were 'piled up by the ditches' to use the exact words of my informant." From Enniskean in Cork: "Old people said it was God's will to have the famine come, for people abused fine food when they had it aplenty. I heard it for a fact, that spuds were so plentiful that they were put out on the fields for manure."

According to another account from the same area, "it was remarked by many old wise heads at the time that great want would surely follow great waste, and their words came only too true." In Stradbally, County Laois, "most people think [the blight] was a punishment from God for the careless manner in which they treated the crops the years previous when there was a very plentiful supply of potatoes."[55] In Uíbh Ráthach in south Kerry the following story was told:

> Do bhí na prátaí cómh flúirseach gur chaitheadar leis a' bhfaill iad . . . . Potatoes were so plentiful that they dumped them over the cliff. They used to ship them out from this place long ago, from Carraig a' Bhacaigh here, and they had pits [for potatoes] there. They were waiting for the boat—before the bad times—they would ship them to Cork—the potatoes were so plentiful that you would be better off with one ridge of them than with three. The boat wasn't showing up and they shoved them over the cliff edge with shovels.
>
> But there was this wandering beggar passing west from an Rinn Iarthaigh with a bag of potatoes, and when he saw them shovelling the potatoes over the cliff he said: "if theirs are flotsam, let mine be flotsam too," and he dumped his potatoes over the side with the rest.[56]

Such beggars, of course, were among the first casualties of the slaughter that followed in 1846 and after. Here, finally, is Peig Sayers on a similar note:

> Bhíodar subháilceach go maith roimis a' ndro-shaol . . . . They were happy enough before the Famine. That is the year when potatoes were plentiful, glory be to God, they were never so plentiful again. They had no room for them and they were dumped by the ditches.
>
> But some man from na Raithíneacha was travelling east—a Sullivan, I think, my father said—with a bag of potatoes in front of him on his horse's back. But there was this self-important woman sitting on the bridge at Miltown, knitting. She noticed him passing.
>
> "Is it potatoes you have?" she said.

"It is," was the reply.

"Off to sell them?" she asked.

"Yes, is it how you'd want them?" he replied.

"No," she said, "but wait till I go and ask the pigs if they'd eat them."

"Mhuise, woman, that is a nasty thing to say, and it mightn't be long till you'd be glad of them."

And I used to hear my father say that she died of starvation and, the Lord save us, with her mouth distorted and gaping.

Contemporary price data lend some credence to these claims of a bountiful crop in the year before the blight struck, though the blight probably made people exaggerate their good fortune in 1844.[58]

A related, remarkable feature is the almost complete lack of references to failures of the potato before *Phytophthora infestans*. This could be interpreted as corroboration of claims that the potato was a more reliable crop before 1845 than earlier critics allowed.[59] Or was it merely that previous failures, serious though they may have been, faded into insignificance after 1845?

CONFLICT, RESENTMENT, AND AMNESIA

The hardship forced on people by the famine is bound to have produced its share of harsh decisions, of cruelty and conflict. Nor, as noted in chapter 1, was all this conflict between classes, between landlord and tenant, or between farmer and laborer. Families fought over slender resources, and in the struggles the very young and very old probably lost out. An Ulster poem describes:

> An mac 's an t-athair ag spairn le chéile,
> Ag troid 's ag racán fá'n alpán saolta.
> An iníon de ghnáth ris an mháthair ag aighneas
> Go síor ag rá gur léi-se
> An gé, an chearc, an t-earc, 's a' chaora,
> Agus neithe beag' eile gan mórán féidhme.

> The son and the father bickering
> Fighting and brawling about worldly lumps.
> The daughter always arguing with the mother
> Forever telling her that
> The goose, the hen, the newt, and the sheep,
> And other small useless things belong to her.[60]

Research on famines elsewhere has produced horrible tales of child murder, neglect, apathy, abandonment, and even cannibalism. In Russia in 1921 the Society of Friends stopped distributing cheap sausages when some were found to contain human flesh. In the Warsaw ghetto in January 1942 a rabbi complained that "we see people in the street, without anyone showing compassion for them."[61] The impact on behavior in Ireland, discussed in chapter 1, is also reflected in oral tradition. The widespread terror of fever and cholera led to people shunning stricken neighbors. In Sligo "every man had to do for himself, and when a person died, not even his nearest relation would darken his door." In west Cavan for several days nobody would enter the house of a woman who had died of fever, and the two men who eventually did so "were not allowed into their own homes, clothes were brought out to them and some water to wash themselves and to put on fresh clothes and to leave the cast-offs on a hedge for days."[62] An account from Peig Sayers, who lost an uncle in the famine, conveys some sense of the horror and ensuing guilt:

> *Tháinig an calar are Mhícheál ach go háirithe* . . . . Michael Garvey got the cholera, and he and the entire household succumbed. They perished together. I think he died before his wife. He had a daughter, and had she survived, she would have been the finest girl in the parish of Dún Chaoin. Somebody went to their cottage door, and could see that they were all dead. All they did then was to set fire to the thatch on the cottage, burn it, and knock in the walls. I remember myself in autumn-time how we used to pick blackberries near that spot — because there were lots of bushes where the house used to be — my mother warning us to keep away from the place. "Stay away from there," she used to say, "or you will be harmed."[63]

This is a common enough theme, but folk memory tends to be selective or vague on outright antisocial behavior. As a sixty-six-year-old Corkman recounted in 1945:

> In my young days I used to hear old people discuss the awful cruelty practiced by farmers who were fairly well off against their poorer and less comfortable neighbours. The people who were old when I was young were never tired discussing how some of those taking advantage of the poorest of their neighbours used to offer the rent of their farms to the landlords and grab their farms. . . .
> Several people would be glad if the famine times were altogether forgotten so that the cruel doings of their forebears would not be again renewed and talked about by neighbours.[64]

The same Corkman talked about some of those "cruel doings" in 1945. He told of a man named Denis O'Sullivan from Knocknagree who grabbed all his neighbors' land in those years. There was no trace left of those who lost their land, but according to Buckley the grabber's kin had no luck either, one of them dying "insane in Cork Mental Hospital about fifty years ago." Buckley also mentioned one Johnny Mahony of Bawnard who took over an insolvent neighbor's farm, without even allowing him credit for the crops he had planted. Again, as in other cases where land was obtained this way, we are told that "no luck attended the Mahony family after." Near Castletowngeoghegan in Westmeath, members of the Sheerin clan "were hasping the doors before the people were well outside the door. They were paid for that. . . . That is how the Sheerins are all big farmers now around here, with three big slated houses as you see near the Railway Line as you go on to Johnstown." An account from Offaly describes in some detail a Protestant family of three brothers and a hunchback sister who grabbed a farm in Rahin shortly after the famine, adding (somewhat gratuitously, perhaps) that "names would serve no useful purpose here."[65]

Accusatory stories like these are uncommon in recorded folk memory, however, and mention of names is even rarer. Yet echoes of half-forgotten conflicts probably persisted until recently, subconscious or half-forgotten. Ignoring the shame and the guilt leaves the way open in due course for a version of famine history in which the descendants of those who survived all become vicarious victims. Indeed, this is the version that prevails in popular discourse nowadays.

But the reticence was hardly about guilt only: shared memories about the tragedy were very distressing and sometimes traumatic for those who endured it. In the Clonmel area, famine survivors were taciturn on the matter. According to an account from Glenmore in the Béara peninsula, "all the information you'd get from the old people (about those famine victims) was: 'their graves are there — *cailleav i mbliain a 'ghátair iad* (they died in the year of disaster),'" while in Ballymoe, county Galway, those who had witnessed the horrors of the famine were reluctant to give details, and only an occasional incident was handed down. In 1942 Éamon a' Búrc of Carna, a renowned *seanchaí* or storyteller, confided to a collector how local people had tried to eat embers (*sméarthóideacha*) to ease their hunger during the famine; but he believed that even mentioning this might be sinful ("*ceapa go mbeat sé peacúch á'm*"). The same storyteller said he knew fields where entire households were buried; the present owners stayed away from the burial spots.[66] Elsewhere, survivors were reluctant to admit their dependence on the soup kitchen or *min déirce* (beggar's meal), or to confess that a member of their own household had died of starvation — though "they were considered martyrs if they died of the fever."[67] The record is also almost silent on the identity of alleged soupers, though references to souperism are frequent.

MIRACLES: HOSPITALITY REWARDED

As Roger McHugh noted, several accounts relate how farmers and others who helped their starving neighbors during the famine were rewarded by good luck later on. This account from Rathmore in east Kerry is worth citing for its similarity to that from nearby Knocknagree, cited by McHugh over four decades ago:

> I often heard that old Mrs Cronin grandmother of Father John Cronin, Lissyconnor, Rathmore, was very good and full of charity to the poor and hungry in the bad times. She used always boil a lot of potatoes for the meals and she never used the ones left over after dinner for either pig or cows or poultry, but collected the best of them and put them near the fire to have them for any hungry poor person who might chance to call to the house for some bite to lessen their mad hunger. A few potatoes half cold and a basin of milk was a great boon to such starving people, and often they went away blessing the house and the owners of it. Many were the poor mother and father who came to her for one single head of cabbage she had growing in the field. It was poor fare but it kept many a family from starving in those days. A head or a couple of heads of cabbage boiled with a pinch of salt were divided out among the family and if they had enough of that they'd be very thankful. One day her husband seeing so much cabbage being carried away went into the house to blame her for giving away all the cabbage and asked her did she want to leave themselves with nothing at all? She denied giving away as much of it and said she only gave a few heads to a few poor women who were starving. "Come out now," said the man of the house, "and show me what cabbage is left for ourselves." She went out fearing the worst and hoping he would not blame her too much for helping God's poor. When they reached the cabbage field great was her surprise to find that there was not a single head missing out of the whole field.[68]

The following version from a schoolchild in another part of Kerry has its own charm:

> *Bhí bean de mhuinntir Dubháin i mBaile an Eanaig an uair sin* . . . . There was a woman, one of the Devanes, in Baile an Eanaig at that time, who had two cows. She was very generous, and she gave most of the milk to the poor hungry people who lived nearby. As the proverb says, "*Tabhair rud don ngárlach agus tiocfaidh sé ambáireach* (give to the youth and he'll be back tomorrow)," and the more she gave the more they asked from her. One day she gave away all her milk, and when her husband came in from the fields that night, he said "We'll have to get up early in the morning because we have people in to help with cutting turf." "Lord God," she said, "and we having

no milk." "What did you do with it, you old cow?" he asked. "I gave it away to the poor hungry people," she replied. "Yes, give it to the neighbour and be a laughing stock yourself." "Don't worry," she said, "*Is giorra cabhair Dé ná an doras*. (God's help is closer than the door)." So they went off to bed, and when they got up in the morning the vats were full of milk before them.

Another account tells of the wife of a farmer named Sheehan who lived near Rathmore. Sheehan was "a close fisted chap," his wife "very, perhaps too generous a woman [who] gave nearly all the new milk of her *bawn* of twenty cows to her starving neighbours." Yet another account, "very common in Kilworth forty years ago," could identify the house but not the name of the "*bean truaighmhéileach*" (kind-hearted woman) in question. A Tipperary informant mentioned the grand-mother of a friend, who had run out of grain from feeding the poor. Faced with a further plea for charity, "she prayed hard and went to the barn to find something. When she opened the barn the grain was pour-ing out." In Cill Rialaigh in southwest Kerry, a farmer — grandfather of the informant's friend — who turned a blind eye to those who helped themselves to leaves from his cabbage-patch got his due reward: "the cabbage thrived, and you could hear the plants exploding each night as you passed the road."[70] A variant related by a northwest Mayo school-boy in the 1930s concerns a local landlord family, the Bournes, who earned an enduring reputation for generosity during the famine. One member of the family is supposed to have given away all he had, even his corn seed, so that when spring came he had no oats to plant. In desperation, his wife told him to shake the chaff of the oats over the land, and that with God's help it might grow. According to local lore, the chaff produced a harvest of oats superior to anything witnessed since in the area.[71] In west Cork a generous woman, having given away all her oat seed, planted chaff with similar results: the field where this was done became known as *gort na cátha* (the chaff field).[72] The same motif recurs in Cahirdaniel, county Kerry: a woman who had given away all her oats "got the men to set a handful of the *síol-cháith* (oat-seed) the following spring and it grew." And there is a great deal more in this vein.[73]

These simple, moralistic tales of charity rewarded obviously should not be interpreted as evidence of miracles that really happened. The charity of "old Mrs. Cronin" and "the wife of a farmer called Sheehan" did not save Rathmore, nor could the Bournes save Ceathrú Thaidhg.[74] Such miracle tales are of a type commonly found in European folklore: like urban legends today, they seek plausibility through linking events with living individuals and nearby places. Many variants of this story — the wife with a heart of gold, the cautious and scolding husband — have been collected all over Ireland, often without the Famine setting grafted on. They are a local variant of the Aarne-Thomson folktale type 750B, with obvious links also to medieval religious and even early Irish motifs.[75] Compare the following from "The Life of Saint Brigid the Virgin" by Cogitosus, an obscure seventh-century hagiographer:

> This beautiful maiden, with her generous nature, chose to obey God rather than men. She gave the milk to the poor and to wayfarers, and also handed out the butter. At the end of this period the time came for all to make a return of their dairy production; and it duly came to her turn. Her co-workers could show that they had fulfilled their quota. The blessed virgin Brigid was asked if she too could present the result of her labour. She had nothing to show, having given all away to the poor. She was not allowed any extension of time, and she trembled with fear of her mother. Burning with the fire of an inextinguishable faith, she turned to God in prayer. The Lord heard the voice of the maiden raised in prayer and responded without delay. Through the bounty of the divine will, He who is our help in adversity answered her faith in him by providing a plentiful supply of butter. Marvellous to behold, at the very moment of the maiden's prayer, not only was her quota seen to be filled, but her production was found to be much greater than that of her fellow workers.[76]

Yet though such accounts should not be taken as literally true, their very existence as myths in the context of the famine is surely interesting. That people believed, or wanted to believe, such stories — and that they survived such a long time — is important. Today, some may read them simply as reflections of cultural norms or aspirations, of neighbor helping neighbor. Cold-eyed historians and economists may wish to see them instead as reminders that most people, in Ireland as elsewhere, are far from being saints in times of crisis, and that some of those who had milk and cabbage and grain to spare during the "bad times" kept them for themselves.[77] But surely there is room here for both generosity and restraint?

The Famine in Ballad and Song

In *The Hungry Voice* (1989) Christopher Morash has produced an unusual and very useful compendium of verse on the Great Famine. However, the literary provenance of the material inevitably makes it a better representation of well-intentioned middle-class reactions than of popular attitudes in areas where the famine was most intense. Only the last section of Morash's anthology, which reproduces four broadsheet ballads, touches a truly popular chord, and indeed Morash notes the incongruity of Dublin newspapers preaching rebellion in English to a largely illiterate and Irish-speaking peasantry. Morash claims that "had the Great Famine taken place a half a century earlier, it could have found expression in a native Gaelic tradition that embraced a long history of famine, exile and destitution."[78] Indeed, an earlier famine, that of 1740–41, prompted several poems. Several manuscript copies of Séamus Mac Coitir's "*Ní cogadh ná caragail fhada idir ard righthibh*" have survived; the Jacobite poet Tadhg Ó Neachtain was moved to write "*Má bhí brón romhór gan teimheall*" and "*Fó liag sheaca i ngéibheann tá*," and poems such as "*M'atuirse ghéar, mo phéin, mo nuar, mo bhruid*" and "*Créad an fhuaimsi ar fuaid na tíortha*" also refer to that crisis.[79] However, the claim implies that the Irish language was in a much weaker state on the eve of the famine than was really the case. Garrett Fitz-Gerald's suggestion that half or more of children born in Ireland around 1800 spoke Irish implies an Irish-speaking population of at least 2.5 million.

Though the proportion of Irish speakers dropped thereafter, the number of Irish speakers is likely to have continued to increase. Not only did Ireland's population rise from 5 million circa 1800 to 8.5 million circa 1845, but that rise was greatest in those areas where Irish was strongest. The proportion of Irish-speakers dropped thereafter, but absolute numbers are likely to have continued to increase. Fitzgerald reckons that at least 28 percent of those born in 1831–41 were Irish-speaking, and 41 percent of those born in 1801–11. Allowing for some likely underestimation in the censal data, these percentages imply an Irish-speaking total of 3–3.5 million on the eve of the famine, an all-time high.[80]

Alternatively, one might surmise that the sheer scale of both the 1740–41 famine and the Great Famine would have been enough to silence the Muse in any language. In his introduction to Morash's book, critic Terence Brown writes of "silence as our truest language." Yet the record on the 1840s is not completely mute. The rest of this chapter offers a sampling from a few contemporary and near-contemporary songs and ballads about the famine.[81] With a few obvious exceptions, the verses were probably composed rather than written down, because their authors were almost certainly illiterate. In this sense they differ from those that have survived from the 1740s, which belong to the Gaelic literary tradition. Famine songs in the English language are rarer, though a few have survived.[82]

The Irish Folklore Commission recorded songs and verse about the famine in most counties where Irish survived as a vernacular in the 1930s and 1940s. None of it deserves to be called great poetry; the surviving versions of several are clearly defective, the tunes and the precise context and authorship of most have been lost. Nevertheless, these poems and songs constitute a useful record in their own right, fossilized like contemporary written documents, without subsequent filtering.[83]

Peatsaí Ó Callanáin (1791–1865), a farmer-poet from Craughwell in east Galway, was the author of "*Na Fataí Bána*" (The White Potatoes), sometimes remembered as "*Rann na bhFataí nDubh*" (The Ballad of the Black Potatoes). Ó Callanáin was "a nice respectable man . . . with cows and sheep," and the Callanáins were relatively comfortable and well-educated people by local standards: their twenty-acre farm was valued at £6 (about $30) in 1840.[84] The poem, which shows signs of having been composed in Black '47, contains thirty-three verses in all: as an old woman from Kilchreest informed Lady Gregory a century ago, "some used to say that Callinan's songs were too long." Several versions of the poem survive in manuscript; one, incorrectly attributed to "Michael Callanan," was collected by the Gaelic scholar Eugene O'Curry soon after its composition.[85]

Ó Callanáin's wistful paean to the white potatoes, "generous and cheerful, laughing at us from the head of the table," recalls themes discussed in chapter 1. They were "*an bhanaltra a bhíodh ár mbréagadh in aimsir béilí de ló is d'oíche*" (the nurse that kept us amused at meals, daytime and nighttime), sustaining the young and the old, the weak and the strong. Sadly, these former harbingers of good company and mirth had now rotted for no obvious reason. The year 1846 — not 1845, interestingly enough — would always be remembered as the year when the potato failed all over the world.

> Mo mhíle slán do na fataí bána,
> Ba shúbhach an áit a bheith in aice leo,
> Ba fáilí soineannta iad at tíocht chun láithreach,
> Agus iad ag gáirí linn ar cheann an bhoird.
>
> Ba chabhair don bhanaltra iad, don fhear is don gharlach,
> Don lag is don láidir, don óg is don chríon,
> Ach fáth no dhocharna is ábhar m'angair,
> Gur lobh na preátaí gan sioc ná síon.[86]

In an awkward, metrical translation of part of the poem by one Thomas Chapman appended to Eugene O'Curry's version, the above two quatrains were rendered as follows:

> A long farewell to the white potatoes, how great the happiness they could afford
> How glad they made us when they came before us, with faces smiling at us from the board;

They fed the mother and the son from childhood, the strong the weak, the young and the old

But oh! my misery and endless anguish, for they have perished without frost or cold.[87]

Ó Callanáin then turns to the famine proper. The workhouse and the fever hospital are full, corpses are being laid out, and the survivors are fed on yellow meal twice a day. There follows a complaint about low wages on the public works for those outside:

Is iomaí teach a bhfuil ochtar daoine ann,
Is gan fear le saothrú ach aon duine amháin,
Siúd pingin don duine acu, gan caint ar an tSaoire,
Agus lá na díleann níl faic le fáil.

(It is many a household that contains eight people, and with only men working, that's a penny each, taking no account of Sunday, and on wet days there is no work.)

The quatrain accurately echoes the complaint of a Roscommon inspecting officer who wondered in 1847 "what was a man to do on eight pence with a large family, and he the only one to work out of it . . . a question I would earnestly call the attention of the Government to."

Folklore attributes a second Galway famine song, "*Johnny Seoighe*" or "Johnny Joyce," both to Tomás Shiúnach and to Micheál Mharcuis Mac Con Iomaire, both Carna men with a gift for impromptu compositions,[88] and to Brídín Ní Mháille, a widow with young children. The song reveals little about Johnny Joyce, the object of its praises, except that he would seem to have played some part in doling out Indian meal in the area around Carna during the famine. The context is the workhouse and outdoor relief: there is no room in the workhouse for the singer and his family, so the singer appeals to Joyce for some food. The first stanza pleads to Joyce for help, the second describes the plaintiff's plight. The third stanza, on the face of it, is in fulsome praise of Joyce and his betrothed. The praise is stylized and conventional: the people of Carna may be proud of Joyce and his beloved, a hug from him would cure a sickly queen, and so on.

However, this song is also open to a less flattering reading. According to a local source, audiences around Carna would have known Joyce as a dishonest schemer, and they would have readily recognized the "queen" as Joyce's mistress, Peg Barry, the daughter of a land agent on the Martin estate. Joyce, in this version, was an interloper from Oughterard, who had sought to replace a respected local man as distributor of relief tickets in Carna. The reference to the queen's illness is taken to be an allusion to Peg Barry's mock collapse in the courthouse in Roundstone, as she was about to appear as a witness for Joyce. In this interpretation *"Johnny Seoighe"* should be seen as a satire. *"Ní raibh aon bheirt eile i bpobal Carna a raibh an oiread gráin orthu leis an mbeirt"* (no other two people in the community of Carna were detested as much), and *"ní raibh aon tslacht chor ar bith ar ceachtar den bheirt acu"* (they were both pretty seedy characters). Another local account relates that Joyce had turned down the singer's request for half a stone of meal, but that Joyce's wife was moved to charity by the final few lines. Such remarks, with their resonances of local conflict, may explain why the song was not considered "safe" to sing in public until quite recently.[89]

Another Carna ballad maker, Seán Ó Guairim, is credited with a longer, almost-forgotten song in praise of a soup kitchen in neighboring Muigh Iorrus.[90] Surviving versions are defective and garbled, but the sense of desperation and horror is clear. *"Scaip' ar bith ná scaoileadh,"* it began, *"nár thaga ar shoup house Mhuigh Iorruis"* (let no harm befall the soup house at Muigh Iorras), in describing a tragedy that had *"gur léithe fear maith sínte ná leag an taoille i snámh an Áirc"* (taken away more good men than the flood in Noah's time). Indeed, according to Ó Guairim, *"níl fear ar bith amach ó Mhuíghros nach é a bhfocal 'cuirí' síos mé, nó mara gcuire, dhiún blas íosfas mé a choídhchin ná go bráthach!'"* (because there isn't a man from Muigh Iorras who isn't shouting 'put my name down, for if you don't, I will never eat a morsel again!'). The plea of one poor old woman, as she kept a tight grip on her little bag, was "are my children included in your list, or do I get only enough for myself?"

> *Dá bhfeictheá an tsean-bhean chríon liath bhocht*
> *'S a máilín go cruaidh fíllte aici,*
> *'Bhfuil mo mhuirín thíos dom*
> *Nó a' bhfuigh mé ach mo chion féin?*

Hunger was the abiding concern of all:

> *Níl duine ar bith sách láidir ag an ocras ach aon lá amháin,*
> *Scaipeann sé na cnámhaí agus leaghann sé an fheoil.*

(Nobody is strong enough to withstand hunger for more than a day, it slackens the bones and dissolves the flesh.)

Ó Guairim's passing references to Hector and Venus, "Deirdre of the fair women," and *Bínn Éadair* (Howth) are the only concessions to classical literary adornment in these songs. Another evocative feature is the illiterate Jack Bacach (or lame Jack) Ó Guairim's awe at the writing skills of those doling out relief; *"an t-am a bhfeicfeá an pencil i láimh Johnnie Liam le bheith ag scríobh síos, nach againn a bhéas an meeting 'guil timpeal teach an stóir"* (when you'd see the pencil in Johnnie Liam's hand, won't we have fun [following him] around the warehouse) or *"Peatsaí King siar, sin é an fear a scríobhfas síos gach ní díobh mar is cóir"* (Patsy King over there, he is the man who will write down everything properly). But the awe is hardly surprising in an area where over nine in ten of the people could neither read nor write.[91]

Máire Ní Dhroma of Ring in County Waterford was responsible for a long song called *"Na Prátaí Dubha"* (The Black Potatoes). The song combines a conventional plea for divine mercy and intervention with social protest. Ní Dhroma was critical of the poorhouse for splitting families apart, even separating dying children from their mothers, and of *"na huaisle go bhfuil mórán coda acu"* (the well-heeled) for growing rich as the poor lie in their beds of clay in *"Reilig an tSléibhe"* (the mountain cemetery). It is said that the sentiment *"ní hé Dia a cheap riamh an obair seo"* (this was not God's work) caused the song to be frowned on by the local clergy. *Reilig an tSléibhe* is located in the parish of Ring, but the song made it as far north as south Tipperary, perhaps through people who came to Dungarvan to trade. *"Na Prátaí Dubha"* is a memento of hard years in Ring: the population of the parish fell by 22 percent between 1841 and 1851.[92]

Cork also produced a few famine songs. The most interesting two were taken down from a farmer in Baile Mhacóda in southeast Cork in 1934. In the first, the potato blight prompts the narrator, a farmer, to spend the money set aside for rent on potatoes for seed and food. He travels some distance from home on horseback to an unpleasant old woman who is charging famine prices—seven shillings ($1.75) a barrel for seed potatoes—with the result that he ends up with little for his trouble. The song finishes with a supplication to God and a lament for the potato in the pre-blight era. Before the famine, the potato could be shared with the poor, and every beggar who passed the way was fed and given *"lóistín seachtaine"* (a week's lodging). Now, however, the sight of thousands lying in ditches had hardened people's hearts:

> *Ba mhaith é an práta, dob fhial is dob fhairsing é*
> *Chun é a roinnt ar bhochtaibh Dé,*
> *Is gach stróire gheobhadh a tslí bhíodh lóistín seachtaine 'ge*
> *'S suí go daingean istigh Ón spéir,*
> *Nú gur laghadaigh a gcroí 's gur dh'iompaigh a gcrathacha*
> *Nuar a chonaiceadar na mílte sínte cois na gclathacha*
> *"Imigh, bí ar siúl, níl aon tslí leapan againn"*
> *Ar eagla go mblaisfimis an mhin bhuí féin.*

(The potato was good and generous, leaving plenty to share among God's poor; and every stranger who passed the way had a week's lodging and shelter from the elements; till their hearts hardened when they saw thousands stretched by roadside ditches; "Be off with you, we have no room here," for fear we might even taste the yellow meal.)

"*Amhrán a' tSúip*" (The Soup Song) refers to the same part of east Cork. Composed by a wandering minstrel known as "*Píobaire na Gruaige*" (The Hairy Piper), its topic is souperism—charity given in the hope of, or conditional on, conversion to the Established Church—in Baile Uí Chríonáin (a townland in the parish of Kilcredan). *Píobaire na Gruaige* did not approve of this "sour soup" and "dearly bought broth," nor of those people "who pay no heed to the second commandment but hope for gains that injure hundreds"; he reminded listeners who were tempted by the prospect of such soup that "*go mbeirtear ar na franncaig fé bhrannra 'n chréithir, 's mheallfaí's an madra sa tseamlas is géire*" (rats are caught under sieve-pots and the nastiest shambles will tempt a dog).[93]

Several versions of another song from Galway, "*Dúchan na bPrátaí*" (The Potato Blight), survive. The tune seems to have been lost, but some folklore about the song's background survived into the 1950s. One account attributes the song to a man named Breatnach from Oranmore, another to a woman from the Cois Fharraige district west of Galway City. In 1951 Nora Costello from Claregalway remembered a neighbor singing it at wakes long ago; he could move his audience to tears with it.[94] As for Breatnach, when the ship set sail: "*An-bhuachaill a bhí ann* . . . . He was a fine lad. He brought his hurley and ball with him on board, and tapped the ball upwards twenty-one times with the hurley; then, next time as it came down, he doubled on it into the ocean and threw the hurley after it." A poetic departing gesture in itself! The song refers to over two hundred famine emigrants of all ages who made the Atlantic crossing from Galway Bay to Baltimore ("*dhá chéad agus naonúr, an t-óg 's an críonna*")—very late in the sailing season ("*tráthnóna oích' Nollag sea d'ardaigh gaoithe*"), probably in 1847 or 1848. An accompanying priest kept up the spirits of those on board: "*bhí sagart beannuí' a labhair ó chroí linn gur thug sé saor sinn go Baltimore*" (there was a saintly priest who spoke to us from the heart and who brought us safe to Baltimore).[95]

The final song discussed here, "*Amhrán an Ghorta*" (The Famine Song), refers to the area west of Dingle in county Kerry.[96] A Cill Maol Chéadair schoolchild, who contributed a version to the school's collection in 1937, introduced it as "*amhrán a dhein bean*" (a song by a woman), but neither author nor precise provenance can now be identified, and the tune has been lost. Presumably it originated around Baile na nGall, where it was later collected.[97] Again the song combines belief that the failure of the potato was *"toil an Ard-Mhic do cheap gach n-aon"* (the will of God who created all) with populist resentment against people who could have helped to relieve hardship, but did not, especially the Poor Law Guardians *"a bhí os cionn súip, is ná roin-nfeadh é"* (who had charge of soup, and who would not share it). Since work on the construction of the Dingle poorhouse did not begin until early 1848, the reference here could be to the Tralee Board of Guardians, which was responsible for Corca Dhuibhne at the height of the crisis. This would also explain the reference to *"lucht Búird dá insint don bhfánaí fíorbhocht, 'ní linne a luíonn sibh, is ní bheidh sibh ann'"* (and the Board people telling the impoverished wanderer, 'You are not our concern, and you will not stay here'). This is a strong and vivid ballad, full of arresting lines about the effect of the tragedy on people's behavior. The famine not only did away with the usual enthusiasm for music and socializing: people hardly recognized one another any more; there were no marriages, *"ná suim ina dhéanamh"* (nor any interest in arranging them), and those young people who might normally be considering marriage now wanted to spend their dowries on a passage to America instead. Young men had lost their vigor (*tréine*), so that *"ní miste spéirbhean bheith amuigh go déanach"* (it is safe for young beauties to be out alone late). The result would be a thinly populated land inhabited by *"daoine aosta i mbun stoic ag aoireacht cois fallaí i ndrúcht"* (old folk tending livestock in dewy fields).

Taken together, the songs suggest both resignation and resentment. Several plead for divine intervention and forgiveness, but others such as *"Na Fataí Bána"* and *"Na Prátaí Dubha"* give vent to populist indignation. Salvoes at *"muintir Shasana"* (the English) and *"lucht Béarla"* (English speakers), or at *"daoine uaisle i mbuaic an tsaoil seo"* (the rich who rule the roost) and at *"uaisle a bhfuil mórán cuid acu"* (posh people who have everything) have a Mitchelite ring to them. Yet though these songs represent the perspectives of those most at risk, it would be quite wrong to force them into a common thematic straitjacket.

The Muses might be forgiven for losing their voices during the Great Famine.[98] The rhetoric of fatalism is silence, and as the crisis deepened communal fatalism was an understandable response. Still, the trawl is more than might have been expected at the outset.

One reason why historians object to folk memory is its antiquarianism and alleged sentimentality, "its attachment to a bygone past." A more important reason in the present context, I suspect, is the belief that folklore evidence was flawed by populist and nationalist biases: in his ghosted introduction to Edwards and Williams, Kevin Nowlan chided folklore for seeing "the failure of the British government in a sinister light."[99] This chapter has attempted to show that folklore's biases are different. The evidence, despite and sometimes because of its biases and silences, has something distinctive to contribute to our understanding of the Great Irish Famine.

APPENDIX: REFERENCES TO RATES OF PAY ON THE PUBLIC WORKS

A. In Cathal Póirtéir, *Glórtha ón nGorta* (Dublin, 1996) [my translations].

Page, County

67, Donegal	This was relief work and the best and the strongest men in the parish were getting a groat (i.e., fourpence) a day.
154, Donegal	The poor men had only a groat a day, or if they preferred, a stone of meal east in Fall Charrach on Saturday evening.
157, Clare	A groat a day.
159, Kerry	A groat or a few pence a day was the pay or a stone of meal per week and work from dawn to dusk.
159, Kerry	There was no pay but such an amount of yellow meal, a stone of meal, I think.
159, Kerry	I remember[100] the Board of Works being done. A stone of meal per man per week, of coarse meal. That was their pay.
162, Kerry	A groat a day was what they got and they earned many pennies there. Some of them earned enough to bring them to America.
163, Clare	They got fourpence a day for lifting stone out of that quarry there.
164, Tipperary	As far as I can recall, I think workmen got three sixpences a week there. It just occurs to me that I heard it said that they got meal in return for their labors. There were men on the lookout in case somebody dropped dead so that they could take their place.

165, Waterford   Most of those who were getting meal for 1/6 per week were on task work.

166, Kerry   An old Sullivan man here saw the girls removing surface matter from the roadsides for the Board of Works and carrying it in baskets for fourpence a day.

B. In Cathal Póirtéir, *Famine Echoes* (Dublin, 1995).

Page, County

151, Westmeath   My father worked on the Relief Scheme splitting the Hill of Dromore. . . . The pay was 8d, 6d, or 4d, hardly anyone got as much as 10d a day. It was all task work.

152–3, Westmeath   The pay was 10d a day for the common laboring man. The overseer or ganger got 2d a day more, that was the highest pay. . . . Only the strongest ablest men earned 10d a day, most of them got only 5d or 6d or even 4d.

155, Carlow   They got 4d a day for working on the road.

155, Wicklow   His grandfather worked for 4d per day building the ditch at the straight mile near Aughrim.

156, Armagh   The ditch up Slieve Gullion was done then for fourpence a day.

158, Mallow   The pay was from 2d to 4d a day, while the overseers had the lion's share.

158, Mayo   They received from 2d to 4d per day or a quart of Indian meal.

159, Mayo   The workman got 4d a day and the ganger 8d. My father was ganger on these works, just because there were few men could write or keep men's time in those days.

159, Galway   A woman he knew worked for 4d a day.

161, Monaghan   Wages on these schemes were very small, 4d per day for an 11 or 12 hour day.

161, Tyrone	Any person working on the scheme received in return one pound of yellow meal per day.
164, Tipperary	4d a day.
165, Leitrim	The women 1.5 pence a day and the men 2d.
165, Sneem	4d was the daily wage then.

Chapter Seven

THE LEGACY

> *Ní bheidh in Éirinn ach daoine aosta,*
> *I mbun stoic ag aoireacht cois fallaí i ndrúcht;*
> *Ní bheidh pósadh in aon bhall ná suim ina dhéanamh,*
> *Ach 'tabhair dom an spré' agus 'raghad anonn.'*
>
> [Ireland will be left with only the elderly, tending
> livestock by walls in the morning due; there will be no
> marriages, nor interest in them, but "give me the dowry"
> and "I'll head off."]
> (From a Kerry famine song, c. 1847)
>
> Will you come down to Tullamore and see the hunger there?
> (Irish politician on a plea from Bengal in 1944)

THIS BOOK has been mainly about economic and demographic aspects of the Irish famine. The long-term impact of the famine on the Irish psyche and on Irish culture, much commented on in the media during the sesquicentennial commemorations of 1995–96, is beyond its scope. So is research on the impact, if any, on the physical and mental health of post-famine generations. Still, it bears remembering (as already noted in chapter 3) that the main victims of famines are typically the poor and the weak. In that sense famines leave a healthier population in their wake. A problem with this simple inference is that it fails to take account of any knock-on effects on the physical and mental performance of those born during the crisis. Such a link is by no means farfetched: the possibility was the subject of an ambitious study of people born in the western Netherlands during and immediately after the Hunger Winter of 1944–45. The study, which took a team of U.S.-based epidemiologists seven years to complete, found that "prenatal exposure to famine had no direct effect on body size in terms of height or weight." Moreover, though fetuses exposed to famine may have suffered some brain cell depletion at the time, the authors could find no evidence of reduced mental competence in adulthood. The implication that the Hunger Winter did not reduce the productivity of those born in its wake is consistent with the unprecedented dynamism of the postwar Dutch economy. The presence of such a famine echo would also have been difficult to square with the postwar growth in the average heights of Dutch people: by the 1990s the Dutch were among the tallest, if not the tallest, in the world.[1] It is true that the Dutch famine, in which about ten thousand people died, was mild and short-lived compared to the Irish famine. Yet perhaps what matters is that it was big enough to produce significant famine amenorrhea (hunger-induced absence of menstruation), which is a stage beyond the prenatal impact on later mental and physical health at stake here. Another recent study of such cohort effects refers to Bangladesh in the wake of the famine in 1974–75. Comparing the death rates of children born and conceived during the famine with those from a post-famine cohort, it finds that mortality in the famine-born cohort was higher in both the first and second years of life, and in the famine-conceived cohort higher in the first year only. However, the effect was short-lived: no significant differences were found in children aged between two and five years.[2] This evidence from Holland and Bangladesh reduces the likelihood of long-lasting cohort effects in post-famine Ireland. More generally, the claim that Ireland's famine impeded the later growth of its economy is not easy to sustain. In the half-century or so after the famine, as noted in chapter 3, living standards in Ireland converged on those in Britain and in northern Europe. Migration was partly responsible, though hardly the whole story. The subsequent divergence in the Irish Free State is best explained as the price paid for political sovereignty, not as a product of the famine.[3]

Nonetheless, the economic impact of the famine on the Irish economy long outlasted the crisis itself. By the time a new normality had been established, in 1853 or 1854, Ireland contained about two million fewer people than in 1845. For those men and women who stayed on, the departure of others through death and emigration meant a tighter labor market, higher wages, and a higher land-labor ratio. Landlords might well have been the losers in such a process; luckily for them, the switch toward a more pastoral agriculture induced by rising livestock and butter prices increased the demand for land, and rents would soon bounce back to their pre-famine levels and beyond. A survey carried out in 1850 suggests that wages did not rise much during the famine, but they did rise thereafter. The rise was greatest in counties where wages had been lowest before the famine.[4]

The nature of the potato blight meant that there was no question of a return to the *status quo ante* in agriculture. Potato yields, which had averaged over six tons per acre before 1845, were little more than half that in the 1860s and 1870s, and still averaged only 3.7 tons in the 1880s and 1890s. Not all the decline was due to the blight; the switch away from the high-yielding Lumper to tastier but less prolific varieties and from spade to plough cultivation played a part. But the big rise in potato yields that followed the introduction of the anti-blight bluestone solution — an average of 4.5 tons per acre in the 1900s, 5.4 tons in the 1910s — tells its own story. How important was the blight's impact? Kevin O'Rourke's general equilibrium simulations suggest that had the potato remained healthy, but allowing for exogenous price shocks and a one percent annual rise in real wages, agricultural employment would have fallen by 2 percent instead of the actual 45 percent between 1845 and 1876, and potato output would have risen marginally instead of falling by four-fifths. These numbers are only approximations based on a series of judicious assumptions, both technical and conjunctional. Still, it seems clear that by increasing year-to-year yield variability and reducing average yield, the potato blight inflicted significant and enduring damage on Irish agriculture's capital stock. This ecological aspect differentiates the Irish famine from most other famines.[5]

The famine also had an enduring impact on the nature and extent of overseas migration. Long-distance emigration had long been an important feature of Irish life. Between 1815 and 1845, about eight hundred thousand Irish people, about two-thirds of them men, had emigrated to North America. That outflow accounted for almost one-third of all trans-Atlantic emigration from Europe in these decades. Before the famine the correlation across Irish counties between the emigration rate and living standards (crudely measured by weekly wage rates in agriculture) was very weak. Presumably some kind of poverty trap, budgetary or psychic, was at work. Though hard evidence is scarce, it is likely that the cost of the passage, coupled with the expenses of searching for employment in the receiving country, ruled out the option of emigration to North America for many of those without land. Such costs would not have prevented emigration to Britain; indeed, hundreds of thousands emigrated there also before 1845. But the role of a psychic barrier is suggested by the importance of temporary, seasonal migration across the Irish Sea from poorer counties in the west of Ireland. In the 1850s and 1860s such seasonal migration would complement permanent emigration, but before the famine it seems to have substituted for it. Like cottage industry, fishing, and kelp burning, seasonal migration underpinned the smallholding economy. However, the famine changed all that. The correlation between wages and the emigration rate was already strongly negative by 1850, and the following decades brought increasing internal convergence in living standards. The coefficient of variation of agricultural wages across counties fell from 0.16 in 1850 to 0.11 in 1870 and 0.8 in 1911.[6]

By producing a huge one-time stock of emigrants, mostly settled in a relatively small number of cities and countries, the famine gave an added spur to emigration in its wake. By guaranteeing accommodation

on arrival, easing job searches, and providing a supportive social network, the concentration of migration in such a short period made life in
their new abodes easier for those who followed. New immigrants relied
heavily on family and neighborhood ties, and the study of Irish settlement patterns in places such as New York City highlights the importance of such ties. The size of the impact of migrant stock on subsequent migrant flow can be debated — according to one estimate it
accounts for the entire gap between pre- and post-famine migration
rates — but it remains clear that in this sense, too, the famine mattered.[7]
The persistence of the blight and the impact of such a concentrated rush
of emigration between 1847 and the mid-1850s meant that the famine
did much more than merely accelerate demographic and economic processes that were under way in any case.

Nor did famine return to Ireland after the 1840s. In 1860–62, despite
a potato crop less than two-thirds of even the post-famine average, reduced livestock numbers, poor prices, and a big increase in workhouse
admissions, starvation and its associated diseases did not reappear. In
1879–81, another series of bad potato crops, low prices, and poor grain
harvests also produced hardship and a big increase in emigration, but
once again there was no mortality on a mass scale. As historian Tim
O'Neill has noted, "If widespread death from starvation is regarded as
an essential ingredient of famine then there were few, if any, famines in
Ireland after the Great Famine." O'Neill's quest for the last victims of
famine in Ireland in the 1880s and 1890s concentrated on the remoter
regions of south Conamara. It found that claims of starvation generally
remained unproven, with isolated incidents indicating pockets of acute
distress rather than famine proper.[8]

Thomas Malthus famously referred to famine as "the ultimate recourse of nature," the positive check of last resort. Some historians
counter that famines are ineffective Malthusian correctives, in the sense
that their impact on population is purely transitory. In Finland, for example, the demographic damage done by a major famine in 1867–68
was made good within a few years, and population growth there in
1870–1900 was much faster than in the decades leading up to the famine. The demographic impacts of other famines such as those affecting
England in the 1550s, France in the 1690s, much of Europe in the late
1810s, or Ireland in the 1740s were also swamped by rapid population
growth in their wake.[9] In Ireland after the 1840s, by contrast, population did not rise again to fill the vacuum left by the Great Famine. It
would take half a century before a census would register an increase in
population in Ireland as a whole, and a full century before a census
would do the same for the twenty-six-county area. Some pockets in the
west, it is true, showed some signs of the vacuum created by the famine

being filled in its wake. For example, the populations of the Mayo electoral divisions of Knocknalower (in Belmullet union) and Callow (in Swinford union) fell by 42 percent and 28 percent, respectively, between 1841 and 1851 but bounced back by 29 percent and 22 percent in the following decade. Even in such areas, however, population would soon begin to tumble. By and large, population decline was greatest where living standards were lowest, a pattern that would endure into the late twentieth century. In a series of classic papers, K. H. Connell attributed this radical, long-lasting demographic adjustment to the lessons learned the hard way by the Irish in the 1840s. A lower marriage rate reduced the birthrate, as Connell argued: the proportion of women still unmarried at ages 45–54 years rose from 12.5 percent in 1841 to 14.3 in 1861 and 17.1 percent in 1881, while the proportion of children aged 0–4 years in the total population fell from 12.6 percent in 1841 to 12 percent in 1861 and 11.1 percent in 1881. However, the adjustment was less the product of these classic Malthusian preventive checks of lower nuptiality and lower marital fertility through sexual abstinence than of massive, continuing, and permanent emigration.[10]

Inevitably, economic trends in Ireland reflected world market forces. The post-famine decades saw big increases in the demand for immigrant labor in the United States, in Australia, in Canada, and in Great Britain, and also big increases in the demand for meat and dairy products. The impact of these exogenous factors, with conflicting implications for workers' welfare, is not so easy to disentangle from the impact of the famine. The rise in real wages after 1850 might be attributed in part to the pull of foreign labor markets, but the rise in landlords' share of agricultural net value added in the 1850s and 1860s, and the relatively light impact of the post-1876 agricultural depression on Irish agriculture generally, both stemmed largely from relative price shifts on world food markets.[11]

A whiggish, neo-Malthusian interpretation of famines might posit that before they permanently disappear from a region or a country, they become gradually less frequent and less murderous. This is because a gradual improvement in living standards entails an ever-smaller proportion of the population at risk. Famines thus disappear from history with a whimper, not a bang. The historical record on this is mixed. Historian John Iliffe's claim that between 1927 and the end of the colonial era, Africa (Ethiopia apart) saw very few "famines that kill" fits such a scenario. Iliffe points to a variety of factors — effective government, better transport, better medicine, better access to markets, cassava, and some increase in average wealth — as the reasons for this. Wrigley and Schofield's analysis of years of crisis mortality in England between the 1540s and the 1860s (years when the crude death rate was at least 10 percent above a twenty-five-year moving average) also suggests that both the size and duration of famines declined gradually over time.[12] The experience of Ireland between the 1740s and 1840s also broadly supports the whiggish model. The massive famine of 1740–41 was followed by a gap in famines, in effect a series of smaller famines, notably in the mid-1750s, 1783–84, 1800–1801 and 1817–19. Mortality was significant in the last two cases (perhaps 40,000–60,000 in each), but the famines that followed in 1822 and 1831 were more localized and on a much smaller scale.[13] In Ireland, however, the Great Famine brought the era of famines to a cataclysmic end. In Finland too the Great Famine of 1867–68 brought the era of famines in that country to a dramatic halt.

Modern evidence also fails to square with a neo-Malthusian analysis, though for a different reason. In recent decades the threat of famine has been eradicated in Russia and in China, but the last of the "famines that kill" in those countries were major ones indeed. The Great Bengali Famine of 1943–44 also upset a pattern of gradually less murderous famines in India between the 1890s and the 1980s. In many parts of Africa, too, war and political instability brought the return of famines after independence.[14] In sum, tyranny, war, and civic mayhem, rather than the lack of food and medical relief in the strict sense, are the main reasons for twentieth-century famine mortality. Agency is more important than a food production shortfall. Mars counts for more than Malthus. That is partly why Amartya Sen's entitlements interpretation of the economics of famines seems to fit modern famines better than historical famines.

In the late 1840s the famine was synonymous with places like Schull and Skibbereen in west Cork. A century and a half later, its horrors are not easily captured in what have become an expensive tourist spot and a bustling, traffic-choked town. The prosperity of Schull and "Skib" is striking evidence of a broader economic transformation in Ireland. Even in such places the famine has left few surviving physical traces. Elsewhere there is little for the casual outsider to see apart from the occasional abandoned potato ridge. The folk memories of the 1930s and 1940s, reviewed in chapter 6, are much dimmer and contaminated now. The heritage industry seeks, with limited success, to fill the gap. In Skibbereen in late 1993 a local group proposed to build a Wall of Remembrance whereby "we, the decendants [sic] of the Famine victims . . . remember our kinfolk," forgetting that the victims were much less likely to leave descendants than their oppressors. Brutal photographic and screen images of modern or near-modern famines provide most Irish people with a better sense of what it was like to have been there during the famine than any museum or interpretative center.[15]

As noted at the beginning of this book, not so long ago a respected historian described the Irish famine as no more than a detail in European history: "Even the scale of the great famine was not unique when seen in the context of contemporary European experience." Even then a little research would have shown the opposite to have been true: a comparative perspective on the famine makes it stand out, not only in nineteenth-century European history, but in world history. This baffling claim reflected the tendency of some historian quarters in the 1970s and the 1980s to talk down or marginalize the Irish famine.[16] This book, in common with most recent research, has tended to talk it back up. It has shown that the Irish famine was much more murderous, relatively speaking, than most historical and most modern famines, that it lasted long beyond when most general accounts used to end, and that its ravages reached all counties, classes, and creeds. Its enduring impact is reflected in a continued desire in Ireland "to remember those things we never knew" and an eagerness in some quarters further afield, particularly in the United States, to invoke the famine as a means of stoking up old resentments. There is, indeed, evidence aplenty in the record of neglect and harshness and brutality on the part of policymakers of the day—and on the part of others too. But economists and historians will continue to study the famine, not because they delight in confirming or debunking preconceived ideological positions, but because it is central not only to Ireland's history, but to British political and European demographic history, and to the world history of famines.

NOTES

ABBREVIATIONS USED IN NOTES AND BIBLIOGRAPHY

BPP	British Parliamentary Papers
CUP	Cambridge University Press
CC	Cork Constitution
CE	Cork Examiner
DMP	Dublin Medical Press
DQJMS	Dublin Quarterly Journal of Medical Science
EEH	Explorations in Economic History
EHR	Economic History Review
ESR	Economic and Social Review
FJ	Freeman's Journal
G&M	Gill & Macmillan
IAP	Irish Academic Press
IDS	Institute of Development Studies
IESH	Irish Economic and Social History
IFC	Irish Folklore Commission
IHS	Irish Historical Studies
IUP	Irish University Press Famine Series
JCHAS	Journal of the Cork Historical and Archaeological Society
JKAHS	Journal of the Kerry Archaeological and Historical Society
JEH	Journal of Economic History
JEL	Journal of Economic Literature
JIH	Journal of Interdisciplinary History
JME	Journal of Monetary Economics
JPE	Journal of Political Economy
MUP	Manchester University Press
NAD	National Archives Dublin
NLI	National Library of Ireland
OUP	Oxford University Press
PDR	Population and Development Review
PRIA	Proceedings of the Royal Irish Academy
PRO	Public Record Office (London)
PRONI	Public Record Office Northern Ireland
PS	Population Studies
PUP	Princeton University Press
RPE	Research in Population Economics
TRHS	Transactions of the Royal Historical Society

INTRODUCTION

1. According to Eddie Holt (*Irish Times*, 30 December 1995), the arguments had been thrashed to death. For an overview of recent research, see C. Ó Gráda,

"Making famine history in Ireland in 1995," *History Workshop Journal*, no. 42 (Autumn 1996).

2. In Stephen Campbell, *The Great Irish Famine* (Strokestown, 1994), 7; also Mary Robinson, *A Voice for Somalia* (Dublin, 1992), 11–12.

3. Niall Ó Ciosáin, "Dia, bia agus Sasana: an Mistéalach agus íomhá an Ghorta," in C. Póirtéir, ed., *Gnéithe den Ghorta* (Dublin, 1995), 151–63; Edmund M. Hogan, *The Irish Missionary Movement: A Historical Survey 1830–1980* (Dublin, 1990). The famine informs both Galway-born playright Thomas Murphy's *Famine* (1968) and Séamus Heaney's "For the Commander of the Eliza" (in *Death of a Naturalist* [Dublin, 1966], 34). Neither, it seems, owed much to folk memory: a passage in Woodham-Smith was Heaney's inspiration, while Murphy first read the facts of the Irish famine in *The Great Hunger* (introduction to *Thomas, Murphy: Plays One*).

4. However, the link between Irish missionary activity and generosity in face of Third World famines is not completely straightforward, either. Until relatively recently, the emphasis in charities organized by Irish missionary societies was on souls rather than bodies. The widely sold *Far East*, for example, contained little about economic development or the relief of poverty in the mid-1940s, and concentrated on seeking support for missionary personnel and church buildings. Nor, despite articles about Christ's poor in Nancheng City or how tribesmen in Upper Burma subsisted on a diet of rice, did it refer to the Great Irish Famine between 1945 and 1947.

5. *Freeman's Journal*, 4 February 1848.

6. Iliffe, *The African Poor* (Cambridge, U.K., 1987), 157, 255; Alex de Waal, "Famine mortality: A case study of Darfur, Sudan in 1984–5," *Population Studies*, 43 (1989), 5–24; John Seaman, "Famine mortality in Africa," *IDS Bulletin*, 24(4) (1993), 29; Gopalakrishna Kumar, "Ethiopian famines 1973–1985: A case-study," WIDER Working Paper No. 26, November 1987, 23; Asmerom Kidame, "Demographic consequences of the 1984–85 Ethiopian famine," *Demography*, 26 (1989), 515–22; Megan Vaughan, *The Story of an African Famine: Hunger, Gender and Politics in Malawi* (Cambridge, U.K., 1987), 162.

7. Iliffe, *African Poor*, 251; Kumar, "Ethiopian famines," 42; Seaman, "Famine mortality in Africa," 30–31; Amartya Sen, *Poverty and Famines* (Oxford, 1981), 86, 116, 134, 195–216; S. G. Wheatcroft and R. W. Davies, "Population," in R. W. Davies, M. Harrison, and S. G. Wheatcroft (eds.), *The Economic Transformation of the Soviet Union, 1913–1945* (Cambridge, U.K., 1994), 62–63, 67–77; B. Ashton *et al.*, "Famine in China, 1958–61" *PDR*, 10(4) (1984), 613–46; Penny Kane, *Famine in China, 1959–61: Demographic and Social Implications* (New York, 1988); Kari Pitkänen, "The patterns of mortality during the Great Finnish Famine in the 1860s," *Acta Demographica 1992* (Physica-Verlag, Heidelberg), 81–102; *id.*, *Deprivation and Disease: Mortality during the Great Finnish Famine of the 1860s* (Helsinki, 1993), 7. John Iliffe (in *Africa: The History of a Continent* [Cambridge, U.K., 1995], 68) notes that in Cape Verde between 1773 and 1866 three well-documented famines each killed about two-fifths of the entire population. But he adds that such mortality was rare. According to Wheatcroft and Davies, deaths from famine and disease in the

Soviet Union in 1918–22 may have reached 14 million in a population of 140 million in 1914.

8. Joel Mokyr, *Why Ireland Starved* (London, 1985), ch. 2; David Johnson and Liam Kennedy, "Irish national income on the eve of the famine" (mimeo, 1995); B. R. Mitchell, *British Historical Statistics* (Cambridge, U.K., 1988), 837–41; Robert Summers and Alan Heston, "The Penn world table (mark 5): An expanded set of international comparisons," *Quarterly Journal of Economics*, 106(2) (1991), table 2; United Nations, *Human Development Report 1995* (New York, 1995), table 1.

9. Ruth Dudley Edwards, *The Age of Reason: A History of the Economist* (London, 1994), ch. 4; Peter Gray, "Potatoes and providence: British government's responses to the Great Famine," *Bullán: An Irish Studies Journal*, no. 1 (1994), 75–90; id., "Ideology and the famine," in Póirtéir, *The Great Irish Famine*, 86–103.

10. Ó Gráda, *Ireland before and after the Famine* (Manchester, 1993), ch. 3; id., *Ireland* (Oxford, 1994), ch. 8; P. Gray, "Punch and the Great Famine," *History Ireland*, 1(2) (1993); Ira Klein, "When the rains failed: Famine relief and mortality in British India," *Indian Economic and Social History Review*, 21 (1984), 189; M. Bergman, "The potato blight in the Netherlands and its social consequences (1845–1847)," *International Review of Social History*, 17(3) (1967), 391–431; Peter Gray, "Famine relief in comparative perspective: Ireland, Scotland, and North-western Europe, 1845–50," paper presented to the NYU/Ireland House Conference on Famine and World Hunger, May 1995; Richard G. Robbins, Jr., *Famine in Russia, 1891–1892: The Imperial Governments Response to a Crisis* (New York, 1975).

11. S. Devereux, *Theories of Famine* (London, 1993), 95–97, 133–47; information from Trócaire; W. A. Dando, *The Geography of Famine* (London, 1980), 101–2; Iliffe, *African Poor*, 256.

12. De Waal, "War and famine in Africa," *IDS Bulletin*, 24(4) (1993), 33.

13. Jean Drèze and Amartya Sen, *Hunger and Public Action* (Oxford, 1989), 274–7; de Waal, "War and famine in Africa"; Michael Watts, "Entitlements or empowerment? Famine and starvation in Africa," *Review of African Political Economy*, 51 (1991), 13–14; John Iliffe, *Famine in Zimbabwe* (Gweru, 1990), 111; Food and Agricultural Organization, *Food Security and Food Assistance* (WFS 96/TECH/14), July 1996, 4.

14. A. Martin Freeman (ed.), *Annála Connacht: The Annals of Connacht* (Dublin, 1944), 241, 253, 283.

15. North Korea in 1997 seems a likely exception; ideology also constrained relief both from within and from abroad in Ethiopia in the mid-1980s.

16. Amartya Sen, "Nobody need starve," *Granta*, no. 52 (Winter 1995), 213–20; J. D. Post, *Food Shortage, Climatic Variability and Epidemic Disease in Preindustrial Europe* (Ithaca, N.Y., 1985), 145, 177; Peter Solar, "The potato famine in Europe," in Ó Gráda, *Famine 150*, 113–27.

17. See Timothy W. Guinnane, "Ireland's famine wasn't genocide," *Washington Post*, 17 September 1997.

CHAPTER 1
CONTEXTS AND CHRONOLOGY

1. David Ricardo, *Works and Correspondence*, vol. 9, ed. Piero Sraffa (Cambridge, U.K., 1952), 23.

2. R. N. Salaman, *The Influence of the Potato on the Course of Irish History* (Dublin, 1943); id., *The History and Social Influence of the Potato* (Cambridge, U.K., 1949), chs. 11–13; Connell, *The Population of Ireland*, ch. 5; Cullen, "Irish history without the potato"; Charles Heiser, *Seed to Civilization: The Story of Food* (Cambridge, Mass., 1990), 136.

3. Nicholas Williams (ed.), *Pairlimint Chloinne Thomáis* (Dublin, 1981), 62–63, 115; J. C. McErlean, *Duanaire Dháibhidh Uí Bhruadair*, vol. 1 (London,1913), 66–67. Compare L. M. Cullen, *The Emergence of Modern Ireland* (London, 1981), 159–60.

4. D. Dickson, "The potato and Irish diet before the famine," in Ó Gráda, *Famine 150*; Ó Gráda, *Ireland before and after the Famine*, 9–14; W. J. Smyth, "Making the documents of conquest speak: The transformation of property, society, and settlement in seventeenth-century Tipperary and Kilkenny," in Marilyn Silverman and P. H. Gulliver (eds.), *Approaching the Past* (New York, 1992), 248 (map of population density c. 1680).

5. Robert McKay, *An Anthology of the Potato* (Dublin, 1961), 25–27; Pádraig Breathnach, "Togha na héigse," *Éigse*, 27 (1993), 121. Also C. Ó Gráda and Diarmaid Ó Muirithe, "Representations of the famine of 1740–41 in Gaelic poetry," in prep.

6. Austin Bourke, *The Visitation of God* (Dublin, 1993), 25; T. P. McIntosh, *The Potato: Its History, Varieties, Culture and Diseases* (Edinburgh, 1927), 13; Sir John Forster, *England's Happiness Increased ... by a Plantation of the Roots Called Potatoes* (London, 1664), 2–3.

On the diffusion of the potato on the Continent, see Max Labbé, *Cette étonnante pomme de terre* (Paris, 1988), 27–29; Christiaan Vanderbroeke, "Aardappelteelt en aardappelverbruik in de 17e en 18e eeuw," *Tijdschrift voor Geschiedenis*, 82 (1969), 49–68; Michael Drake, *Population and Society in Norway* (Cambridge, U.K., 1969), 54–65; Javier López Linage (ed.), *De Papa a patata: La diffusion española del tubérculo andino* (Madrid, c. 1991); V. Falbe Hansen and W. Scharling, *Danmarks Statistik* (Copenhagen, 1887), 136–37, 185; Dietrich Denecke, "Innovation and diffusion of the potato in central Europe in the seventeenth and eighteenth centuries" in Buchman et al., *Fields, Farms*, 107–17.

7. Archives Nationales (Paris), F/10/210 (my translation).

8. Etienne Juillard, *La vie rurale en Basse-Alsace* (Strasbourg, 1992), 214; Paul Leuilliot, *L'Alsace au début du XIXe siècle: Les transformations économiques* (Paris, 1959), 83.

9. Bourke, *Visitation*, 12; Juillard, *La vie rurale*, 213–15.

10. Alexis Jacquemyns, "Histoire de la crise économique des Flandres," *Académie Royale de Belgique, Mémoires*, 26 (1929), 11–472; Joel Mokyr, "Industrialization and poverty in Ireland and the Netherlands: some notes towards a comparative case study," *Journal of Interdisciplinary History*, 10(3) (1981), 429–59; Solar, "Potato famine in Europe," 113–27; H. M. Waidson, *Jeremias*

Gotthelf (London, 1954), 117–21; Jean-Michel Selig, *Malnutrition et développement économique dans l'Alsace du XIXe siècle* (Strasbourg, 1996), 660–61; Hans-Heinrich Bass, *Hungerkrisen in Preussen während der ersten Hälfte des 19. Jahrhunderts* (St. Katherinen, 1991), 213–69.

11. T. Devine, "Why the Highlands did not starve: Ireland and Highland Scotland during the potato famine," in S. J. Connolly, R. Houston, and R. J. Morris (eds.), *Conflict, Identity, and Economic Development* (Carnegie Publishing, 1995), 78–81. See also Chapter 3 below.

12. Forster, *England's Happiness Increased*, 12.

13. Young's data are given in his *Tour in Ireland* (Dublin, 1780), vol. 2, 28–29. For more on Young, see C. Ó Gráda, "Notes on the potato," mimeo; R. C. Allen and C. Ó Gráda, "On the road again with Arthur Young: English, Irish and French agriculture during the Industrial Revolution," *Journal of Economic History*, 47 (March 1988), 93–116.

14. Bourke, *Visitation*, 120; Ó Gráda, "Notes on the potato."

15. Bourke, *Visitation*; Allen and Ó Gráda, "On the road again."

16. Brendan McWilliams, "The kingdom of the air: The progress of meteorology," in J. W. Foster (ed.), *Nature in Ireland: A Scientific and Cultural History* (Dublin, 1997), 118; Bourke, *Visitation*, ch. 4; Mokyr, "Irish history with the potato" *Irish Economic and Social History* 8 (1981), 3–29; Michel Demonet, *Tableau de l'agriculture française au milieu du 19e siècle: L'enquête de 1852* (Paris, 1990), 187; M. Drake, *Economy and Society in Norway* (Cambridge, U.K., 1969), 64; S. Vissering, *Eenige opmerkingen ter zake der aardappelziekte* (Amsterdam, 1845), 9–12 (cited in Bourke and Lamb, *Spread of the Potato Blight in Europe*, 40).

17. Vandenbroeke, "Aardappelteelt en aardappelverbruik," 49–68; Martine Goossens, *The Economic Development of Belgian Agriculture: A Regional Perspective, 1812–1846* (Brussels, 1992); Selig, *Malnutrition et développement économique*, 527; Bass, *Hungerkrisen in Preussen*, 52. The table shows the story for Belgium as a whole.

Year	hl/ha	Output (hl)	Population (1,000s)	Daily Consumption Per Capita (kilos)
1812	130.9	5,225,082	4,166	0.26
1846	197.87	12,908,139	4,337	0.64

Source: Goossens, *Economic Development of Belgian Agriculture*, 89, 146; Mitchell, *European Historical Statistics*, 19. A hectoliter of potatoes was assumed to weigh 75 kilograms.

18. Compare data on the price of potatoes and oats in Peter Solar, "Growth and distribution in Irish agriculture" (Ph.D: diss., Stanford University, 1987); Gunnar Myrdal, *Wages, Cost of Living and National Income in Sweden, 1860–1930, vol. 1: The Cost of Living in Sweden, 1830–1930* (London, 1933), 200; Preston price data in Joan Thirsk (ed.), *The Agrarian History of England and Wales*, vol. 6 (Cambridge, U.K., 1989), 984–85; Svend Aage Hansen, *Øko-*

nomisk Vaekst i Danmark: Bind II: 1914–1983 (Copenhagen, 1984), 301–2; Wilhelm Abel, *Agricultural Fluctuations in Europe from the Thirteenth to the Twentieth Centuries* (London, 1980), 279, 286.

19. Denis Knight, *Cobbett in Ireland: A Warning to England* (London, 1984), 95, 110, 185; Cullen, *Emergence of Modern Ireland, 1600–1900*, 159–160; *Sixth Annual Report of the Bureau of Statistics of Labour* (Boston, 1875), "Condition of workingmen's families," 221–354; Robert P. Skinner, *Utilization of Potatoes in Europe: Special Consular Reports no. 64* (Washington, D.C., Department of Commerce, 1914).

20. As suggested by Bourke, *Visitation*, 12. Also Kevin Whelan, "The modern landscape," in Aalen *et al.*, *Atlas of the Irish Rural Landscape*, 85.

21. The Irish potato yields discussed above may be compared with those in Young's *Tour of the North of England*, where he presented about thirty independent observations on yields. Excluding the extreme estimates at the top and bottom (two or three at each end), these data imply a yield of about 250 bushels per acre. Taken together, Young's numbers suggest that the Anglo-Irish gap in potato yields was less than that in grain. Applying standard conversion ratios to produce Irish volume measures, and comparing to Belgian and French yields in the 1840s, suggests a similar outcome. See Young, *A Six Month's Tour through the North of England*, 2d ed. (London, 1771), vol. 3, 413; id., *Tour in Ireland* (Dublin, 1780), vol. 2, 15 (appendix); Goossens, *Belgian Agriculture*, 87, 89; B. R. Mitchell, *European Historical Statistics* (London, 1975), 199, 203, 237, 240.

22. A. W. Sutton, "The potato," in T. Johnson (ed.), *Report on the Conference and Exhibition of the Tercentenary of the Potato* (Dublin, 1897), 57; McIntosh, *The Potato*, 16; P. Joigneaux, *Le livre de la terre*, 3d ed. (Paris, 1860–65), 1, 267 (my translation).

23. There is hardly a mention of potato varieties in the studies of Juillard, Vandenbroeke, or Morineau cited earlier. On names, see, e.g., Labbé, *Cette étonnante pomme de terre*, 30–32.

24. W. D. Davidson, "History of potato varieties," *Journal of the Department of Agriculture*, 33 (1935), 57–81; Bourke, *Visitation*, 28–42; Tighe, *Kilkenny*, 234–35.

25. From "Patrick Read's Second Notice to the Rev. F.W.F. Rector of Kilbeacon to draw his Tithes" (*Faulkner's Dublin Journal*, 19 May 1798).

26. B. Merriman, *Cúirt an Mheon-Oíche*, ed. Liam P. Ó Murchú (Dublin, 1982), 29.

27. P. Kennedy, *By the Banks of the Boro* (Dublin, 1875), 5. According to Bourke (*Visitation*, 36), the first Irish reference to the Lumper is in Hely Dutton, *Statistical Survey of the County of Clare* (Dublin, 1808), 43. References between then and the 1820s were few.

28. Bourke, *Visitation*, 109; W. S. Trench, *The Realities of Irish Life* (London, 1966 (1868), 47. See too Ó Gráda, *Ireland before and after the Famine*, 11–12; E. Hoffman and J. Mokyr, "Peasants, potatoes and poverty: Transactions costs in prefamine Ireland," in G. Saxonhouse and G. Wright (eds.), *Technique, Spirit, and Form* (Greenwich, Conn., 1984).

29. The data are taken from Solar, "Growth and distribution."

30. P. Solar, "The great famine was no ordinary subsistence crisis," in E. M.

Crawford (ed.), *Famine* (Edinburgh, 1989). 114–18; J. Mokyr, "Uncertainty in prefamine Irish agriculture," in Devine and Dickson, *Ireland and Scotland*. The potato price data used in figure 1.1 were taken from Solar, "Growth and distribution."

31. Bourke, *Visitation*, 150–54.

32. E. Wakefield, *Ireland, Political and Statistical* (London, 1812), vol. 2, 838; Henry D. Inglis, *Ireland in 1834* (London, 1835), vol. 2, 322–24; J. G. Kohl, *Travels in Ireland* (London, 1844); G. De Beaumont, *Ireland: Social, Political and Religious*, 2 vols. (London, 1839); C. Ó Gráda, *Ireland: A New Economic History* (Oxford, 1994), 80–85.

33. Campbell Foster, *Letters on the Condition of Ireland*, 202; Ó Gráda, *Ireland*, ch. 4. Mokyr's *Why Ireland Starved* submits many of the data produced by these investigations to ingenious cliometric analysis. For an accessible sampling of the Poor Inquiry's evidence, taken from one county, see CLASP (Close Local Studies Project), *Poverty before the Famine: County Clare 1835* (Ennis, 1996).

34. Ó Gráda, *Ireland before and after the Famine*, 78–79.

35. Kevin Whelan, "Pre- and post-famine landscape change," in Póirtéir, *The Great Irish Famine*, 19–33; Campbell Foster, *Letters on the Condition of the People of Ireland*, 202.

36. N. W. Senior, *Journals, Conversations and Essays*, vol. 2 (London, 1868), 277. See too S. G. Osborne, *Gleanings from the West of Ireland* (London, 1850), 140–42.

37. Andrés Eiríksson and C. Ó Gráda, "Bankrupt landlords and the Irish famine" (1996); Mary C. Lyons, *Illustrated Encumbered Estates* (Whitegate, Co. Clare, 1993), 23, 25; see too Osborne, *Gleanings from the West of Ireland*, 45–46; *Transactions of the Society of Friends*, 207.

38. IUP7/406–7 (Waterford), 538 (Westmeath); *Report of the British Association for the Relief of Extreme Distress*, 96 (Count Strzelecki from Clifden, 4 March 1847). See too Campbell Foster, *Letters on the Condition of the People of Ireland*, 482–85.

39. Ó Gráda, *Ireland*, 124–25.

40. Campbell Foster, *Letters on the Condition of the People of Ireland*, 473–82; Richard Roche, "The famine years in Forth and Bargy," *Journal of the Wexford Historical Society*, no. 15, 1–14. See too Anna Kinsella, *County Wexford in the Famine Years* (Enniscorthy, 1995), 69–70.

41. Ó Gráda, *Ireland before and after the Famine*, 24–25; Trevor McCavery, "The wealthy found wanting: Controversies over famine relief in Newtownards Poor Law Union," *Ulster Local Studies*, 17(2) (1995), 50–74; Ó Gráda, *Ireland before and after the Famine*, 24–25; James Grant, "The Great Famine in county Down," in L. Proudfoot (ed.), *Down: History and Society* (Dublin, 1997), 370.

42. On this point see the maps and the correlations reported in Desmond McCabe, "The Great Famine in Ballina," typescript, National Famine Research Project (Dublin, 1997).

43. The underrecording of population in 1841 in remoter areas may also have played some part. In county Mayo, for example, 26.3 percent of women aged 17–25 years and 81.8 percent of women aged 26–35 years were married

or widowed, compared to percentages of 19.3 and 71.1 for Ireland as a whole. The rate of emigration nationally in the 1830s was almost certainly higher than that from Mayo. Yet recorded population growth in Mayo in 1831–41 was only marginally higher than that in Ireland (6.2 percent versus 5.2 percent).

44. Mokyr, *Why Ireland Starved*, ch. 3; Ó Gráda, "Malthus and the pre-famine economy," in A. Murphy (ed.), *Economists and the Irish Economy* (Dublin, 1983), 75–80; *id., Ireland before and after the Famine*, ch. 1.

45. According to data given in Mitchell, *European Historical Statistics*, the percentages were Belgium 53 percent in 1846, Denmark 49 percent in 1860, Netherlands 45 percent in 1849, and Sweden 66 percent in 1860. The population data are also given in Mitchell.

46. Assuming that Irish income per capita rose from less than half to about two-thirds that of Great Britain between 1845 and 1914, and comparing the outcome with data for the other countries in Angus Maddison, *Dynamic Forces in Capitalist Development* (Oxford, 1991), app. A and B.

47. Patrick McGregor, "Demographic pressure and the Irish famine: Malthus after Mokyr," *Land Economics*, 65 (1989), 228–38.

48. The results for Ireland as a whole are also summarized in C. Ó Gráda and K. O'Rourke, "Mass migration as disaster relief," *European Review of Economic History*, 1 (1997): 3–27.

49. One of the most frequently asked questions about the famine is why the poor did not substitute fish for potatoes. On this, see C. Woodham-Smith, *The Great Hunger* (London, 1962), 289–93; Ó Gráda, *Ireland*, 146–52. On 29 December 1846 the *Cork Constitution* reported that "the rivers throughout this county are every night ablaze, from the lights carried along them for the purpose of catching salmon." The statistical analysis is discussed more fully in Ó Gráda, "The Great Irish Famine: Some economic aspects," typescript (1995).

50. T. W. Freeman, *Ireland: A General and Regional Geography*, 4th ed. (London, 1969), 44.

51. Bourke, *Visitation*, 47–48; Mokyr, *Why Ireland Starved*, 214–16; Ó Gráda, *Ireland*, 17, 50 42.

52. CLASP, *Poverty before the Famine*, 26, 48, 71, 91, 108, 127, 137, 162.

53. *Poor Inquiry*, app. E ("Clothing and furniture"), 68–92; *Census 1841*; Alexis de Tocqueville, *Journey in Ireland, July–August 1835* (Washington, D.C., 1990), 112.

54. *Poor Inquiry*, app. E, 70 (Murrisk); (IUP7/30); Ciarán Ó Murchadha, personal communication. In John Millington Synge's *Riders to the Sea*, Maurya talks of "the great rest I'll have now, and great sleeping in the long nights after Samhain, if it's only a bit of wet flour we do have to eat, and maybe a fish that would be stinking."

55. Bourke and Lamb, *Spread of the Potato Blight*, 47; Mitchell, *European Historical Statistics*, 199, 203, 237, 240 (on French yields); Jacquemyns, "Crise économique," 248–55 (on 1845 in Belgium); Goossens, *Belgian Agriculture*, 88–89 (on 1846); T. M. Devine, *Great Highland Famine*, (Edinburgh, 1988). 34–36.

56. Stephen A. Royle, "Irish famine relief in the early nineteenth century: The 1822 famine on the Aran Islands," *IESH*, 11 (1984), 44–59; Peter Gray, "Brit-

ish politics and the Irish land question, 1843–50" (Ph.D. diss., University of Cambridge, 1992), 209–14.

57. Bourke and Lamb, *Spread of the Potato Blight in Europe*, 22–24. Check too (for Sligo) *Quarterly Journal of the Royal Meteorological Society*, 10 (1884), 158–61; Ordnance Survey of Ireland, *Meteorological Observations Taken during the Years 1829 to 1852 at the Ordnance Survey Office, Phoenix Park, Dublin* (Dublin, 1856); H. D. Jones, "Daily observations on the weather and on the rise and fall of the Shannon during the years 1845–48," *PRIA* 4 (app. 6) (1849).

58. Pat McGregor, "The Great Irish Famine: A failure of development or policy?" University of Ulster, typescript, 1997.

59. PRO T64/367A/1 (Douglas to Routh, 11 December 1846); Captain Wynne in IUP7/170; Colonel Vandeleur, cited in Ignatius Murphy, *A People Starved: Life and Death in West Clare, 1845–51* (Dublin, 1996), 76.

60. IUP5/565, 890 (Clare); IUP7/413 (Clare); also IUP6/477 (Leitrim); W. Wilde, "Epidemics," *DQJMS*, 7 (1849), 89 (citing Dr Cullinan of Ennis, who blamed the increase in deaths on a combination of inadequate food and "the exposure to cold and wet to which the peasantry were exposed to an unusual degree"); IUP7/439 (Clare); D. Thomson and M. McGusty (eds.), *The Irish Journals of Elizabeth Smith* (Oxford, 1980), 114; Hugh Dorrian, "The years of the famine" (typescript), 4 (also cited in Noel Kissane, *The Irish Famine*, 70). See too C. Kinealy, *This Great Calamity* (Dublin, 1994), 95, 159, 174; *Report of the British Association for the Relief of the Extreme Distress in Ireland and Scotland* (London, 1849), 93. Compare Maharatna, *Demography of Famines*, 54.

61. NLI Ms. 12,201 (Ballina poor-law union Board of Guardians' minutes, 30 May 1846); Campbell Foster, *Letters on the Condition of the People of Ireland*, 441; IUP5/32–3; T.P. O'Neill, "The organisation and administration of relief," in Edwards and Williams, *The Great Famine*, 222. On the death from starvation in July 1846 of a young man in Inagh, north Clare, see Ciarán Ó Murchadha, "The onset of famine: County Clare, 1845–1846," *Old Limerick Journal*, 32 (1995), 30.

62. Bourke and Lamb, *Spread of the Potato Blight*, 40.

63. Thirteenth Annual Report of the Poor Law Commissioners (quotation); IUP5/890; IUP6/284–85 (Skibbereen), 5/919 (Dingle), 5/754 (Kilkenny); M. O'Connell (ed.), *The Correspondence of Daniel O'Connell*, vol. 8 (Dublin, 1980), 156; John Killen, *The Famine Decade* (Belfast, 1995), 76; Murphy, *A People Starved*, 37.

64. Thirteenth Annual Report of the Poor Law Commissioners gives weekly deaths up to 1 May 1847; Gerry McAtasney, "The famine in Lurgan and Portadown," *Ulster Local Studies*, 17(2) (Winter 1995), 80.

65. IUP1/39, 1/45; R. Mayne, "Observations on the late epidemic of dysentery in Dublin," *DQJMS*, 7 (1849), 294–308.

66. Margaret Kelleher, "The female gaze: Asenath Nicholson's famine narrative," in C. Morash and R. Hayes (eds.), *Fearful Realities* (Dublin, 1996), 127–28; McCorry, "The famine in the Montiaghs," in McCorry et al., *Armagh* (Dublin, 1998).

67. C. Ó Gráda, *An Drochshaol* (Dublin, 1994), 73–74; Irish Folklore Commission, Ms. 1480/383–84; *The Times*, 26 April 1849 (citing *the Mayo Constitution*), 27 April 1849 (citing *FJ*), 30 April 1849 (citing *the Evening Mail*), 11 May 1849 (citing *The Cork Examiner*); *Tipperary Vindicator*, 27 January 1847, 20 March 1847, 31 March 1847.

68. *The Times*, 15 January 1847; *FJ*, 13 March 1847; Dorothy Howell-Thomas, *Duncannon: Reformer and Reconciler, 1781–1847* (Norwich, 1992), 306–8.

69. Mary Daly, *The Great Famine* in Ireland (Dandalk, 1986), 113.

70. P. Gray, *Ireland's Famine* (London and New York, 1995), 82; Second Annual Report of the Poor Law Commissioners, 10.

71. P. Hickey, "Famine, mortality and emigration," in O'Flanagan and Buttimer (eds.), *Cork*, 910–11; Sixth Annual Report of the Poor Law Commissioners, 7. Joan Vincent, "A political orchestration of the Irish famine: County Fermanagh, May 1847," in M. Silverman and P. Gulliver (eds.), *Engaging the Past: Historical Anthropology through Irish Case-studies* (New York, 1992), 94), claims that mortality continued "high" in Fermanagh until 1856.

72. Compare Ó Gráda, *Ireland before and after the Famine*, 108–9; IUP4/292, 293, 301, 306, 363.

73. PRO T64/370A/2 (Henry Brewster, "General observations on the state of Mayo in the month of December 1849"); Desmond McCabe, "Ballina and the Great Famine," table 22a; Ciarán Ó Murchadha, "One vast abbatoir."

74. *The Times*, 4 May 1849; other data derived from Andrés Eiríksson, *Parsonstown Union and Workhouse during the Great Famine: A Statistical Report* (Dublin, 1996), app. 3; BPP 1851, vol. 19 [484.], *Return of the Deaths in Kilrush and Ennistymon Workhouses. 25th Day of March 1851*; worksheets kindly supplied by Andrés Eiríksson.

75. Gray, *Ireland's Famine*, 84; Murphy, *A People Starved*, 1996; Kinealy, *This Great Calamity*, 286–93.

76. BPP 1852/3 (L). The commissioners' year ran from May to April. App. B, no. 16, gives data on wages by district, indicating no big rise between 1846 and 1853.

77. K. Pitkänen, *Deprivation and Disease: Mortality during the Great Finnish Famine of the 1860s* (Helsinki, 1993); Sen, *Poverty and Famines*, 215; Tim Dyson, "Demographic responses to famines in South Asia," *IDS Bulletin*, 24(4) (1993), 17–26; Dali L. Yang, *Calamity and Reform in China: State, Rural Society, and Institutional Change since the Great Leap Famine* (Stanford, 1996), 38.

78. 16 October 1847; Gray, "Punch and the famine," 26–32; J. S. Donnelly, "Irish property must pay for Irish poverty: British public opinion and the Great Irish Famine," in Morash and Hayes, *Fearful Realities*, 60–76.

79. Kinealy, *This Great Calamity*, 165.

80. James Grant, "The Great Famine and the Poor Law in the province of Ulster: The rate-in-aid issue of 1849," *IHS*, 27, no. 105 (1990); G. McAtasney, *This Dreadful Visitation* (Belfast, 1997), 83–92; *Times*, 5 March, 7 March, 29 May 1849. On the reluctance of the better-off in Ireland to help, see e.g. Denis Marnane, "The famine in south Tipperary—part 1," *Tipperary Historical Journal*, 9 (1996), 33.

81. For more on famine and post-famine migration, see chapter 3; Oliver MacDonagh, "Irish emigration to the United States of America and the British colonies during the famine," in Edwards and Williams, *The Great Famine*, 319–88; D. Fitzpatrick, *Irish Emigration, 1820–1921* (Dundalk, 1984).

82. Murphy, *A People Starved*, 53; W. E. Vaughan, *Landlords and Tenants in Mid-Victorian Ireland* (Oxford, 1993), 230–31; Mary Daly, "Farming and the famine," in Ó Gráda, *Famine 150*, 42; Kinealy, *This Great Calamity*, 218; J. Donnelly, "Mass evictions," in Póirtéir, *Great Irish Famine*; T. Yager, "Mass eviction in the Mullet peninsula," *IESH*, 23 (1996), 24–44; Eugene Broderick, "The famine in Waterford as reported in the local newspapers," in Cowman and Brady, *Teacht na bPrátaí Dhubha*, 184–85; *Report of the Select Committee on the Kilrush Union*, BPP 1850, vol. 3; Tim P. O'Neill, "Famine evictions," typescript, April 1997. J. H. Tuke, *Visit to Connaught in the Autumn of 1847*, 2d ed. (London, 1848), 61–71, contains a detailed account of the clearances in Erris.

83. *Transactions of the Society of Friends*, 208; IUP7/38, 171, 444–45. Between 1846 and early 1849, the number of tenements valued at under £4 in Ballina union fell by two-fifths (from 17,216 to 10,354), that of tenements valued above £4 by a ninth (from 5,779 to 5,111).

84. J. S. Donnelly, "The journals of Sir John Benn-Walsh relating to the management of his Irish estates," *JCHAS*, 79 (1974), 103, 105–7, 109.

85. Typically emigration was not an option for the elderly, nor was payment in return for possession enough to pay for large families. See NLI Ms. 3773 (commonplace book of an east Clare proprietor).

86. PRO, T64/365B (Captain Mann to Hewetson, 28 April 1848); also Osborne, *Gleanings from the West of Ireland*, 151; W. Aykroyd, *The Conquest of Famine* (London, 1974), 16.

87. Póirtéir, *Glórtha*, 158–59, also *ibid.*, 128; Osborne, *Gleanings from the West of Ireland*, 25; Colman O'Mahony, *In the Shadows* (Cork, 1997), 167 (citing *CE*, 26 May 1847). Compare the famine poem "Caora an tSagairt (The Priest's Sheep)," in Énrí Ó Muirgheasa, *Dánta Diadha Uladh* (Dublin, 1936), 217, lines 5–8; L. M. Geary, "The living were out of their feeling," *Comhdháil an Chraoibhín 1997*.

88. See, e.g., R. Dirks, "Resource fluctuations and competitive transformations in West Indian slave societies," in Laughlin and Brady, *Extinction and Survival*, 167–77; *id.*, "Social responses during severe food shortages and famine," *Current Anthropology*, 21 (1980). According to John Iliffe (in *Africa: The History of a Continent*, 113), when famine struck "family ties dissolved, and humans became animals."

CHAPTER TWO
RELIEF

1. Marie C. Nelson, *Bitter Bread: The Famine in Norrbotten* (Uppsala, 1988), 143, 150; Antti Häkkinen *et al.*, *Kun Hallen nälän tuskan to* (Helsinki, 1991), 195–200; Robbins, *Famine in Russia, 1891–1892*, 24–25; Henry F. Deng and Larry Minear, *The Challenges of Famine Relief: Emergency Opera-*

tions in the Sudan (Washington, D.C., 1992), 32; World Bank, *World Development Report* (Washington, D.C., 1987), 202. Compare *Hungerkrisen in Preussen*, 274; W. O. Henderson, *The Lancashire Cotton Famine, 1861–1865* (Manchester, 1934), 85–87; Peter Keen, *The Benefits of Famine: A Political Economy of Famine and Relief in Southwestern Sudan, 1983–1989* (Princeton, N.J. 1994); Jean-François Bayart, *The State in Africa: The Politics of the Belly* (London, 1993). In 1985 Sudan's population was 21.9 million, and its GNP per capita was $300. For a recent survey of the literature on the economics of corruption, see Pranab Bardhan, "Corruption and development: A review of issues," *JEL*, 35(3) (1997), 1320–46.

2. Drèze and Sen, *Hunger and Public Action, passim*, but especially ch. 7 and pp. 113, 115, 117; FAO, *Food Security and Food Assistance* (WFS/TECH/14), 8–9; Keen, *The Benefits of Famine*, 159–60; Alex de Waal, "Sorry St Bob, but it's time we banned aid," *The Observer*, 20 October 1996; "Not by bread alone," *The Economist*, 13 January 1990. On the political economy of U.S. food aid, see Vernon Ruttan (ed.), *Why Food Aid?* (Baltimore, 1993).

3. "Food, economics, and entitlements," in Jean Drèze, Amartya Sen, and Athar Hussain (eds.), *The Political Economy of Hunger: Selected Essays* (Oxford, 1995), 59–61; Aykroyd, *The Conquest of Famine*, 76.

4. This has been amply documented by the late Thomas P. O'Neill in "The organisation and administration of relief, 1845–52," in Edwards and Williams, *The Great Famine*, 209–60, and by Christine Kinealy, *This Great Calamity*. Ó Gráda, *Great Irish Famine* (ch. 2), and Gray, *The Irish Famine*, provide summaries.

5. *The Economist*, 16 January 1847. On 21 January 1847 the *Times* editorialized that "it is because such exertions could, under present circumstances, administer a temporary mitigation to an enormous and growing calamity — because whatever might be done now would only increase the necessity and hasten the occasion for doing more hereafter — that the hand of charity has paused in executing a work which we believe the intelligence and humanity of many of our countrymen have for some time been contemplating." Compare Michael Watts, *Silent Violence* (Berkeley, 1983), 302.

6. On relief committees, see Kinealy, *This Great Calamity*, 82–89; Jim Grant, "Studying local relief committees," *Ulster Local Studies*, 17(2) (1995), 27–33.

7. Mary Daly has written of "undeserving large farmers employed at the expense of labourers" and David Fitzpatrick of "widespread and systematic imposture" on public works schemes. James Grant describes their contribution in Ulster as "vital." See O'Rourke, *Great Irish Famine*, 211; Kinealy, *This Great Calamity*, 103–4; Daly, *The Famine in Ireland*, 82–83; "The operations of famine relief, 1845–47," in Póirtéir, *Great Irish Famine*, 131; David Fitzpatrick, "Famine, entitlements and seduction," *English Historical Review* 110 (1995), 598; James Grant, "Local relief committees in Ulster," in Crawford, *The Hungry Stream*, 194.

In an assessment that anticipates O'Rourke's novelist Anthony Trollope, who lived in Ireland during part of the famine, found that "the work was done; the men were got on the roads . . . and though hundreds upon hundreds doubtless succeeded in cheating . . . these peculations were not so great as might have been expected on considering the extent and nature of the works"; *The Examiner*, 6 April 1850, 217 (reprinted in L. Tingay, ed., *The Irish Famine: Six Letters to the Examiner 1849/1850 by Anthony Trollope* [London, 1987], 16).

8. George Nicholls, *A History of the Irish Poor Law* (London, 1856), especially chs. 4 and 5; Gerard O'Brien, "The New Poor Law in pre-famine Ireland," *IESH*, 12 (1985), 33–49; *id.*, "The establishment of poor law unions in Ireland, 1838–43," *IHS*, 23 (1982–83), 97–120; *id.*, "Workhouse management in pre-famine Ireland," *PRIA*, 86C (1986), 113–34; O'Mahony, *In the Shadow*, 141–144; Ó Gráda, *Ireland*, 98–99.

9. NLI, Ms.12,001, 17 October 1847; CJL, "The present condition of the Irish poor," *The Economist*, 2 January 1847.

10. 13th Annual Report of the Poor Law Commissioners, 24, 27; Eva Ó Cathaoir, "The Poor Law in county Wicklow," in Ken Hannigan and William Nolan (eds.), *Wicklow: History and Society* (Dublin, 1994), 533–47.

11. For an analysis of the trend in real wages on the works in 1846–47, see Pat McGregor, "The Great Irish Famine: A failure of development or policy?" (typescript, University of Ulster, 1997).

12. On the administrative details, see O'Neill, "The organisation and administration of relief"; Kinealy, *This Great Calamity*, 52–54, 138–43.

13. IUP5/772, 8/12/46; Dorrian, "The years of the famine," 5.

14. Though often demanding, these jobs were much sought after. The top jobs were reserved exclusively for former army officers, and allocated on the basis of patronage. See Dermot Power, "Public works in Waterford, 1846–7," *Decies*, no. 51 (1995), 59.

15. Kinealy, *This Great Calamity*, 103–4; IUP6/344 (Skibbereen); IUP5/772 (circular); IUP6/306–8, 322 (Clare), 415 (east Galway), 475 (Tinnahinch), 477 (Leitrim); IUP7/112 (Donegal), 140 (Galway); 122–23 (Kerry).

16. E.g., IUP5/794 (Donegal); IUP7/123 (Kerry); "Fr Thomas O'Carroll's diary, 1846," 6 December 1846; Dorrian, "The years of the famine," 6.

17. IUP6/344 (Skibbereen); IUP5/846 (Clare).

18. C. Póirtéir, *Famine Echoes* (Dublin, 1995), 153–67; *id.*, *Glórtha ón nGorta* (Dublin, 1995), 77–78. The latter, an account from south Kerry, describes how the local relief committee refused one Tadhg Mac Cárthaigh meal on the grounds that he was hoarding potatoes which he intended to sell in the spring. However, the narrator, whose own grandmother had been refused, held that favoritism and injustice were rife: "We have the evidence of the people's memories, and it is no use for the historian to seek to hide the truth."

19. IUP7/191 (Captain Fishbourne, Ennistymon); BPP 1847(L), 64 (Captain Wynne). Such criticisms were a little rich, coming from men who were paid £1 a day.

20. National Archives, Relief Commission Papers, Cavan; cited in Kissane, *The Irish Famine*, 67; IUP5/826, 22 December 1846; IUP7/170 (Mayo).

21. BPP 1847, vol. 54.

22. IUP7/439 (Ennis); IUP7/170 (Blake Galway); IUP6/321 (Col. Jones); also 5/698 (Longford); Gray, "Punch and the Great Famine," 26–33; *id.*, "British public opinion and the great Irish famine 1845–49," *Comhdháil an Chraoibhín 1995*, 56–74; Kinealy, *This Great Calamity*, 106; Donnelly, "British public

opinion," *The Times*, October 1847 (as cited in Kinealy, *This Great Calamity*, 165).

23. Bourke, *Visitation of God*, 78–80; Daniel O'Connell to Maurice O'Connell, 18/11/1846, in M. O'Connell (ed.), *The Correspondence of Daniel O'Connell*, vol. 8 (Dublin, n.d.), 140; C.W.P. MacArthur (ed.), "James Hack Tuke's narrative of a visit to some of the distressed districts in Ireland," *Donegal Annual*, no. 46 (1994), 69–70; "Condition of the county Mayo, III," *Freeman's Journal*, 7 January 1847.

24. PRO T64/367A/1 (Roscrea); IUP7/37 (17/1/47); also IUP5/482.

25. W. H. Smith, *A Twelvemonth's Residence in Ireland during the Famine* (London, 1848), 55–56; Central Relief Committee of the Society of Friends, *Distress in Ireland, no. 2* (Dublin, 1847), 19; IUP7/580 (Valentia), 281 (Dublin), 288 (Roscommon).

26. IUP7/116 (Tyrone), 124 (Limerick), 129 (Carlow), 131 (Ballyraygal, Kilkenny), 134 (Meath), 136 (Queen's), 261 (Tyrone).

27. IUP5/445, 447, 473, 474, 480, 481, 482; IUP6/382 (Meath); IUP7/291 (east Galway).

28. IUP7/270 (13 February 1847).

29. IUP7/127 (Waterford), 135 (Queen's), 140 (Galway), 142–43 (Leitrim), 405 (Routh to Trevelyan).

30. Smith, *A Twelvemonth's Residence*, 43; Central Relief Committee, *Transactions*, 50, 178–79; IUP7/272 (Cork); *Report of the Proceedings of the General Central Relief Committee for All Ireland* (Dublin, 1848), 18–19; Murphy, *A People Starved*, 39, 44; Thomas P. O'Neill, "The Catholic clergy and the Great Famine," *Reportorium Novum*, 1 (1956), 461–69; Osborne, *Gleanings from the West of Ireland*, 190–91; Donal Kerr, *A Nation of Beggars* (Oxford, 1994), 47, 49; Séamus Ó Canainn, "An Gorta i nDún Fionnachaidh," in Póirtéir, *Gnéithe den Ghorta*, 183; Trench, *Realities of Irish Life*, 252–53; David C. Sheehy, "Archbishop Daniel Murray and the response of the Catholic Church to the Great Famine in Ireland," *Linkup: A Journal for the Dublin Diocese*, no. 76 (December 1995), 38–42; "Fr Thomas O'Carroll's diary, 1846," 4 April 1846, 4 October, 12 November, 10 December, 21 December 1846; Raymond Browne, *The Destitution Survey: Reflections on the Famine in the Diocese of Elphin* (Boyle, 1997), 26–46, 74–85. For a broader evaluation, see Donal Kerr, *The Catholic Church and the Famine* (Dublin, 1996). See too, however, Laurence M. Geary, "The Great Famine and Fethard temporary fever hospital," *Tipperary Historical Journal*, 10 (1997), 151–65.

31. W. J. Lowe, "Policing famine Ireland," *Éire-Ireland*, 29(4) (1994), 47–67; O'Mahony, *In the Shadow*, 161. See too Stanley H. Palmer, *Police and Protest in England and Ireland, 1780–1850* (Cambridge, U.K., 1988); W. J. Lowe and E. L. Malcolm, "The domestication of the Royal Irish Constabulary," *IESH*, 19 (1992), 27–48; Mokyr, *Why Ireland Starved*, 290.

32. *Hansard*, 89 (1847), col. 927.

33. I am grateful to Joel Mokyr for the county income data, which are the basis for the analysis in *Why Ireland Starved* (rev. ed.), ch. 2.

34. Ó Murchadha, "The onset of famine," 25; Daly, *The Famine in Ireland*, 53–54; *Hansard*, 88 (1846), col. 770.

35. For how these figures were derived, see Ó Gráda and O'Rourke, "Mass migration as disaster relief."

36. Suppose that, in the absence of a famine, population growth in the different baronies would have been one-third that recorded in 1821–41. By this necessarily crude measure, the east still lost marginally more; the worst-hit barony was Burren in the north, and the least affected were Islands and Moyarta (which included the towns of Ennis and Kilrush, respectively).

37. *Transactions of the Central Committee* . . . , 179 (report from Limerick by James Harvey and Thomas Grubb, 22 February 1847).

38. On Wynne, see John O'Rourke, *History of the Great Irish Famine* (Dublin, 1902), 210–2; Fitzpatrick, "Famine." The parish priest of Ennistymon gave the following account of Wynne (in a letter to *The Clare Journal*, 17 December 1846; I am grateful to Ciarán Ó Murchadha for this reference):

An intrepid fire eater, it is said, who would be more at home in the field of Mars, enjoying the pomp and honor of glorious war, than in a commmittee of relief, who would be more quick in dealing out slugs and bullets, than work tickets — this paid officer, in the performance of his duty, told one of the committee, and a member of parliament, that he could treat his observation with contempt. After exhibiting in this manner, after this insult to a man, perhaps more brave and resolute than himself, he had the coolness to say that he kept his temper, upon which another of the committee replied that he was the more dangerous on that account, and the more to be dreaded. The scene became curious, perhaps startling, it was one in real life. . . . A clergyman looking on, a mere silent spectator, witnessing the outrageous conduct indulged in became indignant, and remarked that the official thus conducting himself ought to be turned out of the room, and would soon suit the action to the word, if he had not respected the law and been kept in check by his clerical character. The Clergyman was told to hold his tongue, but he replied that he stood there as a member of the committee, on the same vantage ground with the government officers, and would not be silenced or put down like the Priest of Corofin.

39. Fitzpatrick, "Famine"; IUP6/202.

40. IUP6/323; IUP7/170.

41. These included a specimen of a list from Clondagad in Clare. Wynne's doubts about it were strengthened by the mean size of the fifty-nine families concerned, and indeed the gap between that mean (8.7) and mean family size in Clondagad in 1841 (5.4) was suspiciously large. See IUP6/465; BPP 1847 (L), 30, 66. Few relief lists from other areas seem to have survived. One from Killoughy (King's county) in spring 1847 shows that the vast majority of the thousand or so listed held little or no land, and the applicant with the largest farm on the relief lists held only nine acres of poor land. See Tim O'Neill, "The famine in Offaly," in O'Neill (ed.), *Offaly*.

42. Wynne's proposal to build a road next to Ennistymon's Catholic chapel "but without encroaching on the grounds attached thereto" was meant to embarrass the local parish priest. An associate claimed that the same priest was

overdramatizing suffering in the area, even as he noted that "deaths from dysentery, inflammation, and colds contracted on the public works are of frequent occurrence." BPP 1847(L), 47–48; *Hansard*, 89 (1847), cols. 926–30, 1171–75; 90 (1847), col. 499; O'Rourke, *Great Irish Famine*, 210–11; IUP7/30.

43. This incident and the response to it are cited in both O'Rourke, *Great Irish Famine*, 206–7, and Woodham-Smith, *Great Hunger*, 153–54. See also IUP6/341 (Wynne to Board of Works); NAD, RLFC3/2/5/26 (O'Brien to Routh); IUP5/891; PRO T64/363D (report from Wynne, 2 January 1847).

44. PRO T64/368B (Russell to Trevelyan, 29 December 1846). I am grateful to Ciarán Ó Murchadha for the plausible suggestion that Wynne may have suffered a nervous collapse of some kind.

45. IUP7/55, 7/118, 7/169–170 (north Mayo); on Wynne in Carrick-on-Shannon, see David Thomson, *Woodbrook* (London, 1974), ch. 8; Fitzpatrick, "Famine."

46. IUP5/846.

47. IUP6/447; IUP7/204–5.

48. IUP6/217; also IUP 7/118.

49. IUP6/217, 478. A headline-grabbing report in the *Sligo Champion*, "The jobbing on the public works," relayed in the *Morning Chronicle* (24/2/47), *Northern Whig* (6/3/47), and in other newspapers, prompted a plea from the Office of Public Works in Dublin for O'Brien to investigate. O'Brien effectively dismissed the report as without foundation (IUP7/206–8).

50. IUP7/117–18 (Newmarket-on-Fergus); IUP7/393 (Macroom).

51. IUP7/203.

52. NA, RLFC 3/2/5/25 (excerpt from the report of Captain H.H.D. O'Brien, 4 January 1847). The point about wages is well corroborated in the statement of an engineer employed by the Board of Works in Roscommon, who "consider[ed] all who sought employment should have had it, for surely men who would accept work at 5s per week, a sum equivalent to 3s in seasons of plenty, surely such men could not be too opulent for employment" (Smith, *A Twelvemonth's Residence*, 57).

53. IUP6/448; IUP5/845.

54. IUP7/166–67; IUP7/271 (27 February 1847).

55. IUP5/571, 883, 885, 891.

56. IUP7/411–12, IUP5/891.

57. O'Rourke, *Great Irish Famine*, 211.

58. IUP5/476.

59. IUP7/287.

60. IUP7/38 (Castlebar); IUP7/30 (Ennis).

61. IUP7/137, 7/39.

62. IUP7/38, 39 (18 January 1847); compare *Transactions of the Society of Friends*, 138 (2 December 1846).

63. Kinealy, *This Great Calamity*, 93, 100; IUP6/329 (Jones to Trevelyan); IUP6/527 (Report for December 1846); IUP7/35–40; IUP7/61 (Report for January 1847); Jones to Trevelyan 27/2/47; IUP8/383.

64. T. H. Marmion in the *Cork Constitution*, 17 December 1846.

65. IUP6/497 (Trevelyan to Jones); IUP6/309, 321, 323; Trevelyan, *The Irish Crisis* (London, 1848), 62–63.

66. IUP1/4.

67. NLI Ms. 7680 (Tralee); Ms. 2,202 (Ballina); Kinealy, *This Great Calamity*, 122.

68. *Report of the British Association*, 101; Gerry McAtasney, "The famine in Lurgan and Portadown," *Ulster Local Studies*, 17(2) (1995), 75–87; id., "*This Dreadful Visitation*" F. X. McCorry, "The famine in Lurgan," forthcoming. Curiously, McCorry found that it was the poorest parishes that supplied the fewest admissions, and that there were more Protestant than Catholic admissions and deaths.

69. This statement is based on an analysis of the North Dublin Union's registers (National Archives, Dublin, BG 78/5), which describe the health of inmates on admission.

70. NLI Ms. 7860 (Tralee); NLI Ms. 12,202 (Ballina); Kinealy, *This Great Calamity*, 133.

71. IUP2/648 (Milford); IUP2/844 (Kenmare); see too IUP2/697 (Ballinrobe).

72. IUP4/92–100 (Boyle union).

73. This is also the main message of S. G. Osborne's *Gleanings from the West of Ireland*. Osborne traveled through much of the west in the summer of 1849. See too G. P. Scrope, *Draft Report Proposed to the Select Committee of the House of Commons on the Kilrush Union* (London, 1850).

74. NLI Ms. 12203 (letter of 9 December 1847).

75. NLI Ms. 7860 (2 March and 27 April 1847); NLI Ms. 12202 (March 1847).

76. NLI Ms. 7860, duplicate of Tralee Board of Guardians Minute Book (April 1847). Compare Daniel Hegarty and Brian Hickey, "The famine graveyard on Carr's hill near Cork," *JCAHS*, 101 (1996), 15–25.

77. IUP8/83, 111–12.

78. Daly, *The Famine in Ireland*, 88; Kinealy, *This Great Calamity*, 143–46; A. Eiríksson, "Food supply and food riots," in Ó Gráda, *Famine 150*, 67–93; Eugene Broderick, "The famine as reported in the local newspapers," in Cowman and Brady (eds.), *The Famine in Waterford*, 175–77; Donnelly, "The soup kitchens," in Vaughan, *New History of Ireland*, 307–10; *Tipperary Vindicator*, 20 March 1847; *FJ*, 7 June 1847; *The Times*, 2 April 1847. Folk memory of the famine is assessed in some detail in chapter 6. Only once in the dozens of references to soup kitchens in Cathal Póirtéir's compendia is there mention of a family member relying on soup (*Glórtha ón nGorta*, 68). Later an Erris landlord would identify another hiatus, reporting that mortality had been considerable "between the expiration of the Relief Commission operation [and] the commencement of the Poor Law relief" (House of Lords S.C. on the Operation of the Irish Poor Law, Minutes of Evidence, BPP 1849, vol. 16).

79. O'Neill, "Organisation and administration of relief," 235–46; Kinealy, *This Great Calamity*, 148–49, 169.

80. Daly, *The Famine*, 82–84; compare Kinealy, *This Great Calamity*, 364–65; Ó Murchadha, "The onset of famine," 30; IUP6/562, 591 (grants to Clonderlaw and Ibrickane).

81. The county totals on the public works were taken from the *Tipperary Vindicator*, 13 March 1847. The statement about correspondence is based on analysis of the catalogues in the National Archives.

82. NLI Ms. 7850, entry for 14 December 1847; Ó Gráda, *An Drochshaol*, 72, 74; *Minutes Taken before the Select Committee on the Operation of the Irish Poor Law*, BPP 1849 (16), Q. 3483; Tomás Ó Caoimh, "Tigh na mBocht, an Daingean," in Ó Fiannachta (ed.), *An Gorta Mór*.

83. PRO T64/365B (3 February 1848).

84. Denis Bingham attended once in 1845 and once in 1846; three of the Reilly family of Belmullet served on the board, but between them they attended only three meetings in 1845–46 (NLI Mss. 12,200–201). In all, the four Erris guardians made it to Ballina only eight times in 1845 and 1846, and not once in 1847.

85. IUP2/94–98; Tuke, *Visit to Connaught*, 15fn; *Report of the British Association* (report of M. J. Higgins from Belmullet, 13 April 1847).

86. O'Neill, "The organisation and administration of relief," 255–56.

87. BPP 1847, vol. 54, 37; IUP5/822. For more on contemporary criticism, see Ó Gráda, *Ireland*, ch. 8. Compare Michael Watts, "Entitlements or empowerment? Famine and starvation in Africa," *Review of African Political Economy*, 51 (1991), 10.

88. IUP7/203–4 (resolution of Clare relief committees, 5 February 1847); McHale, cited in Kerr, *A Nation of Beggars*, 62–63; Browne, *The Destitution Survey*, 60–61 (citing *The Catholic Registry*, 1852); Bentinck, cited in Ó Gráda, *Ireland before and after the Famine*, 104; Trevelyan, cited in Kinealy, *This Great Calamity*, 348.

89. Gray, "Ideology and the famine," in Póirtéir, *Great Irish Famine*, 103; Mokyr, *Why Ireland Starved*, 292; *Hansard*, vol. 89 (19 January 1847), 76–84; *The Times*, 1 February 1847 (comparing the £20 million "with what we purchased the liberty of the negro").

90. R. J. Barro, "Government spending, interest rates, prices, and budget deficits in the United Kingdom, 1701–1918," *JME*, 20 (1987), 221–47.

91. The data on public spending and interest rates are given in B. R. Mitchell and P. Deane, *Abstract of British Historical Statistics* (Cambridge, 1962). See too C. N. Ward-Perkins, "The commercial crisis of 1847," *Oxford Economic Papers*, n.s. 2 (1950), 75–92; Rudiger Dornbusch and Jacob Frenkel, "The gold standard crisis of 1847," *Journal of International Economics*, 16 (1984), 1–27.

92. Ward-Perkins, "Commercial crisis," 88–89. The sources for the data in figure 2.2 are B. R. Mitchell, *British Historical Statistics* (Cambridge, U.K., 1980), 818, 838; and N.F.R. Crafts, S. J. Leybourne, and T. Mills, "Trends and cycles in British industrial production, 1700–1913," *Journal of the Royal Statistical Society, Series A*, 152 (1989), 58. GNP and gross capital formation (GCF) are in 1900 prices, industrial production is set at 1913 = 100. My thanks to Joel Mokyr for the consumption data behind figure 2.1. Their construction is explained in Mokyr, "Is there still life in the pessimist case? Consumption during the industrial revolution, 1790–1850," *JEH*, 48 (1988), 90–92.

93. Mitchell and Deane, *British Historical Statistics*, 450. The English data include the Bank of England.

94. Post, *Food Shortage, Climatic Variability and Epidemic Disease*, 145;

Sen, "Nobody need starve," in *Granta*, 52 (Winter 1995), 220; Solar, "Potato famine in Europe."

95. Compare Indian famine historian B. M. Bhatia's remark that "it had been proved repeatedly in the past that, once a famine got out of hand, even a lavish expenditure on relief later would fail to save life and prevent distress" (Bhatia, cited in Maharatna, *Demography of Famines*, 236). Also Famine Inquiry Commission, *Report on Bengal*, vol. 1, 132.

96. E.g., in the *Times* toward the end of a month that brought ten thousand deaths in Irish workhouses: "But what art, what policy, what wealth is cunning enough, wise enough, rich enough to assuage the moral evils and stay the moral disease of a vast population steeped in the congenial mire of voluntary indigence and speculating on the gains of a perpetual famine?" *The Times*, 26 March 1847 (as cited in Donnelly, "Irish property"); Gray, "British public opinion and the great Irish famine."

97. Robbins, *Famine in Russia*, 168–69; Theodore von Laue, *Sergei Witte and the Industrialization of Russia* (New York, 1963), 31–32; S. G. Wheatcroft, "The 1891–92 famine in Russia: Towards a more detailed analysis of the scale and economic significance," in Linda Edmundson and Peter Waldron (eds.), *Economy and Society in Russia and the Soviet Union* (London, 1992), 44–64. Compare too the £1.5 million in subsidized loans for public works sanctioned during the Lancashire "cotton famine" of the early 1860s (Ó Gráda, *Ireland*, 191).

CHAPTER THREE
THE DEMOGRAPHY OF THE IRISH FAMINE

1. E. A. Wrigley and R. Schofield, *The Population History of England* (London, 1981), 496–502; Marcel Lachiver, *Les années de misère: La famine au temps du grand roi* (Paris, 1991), 480; R. Tomasson, "A millennium of misery: The demography of the Icelanders," *Population Studies*, 31 (1977), 405–25; D. E. Vasey, "Population, agriculture, and famine: Iceland, 1784–85," *Human Ecology*, 19 (1991), 323–50; Kari Pitkänen, "The patterns of mortality during the great Finnish famine in the 1860s", *Acta Demographica 1992*; id., *Deprivation and Disease*.

2. William Chester Jordan, *The Great Famine: Northern Europe in the Early Fourteenth Century* (Princeton, N.J., 1996), 114, 148; Michael Flinn *et al.*, *Scottish Population History from the Seventeenth Century to the 1930s* (Cambridge, U.K., 1977), 164–85; D. Dickson, C. Ó Gráda, and S. G. Daultrey, "Hearth tax, household size and Irish population change, 1672–1821," *Proceedings of the Royal Irish Academy*, ser. C, 82 (1982), 125–81; D. Dickson, "The gap in famines: A useful myth?" in Crawford (ed.), *Famine: The Irish Experience*, 97–98; John Seaman, "Famine mortality in Africa," *IDS Bulletin*, 24(4) (1993), 27–32; Basil Ashton et al. "Famine in China, 1958–61," *Population and Development Review*, 10(4) (1984), 613–45; Barbara Sands and Sven Buelow, "Recounting China's Great Leap Forward deaths," University of Arizona, typescript, 20 June 1996. Jasper Becker's rather histrionic *Hungry Ghosts:*

China's Secret Famine (London, 1996), 266–74, adds nothing new on the Great Leap's demographic toll.

3. Introduction to Edwards and Williams, *The Great Famine*, vii. A plea from William Smith O'Brien M.P. in March 1847 for a register of famine deaths came to nought when Lord John Russell threw cold water on the proposal (*FJ*, 12 March 1847).

4. Compare Mary Daly, *Economic History of Ireland since 1800* (Dublin, 1980), 20–21; Tom Garvin, *The Evolution of Irish Nationalist Politics* (Dublin, 1981), 54; Woodham-Smith, *Great Hunger*, 411; S. H. Cousens, "Regional death rates in Ireland during the Great Famine," *PS* 14 (1960), 55–74; J. Mokyr, "The deadly fungus," *RPE*, 2 (1981), 429–59; P. P. Boyle and C. Ó Gráda, 'Fertility trends, excess mortality, and the Great Irish Famine," *Demography*, 23 (1985), 543–62.

5. O'Neill, "The famine in Offaly"; McCorry, "Famine in the Montiaghs." Burials in three Protestant parishes in Offaly (Edenderry, Clonsast, and Tisseran) rose from an annual average of 17 in 1841–45 to 20 in 1846, 39 in 1847, and 25 in 1848. I am grateful to Tim O'Neill for these data.

6. A Yorkshire newspaper proprietor noted soon afterwards (Anon., *Brief Notes of a Short Excursion in Ireland, in the Autumn of 1852, by the Editor and Sole Proprietor of the Hull Advertiser* (London, 1854), 34): "Bandon is a clean town, and has a rather prosperous appearance. But it suffered severely during the Famine, and one street was pointed out to us in which not a single inhabitant was left. Those who escaped death fled to distant lands, and when we saw it, every house was desolate; the garden fences were broken down; the doors and windows were partially in a state of visible decay; and the rank grass was growing about the thresholds. Altogether, it was one of the most saddening sights we ever looked upon."

7. Patrick Hickey, "Famine, mortality, and emigration," in O'Flanagan and Baltimer (eds.), *Cork.* Marshall's numbers are discussed further below.

8. *Report of the Proceedings of the General Central Relief Committee for All Ireland* (Dublin, 1848).

9. Mokyr, "Deadly fungus"; Boyle and Ó Gráda, "Fertility trends."

10. Cited in Hickey, "Famine, mortality, and emigration," 890; W. A. Mac-Arthur, "Medical history of the Famine," in Edwards and Williams (eds.), *The Great Famine*, 308–12. See too J. Mokyr and C. Ó Gráda, "Famine disease and famine mortality: Lessons from the Irish experience, 1845–50," typescript, University College Dublin, 1996.

11. MacArthur, "Medical history," 311.

12. Mokyr, and Ó Grada, "Famine disease and famine mortality: Lessons from the Irish experience, 1845–1850," typescript, 1996.

13. MacArthur, "Medical history," 265–68.

14. The proportion of deaths from these causes was 55 percent in 1846, 54 percent in 1847, 57 percent in 1848, 50 percent in 1849, and 48 percent in 1850.

15. De Waal, "Famine mortality"; Tim Dyson, "On the demography of South Asian famines," *PS*, 45 (1991); Ann Bowman Janetta, "Famine mortality in nineteenth-century Japan," *PS*, 46 (1992); E. Jutikkala and M. Kauppinen,

"The structure of mortality during catastrophe years in a pre-industrial society," *PS*, 25 (1971); On the somewhat different outcome in Finland in the 1860s, see Pitkänen, *Deprivation and Disease*, 90–91.

16. For a full discussion, see Mokyr and Ó Gráda, "Famine disease and famine mortality."

17. Deaths of non-Dubliners in the North Dublin union rose from 132 in 1845 to 263 in 1846 and 514 in 1847. These numbers are based on tables prepared by Catherine Cox for the National Famine Research Project.

18. In the jargon of time-series econometrics, the rise in pauper burials "Granger-caused" the rise in other burials. See the note at the end of chapter 5 below.

19. Cited in Jordan, *The Great Famine*, 147. Compare Flinn, *Scottish Population History*, 171.

20. IUP5/842 (Assistant Commissary Inglis to Deputy Assistant Commissary-General Routh, 23 December 1846).

21. *DQJMS*, 8 (1849), 8, 16.

22. *The Times*, 24 April 1847 (Gregory); *The Times*, 3 May 1847 (Lord Lurgan); *FJ* , 25 May 1847 (Stepney St. George and other "gentlemen of station"); Marnane, "The famine in south Tipperary — part 2," 134.

23. MacArthur, "Medical history," 310–11; *DQJMS*, 5 (1848), 282; *Transactions of the Society of Friends*, 208 (Belmullet, 20 February 1848); PRO T64/368B (letter from Bishop John O'Sullivan to Trevelyan, 2 December 1847); T. P. O'Neill, "The Catholic clergy and the great famine," *Reportorium Novum*, 1 (1956), 461–69; Kerr, *A Nation of Beggars*, 43; Hickey, "The famine in Skibbereen union," in Pórtéir (ed.), *The Great Irish Famine*, 201; Daniel Grace, "Priests who died in the Great Famine," *Tipperary Historical Journal*, 10 (1997), 178–79. Bishop O'Sullivan gave the ages of twenty-five priests: they averaged under forty-one years.

24. Eugene Broderick, "The famine in Waterford as reported in local newspapers," in Cowman and Brady, *The Famine in Waterford*, 165 (citing *Waterford Mirror*, 12 May 1847); E. Ó Cathaoir, "The poor law in county Wicklow," 544; O'Mahony, *In the Shadows*, 158; Donal Kerr, *The Catholic Church and the Famine* (Dublin, 1996), 24–25; *The Economist*, 2 January 1847. In their first report, the Irish Relief Commissioners noted that between April 1847 and April 1848 ninety-four workhouse officers had died, mostly of fever, as well as two inspectors, and a vice-guardian in Scariff (p. 16). On deaths of medical men, see P. Froggatt, "The response of the medical profession to the Great Famine," in E. M. Crawford (ed.), *Famine* (Edinburgh, 1989), 148–49. During the Great Finnish Famine of the mid-1860s, one-tenth of the medical community perished, which also meant a higher rate than for the population as a whole; see Oiva Turpeinen, *Nälkä Vai Tauti Tappoi? Kauhunvuodet 1866–1868* (Helsinki, 1986), 307.

Differences in death rates from famine-related diseases across social classes are unavailable except for the city of Dublin. There the proportion of reported deaths in 1841–51 due to fever, dysentery, and diarrhea was not much higher in Inns Quay, one of the poorest districts, than in houses on the "first-class streets" north and south of the Liffey. Cross-tabulation by first-class, second-class, and third-class families returns an even narrower differential (5,7, 6.1, and 6.4 percent, respectively). However, both comparisons are seriously biased by the exclusion of workhouse deaths. See 1851 Census, "Tables of death," vol. 1, 492–97, 501.

25. T. McKeown, *The Role of Medicine: Dream, Mirage, or Nemesis?* (Princeton, N.J., 1979). For a summary and an interesting case study, see Sumit Guha, "Nutrition, sanitation, hygiene, and the likelihood of death: The British army in India c. 1870–1920," *PS*, 47 (1993), 385–401.

26. *DQJMS*, 8 (1849), 25.

27. *DMP*, 29 November 1848; 17 March 1847.

28. *DMP*, 16 June 1847. This did not prevent the same editor from claiming some months later (13 October 1847) that excess mortality from fever in the medical profession was due to "the want of the comforts and necessaries of life, and of the means of making visits without bodily fatigue."

29. Froggatt, "The response of the medical profession to the Great Famine," 134–56; id., "Doctors in the Great Famine," *The Recorder*, 8(2) (1995), 1–9. The impression gained by a perusal of the *Dublin Medical Press* in the late 1840s is less exalted. Issue after issue provides evidence that the editor's accusation against Dominic Corrigan and Sir Philip Crampton—that "neither of them is distinguished for disregard of his own interests" (3 February 1847)—had a much wider application.

30. Meanwhile, see MacArthur, "Medical history"; Laurence Geary, "Famine, fever, and the bloody flux," in Póirtéir, *The Great Irish Famine*, 74–85.

31. See S. Wheatcroft, "Famine and factors affecting mortality in the USSR: The demographic crises of 1914–1922 and 1930–1933," Centre for Russian and East European Studies Discussion Paper, no. 20 (1981); "Famine and factors affecting mortality in the USSR: the demographic crises of 1914–1922 and 1930–1933: Appendices," ibid., no. 21 (1981); "Famine and epidemic crises in Russia, 1918–1922: The case of Saratov," *Annales de Démographie Historique*, (1983), 329–52; K. David Patterson, "Typhus and its control in Russia, 1870–1940," *Medical History*, 37 (1993), 376–81; Dyson, "On the demography of south Asian famines," parts 1 and 2, 5–25, 279–97; A. Maharatna, *The Demography of Famines* (Delhi, 1996); Hionidou, "The demography of a Greek famine," 293; Pitkänen, *Deprivation and Disease*, 77.

32. M. Livi-Bacci, *Population and Nutrition* (Cambridge, 1991), 436; Myron Winick, "Hunger disease: Studies by Jewish physicians in the Warsaw ghetto," *Nutrition*, 10(4) (1994), 365–80 (also see Winick, *Hunger Disease* [New York, 1979]); Zena Stein et al., *Famine and Human Development: The Dutch Hunger Winter of 1944–1945* (New York, 1975).

33. Winick, "Hunger disease," 380.

34. *FJ*, 22 May 1847 (letter from P. Murphy); Aykroyd, *The Conquest of Famine*, 13.

35. *FJ*, 1 January 1848; P. Harkan, M.D., *Medical Report of the House of Recovery and Fever Hospital, Cork Street, Dublin for . . . 1842* (Dublin, 1843), 12.

36. The case for the role of better nutrition has long been associated with Thomas McKeown, that for hygiene with Peter Razzell. See, e.g., McKeown,

The Modern Rise of Population (London, 1976); Razzell, "The growth of population in eighteenth-century England," *JEH*, 53(4) (1993). On the continued damage caused by diseases such as typhus and dysentery among the poor in certain less developed countries, compare the studies by K. David Patterson, Herbert L. DuPont, and Charles W. LeBaron and David W. Taylor in Kenneth F. Kiple, *The Cambridge World History of Human Disease* (Cambridge, U.K., 1993), 447–53, 676–79, 1071–77. For her insights into the role of medicine in famine-affected regions today, I wish to thank Sister Geneviève van Waesberghe M.M.M.

37. Raymond McClean, *A Cross Shared* (Ballyshannon, 1988), 22, 34–38.

38. Osborne, *Gleanings from the West of Ireland*, 19.

39. Boyle and Ó Gráda, "Fertility trends"; David Fitzpatrick, "Gender and the famine," in Kelleher and Murphy (eds.), *Gender Perspectives*; Hickey, "Famine, mortality, and emigration," 892; Ó Cathaoir, "The poor law in county Wicklow," 544; Liam Kennedy, "Adam and Aoife: Gazing at gender ratios," unpublished typescript, October 1997; Proinsíos Ó Duigneáin, *North Leitrim in Famine Times* (Manorhamilton, 1986), 32–33.

40. Drèze and Sen, *Hunger and Public Action*, 55–56, 79–80; de Waal, "Famine mortality," 5–24; Dyson, "On the demography of South Asian famines—parts 1 and 2," 5–25 and 279–97; Maharatna, *Demography of Famines*, 74–78, 170–71; Famine Inquiry Commission, *Report on Bengal* (Delhi, 1945), 110; Hionidou, "The demography of a Greek famine," 294; Thomasson, "A millennium of misery," 420; Vasey, "Population, agriculture, and famine"; Bowman Jannetta, "Famine mortality in nineteenth-century Japan," 2; H. A. van der Zee, *The Hunger Winter: Occupied Holland 1944–45* (London, 1982), 304; K. Pitkänen and J. Mielke, "Age and sex differentials in mortality during the two nineteenth-century population crises," *European Journal of Population*, 9 (1993); Pitkänen, *Deprivation and Disease*, 90–92; Stein et al., *Famine and Human Development*, 53.

41. Jane E. Brody, "Sex and the survival of the fittest: Calamities are a disaster for men," *New York Times*, 24 April 1996.

42. Sara M. Hunt and James L. Groff, *Advanced Nutrition and Human Metabolism* (New York, 1990), 389 (reporting data in A. R. Behnke and J.H. Wilmore, *Evaluation and Regulation of Body Build and Composition* [Englewood Cliffs, N.J., 1974]).

43. T. H. Clutton-Brock, E. E. Guinness and S. D. Albon, *Red Deer: Behavior and Ecology of Two Sexes* (Chicago, 1982); E. M. Widdowson, "The response of the sexes to nutritional stress," *Proceedings of the Nutritional Society*, 35 (1976), 1175–80.

44. Fitzpatrick, "Gender and the famine." For a numerical example, see Ó Gráda, "The Great Irish Famine: Some demographic aspects," UCD Centre for Economic Research, WP96/12. Thaddeus Sunseri, "Famine and wild pigs," *Journal of African History* 38 (1997), touches on issues of gender and culture, but is not concerned with relative demographic impact.

45. Sen, *Poverty and Famines*, 98, 205; Susan C. Watkins and Jane Menken, "Famines in historical perspective," *PDR*, 11 (1985), 652; Sally E. Findley, "Does drought increase migration? A study of migration from rural Mali during

the 1983–1985 drought," *International Migration Review*, 28 (1994), 539–53; Pierre-Etienne Will, *Bureaucracy and Famine in Eighteenth-Century China* (Stanford, 1990), 38–42; Kari Pitkänen, "The road to survival or death? Temporary migration during the Great Finnish Famine in the 1860s," in Häkkinen (ed.), *Just a Sack of Potatoes?*

46. *Cork Constitution*, 26 April 1847.

47. Flinn, *Scottish Population History*, 180; Devine, *Great Highland Famine*, chs. 7–12. In northern India in the 1870s the lieutenant governor of Bengal sought to use emigration as a weapon against famine. He sought to link the colonization of wasteland with the migration of poor agrarian caste families across the Bengal Sea to Burma. Neither of these suggestions came to anything: the locals refused to move to the wastelands because they were disease-ridden, and moving to Burma would have entailed losing caste status. Moreover, the local *zamindars* (landlords) were reluctant to see good *raiyats* (tenants) go; C. V. Hill, "Philosophy and reality in riparian south Asia: British famine policy and migration in colonial north India," *Modern Asian* Studies, 25 (1991).

48. Scally, *End of Hidden Ireland* (New York, 1995), 218.

49. Donnelly, "The journals of Sir John Benn-Walsh," 108. On the fate of famine emigrants from Ballykilcline in Roscommon, compare Scally, *End of Hidden Ireland*, 226–29, and Ruth-Ann Harris, "Ballykilcline and beyond," *Irish Studies Review*, no. 15 (Summer 1996), 39–42.

50. One recent analysis of slave mortality on the middle passage in the 1790s reports a mean mortality rate of 11.6 percent, while the lowest *daily* mortality rate reported in another analysis of the 1837–63 period is 1.81 percent on ships leaving the Bight of Benin. See D. Eltis, "Mortality and voyage length in the middle passage: new evidence for the nineteenth century," *JEH*, 44 (1984), 301–19; R. Steckel and R. A. Jensen, "New evidence on the causes of slave mortality and crew mortality in the Atlantic slave trade," *JEH*, 46 (1986), 57–77.

51. Stephen Campbell, *The Great Irish Famine* (Strokestown, 1994), 40–42.

52. Pádraig B. Ó Laighin, "Grosse-Isle: Samhradh an bhróin, 1847," in Póirtéir, *Gnéithe den nGorta*; Raymond Cohn, "Mortality on immigrant voyages to New York, 1836–1853," *JEH*, 44 (1984), 289–300; Mokyr, *Why Ireland Starved*, 267–68.

53. *The Times*, 2 April 1847; *FJ*, 12 March 1847 (Skibbereen); Póirtéir, *Glórtha ón nGorta*, 241–42, 243; *The Times*, 14 April 1847 and 26 April 1847 (citing *the Cork Reporter, the Galway Mercury, the Cork Examiner*). For more on the migrants, see Ira A. Glazier, Deirdre Mageean, and Barnabus Okeke, "Socio-economic characteristics of Irish emigrants, 1846–1851," in Klaus Friedland (ed.), *Maritime Aspects of Migration* (Cologne, 1989), 243–78; O. MacDonagh, "Irish emigration to the United States of America and the British colonies during the famine," in Edwards and Williams, *The Great Famine*, 319–90.

54. *FJ*, 8 May 1847.

55. Glazier et al. "Socio-economic characteristics of Irish emigrants"; Ó Gráda, "Across the briny ocean: Some thoughts on Irish emigration to America, 1800–1850," in Devine and Dickson, *Ireland and Scotland*, 118–30.

56. J. P. Ferrie, "The wealth accumulation of antebellum immigrants to the U.S., 1840–1860," *JEH*, 54 (1994), 1–33; "Up and out or down and out? Immigrant mobility in the antebellum United States," *JIH*, 26 (1994), 33–55.

57. IUP6/518; Lord Dufferin and G. F. Boyle, *Narrative of a Journey from Oxford to Skibbereen during the Year of the Irish Famine* (Oxford, 1847; reprinted Cork, 1996), 12–13; IUP7/552 (Sligo), NLI Ms. 12,202 (Ballina); Smith, *A Twelvemonth's Residence*, 56.

58. Smith, *A Twelvemonth's Residence*, 56; Robert Murray, *Ireland: Its Present Condition and Future Prospects* (Dublin, 1847), cited in R.D.C. Black, *Economic Thought and the Irish Question* (Cambridge, U.K., 1960), 229.

59. See Mokyr, *Why Ireland Starved*, 264–65; S. H. Cousens, "Regional death rates in Ireland during the Great Famine," 55–74; id. "The regional pattern of emigration during the Great Irish Famine, 1846–51," *Institute of British Geographers, Transactions and Papers*, no. 28 (1960), 119–34; Ó Gráda and O'Rourke, "Mass migration."

60. Ó Gráda and O'Rourke, "Mass migration." The trouble with the underlying data is that they are based on the implausible assumption of constant underreporting of deaths across counties. The alternative approach of beginning with assumed net famine migration rates produces broadly similar results. However, this method (due to Mokyr, "The deadly fungus") is also open to objection, since it uses county migration shares in 1821–41 and in either 1851 or 1851–55 to gauge famine migration.

61. Hickey, "Famine," 900, 909. The cross-county correlations are reported in Ó Gráda and O'Rourke, "Mass migration."

62. As given in Wrigley and Schofield, *Population History of England*, 501.

63. Frank Neal, "Lancashire, the famine Irish and the poor laws: A study in crisis management," *IESH*, 22 (1995), 26–48; id., "The famine Irish in England and Wales," in Patrick O'Sullivan (ed.), *The Irish Worldwide: Heritage, History and Identity*, vol. 6, *Meaning of the Famine* (London, 1996), 56–80; id., "Black '47: Liverpool and the Irish famine"; Jona Schellekens, "Irish famines and English mortality in the eighteenth century," *JIH*, 27(1) (1996), 29–42; Horace Mann, "Statement of the mortality prevailing in Church Lane," *Journal of the Statistical Society of London*, 11 (March 1848), 19–24; E. M. Crawford, "Migrant maladies: unseen lethal baggage," in Crawford (ed.), *Hungry Stream*.

Note that for several generations before 1846–48 the impact of economic hardship and subsistence crises on births in England had been greater than that on deaths, reflecting what Wrigley and Schofield dubbed England's "low pressure" demographic regime. The greater impact of the crisis of the 1840s on deaths than on births may thus signal that most of the excess deaths were among the Irish immigrants. Compare Wrigley and Schofield, *Population History of England*, 501, 683–85.

64. Flinn *et al.*, *Scottish Population History*, 373, 303. Unfortunately for the demographic historian, in Scotland civil registration came a decade or so too late.

65. Cousens, "The regional variation in emigration." See too J. G. Williamson, "Regional inequality and the process of national development: A description of the patterns," *Economic Development and Cultural Change*, 13 (1965), 3–45.

66. Marion R. Casey, "Friends in need: Financing emigration from Ireland, the Irish Emigrant Society and the Emigrant Industrial Savings Bank," *Seaport Magazine*, May 1996. The author is currently engaged in a larger study of the Emigrant Savings Bank with Eugene N. White of Rutgers University.

67. J. P. Ferrie, *Yankeys Now* (New York, 1997), 108–9; Thomas Mooney, *Letters on Emigration* (Dublin, 1851), 83–84, 93–94. For an up-to-date introduction to the literature on the Irish in mid-nineteenth-century New York, see Edward T. O'Donnell, "The scattered debris of the Irish nation," in Crawford, *Hungry Stream*.

68. Mooney, *Letters on Emigration*, 84–85.

69. Oliver MacDonagh, "Irish emigration to the United States and the British colonies during the famine," 335; D. Fitzpatrick, *Irish Emigration 1801–1921* (Dundalk, 1984), 20; *id.*, "Emigration, 1801–1870," in Vaughan, *New History*.

70. Cited in Lyne, "William Steuart Trench," *JKAHS*, no. 25 (1992), 86.

71. Ibid., 104–5. Compare P. J. Duffy's analysis of Trench's management of an earlier assisted emigration scheme on the Shirley estate, "Emigrants and the estate office in the mid-nineteenth century: A compassionate relationship?" in Crawford, *Hungry Stream*, 71–86.

72. Ferrie, *Yankeys Now*, 44–45.

73. "Ladies of the Mission," *The Old Brewery and the Mission House at the Five Points* (New York, 1854), 34.

74. Further details are given in C. Ó Gráda, "Fleeing from famine: Irish immigrants in New York in the 1850s," mimeo.

75. Carol Groneman Pernicone, "The 'Bloody Ould Sixth': A social analysis of a New York City working-class community in the mid-nineteenth century" (Ph.D. diss., University of Rochester, 1973), 155, table V-2; Robert Ernst, *Immigrant Life in New York City* (New York, 1949).

76. Rebecca Yamin, "New York's mythic slum: Digging lower Manhattan's infamous Five Points," *Archaeology*, March-April 1997, 46–53.

77. Heather Griggs, who kindly gave me a copy of the Transfiguration Church data and whose research focused particularly on a block of tenement houses in the Sixth Ward, notes that very few of the individuals recorded in the marriage registers were included in the censuses of 1855 or 1860. This highlights "the necessity for using other primary sources to supplement census data." See Heather Griggs, "Emigrant Bank and Transfiguration Church records as supplementary historical sources: A statistical analysis," mimeo, 1996, 37.

78. Mokyr's estimates of the singulate mean age at marriage on the eve of the famine are 26.3 years for females and 29.9 years for males (*Why Ireland Starved*, 37).

79. MacDonagh, "Emigration during the famine," 361–62; Bayard Tuckerman (ed.), *The Diary of Philip Hone*, vol. 2 (New York, 1889), 300. The classic source on contemporary economic thought about emigration is Black, *Economic Thought and the Irish Question*, ch. 7.

CHAPTER FOUR
WINNERS AND LOSERS

1. Amartya K. Sen, *Poverty and Famines* (Oxford, 1981), chs. 6–7; also Jean Drèze and Amartya Sen, *The Political Economy of Hunger*, 3 vols. (Oxford, 1991), ch. 2.

2. For discussion and references, see Devereux, *Theories of Famine*, 76–81.

3. Drèze and Sen, *Hunger and Public Action*, 22; Woodham-Smith, *The Great Hunger*, 165; CC, 19 December 1846.

4. M. Ravallion, "Trade and specialization: Another look at India's controversial foodgrain exports," *EEH*, 24 (1987). However, Ravallion's findings are rather marred by reliance on dubious agricultural output data and failure to focus on net rather than total exports of foodstuffs.

5. Irish beer output totaled 732,000 barrels in 1846 and 617,000 barrels in 1847. Allowing 6 stones of barley per gallon implies about 0.5 million barrels of barley (of 16 stone each) over the two years. Compare P. Lynch and J. Vaizey, *Guinness's Brewery* (Cambridge, U.K., 1960), 129; J. Lee, "Money and Beer in Ireland, 1790–1875," *EHR* (1966), 185.

6. National Archives (Washington, D.C.), Micr. D359 ("Despatches from United States consuls in Cork"). See too Christine Kinealy, "Food exports from Ireland, 1846–47," *History Ireland*, 5(1) (1997), 32–36. I am grateful to Ed McCarron for sending me the consular data.

7. For an overview of the potato's importance and the shortfalls in 1845, 1846, and later, see Bourke, *Visitation*, chs. 4–8; Solar, "The great famine."

8. Compare Sidiqq Osmani, "The entitlement approach to famine: An assessment," in K. Basu, P. Pattanaik, and K. Suzumura (eds.), *Choice, Welfare, and Development: A Festschrift in Honour of Amartya K. Sen* (Oxford, 1995), 276–77; Ravallion, "Famines and economics," 1207–19.

9. Sheila Fitzpatrick, in *Stalin's Peasants: Resistance and Survival in the Russian Village after Collectivization* (Oxford, 1994), 69–76, explains how both contemporaries and historians have seen the Soviet famine of 1932–33 as the outcome of the struggle over grain procurements between peasants and the authorities in the wake of collectivization.

10. Maharatna, *The Demography of Famines*, 174.

11. O. Robinson, "The London companies as progressive landlords in the nineteenth century," *EHR*, 15(1) (1962), 103–18; W. A. Maguire, *The Downshire Estates in Ireland, 1801–1845* (Oxford, 1972); Vaughan, *Landlords and Tenants in Mid-Victorian Ireland*; R. B. McCarthy, *The Trinity College Estates, 1800–1923* (Dundalk, 1993); Lindsay J. Proudfoot, *Urban Patronage and Social Authority: The Management of the Duke of Devonshire's Towns in Ireland, 1764–1891* (Washington, D.C., 1995). J. S. Donnelly's researches on Cork and Kerry landed estates are exceptional in this respect. See his *The Land and the People of Nineteenth-century Cork* (London, 1975); *id.*, "The journals of Sir John Benn-Walsh"; *id.*, "The Kenmare estates during the nineteenth century," *JKAHS*, 21 (1988), 5–41.

A precise enumeration of landlords around this time is lacking. An appendix to a House of Lords Inquiry into the Irish Poor Law in 1849 (BPP 1849, vol. 16) returned a total of 21,437 estates, but over half of these were valued at less than £300.

12. P. G. Lane, "The Encumbered Estates Court, Ireland, 1848–49," *ESR*, 3 (1972), 424; Póirtéir, *Glórtha ón nGorta*, 216. D'Arcy had borrowed £60,000 from a London banker when building Clifden (see P. G. Lane, "The impact of the Encumbered Estates Court upon the landlords of Galway and Mayo," *Journal of the Galway Archaeological and Historical Society*, 38 (1981–82), 46;

Donnelly, "The journals of Sir John Benn-Walsh," 106–7; "Report of Richard Bourke, 15 July 1847," in *Papers Relating to the Relief of Distress*, 4th ser. (1847), 67; reprinted in IUP, *Famine Relief in Ireland*, vol. 2 (1968), 74.

13. [John Locke], *Ireland, Observations on the People, the Land and the Law in 1851* (London, 1852), 30. The reference is to Mary Martin, who inherited the estate when her brother Thomas died from famine fever. Thomas had caught the fever when visiting former tenants in the workhouse. See Tim Robinson's introduction to Thomas Colville Scott, *Connemara after the Famine: Journal of a Survey of the Martin Estate* (Dublin, 1995), xi.

An account in the archive of the Irish Folklore Commission describes "a landlord named Freeman Dave of Castle Cor, Kanturk [who] is believed to have given all he had to feed the poor. His property was sold after the Famine" (Irish Folklore Commission Archive, Dublin, vol. 1,068, pp. 235–39).

14. Cited in Lane, "The Encumbered Estates Court," 416. See too W. L. Burn, "Free trade in land: An aspect of the Irish question," *TRHS*, 4th ser. (1945), 61–74.

15. Lane, "The Encumbered Estates Court"; Vaughan, *Landlord and Tenant in Mid-Victorian Ireland*, 133.

16. Black, *Economic Thought and the Irish Question*, 130; F.S.L. Lyons, *Ireland since the Famine* (London, 1973), 26; Donal McCartney, *The Dawn of Democracy* (Dublin, 1987), 173; R. Foster, *Modern Ireland* (London, 1988), 336; D. G. Boyce, *Ireland 1828–1923: From Ascendancy to Democracy* (London, 1992), 37–38. Compare Donnelly, *The Land and the People*, 131.

17. Proudfoot, *Urban Patronage and Social Authority*, 43; K. T. Hoppen, *Ireland since 1800: Conflict and Conformity* (London, 1989), 87.

18. See Woodham-Smith, *The Great Hunger*, 409–10.

19. BPP 1847–48. *Abstract of Return from the Registrar's Office of the Court of Chancery in Ireland* (226), vol. 62 [.213].

20. Raymond D. Crotty, *Irish Agricultural Production: Its Volume and Structure* (Cork, 1966), 303.

21. *Thom's Commercial Directory 1851*; also BPP, *Report from H.M. Commissioners to Inquire into the State of the Law and Practice in Respect of the Occupation of Land in Ireland* (672), vol. 22 [.1] 1845 (Devon Commission), app. 98.

22. *Thom's Commercial Directory . . . 1853*, 277.

23. Lyons, *Illustrated Encumbered Estates*, 23, 25; see too Osborne, *Gleanings from the West of Ireland* (London, 1850), 45–46.

24. David Large, "The wealth of the greater Irish landowners, 1750–1815," *Irish Historical Studies*, 15 (1966); L. P. Curtis, Jr., "Incumbered wealth: Landed indebtedness in post-famine Ireland," *American Historical Review*, 85(2) (1980), 337. For an interesting case study of one hard-pressed landed family, see Timothy P. O'Neill, "The Rices of Mountrice: Solicitors' records of an epigonal family," *Journal of the Kildare Historical and Archaeological Society*, 18(3) (1996–97), 351–66.

25. John Habakkuk, *Marriage, Debt, and the Estates System: English Landownership, 1650–1950* (Oxford, 1994), 353–58.

26. *Mayo Constitution*, 11 July 1854; cited in Lane, "The Encumbered Es-

tates Court," 50; Donnelly, *The Land and the People*, 72, 164; see too Ian D'Alton, *Protestant Society and Politics in Cork, 1812–1844* (Cork, 1980), 21, 26; Ó Gráda, *Ireland*, 29–30; W. A. Maguire, "Lord Donegal and the sale of Belfast: A case study from the encumbered estates court," *Economic History Review*, 29(4) (1976); E.R.R. Green, "The Great Famine and its consequences" (undated and incomplete typescript, PRONI, D3561/B/54).

27. Cited in John McArthur, *Incumbered Estates Court Ireland: Summary of Proceedings* (Dublin, 1854).

28. Donnelly, *The Land and the People*, 71.

29. BPP 1854–55. *Report of H.M. Commissioners Appointed to Inquire into the Incumbered Estates Court . . . with an Appendix Containing Evidence and Returns* (1938), vol. 19 [.527]; see too Mokyr, *Why Ireland Starved*, 93–94.

30. For a breakdown of the underlying data by barony and a map of the outcome, see Eiríksson and Ó Gráda, *Estate Records of the Irish Famine* (Dublin, 1996). Compare Ó Gráda, *Ireland before and after the Famine*, 39, 184.

31. As a check on the accuracy of the index, Eiríksson and I tested three volumes of the rentals. These volumes included 159 rentals (Dublin City excluded), covering 781 townlands. Out of these 781 townlands, 656 are marked in the index to the O'Brien Rentals, while 125 are not. This means that the index underestimates the number of townlands auctioned by about 16 percent. Furthermore, there is a certain geographic bias as to the accuracy of the index. The percentage of townlands missing from each province is Leinster 21%, Munster 17%, Ulster 13%, and Connacht 12%. The reason for the bias seems to be the size of the baronies, the size of the rentals, and how well the index for each county was organized. Our impression is that counties Cork, Tipperary, Limerick, Kilkenny, Kildare, Dublin, and Meath are those most underestimated in the index to the O'Brien rentals. As for Donegal, singled out above, there is no sign of particularly poor recording in the index. See Eiríksson and Ó Gráda, "Bankrupt landlords."

32. BPP 1854–55. *Report of H.M. Commissioners Appointed to Inquire into the Incumbered Estates Court . . . with an Appendix Containing Evidence and Returns* (1938), vol. 19 [.527], 82, 83.

33. Compare Osborne, *Gleanings From the West of Ireland*, 245.

34. Such massive indebtedness also indicates that even in depressed conditions the well-organized landlord, unencumbered with debt when the famine struck, would almost certainly have been able to borrow short-term during the crisis.

35. Donnelly, "Irish property must pay for Irish poverty, 60–76.

36. Donnelly, *The Land and the People*, 106–7; Vaughan, *Landlord and Tenant*, 246; Proudfoot, *Patronage and Authority*, 107–8.

37. E.g., Barbara L. Solow, *The Land Question and the Irish Economy* (Cambridge, Mass. 1971); Vaughan, *Landlord and Tenant*.

38. Megan Vaughan, *The Story of an African Famine: Hunger, Gender and Politics in Malawi* (Cambridge, U.K., 1987), 106–10; Ravallion, *Markets and Famines*, 7; David Hardiman, "Usury, dearth and famine in western India," *Past and Present*, no. 152 (August 1996), 134; J. Steele, "Millionaire 'grain barons' hoarding supplies in Sudan," *The Guardian Weekly*, 20 October 1985 (cited in Ravallion, "Famines and economics," 1219).

39. Pierre-Etienne Will, *Bureaucracy and Famine in Eighteenth-Century China* (Stanford, 1990); Lachiver, *Les années de misère*, 126, 141–42; Shoko Okazaki, "The great Persian famine of 1870–71," *Bulletin of the School of Oriental and African Studies*, 49 (1986), 192; Cobb, cited in F. Aftalion, *The French Revolution: An Economic Approach* (Cambridge, U.K., 1990), 169–70. See too Jordan, *The Great Famine*,136–37, on allegations of hoarding and speculation in Europe in the 1310s.

40. S. L. Kaplan, *Bread, Politics, and Political Economy in the Reign of Louis XV* (The Hague, 1976), 192.

41. Alexander Somerville, *Letters from Ireland during the Famine of 1847* (Dublin, 1994), 34; Daly, "Farming and the famine," 41.

42. Woodham-Smith, *The Great Hunger*, 167; Black, *Economic Thought and the Irish Question*, 118–19.

43. Adam Smith, *Wealth of Nations* (London, 1961), 32–33.

44. Drèze and Sen, *Hunger and Public Action*, 89; Sen, *Poverty and Famines*, 76–77, 159; B. M. Bhatia, *Famines in India, 1860–1965*, 2d ed. (Bombay, 1967), 323–24.

45. Bhatia, *Famines in India*, 9, 61; Hardiman, "Usury, dearth and famine in western India," 134; Ravallion, *Markets and Famines*, 57.

46. Ravallion, *Markets and Famines*, 82, 112, 19.

47. Ó Gráda, *Ireland*, 131–38.

48. E.g., Ravallion, *Markets and Famines*, 103–4, 114.

49. Hoffman and Mokyr, "Peasants, potatoes, and poverty," 131–34; Ó Gráda, *An Drochshaol*, 20–23; J. Coombes, "The sea trade in potatoes in south west Cork, 1730–1850," *Seanchas Chairbre*, 3 (1993), 3–16; Ó Gráda, *Famine 150*, 11, 56, 72 (for contemporary illustrations of potato markets); Ó Gráda, *Ireland before and after the Famine*, 144 (on the regional spread of potato prices).

50. BPP, "Highest price of potatoes . . . in the week ending 24 January for the last seven years as well as can be estimated" [110] (1846), vol. 37, 489.

51. BPP, "Return of the price of potatoes agreed for at the last Contract entered into by each Board of Guardians, in Ireland, previously to the 1st of May in the Years 1844, 1845, and 1846, respectively" (app. B, no. 26, in the twelfth annual report of the poor-law commissioners) [745], vol. 19 (1846), 467.

For example, the Bandon data for 1844, 1845, and 1846 refer to Minions, Whites, and Quaries, respectively. In Dublin South, contract prices refer to Cups, Pink Eyes, and Apples (though only very late in the season in this case, between June and August).

52. The rises in the standard deviations of rye and barley prices during the Finnish famine of the 1860s were much greater and account for some of the regional variation in excess mortality. See Pitkänen, "The patterns of mortality during the Great Finnish Famine."

53. The Irish data were supplied by "James O'Hea, malt and corn factors." For some background on the socioeconomic context in mid-nineteenth-century Cork city, see John B. O'Brien, "Glimpses of entrepreneurial life in Cork, 1800–1870," *JCAHS*, 82 (1985), 150–57, and Andy Bielenberg, *Cork's Industrial Revolution, 1780–1880* (Cork, 1991).

54. The material cited here is to be found in Cork Archives Council, B501/55/2 and B501/55/3.

55. In early December an ailing Daniel O'Connell informed his son Maurice that "there was no Indian corn in Cork" (5/12/1846). I am grateful to Giuliana Biagoli and Giovanni Federico for the Tuscan data.

56. The *Cork Examiner* reported that seventy-two vessels had entered Cork harbor between 20 March and 23 March, carrying nearly 20,000 tons of bread-stuffs; a similar number had arrived in the previous week. The imports had been operating in "a most beneficial manner on our markets and prices" (cited in *FJ*, 26 March, 1847). See too *Hunt's Merchants' Magazine*, June 1847, 607.

57. James Murphy (1769–1855), who lived in Ringmahon Castle in Black-rock, had twelve children. The eldest, Jeremiah James (1795–1851), had fifteen children—nine daughters and six sons. Five of his six sons—James Jeremiah (the eldest), William, Jerome, Francis, and Nicholas—founded James J. Murphy & Co. at Lady's Well Brewery, Cork, in 1856.

58. For a list of the principal corn merchants in Cork around this time, see Bielenberg, *Cork*, 45 (citing CAC, Murphy to Buchanan, 22 May 1839 in Mur-phy letter-book 1837–39, Irish Distillers collection).

59. Murphy and Cork fit well Adam Smith's classic depiction of the specula-tor (*Wealth of Nations*, Book 1, ch. 10):

The speculative merchant exercises no one regular, established, or well known branch of business. He is a corn merchant this year, and a wine merchant the next, and a sugar, tobacco or tea merchant the year after. He enters into every trade when he foresees that it is likely to be more than commonly profitable, and he quits it when he foresees that its profits are likely to return to the levels of other trades. . . . A bold adventurer may sometimes acquire a consid-erable fortune by two or three successful speculations; but is just as likely to lose one by two or three unsuccessful ones. This trade can be carried on no where but in great towns. It is only in places of the most extensive commerce and correspondence that the intelligence requisite for it can be had.

In the mid-1840s Cork had dozens of flour and grain merchants, large and small.

60. Sen, *Poverty and Famines*, 76–77, 148–49; Ravallion, *Markets and Fam-ines*, ch. 3; compare Salim Rashid, "The policy of laissez-faire during scar-cities," *Economic Journal*, 90 (1980), 493–503.

61. *Ireland before and after the Famine*, 111–21; D. N. McCloskey and J. Nash, "Corn at interest: The extent and cost of grain storage in medieval En-gland," *American Economic Review*, 74(1), (1984), 174–87. The underlying in-sight is in Paul Samuelson, "Intertemporal price speculation: A prologue to the theory of speculation," *Weltwirtschaftliches Archiv*, December 1957, 181–219.

62. CC, 22 October 1840.

63. Mokyr, "Irish history with the potato."

64. I assumed that weekly sales were divided into the following proportions: Monday, .06; Tuesday, .12; Wednesday, .13; Thursday, .14; Friday, .09; Satur-day, .46.

65. In his report on the laws governing pawnbroking in Ireland, William Neilson Hancock presents data implying that the returns were reasonably complete in the early 1840s at least. Pawnbrokers were supposed to furnish the marshal of Dublin City with monthly returns. Most did, and the marshal presented abstracts (which were usually not printed) to Parliament. However "a correct and perfect list" based on a tour of practically every town in Ireland produced 445 certified pawnbrokers in 1837, and there were 467 in 1844 (see BPP 1837–38, vol. 17 [Report from SC on Pawnbroking in Ireland] [.677]; BPP 1845, vol. 45 [.141]) [Return of the Pawnbrokers in Ireland for the Year ending 31 December 1844]; BPP 1867–68, vol. 32).

66. IUP, 1968, vol. 4. The citations are located as follows: Gort, 138; Roscommon, 119; Tralee, 143; Fermoy, 146; Tipperary, 146; Roscrea, 149; Castlerea, 135.

67. Aidan Hollis and Arthur Sweetman, "Microcredit in pre-famine Ireland," University of Calgary, typescript, April 1997; see too Ó Gráda, "Soláthar creidmheasa don ísealaicme san 19ú aois," Central Bank of Ireland Quarterly Bulletin (1974), 120–35. The aim of the loan funds was to help the industrious poor by offering investment loans. However, the effective interest rates charged by them were quite high (13.6 percent before 1843, 8.8 percent thereafter). This does not allow for how they topped up their charges through various fines and penalties that were difficult to avoid. Such rates may seem low for consumption loans in a poor country like pre-famine Ireland, but it is difficult to think of investment projects that would have been viable at the rates charged.

68. Eleventh Annual Report of the Loan Fund Board, Ireland (in BPP 1849, vol. 23, 27). Connacht's share of the sums lent was always low, but it fell further from 6.6 percent in 1847 to 5 percent in 1848.

69. BPP 1847–48, vol. 57; James O'Shea, "Thurles Savings Bank 1829–71," in William Corbett and William Nolan (eds.), Thurles, the Cathedral Town (Dublin, 1989), 93–116; PRONI D3531/M/3/3; Thom's Irish Almanac 1850 (Dublin, 1850), 192.

CHAPTER FIVE
THE FAMINE IN DUBLIN CITY

1. Mokyr, Why Ireland Starved, ch. 9; Ó Gráda, Ireland before and after the Famine, ch. 3.

2. Mokyr, Why Ireland Starved, 267; Lynch and Vaizey, Guinness's Brewery in the Irish Economy, 166–67.

3. Jan De Vries, in European Urbanization, 1500–1800 (London, 1984), 271, puts Dublin's population in 1750 at 90,000, which is certainly too low. Our higher figure places Dublin comfortably in his "top ten" of European cities in 1750.

4. David Dickson, "The demographic implications of Dublin's growth, 1650–1850," in R. Lawton and R. Lee (eds.), Urban Population Development in Western Europe (Liverpool, 1989); Patrick Fagan, "The population of Dublin in the eighteenth century with particular reference to the proportions of Catholics," Eighteenth Century Ireland, 6 (1991), 121–56.

5. James Whitelaw, *An Essay on the Population of Dublin* (Dublin, 1805), 50–52.

6. Fagan, "The population of Dublin," 149; Ó Gráda, "Dublin's Demography in the Early Nineteenth Century," *PS*, 45 (1991), 43–54; *Census of Ireland . . . 1841*, 18.

7. Cited in John Aldridge, "Review of the Sanitary Condition of Dublin," *DQJMS*, May 1847.

8. Thomas Willis, *Facts Connected with the Social & Sanitary Condition of the Working Classes in the City of Dublin* (Dublin, 1845); Nugent Robinson, "The Condition of the Dwellings of the Poor in Dublin, with a Glance at the Model Lodging Houses," in *Transactions of the National Association for the Promotion of Social Science 1861* (London, 1862), 517–18. See also Jacinta Prunty, *Dublin Slums, 1800–1925* (IAP, 1997), chs. 1–3.

9. Whitelaw, *An Essay on the Population of Dublin*; Dickson, "Demographic Implications"; J. Mokyr and C. Ó Gráda, "The heights of the British and the Irish c. 1800–1815: Evidence from recruits to the EIC Army," in J. Komlos (ed.), *The Biological Standard of Living* (Chicago, 1994).

10. Fernand Braudel, *The Mediterranean and the Mediterranean World in the Age of Philip II* (New York, 1949 [1992]), 237–38; Jordan, *The Great Famine*, 114, 118.

11. E. Evans, "History of Dublin hospitals and infirmaries from 1188 till the present time, No. XXV. Fever Hospital and House of Recovery, Cork Street," *Irish Builder*, 39 (1897), 181–83; John Warburton, James Whitelaw, and Robert Walsh, *History of the City of Dublin*, 2 vols. (London, 1818), vol. 2, 707–16.

12. Post, *Food Shortage, Climatic Variability and Epidemic Disease*, 177.

13. John Swift, *History of the Dublin Bakers and Others* (Dublin, 1948), 371.

14. Dr. Henry Kennedy, cited by William Wilde in *DQJMS*, 8 (1849), 46ff.

15. *Census of Ireland 1851*, "Tables of Death," 36, 82.

16. Ibid., 142–78.

17. The imposition of the Poor Rate Levy in 1839 crowded out many of the subscriptions previously received by the Dublin Mendicity Association. However, the Association's Mendicity Institute would continue to admit hundreds of paupers and was full during the famine. In its 1845 annual report, the Association described how 150 "aged and infirm, and nurses with children, all in poverty and misery, and fit cases for relief" were sent up to the South Dublin union for admission. Only seven were accepted, and the rest returned to the Mendicity.

18. *Thom's Irish Almanac and Official Directory 1848*, 597.

19. NAD, Outrage Reports, 9/16, 9 January 1847.

20. *FJ*, 16 February 1847.

21. NAD, CSOCR 1847/9/47. In April 1847, the death of Ann Magrath, a child who had been trying to subsist on an exclusively liquid diet, prompted the North Dublin union relief committee to switch to a "bread ration alone . . . [as] best calculated to preserve the health and strength of the poor" (*Dublin Evening Post*, 15 April 1847).

22. Sir Randolph Routh, referring to forty-three bundles of old clothing sent

to him by the Association, which he intended to distribute through the clergy, told Trevelyan that "the misery in Dublin is becoming very great" (Routh to Trevelyan, 1 March 1847, in IUP7/548).

23. In Bengal in the early 1940s "it is remarkable that, though a large number of people died of starvation on the pavements of Calcutta, not a single person among the dead belonged to Greater Calcutta." One reason suggested for this is that the needs of industrial labor working in the city's defense-related industries were met first. See Bhatia, *Famines in India*, 324–25.

24. The registers are deposited in the Representative Church Body library in Churchtown. Further evidence that the Protestant poor were not immune is to be found in the city's workhouse records (further discussed below). For example, about 10 percent of those Dubliners who entered the North Dublin union in the early months of 1847 and died there were Protestants.

25. NAD, 1047/3/7.

26. Cousens, "Regional death rates in Ireland during the Great Famine," 55–74.

27. Warburton *et al.*, *History of the City of Dublin*, vol. 2, 1345.

28. M. Craig, *Dublin, 1660–1860* (Dublin, 1980), 309.

29. *Dublin Medical Press*, 29 May 1850. In Cork too the poor crowded into the city; one poor-law guardian deemed the city "in imminent danger from this incursion of Goths and vandals from the wilds of the country, for . . . they were nothing but barbarians" (*CE*, 1 October 1847, cited in O'Mahony, *Shadow of the Steeple*, 169).

30. Somerville, *Letters from Ireland*, 28; Asenath Nicholson, *Lights and Shades of Ireland in Three Parts* (London, 1850), 233; Lord John Manners, *Notes of an Irish Tour* (London, 1849), 8.

31. John East, *Glimpses of Ireland in 1847* (London, 1847), 4; Nicholson, *Lights and Shades of Ireland*, 225, 234, 245.

32. R. Collins, *Observations on the Prevention of Contagious Diseases* (Dublin, 1848), 10.

33. T. Percy Kirkpatrick, *The Book of the Rotunda Hospital: An Illustrated History of the Dublin Lying-in Hospital* (London, 1913); T. D. O'Donel Browne, *The Rotunda Hospital, 1745–1945* (Edinburgh, 1947); C. Ó Gráda, "The Rotunda and the people of Dublin, 1745–1939," *Éire-Ireland*, 30(1) (1995), 49–76.

34. The records for 1826–32 are missing, presumably because Master Robert Collins, whose tenure spanned that period and whose *Practical Treatise on Midwifery, Containing the Result of Sixteen Thousand Six Hundred & Fifty-four Births* (London, 1835) is an analysis of the hospital's caseload at the time, never returned the material to the hospital after finishing his book.

35. Ó Gráda, "Dublin's demography in the early nineteenth century," 43–54.

36. Ó Gráda, "The Rotunda and the people of Dublin."

37. Curiously, this seems to have been the case for most hospitals that did not cater specifically for fever patients. Wilde's "Tables of Deaths" report the numbers below for all general hospitals in Ireland. Twelve of the sixteen listed were in Dublin, and these accounted for most (85 percent) of the deaths. Deaths between 1842 and 1850 were as follows:

Year	1842	1843	1844	1845	1846	1847	1848	1849	1850
Deaths	539	486	546	616	696	824	667	719	594

38. *Dublin Medical Press*, 9 February 1848, 86.

39. Its original two buildings (separated in order to keep ill and convalescent patients apart) still stand and today form part of Brú Chaoimhín geriatric nursing home. Institutions like it bore the brunt of the famine in Dublin.

40. Evans, "History of Dublin hospitals and infirmaries"; C. J. McSweeney, "Short history of the House of Recovery and Fever Hospital, Cork Street, Dublin," *Medical Press and Circular*, 213, no. 5533 (23 May 1945).

41. Richard Carmichael, *An Essay on the Venereal Diseases Which Have Been Confounded with the Syphilis* (Dublin, 1814); Joseph V. O'Brien, *Dear, Dirty Dublin: A City in Distress, 1899–1916* (Dublin, 1982), 118–19.

42. Warburton *et al.*, *History of the City of Dublin*, vol. 1, 698; Great Britain 1852/3, BPP, "Copies of Communications Which Have Passed between the Treasury and the Irish Goverment . . . on the Subject of Grants to the Westmoreland Lock Hospital," H.C. [421.], vol. 94, 3; G.E.P. Meldon, "Some notes on the admissions to the Westmoreland Lock Hospital since 1860," *Dublin Journal of Medical Science*, 37 (1914), 109–18; John Morgan, "Clinical review of cases at the Westmoreland Lock Hospital during the past six months," *DQJMS* (1869), 506–28.

43. J. G. Kohl, *Travels in Ireland* (London, 1844), 278–82; Thackeray, "The Irish Sketch Book," in *Collected Works*, vol. 18 (London, 1888), 344–46. Thackeray would not have been surprised to hear that "procuresses" from the city's brothels had infiltrated the Cork union workhouse in 1841 (*Cork Constitution*, 26 January 1841, cited in O'Brien, "The New Poor Law," 44–45). A few years later another account in the *Constitution* told of how women "who had been improper characters before their entrance into the house seduc[ed] young girls outside its doors" (15 April 1843).

For more on Dublin's workhouses in the 1830s and 1840s, see Prunty, *Dublin Slums*, 217–23. For an analysis of admissions to the South Dublin union, see Helen Burke, *The People and the Poor Law in Nineteenth-Century Ireland* (Littlehampton, Sussex, 1987), 74. The number of widows aged 17–25 years in the whole city in 1841 was 309. In the 26–35-year age group it was 1,931.

44. Great Britain (1842), "Inquiry into the treatment and mortality of infant children in the workhouse of the North Dublin Union," H.C. [370], vol. 36; Willis, *Facts Connected with the Social & Sanitary Condition*, 7–9.

45. *FJ*, 13 April 1847.

46. MacArthur, "Medical history," 311.

47. Deirdre Lindsay, *Dublin's Oldest Charity: The Sick and Indigent Roomkeepers' Society, 1790–1990* (Dublin, 1990); A. E. Farrington, *Rev. Dr. Spratt O.C.C.: His Life and Times* (Dublin, 1893); Peter O'Dwyer, "John Francis Spratt O. Carm. 1796–1871" (Ph.D. diss., Pontifical University, Rome, 1968), 103–16.

48. Compare the subscriptions (to the nearest £) received by the Mendicity Association from inhabitants of Dublin between 1838 and 1849:

1838:	4,793	1842:	564	1846:	1,143
1839:	6,366	1843:	592	1847:	1,569
1840:	1,892	1844:	717	1848:	708
1841:	661	1845:	662	1849:	718

49. Minutes, accounts, and correspondence of the DPA have been deposited in the library of the Representative Church Body, Dublin.

50. On Stanford, see "Proceedings connected with the recent dismissal of Rev. C. S. Stanford from the office of Protestant chaplain of the North Dublin Union," BPP 1852 [120], vol. 46, 59, and Desmond Bowen, *The Protestant Crusade in Ireland, 1800–1870* (Dublin, 1978), 242.

51. *FJ*, 22 May 1849.

52. *FJ*, 27 March 1849.

53. "Twenty-sixth report of the inspectors-general of prisons in Ireland," BPP 1847–48, vol. 34, 253; "Twenty-seventh report . . . ," BPP 1849, vol. 26, 373; 1851 Census, "Tables of Death."

54. Annual Report for 1849, 12.

55. "Return from the county gaols and workhouses in Ireland of the daily diet allowed to an able-bodied man," in BPP 1847–48 (486), vol. 53, 389); "Twenty-sixth report of the inspectors-general," 8. The prisons supplied twice as much milk (two pints daily) but (with the exception of the Richmond) no meat, while the workhouses offered meat soup twice or three times a week. The alleged advantage of prison fare in Cork City greatly concerned the local Grand Jury, who blamed it for increasing vagrancy, theft, malicious injuries to property, and other crimes punishable by imprisonment (*Cork Constitution*, 15 April 1843).

56. Besides Grangegorman, Newgate, and the Richmond (discussed below), records for Mountjoy and Smithfield male convict depot also survive.

57. NAD, V16–8–12.

58. See, e.g., Ó Gráda, *Ireland*, 17–20, 83–84, 105–10; Mokyr and Ó Gráda, "Heights and living standards in the United Kingdom, 1815–1860," *EEH*, April 1996, 1–27.

59. NAD, V16–8–17: 9/45–9/47.

60. NAD, 1064/3/6.

CHAPTER SIX
FAMINE MEMORY

1. Jan Vansina, *Oral Tradition: A Study in Historical Methodology* (London, 1965), 1; id., *Oral Tradition as History* (London, 1985), 199.

2. Vaughan, "Famine analysis and family relations: 1949 in Nyasaland," *Past and Present*, no. 108 (1985), 177–205; id., *Story of an African Famine*; Leah Minc, "Scarcity and survival: The role of oral tradition in mediating subsistence crises," *Journal of Anthropological Archeaology*, 5 (1986), 39–113. See also John J. Cove, "Survival or extinction: Reflections on the problem of famine in

Tsimshian and Kaguru mythology," in Laughlin and Brady, *Extinction and Survival*, 232–44.

3. Vaughan, *Story of an African Famine*, 1. For a sophisticated appplication of folk memory to the history of U.S. slavery, see Stephen Crawford, "The slave family: A view from the slave narratives," in C. Goldin and H. Rockoff (eds.), *Strategic Factors in Nineteenth-Century American Economic History* (Chicago, 1992), 331–50.

4. Gwyn Prins, "Oral History," in Peter Bourke (ed.), *New Perspectives on Historical Writing* (Cambridge, U.K., 1989), 137. For further discussion and examples, see Michael Allen, *Western Rivermen, 1763–1861: Ohio and Mississippi Boatmen and the Myth of the Alligator Horse* (Baton Rouge, 1990); Michael McBane, "Irish famine stories in the Ottawa valley," *Oral History Forum*, 16–17 (1996–97); Mairi MacArthur, *Iona: The Living Memory of a Crofting Community* (Edinburgh, 1990); and the essays by Norwegian folklorists Brynjulf Alver and Birgit Hertzberg Johnson in Reimund Kvideland and Henning K. Sehmsdorf (eds.), *Nordic Folklore: Recent Studies* (Bloomington, 1989). The late Raphael Samuel (in *Theatres of Memory* [London, 1994], 11) noted how John Aubrey loved "to converse with old men as Living Histories."

5. Notably the late K. H. Connell; see his "Peasant marriage in Ireland: Its structure and development since the famine," *EHR*, 14 (1962), and *Irish Peasant Society* (Oxford, 1968), ch. 2. On the historians, see T. W. Moody, "Irish history and Irish mythology," *Hermathena*, 124 (Summer 1978), 7–28; and Séamus Deane, *Strange Country: Modernity and Nationhood in Irish Writing since 1790* (Oxford, 1997), 185–93.

6. Ordnance Survey Letters, 56 (tradition recorded mainly in Kilmacrenan Parish); Richard M. Dorson (ed.), *Folklore and Folklife* (Chicago, 1972), 1.

7. Póirtéir, *Glórtha ón nGorta*, 162. For the details, see app. 6.1. Board of Works records report the following:

Week ending	Spent on Labor (£)	No. Employed	Pence per Worker per Week
6 Mar 1847	235,484	734,792	76.9
24 Apr 1847	120,472	474,650	60.9
29 May 1847	34,851	133,785	62.5

8. Compare James Stewart, *Boccaccio in the Blaskets* (Galway, 1988), and Bo Almqvist, "The mysterious Mícheál Ó Gaoithín, Boccaccio and the Blasket Tradition," *Béaloideas*, 58 (1990), 75–140.

9. Póirtéir, *Glórtha ón Ghorta*, 147–52; id., *Famine Echoes*, 116–31, 150–65.

10. O. S. Letters, Donegal, p. 141, 26 October 1835.

11. IFC1075/548. Here the narrator is confusing the bad times of 1879–80 with those of the 1840s. Similarly, accounts referring to cholera may confuse the first outbreak in 1832 and the second in 1849. See also Roger McHugh, "The famine in folklore," in Edwards and Williams, *The Great Famine*, p. 394.

12. IFC1073/107; IFC1188/267.

13. Edwards and Williams, *The Great Famine*, viii.

14. Lord Landsdowne, IFC1068/102–6; reprinted in Séamus Deane (ed.), *The Field Day Anthology of Irish Writing* (Derry, 1991), vol. 2, 158–60; Sir Richard O'Donnell (IFC1072/162–63); Betsy Barry, Dingle (S420); Gage, Rathlin (IFC1390/228–32); Alexander Hamilton (IFC1072/376–400); Cronin Coltsman (IFC1071/78–80); the Bournes (IFC1072/48–60); the Fitzwilliams (IFC1069/132–40); Freeman Dave (IFC1068/235–39). See too Póirtéir, *Glórtha on nGorta*, 213–21; id., *Famine Echoes*, chs. 13–14; IFC1220/391 (Greencastle); IFC1269/266–67 (Ballymoe).

15. According to Inspector Coffin (Schull, 15 February 1847) "three-fourths of the inhabitants you meet carry the tale of woe in their features and persons, as they are reduced to mere skeletons, all of their physical powers being wasted away" (Commissariat Series, 162–63). Woodham-Smith (*The Great Hunger*, 141, 157–59, 194–96) recalls the harrowing accounts left by Quaker philanthropist William Forster and others.

16. Martin A. Conway, *Autobiographical Memory: An Introduction* (Milton Keynes, 1990), 11–14. For an excellent nontechnical introduction to the field, see John Kotre, *White Gloves: How We Create Ourselves through Memory* (New York, 1995).

17. IFC1070/255; IFC1075/663–66. For the real story of Queen Victoria's donation, see Thomas P. O'Neill, "The Queen and the famine," *Threshold*, 1(2) (1957), 60–63. For articulations of broader anti-English feeling, see Póirtéir, *Glórtha ón nGorta*, 7, 38–39.

18. IFC1009/80.

19. Kerr, "*A Nation of Beggars?*" 56.

20. McHugh, "The famine in folklore"; Ó Gráda, *An Drochshaol*; Póirtéir, *Famine Echoes*; id., *Glórtha ón Ghorta*; Antain Mac Lochlainn, "The famine in Gaelic tradition," *Irish Review*, no. 17/8 (1995); Carmel Quinlan, "A punishment from God: The famine in the centenary folklore questionnaire," *Irish Review*, no. 19 (1996); Patricia Lysaght, "Perspectives on women during the Great Irish Famine," *Béaloideas*, 64/65 (1996–97).

21. On which see Séamus Ó Catháin and Caitlín Uí Sheidhin (1987). *A Mhuintir Dhú Chaocháin, Labhraígí Feasta* (Indreabhán, 1987), xvii–xxvii.

22. A copy of the questionnaire (which is reproduced in Lysaght, "Perspectives on women," 130) was attached inside the front cover of each volume of replies. Several of the replies are more in tune with the guideline provided in Seán Ó Súilleabháin, *A Handbook of Irish Folklore* (Dublin, 1942), 534–35.

23. E.g., IFC1068/49, 100, 212, 219.

24. Compare Ó Súilleabháin, *Handbook*, xi.

25. IFC1188/256–57.

26. IFC668/336; IFC48/121 [Cill na Martra]; *Béaloideas*, 14 (1944), 67–68 [Waterford]; IFC51/19 [Cork]; IFC1072/258 [Dromore West].

27. *Béaloideas*, 24 (1955), 7.

28. IFC1070/12–14. Sayers is best known for her autobiography, *Peig: A Scéal Féin* (Dublin, 1934–36)—in which she also tells this story—and *Machnamh Seanmhná* (Dublin, 1939), trans. as *An Old Woman's Recollections* (Oxford, 1962)). Cf. too Patricia Lysaght, "Perspectives on women," 116–8. Yet

another, corroborative version of the same story was collected by Canon Mic-heál Ó Mainín from Muiris Ó Scanláin of Gleann Luic. In very much the same vein is Seosamh Mac Grianna's fictionalized account of an incident during the famine in "*Ar an Trá Fhoilimh*," reprinted with a translation in Séamus Deane (ed.), *The Field Day Anthology of Irish Writing*, vol. 3 (Dublin, 1994), 845–49.

29. Compare Donnchadh Ó Cróinín, "Eachtra ar an nDroch-Shaol," *Éigse*, 19 (1982–83), 173; IFC667/335; IFC1068/197–203 [Kilworth, Cork], 272–77 [Macroom]; IFC1069/351–54 [Doolin, Clare]; IFC1072/258 [Dromore West, Sligo]; Patricia Lysaght, "Women during the Great Irish Famine," 112–15.

30. Ed. Séamus Ó Duilearga, *Leabhar Stiofáin Uí Ealaoire* (Dublin, 1981), xiii–xiv, xxiii, 309–10; IFC715/457–58 [Cahirciveen]; IFC1069/26–32 [Monaghan]; IFC1069/256 [Ballymoe, Galway]; IFC1070/308–12 [Sneem, Kerry]; IFC1075/171–72 [Hacketstown, Carlow]; IFC1413/177 [Ballycastle]. "I rose from the dead in the year forty-eight" (IFC921/427–29) purports to be a plea by a tramp who narrowly escaped being buried alive.

31. The outbreak of cholera that hit Ireland in December 1848 was most serious in the towns. Many of the rural deaths attributed to cholera were in reality dysentery (MacArthur, "Medical history," 306–7).

32. IFC1073/31–32. For a splendid introduction to Ó Caoidheáin, see Ríonach Uí Ógáin, "Colm Ó Caoidheáin and Séamus Ennis: A Conamara singer and his collector," *Béaloideas*, 64–65 (1996–97), 279–338.

33. E.g., Vincent, "A political orchestration of the Irish Famine," 75–98; Kinealy, *This Great Calamity*.

34. IFCS424/136; Póirtéir, *Famine Echoes*, 90; see also Séamus Ó Duilearga, *Leabhar Sheáin Í Chonaill* (Dublin, 1977), 288.

35. IFC1068/196 [Cloyne]; IFC1069/67 [Donegal]; IFC1068/25 [Grange]; IFC1068/46 [Seskin]; IFC1069/268–9 [Ballymoe]; IFC1071/77 [Knocknagree].

36. Ó Gráda, *Ireland before and after the Famine*, 133–37.

37. IFC685/376. Elsewhere the same informant notes merely that nobody died after turnips became available in 1848. See Tomás Mac Síthigh, *Paróiste an Fheirtéaraigh: Stairsheanchas an cheantair i dtréimhse an Ghorta Mhóir* (Dublin, 1984), 156. This is more plausible.

38. IFCS431 [Liscarney]; IFC1220/385 [Greencastle]; IFC1009/76–77 [Muigh Ros]; IFC1312/162–63, 408 [Kerry].

39. At the other extreme, the memory that "*cailleadh a raibh sa Ghleann Mór ar fad* (all in Gleann Mór perished)" finds support in the drop of that west Kerry townland's population from sixty-seven in 1841 to ten in 1851.

40. IFC1072/217.

41. IFC1069/71 [Fintown]; IFC1069/43 [Inishowen]; IFC1070/20 [Great Blasket]; IFC1070/153 [Cill Mhaol Céadair]; IFC1069/385 [Dubh Thuama].

42. Foster, *Modern Ireland*, 330; Seán Kierse, *The Famine Years in the Parish of Killaloe, 1845–1851* (Killaloe, 1984); Census of Ireland (Tables of Death), 31; Ignatius Murphy, *The Diocese of Killaloe, 1800–1850* (Dublin, 1992), 222–23.

43. Dáithí Ó hÓgáin, "An Stair agus an Seanchas Béil," *Léachtaí Cholm-chille* 14 (1983), 192.

44. Compare Antti Häkkinen "The thieving started in the autumn," in Häk-kinen et al., *Kun Hallen nälän tuskan toi*, 176–94.

45. IFC1070/49–50, 63 [Dún Chaoin]; IFC685/377; Mac Síthigh, *Paróiste an Fheirtéaraigh*, 156 [Ballyferriter]; IFCS420 [Feothanach]; IFC1069/294 [Dunsandle]; IFC1069/276 [Ballymara].

46. IFC1069/154 [Laois]; Ó Duilearga (1977), 286 [Kerry]; IFC1068/23 [Grange]; IFC1069/370–71 [Mayo]; IFC1069/33–40 [Monaghan].

47. Ó Catháin and Uí Sheidhin, *A Mhuintir Dhú Chaocháin* [Mayo]; IFC1075/477 [Westmeath]; IFC1188/256 [Béara]; *Béaloideas*, vol. 2 (193x),139 [Baile'n Sceilg]; IFC1136/299–305 [Creeslough].

48. Conchubhar Ó Muimhneacháin, *Béaloideas Bhéal Átha an Ghaorthaidh* (Dublin, 1935), 94–95.

49. IFC1070/100. See also, e.g., IFC407/404 [Glenbeigh, Kerry]; IFC1070/38–41 [Ballyferriter, Kerry]; IFC1068/151–52 [Carlow], IFC1069/37 [Monaghan]; IFC1073/39 [Galway]; IFC1075/619–21 [Meath]; IFC1188/310 [Glenmore, west Cork]; IFC1075/445, 483 [Westmeath]; IFC1072/294–95 [Sligo-Leitrim border]; IFC1072/335 [Dromintee, Armagh].

50. IFC1278/424–25.

51. Compare Vaughan, *The Story of an African Famine*.

52. IFC1480/383–84; Póirtéir, *Famine Echoes*, 72.

53. IFC1068/286 [Meelick]; IFC1068/329 [Tuamgraney]; Póirtéir, *Famine Echoes*, 78 [Westport].

54. IFC1069/249, 438, 471; IFC1075/688–89; IFC1344/146, 177, 380; IFC1070/93; IFC1068/289; IFC1071/235; see too IFC1075/644; Póirtéir, *Famine Echoes*, 34–48.

55. IFC1071/276 [Enniskean, Cork]; IFC1075/4 [Stradbally, Laois].

56. IFC1070/219.

57. IFC1070/14–15.

58. Ó Gráda, *An Drochshaol*, 22–23.

59. E.g. Ó Gráda, "Malthus and the pre-famine economy"; Solar, "The Great Famine was no ordinary subsistence crisis," in Crawford, *Famine*, 112–33.

60. Enrí Ó Muirgheasa, *Dhá Chéad de Cheoltaibh Uladh* (Dublin, 1936), 217.

61. Aykroyd, *Conquest of Famine*, 93; Charles G. Roland, "A medical school in the Warsaw ghetto," *Medical History*, 33 (1989), 407; Dirks, "Social responses during severe food shortages and famine"; Drèze and Sen, *Hunger and Public Action*, 74.

62. IFC1069/438; IFC1069/215–21.

63. IFC1070/8.

64. IFC1071/90–91.

65. IFC1071/77–154; IFC1075/464–74; IFC1069/182–90.

66. IFC1068/120; IFC1188/309; IFC1269/268; IFC850/306.

67. Compare the following from Greencastle in county Tyrone (IFC1220/399): "The porridge made from (Indian meal) was called 'Indian Buck'. It was a disgrace long after, like I mind this well, to be seen and heard of eating 'Indian Buck.'" The shame surrounding tuberculosis in more recent times provides an analogy.

68. IFC1071/133–34; McHugh, "The famine in folklore," 404–5.

69. IFC419B.

70. IFC1068/131; IFC1068/201–2; IFC1075/245–46; Ó Duilearga, *Leabhar Sheáin Í Chonaill*, 286.

71. Ó Catháin and Uí Sheidhin, *A Mhuintir Dhú Chaocháin*, 148; IFC1072/92; Lysaght, "Perspectives on women during the Great Irish Famine," 87–90.

72. IFC51/110; see too Ó Súileabháin, *Handbook*, 535.

73. IFC1070/395–96. For more, see IFC1068/23–24 (Grange, Clonmel); IFC1068/165 (Lios Póil, Kerry); IFC1068/206 (Kildorrery, Cork); IFC716/26–27 (Waterville, Kerry); Ó Catháin and Uí Sheidhin, *A Mhuintir Dhú Chaocháin*, 153–54 (Ceathrú Thaidhg, Mayo); 1190/289 (Belmullet, Mayo); IFC821/526 (Baile Mhúirne, Cork); Póirtéir, *Glórtha ón nGorta*, 265 (Teilionn, Donegal), 268 (Tuar Mhic Éadaigh, Mayo), 269–70 (Coill Uachtarach, Galway), 277 (Killorglin, Kerry), 279–80 (Cill Maolcéadair, Kerry), 281 (Kilworth, Cork).

74. The population of the largely coterminous civil parish of Nohovaldaly fell from 3,954 in 1841 to 3,036 in 1851. That of the townland of Lissyconnor dropped from 128 to 91. The population of Ceathrú Thaidhg townland fell from 167 to 137.

75. S. Ó Súileabháin and R.Th. Christiansen, *The Types of the Irish Folktale* (Helsinki, 1963), 147; Antti Aarne and Stith Thompson, *The Types of the Folktale* (Helsinki, 1961), 255–56; Frederick C. Tubach, *Exemplorum: A Handbook of Medieval Religious Tales* (Helsinki, 1969), 200; Tom Peete Cross, *Motif Index of Early Irish Literature* (Bloomington, Indiana, 1952), 436; Joan Newlon Radner, *Fragmentary Annals of Ireland* (Dublin, 1978), 23.

76. Liam de Paor, *Saint Patrick's World: The Christian Culture of Ireland's Apostolic Age* (Dublin, 1993), 208–9.

77. Compare Mary Cumiskey, "Folk memories of the Famine," *Creggan: Journal of the Creggan Local History Society*, no. 7 (1994–95), 55–60; McHugh, "The famine in folklore," 407.

78. Christopher Morash, *The Hungry Voice: The Poetry of the Irish Famine* (Dublin, 1989), 18.

79. See Royal Irish Academy Mss. 23 O 39, 23 N 32, 23 C 12, 24 M 5, 23 D 8; Breandán Ó Buachalla, "Seacaibíteachas Thaidhg Uí Neachtain," *Studia Hibernica*, 26 (1991–92), 37n; and P. A. Breatnach, "Togha na hÉigse 1700–1800," *Éigse* (1994), 120–21. "*Amhrán na Mine*," in Mrs. E. Costello, *Amhráin Mhuigh Seola* (Dublin,1923), 23–26, and "Tá Gaedhil Bhocht Cráite," in Donncha Ó Donnchú, *Filíocht Mháire Bhuí Ní Laoghaire* (Dublin, 1931), 64–65, refer to the famine of 1822.

80. Garrett FitzGerald, "Estimates for baronies of minimum level of Irish-speaking amongst successive decennial cohorts: 1771–1781 to 1861–1871," *PRIA*, 84C(3) (1994), 117–55.

81. I exclude later well-known ballads such as "Oh! The Praties They are Small Over Here" or "Remember Skibbereen." See McKay, *An Anthology of the Potato*, 78; George-Denis Zimmermann, *Songs of Irish Rebellion: Political Street Ballads and Rebel Songs, 1780–1900* (Dublin, 1967), 16.

82. E.g., John Moulden, *Thousands Are Sailing: A Brief Song History of Irish Emigration* (Portrush, 1994), 10–1, 22–23.

83. Compare ibid., 3.

84. Lady Gregory, "The Blind Raftery," in *id.*, *Poets and Dreamers: Studies*

and Translations (London, 1974), 239; Ó Ceallaigh, *Filíocht na gCallanán* (Dublin, 1967), 1–2, 11–2. I am told by Hugh Shields that the poem is "singable, rather formulaic," but it is always described as a poem.

85. Ó Ceallaigh, *Filíocht na gCallanán*; Gregory, "The blind Raftery," 239; UCD, Ir. Ms. 14, 345, 347. Another version from Craughwell, noted by Ó Ceallaigh, is given in IFCS35/2–5. For an awkward but literal translation of four of its eight verses by one of O'Curry's friends, see Ó Gráda, *An Drochshaol*, 52–53.

86. According to an account from Ballyferriter, "*lá 'le Michíl a tháinig a' cith i forty five. Aniar dtuaig a tháini sí chuala. Bhí smut dos na prátaí buinte 'cu agus tógach amach as na guirt iad agus dhúbhadar istigh sa tithe an méid a bhí istigh. I forty six a tháinig a' bleaist* (it was on Michaelmas that the shower came in forty-five. From the northwest it came, I heard. They had dug some of the potatoes and they took them in from the fields, but what were in the houses blackened inside. It was in forty-six that the blight came)" (IFC685/375–76). See too Mac Síthigh, *Paróiste an Fheirtéaraigh*, 151.

87. The translation, meant for O'Curry "*exclusively*" as an aid "in giving a *poetical* translation," is found in UCD Ir. Ms. 14/347. Chapman lived at Pearemount, Rathgar.

88. IFC74/248. An interesting song, much favored by Séamus Ennis, who collected it from Colm Ó Caoidheáin. Indeed, the song may owe its survival to Séamus Ennis. Sean-nós singer Seán Chóilín 'ac Dhonncha learned the song from him.

89. Liam Mac Con Iomaire in conversation with Éamonn Ó Conghaola, March 1994; IFC74/248.

90. *An Stoc*, April 1925; see too IFC1073/48, 52–53, and IFC74/241–42.

91. Compare from Mayo (in Póirtéir, *Famine Echoes*, 159): "My father was ganger on these works, just because there were few men could write or keep men's time in those days."

92. Tóibín, *An Duanaire Déiseach* (Dublin, 1978), 19–21. On the local cemetery, see IFC1144/210–27.

93. Ó Gráda, *An Drochshaol*, 62–63, 67; see too Próinséas Ó Ceallaigh, "Amhráin ó Mhuscraí: an Droch Shaol," *Béaloideas*, 7(1) (1937), 31–32.

Folklore is replete with instances of alleged souperism and jumpers. Given the highly charged, far-from-ecumenical atmosphere of the 1840s, such accounts cannot be taken at face value. The widespread *perception* of proselytism linked to charity is interesting, nonetheless, and in the circumstances it is only natural that some donors would make their charity "cautious and conditional." See Irene Whelan, "The stigma of souperism," in Póirtéir, *Great Irish Famine*, 135–54.

94. J. J. Lyons contributed a version to the *Irish American* 5 December 1891. This is reproduced in Ferriter Ms. 8/22 (University College, Dublin). See too Proinsias Ní Dhorchaí, *Clár Amhrán ón Achréidh* (Dublin, 1974), 74–75 and IFC1205/432–34.

95. IFC1205/432–33; IFC72/39–41.

96. The populations of the five parishes of Ballyferriter were as follows in 1841 and 1851:

	1841	*1851*
Dún Chaoin	1,394	722
Dún Urlann	2,125	1,064
Márthain	973	650
Cill Chuáin	1,760	998
Cill Mhaolchéadair	2,333	1,354

97. The version produced here was supplied by the late Micheál Ó Ciosáin, parish priest of Ballyferriter, to Micheál Ó Mainín for editing. See M. Ó Mainín, "Amhrán an Ghorta," in Micheál Ó Ciosáin (ed.), *Céad Bliain* (Baile an Fhir-téaraigh, 1971), 190–93.

98. Compare Antti Häkkinen, "Jos lapsen, vasta näet puunvärisiä arkkuja . . . [If you see wooden coffins, child, you need not ask: they died of famine]," in Häkkinen *et al.*, *Kun Hallen nälän tuskan toi*, 250–72.

99. Radoslav A. Tsanoff, "Folklore and tradition in a growing society," in J. Frank Dobie, Mody C. Boatright, and Harry H Ransom (eds.), *In the Shadow of History* (Austin, Texas, 1939), 1; Edwards and Williams, *The Great Famine*, xi.

100. The narrator was born in 1838.

CHAPTER SEVEN
THE LEGACY

1. Stein *et al.*, *Famine and Human Development*, 220, 236; *Time Magazine*, "Why are the Dutch shooting up fastest?" 14 October 1996, 94.

2. Abdur Razzaque *et al.*, "Sustained effects of the 1974–75 famine on infant and child mortality in a rural area of Bangladesh," *PS* 44 (1990).

3. F. Geary and T. Stark, "Examining Ireland's post-famine economic performance: The distribution of gross domestic product between the countries of the United Kingdom, 1861–1911," typescript, University of Ulster, 1997; George R. Boyer, T. J. Hatton, and K. O'Rourke, "Emigration and economic growth in Ireland, 1850–1914," in Hatton and Williamson, *Migration and International Labour Markets*; Ó Gráda, *A Rocky Road: The Irish Economy since the 1920s* (Manchester, 1997), chs. 3 and 7.

4. "Sixth Annual Report of the Poor Law Commissioners (Ireland)," app. B, no. 16, in BPP 1852/3 (L), 151–56; Ó Gráda, *Ireland*, 236–37.

5. O'Rourke, "Did the Great Irish Famine matter?" 16–20; Solar, "The great famine." On the performance of agriculture more generally, see Turner, *After the Famine*, ch. 5.

6. Ó Gráda and O'Rourke, "Mass migration."

7. For interesting evidence on the strength of Irish family ties in New York's slums in the 1850s, see Pernicone, "The 'Bloody Ould Sixth,'" ch. 3. In their recent econometric study of the determinants of Irish emigration, Hatton and Williamson estimate that for every thousand previous migrants an additional forty-one were attracted over each year. However, this finding refers to the 1880–1914 period; moreover, it is based on a model of emigration in which the

migrants' response to wage gaps is assumed to have been constant over time. Since the stock of migrants fell gradually over the period analyzed, the emigrant stock variable could equally be capturing the reduced sensitivity of the migration rate to a given wage gap as incomes rose. See Hatton and Williamson, "After the famine," 582–85.

8. Ó Gráda, *Ireland*, 251–54; Tim O'Neill, "The persistence of famine in Ireland," in Póirtéir, *The Great Irish Famine*, 205. See also Tim O'Neill, "Minor famines and relief in Galway, 1815–1925," in Moran and Gillespie, *Galway*.

9. S. C. Watkins and J. Menken, "Famines in historical perspective," *PDR*, 11 (1985), 647–76; Pitkänen, *Deprivation and Disease*, 45; Ó Gráda and O'Rourke, "Migration as disaster relief," 17–20.

10. K. H. Connell, "Peasant marriage in Ireland after the Great Famine," *Past and Present*, 12 (1957), 76–91; id., "Peasant marriage in Ireland: Its structure and development since the Famine," 502–23; id., *Irish Peasant Society*, 116–18. Indeed, there is some evidence that emigration delayed the Irish marital fertility decline. See Ó Gráda, *Ireland before and after the Famine*, ch. 5. For a modern reappraisal of Connell and post-famine demography generally, see T. Guinnane, *The Vanishing Irish* (Princeton, N.J., 1997).

11. Ó Gráda, *Ireland before and after the Famine*, ch. 4; J. O'Rourke, "Did the Great Irish Famine matter?" *JEH*, 51 (1991), 1–22.

12. Iliffe, *Africa: The History of a Continent*, 238; id., *The African Poor*, 156–58, 250–53; Jean Drèze, "Famine prevention in Africa," in Drèze and Sen, *The Political Economy of Hunger*; Lord Hailey, *An African Survey: Revised 1956* (London, 1957), 1070; Wrigley and Schofield, *Population History*; R. W. Fogel, "Second thoughts of the European escape from hunger: Famines, chronic malnutrition, and mortality rates," in S. Osmani (ed.), *Nutrition and Poverty* (Oxford, 1992), 246–47. Peter Razzell's recent critique of Wrigley and Schofield increases, if anything, the presumption of a neo-Malthusian tapering off of crisis mortality. See P. Razzell, "The growth of population in eighteenth-century England," *JEH*, 53(4) (1993).

13. Dickson, "The gap in famines: A useful myth?" in Crawford, *Famine*; Ó Gráda, *Ireland before and after the Famine*, 2–8.

14. Iliffe, *The African Poor*, 6, 156–58, 250–53; Drèze, "Famine prevention in Africa."

15. Gwyn Prins, "Oral History," in Peter Bourke (ed.), *New Perspectives on Historical Writing* (Cambridge, U.K., 1989), 137. In Ireland the camera came too late to provide the kind of graphic photographic evidence reproduced in Demetrios Mankriotes, *Thysiai tes Hellades kai Enklemata Katoches Kata ta eté 1941–1944* (Athens, 1944), and Aykroyd, *The Conquest of Famine*.

16. Boyce, *Nationalism in Ireland*, 170; J. Lee, "The famine in Irish history," in Ó Gráda, *Famine 150*.

BIBLIOGRAPHY

Aalen, F.H.A., and Kevin Whelan, eds. (1992). *Dublin City and County: From Prehistory to Present*. Dublin: Geography Publications.

Aalen, F.H.A., Kevin Whelan, and Matthew Stout, eds. (1997). *Atlas of the Irish Rural Landscape*, Cork: Cork University Press.

Aldridge, John (1847). "Review of the sanitary condition of Dublin," *DQJMS*, May.

Allen, Robert C., and C. Ó Gráda (1988). "On the road again with Arthur Young: English, Irish and French agriculture during the industrial revolution." *JEH*, 47, 93–116.

Anon. (1854). *Brief Notes of a Short Excursion in Ireland, in the Autumn of 1852, by the Editor and Sole Proprietor of the Hull Advertiser*. London: Whittaker.

Article 19 (1990). *Starving in Silence: A Report on Famine and Censorship*. London: Article 19. (The author of the section on China is a "a scholar of Chinese history, politics, and contemporary China . . . who wishes to remain anonymous.")

Ashton, Basil, K. Hill, A. Piazza, and R. Zeitz (1984). "Famine in China, 1958–61." *PDR*, 10(4), 613–46.

Aykroyd, W. R. (1974). *The Conquest of Famine*. London: Chatto and Windus.

Balch, William Stevens (1850). *Ireland as I Saw It*. New York.

Bardhan, Pranab (1997). "Corruption and development: A review of the issues," *JEL*, 35(3), 1320–46.

Barrington, Richard M. (1887). "The prices of some agricultural produce and the cost of farm labour for the past fifty years," *Journal of the Statistical and Social Inquiry Society of Ireland*, 137–54.

Barro, R. J. (1987). "Government spending, interest rates, prices, and budget deficits in the United Kingdom, 1701–1918." *JME*, 20, 221–47.

Bass, Hans-Heinrich (1991). *Hungerkrisen in Preussen während der ersten Hälfte des 19. Jahrhunderts*. St. Katherinen: Scripta Mercaturae Verlag.

Bergman, M. (1967). "The potato blight in the Netherlands and its social consequences (1845–1847)." *International Review of Social History*, 17(3), 391–431.

Bielenberg, Andy (1991). *Cork's Industrial Revolution, 1780–1880: Development or Decline?* Cork: Cork University Press.

Bhatia, B. M. (1967). *Famines in India, 1860–1965*. 2d ed. Bombay: Asia Publishing House.

Black, R.D.C. (1960). *Economic Thought and the Irish Question, 1817–1870*. Cambridge, U.K.: CUP.

Bourke, Austin (1993). *The Visitation of God? The Potato and the Irish Famine*. Dublin: Lilliput.

Bourke, Austin, and Hubert Lamb (1993). *The Spread of the Potato Blight in Europe in 1845–46 and the Accompanying Wind and Weather Patterns*. Dublin: Meteorological Office.

Bourke, P.M.A. (1967). "The potato, weather, blight, and the Great Famine." (Ph.D. diss., National University of Ireland, Dublin.

Bowman Janetta, Ann (1992). "Famine mortality in nineteenth-century Japan: The evidence from a temple death register." *PS*, 46, 427–43.

Boyce, D. George (1982). *Nationalism in Ireland*. London: Croom Helm.

Boyer, George E., T. J. Hatton, and K. O'Rourke (1994). "Emigration and economic growth in Ireland, 1850–1914." In T. J. Hatton and J. G. Williamson (eds.), *Migration and International Labour Markets, 1850–1939*. London: Routledge.

Boyle, P. P., and C. Ó Gráda (1985). "Fertility trends, excess mortality, and the Great Irish Famine." *Demography*, 23, 543–62.

BPP (British Parliamentary Papers) (1842). "Inquiry into the treatment and mortality of infant children in the workhouse of the North Dublin union." H.C. [370], vol. 36.

BPP (1846). "Highest price of potatoes . . . in the week ending 24 January for the last seven years as well as can be estimated." H.C. [110], vol. 37, 489.

BPP (1846). "Return of the price of potatoes agreed for at the last contract entered into by each Board of Guardians, in Ireland, previously to the 1st of May in the Years 1844, 1845, and 1846, respectively," app. B, no. 26 in the Twelfth annual report of the Poor Law Commissioners [745], vol. 19, 467.

BPP (1852/3) "Copies of Communications which have passed between the Treasury and the Irish goverment . . . on the Subject of Grants to the Westmoreland Lock Hospital." H.C. [421], vol. 94.

BPP (1856). "The Census of Ireland for 1851, part V. Tables of Death." Vol. 2.

Braudel, Fernand (1992). *The Mediterranean and the Mediterranean World in the Age of Philip II*. New York: HarperCollins. First published 1949.

Browne, O'Donel T.D. (1947). *The Rotunda Hospital 1745–1945*, Edinburgh: Livingstone.

Browne, Raymond, ed. (1997). *The Destitution Survey: Reflection on the Famine in Diocese of Elphin*. Boyle: Herald Printers.

Buchanan, R., R. Butlin, and D. McCourt, eds. (1976). *Fields, Farms, and Settlement in Europe*. Belfast: Institute of Irish Studies.

Burger, G.C.E., et al. (1948). *Malnutrition and Starvation in the Western Netherlands, September 1944–July 1945* (2 parts). The Hague: General State Printing Office.

Burke, Helen (1987). *The People and the Poor Law in Nineteenth-Century Ireland*. Littlehampton, Sussex: Women's Education Bureau.

Campbell Foster, Thomas (1846). *Letters on the Condition of the People of Ireland* (London, 1846).

Campbell, Stephen J. (1994). *The Great Irish Famine: Words and Images from the Famine Museum, Strokestown Park, County Roscommon*. Strokestown.

Carleton, William (1972). *The Black Prophet: A Tale of Irish Famine*. Shannon: IUP. (Originally published in 1847.)

Carmichael, Richard (1814). *An Essay on the Venereal Diseases Which Have Been Confounded with the Syphilis*. Dublin: Cumming.

Casey, Marion R. (1996) "Friends in need: Financing emigration from Ireland, the Irish Emigrant Society and the Emigrant Industrial Savings Bank." *Seaport Magazine*, May.

Central Relief Committee (1848). *Report of the Proceedings of the Central Relief Committee . . . to 31st December 1847*. Dublin: Duffy.

Central Relief Committee (1852 [1996]). *Transactions of the Central Relief Committee of the Society of Friends during the Famine in Ireland in 1846 and 1847*. Dublin: Hodges and Smith [Dublin: Edmund Burke].

Chevet, Jean-Michel, and Cormac Ó Gráda (in progress). "Potato and wheat markets in France in the 1840s."

CLASP (*Clare* Local Studies Project) (1996). *Poverty before the Famine: County Clare, 1835.*

Cobbett, William (1984). *Cobbett in Ireland*. London: Lawrence and Wishart. (Edited by D. Knight. Originally published in the *Political Register* in 1834.)

Cohn, Raymond L. (1984). "Mortality on immigrant voyages to New York, 1836–1853." *JEH*, 44, 289–300.

Cohn, Raymond L. (1987). "The determinants of individual mortality on sailing ships, 1836–1853." *EEH*, 24, 371–91.

Collard, A. (1989). "Investigating 'social memory.'" in E. Tonkin, M. McDonald, and M. Chapman (eds.), *History and Ethnicity*, 89–103. ASA Monograph 27. London: Routledge.

Collins, Robert (1835). *A Practical Treatise on Midwifery, Containing the Result of Sixteen Thousand Six Hundred & Fifty-four Births*. London: Longman.

Collins, R. (1848). *Observations on the Prevention of Contagious Diseases*. Dublin: Hodges and Smith.

Connell, K. H. (1950). *The Population of Ireland, 1750–1845*. Oxford: OUP.

Connell, K. H. (1951). "The History of the Potato," *EHR*, 3, 388–95.

Connell, K. H. (1957). "Peasant marriage in Ireland after the Great Famine," *Past and Present*, 12, 76–91.

Connell, K. H. (1962). "Peasant marriage in Ireland: Its structure and development since the famine." *EHR*, 14, 502–23.

Connell, K. H. (1968). *Irish Peasant Society*. Oxford: OUP.

Connolly, S. J., R. Houston, and R. J. Morris, eds. (1995). *Conflict, Identity, and Economic Development*. Carnegie Publishing.

Conway, Martin A. (1990). *Autobiographical Memory: An Introduction*. Milton Keynes: Open University.

Coombes, J. (1993). "The sea trade in potatoes in south west Cork, 1730–1850." *Seanchas Chairbre*, 3, 3–16.

Cosgrove, Marianne (1995). "Sources in the National Archives for researching the Great Famine: The Relief Commission papers." *Irish Archives Bulletin* (Autumn), 3–12.

Costello, Eibhlín (1923). *Amhráin Mhuighe Seóla: Traditional Folk-Songs from Galway and Mayo*. Dublin: Talbot Press.

Cousens, S. H. (1960). "Regional death rates in Ireland during the Great Famine from 1846 to 1851." *PS*, 14, 55–74.

Cousens, S. H. (1960). "The regional pattern of emigration during the Great

Irish Famine, 1846–51." *Institute of British Geographers, Transactions and Papers*, no. 28, 119–34.

Cousens, S. H. (1965). "The regional variation in emigration from Ireland between 1821 and 1841." *Institute of British Geographers Transactions and Papers*, no. 37, 15–30.

Cove, John J. (1978). "Survival or extinction: Reflections on the problem of famine in Tsimshian and Kaguru mythology." In Laughlin and Brady, *Extinction and Survival in Human Populations*, 232–44.

Cowman, D., and D. Brady, eds. (1995). *Teacht na bPrátaí Dubha: The Famine in Waterford 1845–1850*. Dublin: Geography Publications.

Craig, Maurice (1980). *Dublin, 1660–1860*. Dublin: Figgis. (Originally published in 1952.)

Crawford, E. Margaret, ed. (1989). *Famine: The Irish Experience, 900–1900*. Edinburgh: John Donald.

Crawford, E. M. (1993). "The Irish workhouse diet, 1840–90." In Catherine Geissler and D. J. Oddy (eds.), *Food, Diet and Economic Change, Past and Present*. Leicester: Leicester University Press, 83–100.

Crawford, E. M. (1994). "The Great Irish Famine: Image versus reality." In R. Gillespie and B. Kennedy (eds.), *Ireland: Art into History*, 75–88. Dublin: Townhouse Press.

Crawford, E. M., ed. (1997). *The Hungry Stream: Essays on Emigration and Famine*. Belfast: Institute for Irish Studies.

Crawford, E. M. (1997). "Migrant maladies: Unseen lethal baggage." In Crawford (ed.), *The Hungry Stream*, 137–50.

Crawford, E. M., and L. E. Clarkson (1988). "Dietary directions: A topographical survey of Irish diet, 1836." In Rosalind Mitchison and Peter Roebuck (eds.), *Economy and Society in Ireland and Scotland, 1500–1939*, 171–92. Edinburgh: John Donald.

Crotty, R. D. (1966). *Irish Agricultural Production*. Cork: Cork University Press.

Cullen, L. M. (1968). "Irish History without the Potato." *Past and Present*, no. 40, 70–83.

Cullen, L. M. (1981). *The Emergence of Modern Ireland, 1600–1900*. London: Batsford.

Curtis, L. P. (1980). "Incumbered wealth: Landed indebtedness in post-famine Ireland." *American Historical Review*, 85(2), 332–67.

Daly, Douglas C. (1996). "The leaf that launched a thousand ships." *Natural History* (January), 24–32.

Daly, Mary (1986). *The Great Famine in Ireland*. Dundalk: Dundalgan Press.

Daly, Mary E. (1995). "The operation of famine relief, 1845–47." In Póirtéir (ed.), *The Great Irish Famine*, 123–34.

Daly, M. E. (1995). "Local response to the Great Famine: A question of competence?" Paper presented to the NYU/Ireland House Conference on Famine and Hunger, May.

Daly, Mary E. (1996). "Farming and the Famine," In Ó Gráda, *Famine 150*.

Dando, W. A. (1980). *The Geography of Famine*. London: Edward Arnold.

Davidson, W. D. (1935). "History of potato varieties." *Journal of the Department of Agriculture*, 33, 57–81.

Davidson, W. D. (1937). "The history of the potato and its progress in Ireland." *Journal of the Department of Agriculture*, 34, 286–307.

Davies, John E. (1994). "Giffen goods, the survival imperative, and Irish potato culture." *JPE*, 102(3), 547–65.

Demonet, Michel (1990). *Tableau de l'agriculture française au milieu du 19e siècle: L'enquête de 1852*. Paris: Éditions de l'École des Hautes Études en Sciences Sociales.

Denecke, Dietrich (1976). "Innovation and diffusion of the potato in central Europe in the seventeenth and eighteenth centuries." In Buchanan et al. (eds.), *Fields, Farms, and Settlement in Europe*, 107–17.

Deng, Henry F., and Larry Minear (1992). *The Challenges of Famine Relief: Emergency Operations in the Sudan*. Washington, D.C.: Brookings.

Devereux, Stephen (1993). *Theories of Famine*. London: Harvester Wheatsheaf.

Devine, T. M. (1988). *The Highland Famine: Hunger, Emigration and the Scottish Highlands in the Nineteenth Century*. Edinburgh: John Donald.

Devine, T. A., and D. Dickson, eds. (1983). *Ireland and Scotland: Parallels and Contrasts in Economic and Social Development*. Edinburgh: John Donald.

de Waal, Alex (1989). "Famine mortality: A case study of Darfur, Sudan, in 1984–85." *PS*, 43, 5–24.

de Waal, Alex (1993). "War and famine in Africa." *IDS Bulletin*, 24(4), 33–40.

Dickson, David (1989). "The demographic implications of Dublin's growth, 1650–1850." In R. Lawton and R. Lee (eds.), *Urban Population Development in Western Europe*. Liverpool: Liverpool University Press.

Dickson, D. (1989). "The gap in famines: A useful myth?" In Crawford (ed.), *Famine*.

Dickson, D. (1995). "The other great Irish famine." In Póirtéir (ed.), *The Great Irish Famine*.

Dickson, D. (1996). "The potato and Irish diet before the famine." In Ó Gráda, *Famine 150*.

Dickson, David, C. Ó Gráda, and S. Daultrey (1982). "Hearth tax, household size and Irish population change, 1672–1821." *PRIA*, 82C, no. 6: 125–81.

Dirks, R. (1978). "Resource fluctuations and competitive transformations in West Indian slave societies." In Laughlin and Brady (eds.), *Extinction and Survival in Human Populations*, 161–77.

Dirks, R. (1980). "Social responses during severe food shortages and famine." *Current Anthropology*, 21 (1), 21–44.

Donnelly, J. S. (1974). "The journals of Sir John Benn-Walsh relating to the management of his Irish estates, 1823–64." *JCHAS*, 79, 86–123.

Donnelly, J. S. (1975). *The Land and the People of Nineteenth-Century Cork*. London: Routledge and Kegan Paul.

Donnelly, J. S. (1988). "The Kenmare estates during the nineteenth century." *JKAHS*, 21: 5–41.

Donnelly, J. S. (1989). "Landlords and tenants." In Vaughan (ed.), *A New History of Ireland*, vol. 5, 334–49.

Donnelly, J. S. (1993). "The Famine: Its interpreters, old and new." *History Ireland*, 1(3).

Donnelly, J. S. (1995). "Mass eviction and the Great Famine." In Póirtéir (ed.), *The Great Irish Famine*, 155–73.

Donnelly, J. S. (1996). "'Irish property must pay for Irish poverty': British public opinion and the Great Irish Famine." In Morash and Hayes (eds.), *"Fearful Realities,"* 60–76.

Donnelly, J. S. (1996). "The construction of the memory of the famine in Ireland and the Irish diaspora, 1850–1900." Typescript, March.

Dornbusch, Rudiger, and Jacob Frenkel (1984). "The gold standard crisis of 1847." *Journal of International Economics*, 16, 1–27.

Drake, Michael (1969). *Population and Society in Norway, 1735–1865*. Cambridge, U.K.: CUP.

Drèze, Jean (1991). "Famine prevention in Africa." In Drèze and Sen, *The Political Economy of Hunger*.

Drèze, Jean, and Amartya Sen (1989). *Hunger and Public Action.*, Oxford: OUP.

Drèze, Jean, and Amartya Sen (1991). *The Political Economy of Hunger*. 3 vols. Oxford: OUP.

Dwyer, G. P. and Cotton Lindsay (1984). "Robert Giffen and the Irish potato." *American Economic Review*, 74, 188–92.

Dyson, Tim (1991). "On the demography of South Asian famines," parts 1 and 2, *PS*, 45, 5–25 and 279–97.

Dyson, Tim (1993). "Demographic responses to famines in South Asia." *IDS Bulletin*, 24(4), 17–26.

East, John (1847). *Glimpses of Ireland in 1847*. London: Hamilton Adams.

The Economist. "Famine? What famine?" [Revising the history of the Irish famine], 335 (24 June 1995), 30.

Edwards, Ruth Dudley (1994). *The Age of Reason: A History of the Economist*. London: Hamish Hamilton.

Edwards, R. D., and T. D. Williams, eds. (1956 [1995]). *The Great Famine: Studies in Irish History, 1845–52*. Dublin: Lilliput Press.

Eiríksson, Andrés (1996). "Food supply & food riots." In Ó Gráda, Famine 150 67–93.

Eiríksson, Andrés, and C. Ó Gráda (1995). *Estate Records of the Irish Famine: A Second Guide to Famine Archives*. Dublin: Irish Famine Network.

Eiríksson, Andrés, and C. Ó Gráda (1996). "Bankrupt Landlords and the Irish Famine." University College Dublin Centre for Economic Research Working Paper 96/10.

Eltis, D. (1984). "Mortality and voyage length in the middle passage: New evidence for the nineteenth century." *JEH*, 44, 301–19.

Ernst, Robert (1949). *Immigrant Life in New York City, 1825–1863*. New York: King's Crown Press.

Evans, E. (1897). "History of Dublin hospitals and infirmaries from 1188 till the present time, No. XXV. Fever Hospital and House of Recovery, Cork Street." *Irish Builder*, 39, 181–83.

Fagan, Patrick (1991). "The population of Dublin in the eighteenth century with particular reference to the proportions of Catholics." *Eighteenth Century Ireland*, 6, 121–56.

Farrington, A. E. (1893). *Rev. Dr. Spratt O.C.C.: His Life and Times*. Dublin: James Duffy.

Ferrie, Joseph (1994). "The wealth accumulation of antebellum immigrants to the U.S. 1840–1860." *JEH*, 54, 1–33.

Ferrie, Joseph P. (1997) *"Yankeys Now": Immigrants in the Antebellum U.S., 1840–60*. New York: OUP.

Fewer, Thomas Gregory (1995). "Poverty and patronage: Responses to the Famine of the Duke of Devonshire's Lismore Estate." In Cowman and (eds.), *Teacht na bPrátaí Dubha*, 69–100.

Fitzpatrick, David (1989). "Emigration, 1801–70." In Vaughan (ed.), *A New History of Ireland*, vol. 5.

Fitzpatrick, D. (1995). "Flight from famine." In Póirtéir (ed.), *The Great Irish Famine*, 174–84.

Fitzpatrick, D. (1995). "Famine, entitlements, and seduction: Captain Edmond Wynne in Ireland, 1846–51." *English Historical Review*, 110, 596–619.

Fitzpatrick, D. (1997). "Gender and the famine." In Margaret Kelleher and James H. Murphy (eds.), *Gender Perspectives on Nineteenth-Century Ireland: Public and Private Spheres*. Dublin: IAP.

Fitzpatrick, Sheila (1994). *Stalin's Peasants: Resistance and Survival in the Russian Village after Collectivization*. Oxford: OUP.

Flinn, Michael, et al. (1977). *Scottish Population History since the 1730s*. Cambridge: CUP.

Foley, Mark C., and Guinnane, Timothy (1997). "Did Irish marriage patterns survive the emigrant voyage? Irish-American nuptiality, 1880–1910." Typescript, Yale University, August.

Forster, Sir John (1664). *England's Happiness Increased . . . by a Plantation of the Roots Called Potatoes*.

Foster, Roy (1988). *Modern Ireland, 1600–1972*. London: Allen Lane.

Foster, Thomas Campbell (1846). *Letters on the Condition of the People of Ireland*. London: Chapman & Hall.

Freeman, T. W. (1969). *Ireland: A General and Regional Geography*. 4th ed. London: Methuen.

Geary, Laurence M. (1995). "Famine, fever, and the bloody flux." In Póirtéir, *The Great Irish Famine*, 74–85.

Geary, L. M. (1996). "What people died of during the famine." In Ó Gráda, *Famine 150*.

Geary, L. M. (1998). "The living were out of their feeling: A socio-cultural analysis of the Great Famine in Ireland." *Comhdháil an Chraoibhín 1997*.

Glazier, Ira, Deirdre Mageean, and Barnabus Okeke (1989). "Socio-economic characteristics of Irish emigrants, 1846–1851." In Klaus Friedland (ed.), *Maritime Aspects of Migration*, 243–78. Cologne: Böhlau Verlag.

Goossens, Martine (1992). *The Economic Development of Belgian Agriculture: A Regional Perspective, 1812–1846*. Brussels: Koninglijke Akademie voor Wetenschappen, Lettern en Schone Kunsten van Belgie.

Grace, Daniel (1997). "Priests who died in the Great Famine." *Tipperary Historical Journal*, 10, 78–79.

Grant, James (1990). "The Great Famine and the Poor Law in the province of Ulster: The rate-in-aid issue of 1849." *IHS*, 27, no. 105, 30–47.

Grant, James (1997). "The Great Famine in county Down." In Lindsay Proudfoot (ed.), *Down: History and Society*, 353–82. Dublin: Geography Publications.

Grant, James (1997). "Local relief committees in Ulster, 1845–47." In Crawford (ed.), *The Hungry Stream*, 185–98.

Gray, Peter (1992). "British politics and the Irish land question, 1843–50." Ph.D. diss., University of Cambridge, 209–14.

Gray, Peter (1993). "Punch and the Great Famine." *History Ireland*, 1(2).

Gray, Peter (1994). "Potatoes and providence: British government's responses to the Great Famine." *Bullán: An Irish Studies Journal*, no. 1, 75–90.

Gray, Peter (1995). "Ideology and the famine." In Póirtéir, *The Great Irish Famine*, 86–103.

Gray, P. (1995). *Ireland's Famine*. London and New York: Abrams.

Gray, P. (1996). "British public opinion and the great Irish famine, 1845–49." *Comhdháil an Chraoibhín 1995*, 56–74.

Gray, P. (1997). "Famine relief in comparative perspective: Ireland, Scotland, and North-western Europe, 1845–50." *Éire-Ireland*, forthcoming.

Greenhough, Paul R. (1982). *Prosperity and Misery in Modern Bengal: The Famine of 1943–1944*. Oxford: OUP.

Groneman Pernicone, Carol (1973). " 'The 'Bloody Ould Sixth': A social analysis of a New York City working-class community in the mid-nineteenth century." Ph.D. diss., University of Rochester, Rochester, N.Y.

Guha, Sumit (1993). "Nutrition, sanitation, hygiene, and the likelihood of death: The British army in India, c. 1870–1920." *PS*, 47, 385–401.

Guinnane, Timothy (1997). *The Vanishing Irish: Households, Migration, and the Rural Economy in Ireland, 1850–1914*. Princeton: PUP.

Gwynn, Dennis (1951). *Fr. Luigi Gentili and His Mission (1801–1848)*. Dublin: Clonmore and Reynolds.

Häkkinen, Antti, Vappu Ikonen, Kari Pitkänen, and Hannu Soikkanen (1991). *Kun Hallen nälän tuskan toi. Miten Suomalaiset kokivat 1860-luvun nälkävuodet.* [When the Frost Brought the Agony of Hunger: Finland and the Famine of the 1860s.] Helsinki: Werner Söderström Osakeyhtiö.

Hanse, Hans-Oluf (1979). "Some age structural consequences of mortality variations in pre-transitional Iceland and Sweden." In Charbonneau and Larose (eds.), *Les Grandes Mortalités*, 113–32. Liège: Ordina.

Hardiman, David (1996). "Usury, dearth and famine in western India." *Past and Present*, no. 152, 113–56.

Harkan, P. (1843). *Medical Report of the House of Recovery and Fever Hospital Cork Street Dublin for . . . 1842*. Dublin.

Harris, Ruth-Ann (1996). "Ballykilcline and beyond." *Irish Studies Review*, no. 15, 39–42.

Harrison, Mark (1994). *Public Health in British India, 1859–1914*. Cambridge, U.K.: CUP.

Hatton, T. J., and J. G. Williamson (1993). "After the famine: Emigration from Ireland, 1850–1913." *JEH*, 53(3), 582–85.

Hickey, Patrick (1993). "Famine, mortality, and emigration: A profile of six parishes in the poor law union of Skibbereen, 1846–7." In Patrick O'Flanagan and Cornelius Buttimer (eds.), *Cork: History and Society*, 873–917. Dublin: Geography Pubications.

Hickey, Patrick (1995). "The famine in Skibbereen union (1845–51)." In Póirtéir (ed.), *The Great Irish Famine*, 185–203.

Hill, C. V. (1991). "Philosophy and reality in riparian south Asia: British famine policy and migration in colonial north India." *Modern Asian Studies*, 25, 263–79.

Hionidou, Violetta (1995). "The demography of a Greek famine." *Continuity and Change*, 10(2) (August), 279–99.

Hoffman, Elizabeth, and J. Mokyr (1984). "Peasants, potatoes and poverty: Transactions costs in prefamine Ireland." In Gary Saxonhouse and Gavin Wright (eds.), *Technique, Spirit and Form in the Making of the Modern Economy: Essays in Honor of William N. Parker*, 115–45. Greenwich, Conn.: JAI Press.

Hollis, Aidan, and Arthur Sweetman (1995). "Swift's other modest proposal." Typescript, Institute of Policy Analysis, University of Toronto.

Hurd, John II (1975). "Railways and the expansion of markets in India, 1861–1921." *EEH*, 12, 263–88.

Iliffe, John (1987). *The African Poor: A History*. Cambridge, U.K.: CUP.

Iliffe, John (1990). *Famine in Zimbabwe*. Gweru.

Iliffe, John (1995). *Africa: The History of a Continent*. Cambridge, U.K.: CUP.

Jacquemyns, Alexis (1929). "Histoire de la crise économique des Flandres." *Académie Royale de Belgique, Mémoires*, 26, 11–472.

Johnson, David, and Liam Kennedy (1995). "Irish national income on the eve of the Famine." Typescript, Queen's University, Belfast.

Joigneaux, P. (1860–65). *Le livre de la terre*. 3d ed. Paris.

Jordan, William Chester (1996). *The Great Famine: Northern Europe in the Early Fourteenth Century*. Princeton, N.J.: PUP.

Juillard, Étienne (1953 [1992]). *La vie rurale en Basse-Alsace*. Strasbourg: Presses Universitaires de Strasbourg.

Jutikkala, Eino, and M. Kauppinen (1971). "The structure of mortality during catastrophe years in a pre-industrial society." *PS*, 25, 283–85.

Jutikkala, Eino, and Kauko Pirinen (1974). *A History of Finland*. New York: Praeger.

Kaukiainen, Yrjö (1984). "Harvest fluctuations and mortality in agrarian Finland (1810–1870)." In Tommy Bengtsson, Gunnar Fridlizius, and Rolf Ohlsson (eds.), *Pre-industrial Population Change: The Mortality Decline and Short-Term Population Movements*, 235–54. Stockholm: Amlqvist and Wiksell.

Keen, Peter (1994). *The Benefits of Famine: A Political Economy of Famine and Relief in Southwestern Sudan, 1983–1989*, Princeton, NJ: Princeton University Press.

Kelleher, Margaret (1995). "Irish Famine in literature." In Póirtéir (ed.), *The Great Irish Famine*, 232–47.

Kennedy, Patrick (1875). *By the Banks of the Boro: A Chronicle of the Country of Wexford*. Dublin: McGlashan and Gill.

Kerr, Donal (1994). *"A Nation of Beggars?" Priests, People and Politics in Ireland, 1846–1852*. Oxford: OUP.

Kerr, Donal (1996). *The Catholic Church and the Famine*. Dublin: Columbia Press.

Kidame, Asmerom (1989). "Demographic consequences of the 1984–85 Ethiopian famine." *Demography*, 26, 515–22.

Kierse, Seán (1984). *The Famine Years in the Parish of Killaloe, 1845–1851*. Killaloe: Boru Books.

Killen, John (1995). *The Famine Decade: Contemporary Accounts 1841–1851*. Belfast: Blackstaff Press.

Kinealy, Christine (1994). *This Great Calamity: The Irish Famine, 1845–52*. Dublin.

Kinealy, Christine, and Trevor Parkhill, eds. (1997). *The Famine in Ulster*. Belfast: Ulster Historical Foundation.

Kinsella, Anna (1995). *County Wexford in the Famine Years, 1845–1849*. Enniscorthy: Duffry Press.

Kipple, Kenneth F., ed. (1993). *The Cambridge World History of Human Disease*. Cambridge, U.K.: CUP.

Kirkpatrick, T. Percy (1913). *The Book of the Rotunda Hospital: An Illustrated History of the Dublin Lying-in Hospital*. London: Adlard and Son.

Kissane, Noel (1995). *The Irish Famine: A Documentary History*. Dublin: National Library of Ireland.

Klein, Ira (1984). "When the rains failed: Famine relief and mortality in British India." *Indian Economic and Social History Review*, 21, 185–214.

Knight, Dennis (1984). *Cobbett in Ireland: A Warning to England*. London: Lawrence and Wishart.

Kohl, J. G. (1844). *Travels in Ireland*. London: Bruce and Wyld.

Kotre, John (1995). *White Gloves: How We Create Ourselves through Memory*. New York: Norton.

Kvideland, Reimund, and Henning K. Sehmsdorf, eds. (1989). *Nordic Folklore: Recent Studies*. Bloomington: Indiana University Press.

Labbé, Max (1988). *Cette étonnante pomme de terre: Receuil de connaissances et d'expériences*. Paris: Max Labbé.

Lachiver, Marcel (1991). *Les années de misère: La famine au temps du Grand Roi*. Paris.

Ladies of the Mission (1854). *The Old Brewery, and the New Mission House at the Five Points*. New York: Stringer and Townsend.

Lane, P. G. (1972). "The Encumbered Estates Court, Ireland, 1848–49." *ESR*, 3, 413–53.

Laughlin, Charles D., and Ivan A. Brady, eds. (1978). *Extinction and Survival in Human Populations*. New York: Columbia University Press.

Lee, J. J. (1971). "The Dual Economy in Ireland, 1800–1850." In T. D. Williams (ed.), *Historical Studies VIII*, 191–202. Dublin: G&M.

Lee, J. J. (1973). *The Modernisation of Irish Society, 1848–1918*. Dublin: G&M.

Leuillot, Paul (1959). *L'alsace au début du XIXe siècle: Les transformations économiques*. Paris: SEVPEN.

Lindsay, Deirdre (1990). *Dublin's Oldest Charity: The Sick and Indigent Room-keepers' Society, 1790–1990*. Dublin: Anniversary Press.

Lindsay, Deirdre, and David Fitzpatrick (1993). *Records of the Irish Famine: A Guide to Local Archives, 1840–1855*. Dublin: Irish Famine Network.

Locke, C. G., and F.Z. Ahmadi-Esfahani (1993). "Famine analysis: A study of entitlements in Sudan, 1984–1985." *Economic Development and Cultural Change*, 41, 363–76.

López Linage, Javier (c.1991). *De papa a patata: La diffusion española del tubérculo andino*. Madrid: Ministerio de Agricultura, Pesca y Alimentacion.

Lynch, Patrick, and John Vaizey (1960). *Guinness's Brewery in the Irish Economy, 1759–1876*. Cambridge, U.K.: CUP.

Lyne, Gerard J. (1992). "William Steuart Trench and post-famine emigration from Kenmare to America, 1850–55." *JKAHS*, no. 25.

Lyons, Mary C. (1993). *Illustrated Encumbered Estates, Ireland, 1850–1905: Lithographic and Other Illustrative Material in the Incumbered Estates Rentals*. Whitegate, Co. Clare: Ballinakella Press.

Lysaght, Patricia (1996–97). "Perspectives on women during the Great Irish Famine from oral tradition." *Béaloideas*, 64/65, 63–131.

McAlpin, Michelle Burg (1983). *Subject to Famine: Food Crises and Economic Change in Western India, 1860–1920*. Princeton, N.J.: PUP.

MacArthur, W. A. (1956). "Medical history of the Famine." In Edwards and Williams (eds.), *The Great Famine*, 263–315.

McAtasney, Gerard (1997). *"This Dreadful Visitation": The Famine in Lurgan/Portadown*. Belfast: Beyond the Pale.

McBane, Michael (1996–97). "Irish famine stories in the Ottawa valley." *Oral History Forum*, 16–17, 7–25.

McCavery, Trevor (1995). "The wealthy found wanting: Controversies over famine relief in Newtownards Poor Law Union." *Ulster Local Studies*, 17(2), 50–74.

McClean, Raymond (1988). *A Cross Shared, Ethiopia-Derry: Famine in Ethiopia, a Personal Experience*. Ballyshannon: Donegal Democrat.

McCorry, F. X. (1998). "The famine in the Montiaghs." In F. X. McCorry, Art Hughes, and Roger Weatherup (eds.), *Armagh: History and Society*. Dublin: Geography Publications.

MacDonagh, Oliver (1956 [1995]). "Irish emigration to the United States of America and the British colonies during the famine." In Edwards and Williams (eds.), *The Great Famine*, 319–90.

McGregor, Pat (1989). "Demographic pressure and the Irish famine: Malthus after Mokyr." *Land Economics*, 65, 228–38.

McGregor, Pat (1997). "The Great Irish Famine: A failure of development or policy?" Typescript, University of Ulster.

McHugh, Roger (1956). "The Famine in Folklore." In Edwards and Williams (eds.), *The Great Famine*, 391–406.

McIntosh, Thomas P. (1927). *The Potato: Its History, Varieties, Culture and Diseases*. Edinburgh: Oliver and Boyd.

McKay, Robert (1955). *Potato Diseases*. Dublin: Irish Potato Marketing Co.

McKay, Robert (1961). *An Anthology of the Potato*. Dublin: Figgis.

McKeown, Thomas (1979). *The Role of Medicine: Dream, Mirage, or Nemesis?* Princeton, N.J.: PUP.

McKeown, T. (1987). "Food, infection, and population." In Robert I. Rothberg and Theodore K. Rabb (eds.), *Hunger and History: The Impact of Changing Food Production and Consumption Patterns on Society*, 29–50. Cambridge, U.K.: CUP.

Mac Lochlainn, Antain (1995). "The famine in Gaelic tradition." *Irish Review*, no. 17/8, 90–108.

Mac Síthigh, Tomás (1984). *Paróiste an Fheirtéaraigh: Stairsheanchas an cheantair i dtréimhse an Ghorta Mhóir*. Dublin: Coiscéim.

McSweeney, C. J. (1945). "Short History of the House of Recovery and Fever Hospital, Cork Street, Dublin." *Medical Press and Circular*, 213, no. 5533 (May 23).

Maharatna, Arup (1996). *The Demography of Famines*. Delhi: OUP.

Mann, Horace (1848). "Statement of the mortality prevailing in Church Lane." *Journal of the Statistical Society of London*, 11, 19–24.

Manners, Lord John (1849). *Notes of an Irish Tour*. London: Ollivier.

Marnane, Denis G. (1996–97). "The famine in south Tipperary." *Tipperary Historical Journal*, 9 (1996), 1–42, and 10 (1997), 131–50.

Maxwell, R. (1757). *The Practical Husbandman, Being a Collection of Miscellaneous Papers on Husbandry, etc.* Edinburgh.

Meldon, G.E.P. (1914). "Some notes on the admissions to the Westmoreland Lock Hospital since 1860." *Dublin Journal of Medical Science*, 37, 109–18.

Melville, C. P. (1988). "The Persian famine of 1870–72: Prices and politics." *Disasters*, 12(4), 309–25.

Mercer, Alex (1992). "Mortality and morbidity in refugee camps in El Fasher, Sudan 1982–89." *Disasters*, 16(1) (March), 28–42.

Merriman, Brian (1982). *Cúirt an Mheon-Oíche*, ed. Liam P. Ó Murchú. Dublin: An Clóchomhar.

Miller, Kerby A. (1985). *Emigrants and Exiles: Ireland and the Irish Exodus to North America*. Oxford: OUP.

Minc, Leah (1986). "Scarcity and survival: The role of oral tradition in mediating subsistence crises." *Journal of Anthropological Archaeology*, 5, 39–113.

Mitchell, B. R. (1975). *European Historical Statistics*. London: Macmillan.

Mokyr, Joel (1981). "Industrialization and poverty in Ireland and the Netherlands: Some notes towards a comparative case study." *Journal of Interdisciplinary History*, 10(3), 429–59.

Mokyr, Joel (1981). "Irish history with the potato." *IESH*, 8, 3–29.

Mokyr, J. (1981). "The deadly fungus: An econometric investigation into the short-term demographic consequences of the Irish famine, 1846–1851." *RPE*, 2, 429–59.

Mokyr, J. (1982). "Uncertainty in prefamine Irish agriculture." In Devine and Dickson, *Ireland and Scotland*.

Mokyr, J. (1985). *Why Ireland Starved: An Analytical and Quantitative History of the Irish Economy, 1800–1850.* 2d ed. London: Allen and Unwin.

Mokyr, J. (1995). "Famine disease and famine mortality: Lessons from the Irish experience, 1845–1850." Address to NYU/Ireland House Conference.

Mokyr, J., and C. Ó Gráda (1994). "The heights of the British and the Irish c. 1800–1815: Evidence from recruits to the East India Company's army." In John Komlos (ed.), *Stature, Living Standards, and Economic Development: Essays in Anthropometric History*, 39–59. Chicago: University of Chicago Press.

Mokyr, J., and C. Ó Gráda (1996). "Heights and living standards in the United Kingdom, 1815–1860." *EEH*, April.

Mokyr, J., and C. Ó Gráda (1996). "Disease, mortality, and the Great Irish Famine." Typescript.

Mooney, Thomas (1851). *Letters on Emigration.* Dublin: Pattison Jolly.

Morash, Chris (1989). *The Hungry Voice: The Poetry of the Irish Famine.* Dublin: IAP.

Morash, C. (1995). *Writing the Irish Famine.* Oxford: OUP.

Morash, C., and R. Hayes, eds. (1996). *Fearful Realities: New Perspectives on the Famine.* Dublin: IAP.

Morgan, John (1869). "Clinical review of cases at the Westmoreland Lock Hospital during the past six months." *DQJMS*, 506–28.

Morineau, Michel (1970). "La pomme de terre au 18e siècle." *Annales ESC*, 25: 167–84.

Moulden, John (1994). *Thousands Are Sailing: A Brief Song History of Irish Emigration* (provisional version). Ulstersongs: Portrush.

Murphy, Ignatius (1992). *The Diocese of Killaloe, 1800–1850.* Dublin: IAP.

Murphy, Ignatius (1996). *A People Starved: Life and Death in West Clare, 1845–1851.* Dublin: IAP.

Neal, Frank (1995). "Lancashire, the famine Irish and the poor laws: A study in crisis management." *IESH*, 22, 26–48.

Neal, Frank (1996). "The famine Irish in England and Wales." In O'Sullivan (ed.), *The Irish Worldwide*, vol. 6, 56–80.

Neal, Frank (1997). "Black '47: Liverpool and the Irish famine." In Crawford (ed.), *The Hungry Stream*, 123–36.

Nelson, Marie C. (1988). *Bitter Bread: The Famine in Norrbotten, 1867–1868.* Uppsala: Acta Universitatis Upsaliensis.

Nicholls, George (1856). *A History of the Irish Poor Law.* London: John Murray.

Nicholson, Asenath (1850). *Lights and Shades of Ireland in Three Parts.* London: Gilpin.

O'Brien, Gerard (1985). "Workhouse management in pre-famine Ireland." *PRIA*, 86C: 113–34.

O'Brien, John B. (1979). *The Catholic Middle Classes of Pre-famine Cork.* Dublin: National University of Ireland.

O'Brien, Joseph V. (1982). *Dear, Dirty Dublin: A City in Distress, 1899–1916.* Berkeley: University of California Press.

O'Brien, William (1852). *Dingle: Its Pauperism and Proselytism.* Dublin: O'Toole.

Ó Caoimh, Tomás (1997). "Tigh na mBocht, an Daingean." In P. Ó Fiannachta (ed.), *An Gorta Mór*, 77–102. Dingle: An Sagart.

Ó Cathaoir, Eva. (1994). "The poor law in county Wicklow." In Ken Hannigan and William Nolan, eds., *Wicklow: History and Society*, 503–80. Dublin: Geography Publications.

Ó Ciosáin, Niall (1995–96). "Was there a 'silence' about the famine?" *Irish Studies Review*, no. 13, 7–10.

O'Donnell, Edward T. (1997). "The scattered debris of the Irish nation: The famine Irish and New York City, 1845–1855." In Crawford (ed.), *The Hungry Stream*, 49–60.

O'Dwyer, Peter (1968). "John Francis Spratt O. Carm, 1796–1871." Ph.D. diss., Pontifical University, Rome.

O'Flaherty, Liam (1929). *The House of Gold*. London: Jonathan Cape.

O'Flanagan, Patrick, and Cornelius Buttimer, eds. (1993). *Cork: History and Society*. Dublin: Geography Publications.

Ó Gráda, Cormac (1974). "Soláthar creidmheasa don ísealaicme sa naoú chéad déag." *Central Bank Quarterly Bulletin*, 120–35.

Ó Gráda, C. (1982). "Across the briny ocean: some thoughts on Irish emigration to America, 1800–1850," in Devine and Dickson, *Ireland and Scotland*, 118–30.

Ó Gráda, Cormac (1983). "Malthus and the pre-famine economy." In A. E. Murphy (ed.), *Economists and the Irish Economy*, 75–95. Dublin: IAP.

Ó Gráda, C. (1989). *The Great Irish Famine*. London: Macmillan.

Ó Gráda, C. (1991). "Dublin's demography in the early nineteenth century." *PS*, 45, 43–54.

Ó Gráda, C. (1992). "Making history in Ireland in the 1940s and 1950s: The Saga of *The Great Famine*." *Irish Review*, no. 12 (1992). 87–107; reprinted in Ciarán Brady (ed.), *Interpreting Irish History: The Debate on Historical Revisionism*. Dublin: IAP.

Ó Gráda, C. (1993). *Ireland before and after the Famine: Explorations in Economic History, 1800–1925*. Rev. ed., Manchester: MUP.

Ó Gráda, C. (1994). *An Drochshaol: Béaloideas agus Amhráin*. Dublin: Coiscéim.

Ó Gráda, C. (1994). "The height of Clonmel prisoners, 1840–49: Some dietary implications." *IESH*, 21.

Ó Gráda, C. (1994). *Ireland: A New Economic History, 1780–1939*. Oxford: OUP.

Ó Gráda, C. (1995). "An Gorta san ardchathair (The famine in the capital)." In Póirtéir (ed.), *Gnéithe den nGorta*, 164–75.

Ó Gráda, C. (1995). "The great famine and other famines." In Póirtéir (ed.), *The Great Irish Famine*, 248–58.

Ó Gráda, C. (1996). "Making famine history in Ireland in 1995." *History Workshop Journal*, no. 42, Autumn.

Ó Gráda, C. (1997). *Famine 150: The Teagasc/UCD Lectures*. Dublin: Teagasc.

Ó Gráda, C. (1997). "Markets and famines: A simple test with Indian data." *Economic Letters*, 57, 241–44.

Ó Gráda, C. (1997). *A Rocky Road: The Irish Economy since the 1920s*. Manchester, U.K.: MUP.

Ó Gráda, C., and K. O'Rourke (1997). "Mass migration as disaster relief: Lessons from the Great Irish Famine." *European Review of Economic History*, 1, 3–27.

Okazaki, Shoko (1986). "The great Persian famine of 1870–71." *Bulletin of the School of Oriental and African Studies*, 49(1), 183–92.

O'Mahony, Colman (1997). *In the Shadows: Life in Cork 1750–1930*. Cork: Tower Books.

Ó Mainín, Micheál (1971). "Amhrán an Ghorta." In Micheál Ó Ciosáin (ed.), *Céad Bliain*, 190–93. Baile an Fhirtéaraigh: Muintir Phiarais.

Ó Murchadha, Ciarán (1995). "The onset of famine: County Clare, 1845–1846: *The Other Clare*, 19 (April 1995), 46–53.

Ó Murchadha, Ciarán (1997). "One vast abbatoir: County Clare, 1848–1849." *The Other Clare*, 21, 58–67.

O'Neill, Thomas P. (1956). "The Catholic clergy and the Great Famine." *Reportorium Novum*, 1, 461–69.

O'Neill, Thomas P. (1956). "The organisation and adminstration of relief." In Edwards and Williams (eds.), *The Great Famine*.

O'Neill, Timothy P. (1995). "The persistence of famine in Ireland." In Póirtéir, *The Great Irish Famine*, 204–18.

O'Neill, Timothy P. (1996). "Minor famines and relief in Galway, 1815–1925." In G. Moran and R. Gillespie (eds.), *Galway: History and Society*, 445–87. Dublin: Geography Publications.

O'Neill, Timothy P. (1997). "The famine in Offaly." In id. (ed.), *Offaly: History and Society*. Dublin: Geography Publications.

O'Rourke, John (1902). *History of the Great Irish Famine of 1847*. Dublin: Duffy. (First published 1875.)

O'Rourke, Kevin (1991). "Did the Great Irish Famine matter?" *JEH*, 51, 1–22.

O'Rourke, Kevin (1992). "The causes of depopulation in a small open economy: Ireland, 1856–1876." *EEH*, 28, 409–32.

Osborne, S. Godolphin (1850). *Gleanings from the West of Ireland*. London: Boone.

Ó Súilleabháin, S. (1942). *A Handbook of Irish Folklore*. Dublin: Educational Company.

O'Sullivan, Patrick, ed. (1996). *The Irish Worldwide: Heritage, History and Identity*, vol. 6, *The Meaning of the Famine*. London: Leicester University Press.

Ó Tuathaigh, Gearóid (1995). "An Gorta Mór agus an pholaitíocht" (The Great Famine and politics). In Póirtéir (ed.), *Gnéithe den nGorta*, 26–40.

Passerini, Louisa (1979). "Work ideology and consensus under Italian fascism." *History Workshop*, 8, Autumn.

Patel, Mahesh (1994). "An examination of the 1990–91 famine in Sudan." *Disasters*, 18(4) (December), 313–31.

Pirotte, Fernand (1976). *La pomme de terre en Wallonie au XVIIIème siècle*. Liège.

Pitkänen, Kari (1992). "The patterns of mortality during the Great Finnish Famine in the 1860s." In *Acta Demographica 1992*, 81–102. Physica-Verlag, Heidelberg.

Pitkänen, Kari (1992). "The road to survival or death? Temporary migration during the Great Finnish Famine in the 1860s." In Antti Häkkinen (ed.), *Just a Sack of Potatoes? Crisis Experiences in European Societies, Past and Present*, 87–118. Helsinki: Societas Historica Finlandiae.

Pitkänen, Kari J. (1993). *Deprivation and Disease: Mortality during the Great Finnish Famine of the 1860s*. Helsinki: Finnish Demographic Society.

Pitkänen, Kari, and James Mielke (1993). "Age and sex differentials in mortality during the two nineteenth-century population crises." *European Journal of Population*, 9.

Póirtéir, C. (1995). *Famine Echoes*. Dublin: G&M.

Póirtéir, C. (1995). *Glórtha ón nGorta*. Dublin: Coiscéim.

Póirtéir, C., ed. (1995). *Gnéithe den nGorta*, Dublin: Coiscéim.

Póirtéir, Cathal, ed. (1995). *The Great Irish Famine*. Cork: Mercier.

Post, J. D. (1985). *Food Shortage, Climatic Variability and Epidemic Disease in Preindustrial Europe: The Mortality Peak in the Early 1740s*. Ithaca, N.Y.: Cornell University Press.

Proudfoot, Lindsay (1995). *Urban Patronage and Social Authority: The Management of the Duke of Devonshire's Towns in Ireland*. Washington, D.C.: Catholic University of America Press.

Prunty, Jacinta (1997). *Dublin Slums, 1800–1925: A Study in Urban Geography*. Dublin: IAP.

Quinlan, Carmel (1996). "A punishment from God: The famine in the centenary folklore questionnaire." *Irish Review*, no. 19, 68–86.

Rashid, Salim (1980). "The policy of laissez-faire during scarcities." *Economic Journal*, 90, 493–503.

Ravallion, Martin (1987). "Famines and economics." *JEL*, 35(3), 1205–42.

Ravallion, Martin (1987). *Markets and Famines*. Oxford: OUP.

Ravallion, Martin (1987). "Trade and specialization: Another look at India's controversial foodgrain exports." *EEH*, 24, 354–70.

Razzaque, Abdur, Nurul Alam, Lokky Wai, and Andrew Foster (1990). "Sustained effects of the 1974–75 famine on infant and child mortality in a rural area of Bangladesh." *PS*, 44 (1990), 145–54.

Robbins, Richard D. (1975). *Famine in Russia, 1891–1892: The Imperial Government's Response*. New York: Columbia University Press.

Robins, J. (1995). *The Miasma: Epidemic and Panic in Nineteenth Century Ireland*. Dublin: IAP.

Robinson, Mary (1994). *A Voice for Somalia*. Dublin: O'Brien Press.

Robinson, Mary (1995). "Address at Grosse Isle." In Don Mullan (ed.), *A Glimmer of Light*, 9-13. Dublin: Concern.

Robinson, Nugent (1862). "The condition of the dwellings of the poor in Dublin, with a glance at the model lodging houses." In *Transactions of the National Association for the Promotion of Social Science, 1861*, 517–24. London: Parker, Son and Bourne.

Robinson, T., ed. (1995). *Connemara after the Famine: Journal of a Survey of the Martin Estate, 1853*. Dublin: Lilliput Press.

Roche, Richard (1994–95). "The famine years in Forth and Bargy." *Journal of the Wexford Historical Society*, no. 15, 1–14.

Rodriguez Galdo, Maria Xosé (1991). "Introducción y diffusión de la patata en España," in López Linage, *De papa a patala*, 81–103.

Rosen, Sherwin (1995). "Potato paradoxes." Typescript, University of Chicago.

Royle, Stephen A. (1984). "Irish famine relief in the early nineteenth century: The 1822 famine on the Aran Islands." *IESH*, 11, 44–59.

Roze, E. (1898). *Histoire de la pomme de terre*. Paris: J. Rothschild.

Salaman, R. N. (1943). *The Influence of the Potato on the Course of Irish History*. Dublin: Finlay Lecture.

Salaman, R. N. (1949). *The History and Social Influence of the Potato*. Cambridge, U.K.: CUP.

Scally, R. J. (1995). *The End of Hidden Ireland: Rebellion, Famine and Emigration*. New York: OUP.

Schellekens, Jona (1996). "Irish famines and English mortality in the eighteenth century." *JIH*, 27(1), 29–42.

Scrope, G. Poulett (1850). *Draft Report Proposed to the Select Committee of the House of Commons on the Kilrush Union*. London: Ridgway.

Seaman, John (1993). "Famine mortality in Africa." *IDS Bulletin*, 24(4), 27–32.

Selig, Michel (1996). *Malnutrition et développement économique dans l'Alsace du XIXe siécle*. Presses Universitaires de Strasbourg.

Sen, Amartya K. (1981). *Poverty and Famines: An Essay on Entitlement and Deprivation*. Oxford: OUP.

Sen, A. K. (1995). "Nobody need starve." *Granta*, no. 52 (Winter), 220.

Sen, A. K. (1995). "Starvation and political economy: Famines, entitlements and alienation." Address to the NYU/Ireland House Conference on Famine and World Hunger, New York, May.

Senior, Nassau W. (1868). *Journals, Conversations and Essays Relating to Ireland*. 2 vols. London: Longmans, Green.

Sheehy, David C. (1995). "Archbishop Daniel Murray and the response of the Catholic Church to the Great Famine in Ireland." *Linkup: A Journal for the Dublin Diocese*, no. 76 (December), 38–42.

Shepherd, Jack (1993). "'Some tragic errors': American policy and Ethiopian famine, 1981–85." In John Osgood Field (ed.), *The Challenge of Famine: Recent Experience, Lessons Learned*, 88–125. Hartford, Conn.: Kumerian Press.

Skinner, Robert P. (1914). *Utilization of Potatoes in Europe: Special Consular Reports no. 64*. Washington, D.C.: Department of Commerce.

Smith, William Henry (1848). *A Twelvemonth's Residence in Ireland during the Famine and the Public Works . . . in 1846 and 1847*. London: Longman.

Solar, P. M. (1987). "Growth and distribution in Irish Agriculture, 1780–1860." Ph.D. diss., Stanford University, Stanford, Calif.

Solar, P. M. (1989). "The Great Famine was no ordinary subsistence crisis." In Crawford (ed.), *Famine*.

Solar, P. (1996). "The potato famine in Europe." In Ó Gráda, *Famine 150*, 113–27.

Somerville, Alexander (1994). *Letters from Ireland during the Famine of 1847*. Ed. K.M.D. Snell. Dublin: IAP.

Stein, Zena, Mervyn Susser, Gerhart Saenger, and Francis Marolla (1975). *Famine and Human Development: The Dutch Hunger Winter of 1944–1945*. New York: OUP.

Sunseri, Thaddeus (1997). "Famine and wild pigs: Gender struggles and the outbreak of the Majimaji war in Uzaramo (Tanzania)." *Journal of African History*, 38: 235–59.

Sutton, A. W. (1897). "The potato." In T. Johnson (ed.), *Report on the Conference and Exhibition of the Tercentenary of the Potato*, 54–106. Dublin: Farmer's Gazette.

Swift, John (1948). *History of the Dublin Bakers and Others*. Dublin: Irish Bakers, Confectioners and Allied Workers Union.

Thackeray, W. M. (1888 [1843]). "The Irish Sketch Book." In *Collected Works*, vol. 18. London: Smith, Elder.

Thirsk, Joan, ed. (1989). *The Agrarian History of England and Wales*, vol. 6, *1750–1850*, Cambridge, U.K.: CUP.

Tighe, William (1802). *Statistical Observations Relative to the County of Kilkenney*. Dublin: Graisberry and Campbell.

Tomasson, R. (1997). "A millenium of misery: The demography of the Icelanders." *PS*, 31, 405–25.

Trench, William Steuart (1868 [1966]). *Realities of Irish Life*. Macgibbon and Kee.

Trevelyan, Charles E. (1848). *The Irish Crisis*. London: Longman.

Tuke, James Hack (1848). *A Visit to Connaught in the Autumn of 1847*. 2d ed. London: Gilpin.

Turner, Michael (1996). *After the Famine: Irish Agriculture, 1850–1914*. Cambridge, U.K.: CUP.

Vanderbroeke, Christian (1969). "Aardappelteelt en aardappelverbruik in de 17e en 18e eeuw." *Tijdschrift voor Gescheidenis*, 82, 49–68.

Van der Haegen, Laurence (1993). "Aspects sociaux et médicaux en Irlande au début du dix-neuvième siècle, dans un contexte de famine." Master's diss., University of Paris IV—Sorbonne.

Van der Zee, H. A. (1982). *The Hunger Winter: Occupied Holland, 1944–5*. London: Jill Norman and Hobhouse.

Vasey, D. E. (1991). "Population, agriculture, and famine: Iceland, 1784–85." *Human Ecology*, 19, 323–50.

Vaughan, Megan (1985). "Famine Analysis and Family Relations: 1949 in Nyasaland." *Past and Present*, no. 108, 177–205.

Vaughan, Megan (1987). *The Story of an African Famine: Hunger, Gender and Politics in Malawi*. Cambridge, U.K.: CUP.

Vaughan, W. E., ed. (1989). *A New History of Ireland*, vol. 5, *Ireland under the Union*. Oxford: OUP.

Vaughan, W. E. (1993). *Landlord and Tenant in Mid-Victorian Ireland*. Oxford: OUP.

Vincent, Joan (1992). "A Political Orchestration of the Irish famine: County Fermanagh, May 1847." In M. Silverman and P. H. Gulliver, (eds.), *Approaching the Past: Historical Anthropology through Irish Case Studies*, 75–98. New York: Columbia University Press.

Visaria, Leela, and Pravin Visaria (1983). "Population (1757–1947)." In Dharma Kumar (ed.), *The Economic History of India*, vol. 2, C. 1757–c. 1970, 463–532. Cambridge, U.K.: CUP.

Wakefield, E. G. (1812). *Ireland, Statistical and Political*. London.

Warburton, John, James Whitelaw, and Robert Walsh (1818). *History of the City of Dublin*. 2 vols. London: Cadell and Davies.

Ward-Perkins, C. N. (1950). "The commercial crisis of 1847." *Oxford Economic Papers*, 2, 75–92.

Watkins, Susan C., and Jane Menken (1985). "Famines in historical perspective." *PDR*, 11, 647–76.

Watts, Michael (1983). *Silent Violence: Food, Famine and Peasantry in Northern Nigeria*. Berkeley: University of California Press.

Wheatcroft, Stephen (1983). "Famine and epidemic crises in Russia, 1918–1922: The case of Saratov." *Annales de Démographie Historique*, 329–52.

Wheatcroft, Stephen G. (1992). "The 1891–92 famine in Russia: Towards a more detailed analysis of the scale and economic significance." In Linda Edmundson and Peter Waldron (eds.), *Economy and Society in Russia and the Soviet Union*, 44–64. London: Macmillan.

Whelan, Irene (1995). "The stigma of souperism." In Póirtéir, *The Great Irish Famine*, 135–54.

Whelan, Kevin (1995). "Pre- and post-genuine landscape change." In Póirtéir, *The Great Irish Famine*, 19–33.

Whitelaw, James (1805). *An Essay on the Population of Dublin*. Dublin: Graisberry and Campbell.

Will, Pierre-Etienne (1990). *Bureaucracy and Famine in Eighteenth-century China*. Stanford: Stanford University Press.

Willis, Thomas (1845). *Facts Connected with the Social and Sanitary Condition of the Working Classes in the City of Dublin*. Dublin: O'Gorman.

Winick, Myron, ed. (1979). *Hunger Disease: Studies by the Jewish Physicians in the Warsaw Ghetto*. New York: Wiley.

Winick, Myron (1994). "Hunger disease: Studies by Jewish physicians in the Warsaw ghetto." *Nutrition*, 10(4), 365–80.

Woodham-Smith, C. (1962). *The Great Hunger: Ireland 1845–49*. London: Hamish Hamilton.

Wrigley, E. A., and R. Schofield (1981). *The Population History of England, 1541–1871: A Reconstruction*. Cambridge, Mass.: Harvard University Press.

Xihe Peng (1987). "Demographic consequences of the Great Leap Forward in China's provinces." *PDR*, 13(4), 639–70.

Yager, Tom (1996). "Mass eviction in the Mullet peninsula during and after the Great Famine." *IESH*, 23, 24–44.

Yamin, Rebecca (1996). "New York's mythic slum: Digging lower Manhattan's infamous Five Points." *Archaeology* (March/April), 45–53.

Yang, Dali L. (1996). *Calamity and Reform in China: State, Rural Society, and Institutional Change since the Great Leap Famine*. Stanford, Calif.: Stanford University Press.

Young, Arthur (1770). *A Six Month's Tour through the North of England*. Dublin: Wilson.

INDEX

CORMAC Ó GRÁDA is Professor of Economics, University College, Dublin. He is the author of several books on Irish and European economic history, including *Ireland before and after the Famine* (Manchester University Press, 1993) and *Ireland: A New Economic History* (Oxford University Press, 1994).